S. Sophia Beale

The Churches of Paris from Clovis to Charles X

S. Sophia Beale

The Churches of Paris from Clovis to Charles X

ISBN/EAN: 9783337262501

Printed in Europe, USA, Canada, Australia, Japan

Cover: Foto ©Lupo / pixelio.de

More available books at **www.hansebooks.com**

THE CHURCHES OF PARIS

THE
CHURCHES OF PARIS

FROM CLOVIS TO CHARLES X

BY

S. SOPHIA BEALE

Author of " A Complete and Concise Handbook to the Museum of the Louvre" etc

WITH ILLUSTRATIONS BY THE AUTHOR FROM ORIGINAL SKETCHES
PHOTOGRAPHS AND ENGRAVINGS

LONDON

W. H. ALLEN & CO LIMITED

13 WATERLOO PLACE SW

1893

WYMAN AND SONS, LTD., PRINTERS, LONDON AND REDHILL.

DEDICATED

TO ONE

WHOSE HELP WAS INVALUABLE

BUT WHO IS NOW

TO US

ONLY A MEMORY

" La nef vagant dessus la mer galicque
　Porte dedens soy richesse inestimable
　Justice y est pour patron magnificque
　Raison y sert de Lieutenant notable,
　Gens de scauoir par œuure treslouable
　Sont galliotz qui lamenent a port,
　Marchans y ont tresasseure support.
　Prebstres, Bourgeois, nobles, Clercz et gen-darmes.
　Icelle nef de se'fertile apport,
　Cest de Paris le beau blazon des armes."

PREFACE.

IN a book of this kind, it is difficult to prevent oneself becoming a guide, more or less complete. Dates and facts, architectural details and descriptions, all savour of the handbook; but having determined to keep to the historical and archaeological, rather than the architectural side of the churches, I have tried to rake up quaint and legendary lore, and so add to the interest of an ordinary guide book. I would also pray my readers to bear in mind that, as the work is not intended to be an architectural treatise, I have simply walked in the paths of Viollet-le-Duc and Guilhermy, whenever I have been compelled to describe the technical details of the churches.

My thanks are due to the Editor of the *American Architect*, for his courtesy in allowing me to build these ecclesiastical monographs upon the foundation of some articles which have appeared from time to time in a condensed form in the Boston (U. S. A.) paper; and also to the Editor of the *Magazine of Art*, for a similar kindness.

I should also like to acknowledge my indebtedness to the following authors and their works:

"Histoire de la Sainte-Chapelle." Morand.
"Histoire de Saint-Denis." Dom Millet.

"Histoire de Saint-Eustache." L'abbé Koenig.

"Inscriptions du Diocèse de Paris." F. de Guilhermy.

"Itinéraire Archéologique de Paris." F. de Guilhermy.

"l'Église Saint Julien-le-Pauvre." A. Le Brun.

"Monographie de l'Église Royale de Saint-Denis." F. de Guilhermy.

"Sacred and Legendary Art." Anna Jameson.

"The Early British Church." J. Yeowell.

CONTENTS.

	PAGE
Saint-Antoine des Quinze-Vingts	1
Les Carmes Déchaussées	1
La Sainte-Chapelle	2
Saint-Denis	30
Sainte-Elizabeth	100
Saint-Étienne du Mont	100
Saint-Eustache	116
Saint-François Xavier	158
Sainte-Geneviève	158
Saint-Germain l'Auxerrois	177
Chapelle du Château de Saint-Germain-en-Laye.	189
Saint-Germain des Prés	190
Saint-Gervais	209
La tour Saint-Jacques	213
Saint-Jacques du Haut-pas	215
Saint-Jean-Saint-François	215
Saint-Julien-le-Pauvre	215
Saint-Laurent	232
Saint-Leu-Saint-Gilles	235
Saint-Louis d'Antin	237
Saint-Louis en l'Ile	237
Saint-Louis des Invalides	237
Sainte-Madeleine	239

	PAGE
SAINTE-MARGUERITE ...	243
SAINT-MARTIN DES CHAMPS ...	244
SAINT-MÉDARD ...	248
SAINT-MERRI ...	251
SAINT-NICOLAS DES CHAMPS	256
SAINT-NICOLAS DU CHARDONNET ...	259
NOTRE-DAME (CATHÉDRALE)	260
NOTRE-DAME DE L'ASSOMPTION	299
NOTRE-DAME DE L'ABBAYE AUX BOIS	300
NOTRE-DAME DES BLANCS-MANTEAUX	300
NOTRE-DAME DES CHAMPS ...	301
NOTRE-DAME DE LORETTE ...	302
NOTRE-DAME DES VICTOIRES	303
L'ORATOIRE	303
SAINT-PAUL-SAINT-LOUIS	304
SAINT-PHILIPPE DU ROULE ...	305
SAINT-PIERRE DE CHAILLOT ...	306
SAINT-PIERRE DE MONTMARTRE	306
SAINT-ROCH ...	307
SAINT-SÉVERIN	310
LA SORBONNE	319
SAINT-SULPICE	321
SAINT-THOMAS D'AQUIN	326
L'ANCIEN ABBAYE DU VAL-DE-GRÂCE	326
LA CHAPELLE DU CHÂTEAU DE VERSAILLES ...	328
LA CHAPELLE DU CHÂTEAU DE VINCENNES ...	329
SAINT-VINCENT DE PAUL	331

THE CHURCHES OF PARIS.

SAINT-ANTOINE DES QUINZE-VINGTS.

Saint Louis, always careful in helping his suffering subjects, founded this hospital for the blind in 1260, upon a piece of ground abutting on the Louvre, now traversed by the Rue de Rivoli. In 1780 the hospital was transferred to the Faubourg Saint-Antoine, and took up its abode in the old dwelling place of the Black Musketeers, whose chapel also served as a parish church. It is a little building of no beauty nor interest, although a few inscriptions relating to pious foundations still remain in the chapel, the oldest being dated 1481. One of these tells us of the institution, in 1667, of a somewhat early Mass by one Marie Lambert, maid to the queen mother. It was to be said at 4 a.m. in order that the poor blind people should be able to sally forth a-begging (*d'aller à la quête*) fortified with the Bread of Life.

LES CARMES DÉCHAUSSÉES

The old church of the barefooted Carmelites in the Rue de Vaugirard was commenced in 1613, and dedicated to S. Joseph in 1625. It is now served by the Dominicans. The crypt is the only interesting part of the church, and is a curiosity, as it contains innumerable bones piled up on every side, the remains of the ghastly September massacres of 1792. The frescoes painted by a Liège artist, Bartholet Flamaël, are very much esteemed. Some of the chapels are richly decorated in the gaudy style of the 17th century. The altar is embellished by a 14th century bas-relief in marble representing the Last Supper. A few epitaphs still remain: that of Cardinal de Beausset, the historian of Fénelon and Bossuet; one of Cardinal de la Luzerne; and a marble, covering the heart of Archbishop Affre, who was shot on a barricade in 1848, while endeavouring to make peace with the insurgents.

LA SAINTE-CHAPELLE.

The origin and foundation of this most lovely example of mediæval art is so much a part of S. Louis' life that it may not be out of place to give some account of the Saint's character and habits before proceeding to describe the history of the chapel.

Louis IX. was pious and practical, and inconvenienced his courtiers as much by his punctuality and the assiduity with which he conducted his business, as by his religious duties. These he considered a part of his daily work, hearing all the canonical offices with the same regularity as he attended to the grievances of his subjects. Often, like our own George Herbert, was he found prostrate before the altar wrapped in prayer. Even Gibbon allowed that he united the virtues of a king, a hero, and a man —he might have added those of a just judge and a lawgiver; and Voltaire sums up his character as follows: "Il n'est guère donné à l'homme de pousser la vertu plus loin." When his more worldly friends cavilled at his austerities, he made his case good by retorting: "Si je passais deux fois autant de temps à jouer, ou à courir les bois, pour m'occuper de la chasse, personne n'en parleroit." As in the case of nearly all exceptionally good men, he probably owed everything to the extreme care that his mother had bestowed upon his education—a care which he repaid by a life-long devotion to her memory. Of good Queen Blanche's character we get a glimpse in the following touching anecdote. It is related that one day at Court, the Queen noticed a beautiful youth with long, fair hair, and asking his name, was answered, "Prince Herman, the son of the sainted Elizabeth of Hungary." On hearing this, Queen Blanche rose from her seat, and, gazing at the boy, said to him, "Fair youth, thou hadst a blessed mother; where did she kiss thee?" Whereat Herman, blushing, placed his finger on his forehead between his eyes, and the Queen, reverently pressing her lips upon the spot, looked up to Heaven and breathed the invocation: *Sancta Elisabetha, Patrona nostra dulcissima, ora pro nobis.* That a mother so imbued with admiration for the

THE SAINTE-CHAPELLE FROM THE PONT SAINT-MICHEL.

sainted Elizabeth should have a son who walked in the Hungarian queen's steps, is not very remarkable in those ages of faith. S. Louis' faith was simple, loving, and inextinguishable; and so it came about that when he heard of the Emperor Baldwin II.'s financial difficulties, he decided to purchase the relics which had been given more than once, it is said, as pledges for temporary loans. The Emperor's letter upon the subject would lead one to suppose that it was an act of generosity to *faire passer* the relics to S. Louis; but we know that the King paid very handsomely for them. " Je désire," said the emperor, "ardemment de vous faire passer cette précieuse relique à vous, mon cousin, mon seigneur, et mon bienfaiteur, et au royaume de France ma patrie." Other purchasers seem to have been in the field; for S. Louis only obtained, at that time, the Crown of Thorns and some portion of the True Cross. One of his rivals was our Henry III., who in 1247 summoned all his nobles to London to witness the reception of some of the Holy Blood which had been brought from the East in a crystal vase, by one of the Knights Templars. It was sent by the Master of the Templars and Hospitallers, its genuineness being attested by the Patriarch of Jerusalem and the abbots of the Holy Land. On the 13th October, being the feast of S. Edward the Confessor, the King, after prayer and fasting, carried the reliquary from S. Paul's to Westminster, where it was deposited in the Abbey church. The Bishop of Norwich preached, and celebrated mass; and in his sermon took pains to impress upon his hearers that the Holy Blood was more precious even than the True Cross possessed by the King of France—an argument which points to one of the causes of rivalry between the nations during the Middle Ages. Naturally the assembled prelates accorded indulgences to the faithful who should visit the shrine; but this much coveted privilege seems to have caused certain murmurings among some of the assistants; they objected that, whereas our Lord had ascended into Heaven in the body, He could not have left His blood upon the earth. But Robert Grossetête, Bishop of Lincoln, was equal to the occasion, and replied, that Joseph of Arimathea, having saved it from the precious wounds, more especially from the one in His side, had given some of it to Nicodemus, and thus it had been treasured up, and had passed from father to son, until it came into the possession of the Patriarch Robert of Jerusalem. These disputes seem to have been pretty common in those days, in spite of the unquestioning faith of the multitude. In 1357 we read of a squabble which took place between the Dominicans and the Franciscans, one François Baïle of Barcelona affirming that the blood being separated from the Divinity of our Lord was therefore not adorable. Often, indeed, these wranglings became so violent that the Popes were obliged to interfere in order to settle the matter.

The bringing home of the relics reads like a royal pageant. They were carried to Venice by the " Députés de Saint Louis et les ambassadeurs de l'Empire, accompagnés des plus nobles d'entre les Vénitiens. Le convoi mit à la voile dans le tems de Noël, saison où la mer est le plus orageuse. La confidence des Députés éleva leur ame au dessus de la crainte des périls, et elle fut justifiée ; ils arrivèrent à Venise sans avoir essuyé de tempêtes. Vatace, Empereur Grec, avait détaché plusieurs galères qui croisoient aux différens détroits où les François devoient passer, pour leur enlever ce précieux butin. Sa vigilance fut trompée ; Dieu veilloit sur eux."*

"Arrivée à Venise la Relique fut mise en dépôt dans le Trésor de la Chapelle de Saint-Marc. Le roi instruit du succès de la négociation de ses députés, envoya, ainsi que Baudouin, des Ambassadeurs avec l'argent nécessaire pour se l'approprier. De leur côté les Marchands François établis à Venise, plus riches encore des dons de la foi qu'avantagés de la fortune, ouvrirent leur bourse pour payer la somme stipulée. Les Vénitiens auroient bien desiré garder cette Relique, mais retenus par la foi du traité ils la restituèrent quoique à regret."

"Les Ambassadeurs après avoir reconnu les sceaux se mirent en route, et quoique la saison fût pluvieuse ils n'essuyèrent pas une goutte d'eau. Arrivés en Champagne, le Roi partit aussi-tôt pour les joindre. Il étoit accompagné de la Reine, de ses Frères, de l'Archevêque de Sens, de l'Evêque du Puy, et des Seigneurs les plus distingués de sa cour. Il rencontra la Relique près de Sens ; elle étoit enfermée dans une triple cassette. La première étoit de bois. On l'ouvrit, et on vérifia les sceaux des seigneurs François et du Duc de Venise apposés sur la cassette d'argent dans laquelle se trouva un vase d'or,

---

* I suppose no apology is needed for giving my quotations in the original language. Now that everyone is a good French scholar, it is obviously unnecessary to spoil good work by translations.

contenant la Ste.-Couronne. L'ayant découverte on la fit voir à tous les Assistans, qui fondirent en larmes s'imaginant voir réellement Jésus Christ couronné d'épines. Puis le Roi mit son scelle sur la cassette. Tant de précautions écartent assurément tout soupçon d'infidélité."

"Le lendemain la Relique fut portée à Sens dont on avoit tendu toutes les rues. À l'entrée de la Ville, le Roi et le Comte d'Artois, l'aîné de ses Frères, la portèrent sur leurs epaules, les pieds nuds. Le Clergé alla au-devant, et les principaux Seigneurs chargés à leur tour de ce fardeau honorable la placèrent dans l'Église Métropolitaine de Saint-Etienne. On se mit ensuite en route pour Paris, où la réception de la Relique se fit avec la plus grande solennité. Tout le Clergé régulier et séculier fut convoqué à cette cérémonie. Les Religieux de Saint-Denis dès la pointe du jour se rendirent à l'endroit qui avoit été indiqué hors de Paris du côté de Vincennes ; tous ceux qui assistèrent à cette Procession marchèrent nuds pieds. On avoit dressé un magnifique reposoir près de l'Abbaye Saint-Antoine, où la Châsse fut exposée aux yeux du peuple. Guillaume, Chantre de Saint-Denis, entonna tout ce qui fut chanté pendant la marche et l'Abbé eut place à la droite de l'Autel, avec les Archevêques, Evêques et les autres Abbés, tous en habits pontificaux. Enfin le 18º jour d'Août la Relique arriva, et fut placée au Palais dans la Chapelle de Saint-Nicolas."*

A medal was struck to commemorate this event, with the legend : HÆC REGIS REGUM TOTO PRETIOSIOR AURO, and S. Louis kneeling before an altar upon which is the crown of thorns. As to the particular tree of which the crown was composed, there was much difference of opinion. Clement of Alexandria calls it *ex rubo*, a sort of thicket; other writers a different sort of shrub or bush, called *nerprun*, or wild plum; and others, the white thorn.

The antiphon used every day in the offices of the Sainte-Chapelle began : *Ecce Crux et Corona Spinea Arnia Regis*

---

* *Histoire de la Sainte-Chapelle.* Morand, canon of the chapel.

Gloriae tibi commendantur; and the seal consisted of a cross with the crown of thorns intersecting it, and on each side a *fleur-de-lys*, with the King's crown at the top. Having acquired the holy relics, it was most seemly that a shrine should be constructed wherein they should rest—a shrine worthy the sanctity of such treasures. And so S. Louis commissioned his architect, Pierre de Montereau, to build him a chapel which should be a marvel of lightness and colour, embellished with windows which should glitter like precious stones, and containing a *châsse*, resplendent with enamels, and gold and silver—a shrine, as it were, within a shrine. That the architect was worthy the confidence of his royal master, the chapel testifies to this day, and Maître Pierre's immortal work remains the most perfect example of 13th century architecture in France; one might say, the most exquisite architectural gem which the world has yet seen, or is ever likely to see.

Pierre de Montereau, or Montreau, as it is sometimes written, lived eighteen years after the completion of his *chef-d'œuvre*, and doubtless assisted at some of the splendid ceremonies held in it. He died March 17th, 1266, and was buried in the chapel of the Virgin belonging to the religious of S. Germain des Près, where a splendid monument was erected to his memory. Some of the finest of the buildings attached to the monastery were his work, and up to the last century a stone was to be seen over his burial-place, upon which he was represented with a rule and compass in his hands. His epitaph gives him the titles of *fleur pleine de bonnes mœurs*, and of *docteur des architectes*:

FLOS PLENUS MORUM, VIVENS DOCTOR LATO MORUM,
MUSTEROLO NATUS JACET HIC PETRUS TUMULATUS
QUEM REX COELORUM PERDUCAT IN ALTA POLORUM
CHRISTE MILLENO, BIS CENTENO DUODENO
CUM QUINQUAGENO QUARTO DECESSIT IN ANNO.

Another stone recorded the name of his wife Agnes, and on that he is termed, in old French, mestre Pierre de Montereul. The chapel has disappeared, and with it all trace of the tombs; but one at Reims, erected in honour of Hugues Libergier, architect of the celebrated abbey church of S. Nicaise, who died in 1263, gives some idea of what those of Pierre de Montereau and his wife must have been.

The first stone of the church was laid by S. Louis in 1245,

and three years later, on the Sunday after Easter, *Quasimodo*, 25th April, 1248, it was consecrated by the Pope's legate, Eudes de Châteauroux, Bishop of Tusculum, as the Chapel of the Holy Cross and the Holy Crown. On the same day, Philippe Berruyer, Archbishop of Bourges, celebrated the like ceremony in the lower church, putting it under the patronage of the Blessed Virgin. It seems strange that Joinville should not speak of this event, and yet it must have been an imposing sight; but he does not once mention the Sainte-Chapelle in his life of S. Louis. Perhaps this may be accounted for by what he thus relates: "At Easter-tide, in the year of grace 1248, I summoned my vassals and retainers to Joinville, and on the Easter-eve . . . was born John, my son, Sire d'Ancarville. . . . We had feasting and dancing all that week, in the course of which my brother, the Sire de Vancouleurs and other rich persons who were there, gave banquets one after the other on Monday, Tuesday, Wednesday, and Thursday." And then he goes on to say that he went to Metz on business before he started for the Holy Land; therefore we may suppose that private affairs kept him away from Paris, and that not being present himself at the consecration, he did not consider it necessary to give an account of the ceremony.

Two charters dated Paris, 1245, and Aigues-Mortes, 1248, respectively give the terms of the endowment by the king. The number of ecclesiastics who first formed the college was fixed at twenty-one; five principal priests or *maîtres chapelains*, each having an assistant chaplain (a priest), and a deacon, and three beadles who had as many clerks under them. The number was modified from time to time, during five centuries, and latterly it consisted of a treasurer, twelve canons, and nineteen chaplains. The office of treasurer was generally filled by some important personage, and he had the privilege of wearing the mitre and other insignia of the episcopate, and of giving the Benediction upon great festivals; but he was not allowed to bear the crozier.

The most important event of the 13th century connected with the Sainte-Chapelle was the translation of some of S. Louis' bones from S. Denis, in which church they had been laid twenty-seven years previously upon their arrival from Tunis, where the king had died of fever on the 25th August, 1270. Feeling his last moments to have arrived, he caused his body to be placed upon a bed of ashes, and wearing the habit of the third order of S. Francis, his noble spirit passed away. He was embalmed, according to the fashion of the day; or rather, his bones were relieved of their outer casements, by boiling in wine and water; other parts of his body, which it is unnecessary to specify, being given by his son to the King of Sicily, who placed them in the church of Monreale, Palermo. The young Comte de Nevers had died just before S. Louis; and Alfonso de Brienne, Comte d'Eu, son of John de Brienne, King of Jerusalem, and the Chevalier Pierre, the King's chamberlain, had also succumbed to the unhealthy climate. The funeral procession set out, and wended its way towards France under the care of S. Louis' son, Philippe le Hardi.

Arriving at Paris, the bodies were placed temporarily in Notre-Dame on the 21st of May; and the next day, amidst a large concourse of people, the procession, consisting of clergy, and religious, started early for S. Denis, Philippe, reverently bearing his father's bones, walking like the rest. Up through the city they went, singing and chanting, and taking much the same route as had been traversed by S. Denis and his companions, after their martyrdom, as recorded by the old chroniclers. In an engraving by Boulogne a long procession of monks and knights is seen issuing from the abbey to meet another coming from Paris, the king and bishops being dressed in that peculiar high-wind-blown drapery common to pictorial art in the 17th and 18th centuries. S. Louis' bones were placed in a stone coffin and buried in front of the altar of the Holy Trinity, near the resting place of the bodies of Louis VIII. and Philippe Auguste. Philippe le Hardi's wife, Isabelle, and Tristan, Comte de Nevers, were placed on the right; the chevalier Pierre, who, as chamberlain, had the privilege of sleeping in the King's chamber, was laid at his feet. In 1292, Henri de Luxembourg caused the relics to be placed in a silver shrine and conveyed to the Sainte-Chapelle by the Archbishops of Reims and Lyon; but after some days they were returned to S. Denis, and it was not until 1306 that Philippe le Bel succeeded in his desire of placing the remains of his grandfather in the chapel which was so dear to him, that he felt a *malaise* each time he heard the divine offices elsewhere. The Bull of canonization was promulgated by Pope Boniface VIII. in 1297, and the translation of the king's skull followed nine years later, accompanied by all the picturesque pomp of the 14th century. The reliquary was in the form of a gold bust of natural size, enriched with precious stones, and supported by Angels upon a pedestal which rested upon four silver-gilt lions. The crown and the collar of the vestment were decorated with rubies, pearls, emeralds, and sapphires; and around the socle were representations of the twenty-nine kings of France, and a Latin inscription giving the date of the work, and the name of the smith, Master Guillaume Juliani. Such was the *châsse* which enclosed the principal relic of S. Louis: "Afin que la présence du Chef de ce grand roi, qui pendant sa vie avait eu la justice en singulière recommandation, animat les Juges de ce Parlement à maintenir les loix, protéger les gens du bien, rendre la justice à ses sujets sans exception de personne."*

> L'an mil et trois cens et six ans,
> Ot à Paris joie nouvele,
> Car li rois mit en sa chapele,
> Que S. Loys fist tele faire
> Qu'a tout le monde devroit plaire,
> Le chief de lui si richement
> Et si très-honorablement,

*The bust was given to the chapel by Philippe le Bel in 1304. Another, of silver-gilt, containing the upper part of the head, used to be at the Abbey of Poissy. The little church of la Montjoie rejoices in a portion of the sainted king's hand, enclosed in a 14th century reliquary; and the cathedral of Meaux possesses a chalice said to have belonged to him.

> Que par raison de la bel euvre
> Que li dons saintuaire queuvre
> Le vessel où l'en la mis prisent
> Toutes personnes qui l'avisent. (GUIL. GUIART.)

On the 15th May, 1843, an interesting discovery was made in the chapel. Some workmen, in removing a stone of the pavement of the apse, discovered a tin box containing the remains of a heart, and a *procès-verbal*, stating that it had been previously found on the 21st January, 1803. Although the position of the box (the centre of the apse) indicated that it had belonged to some distinguished person, yet there was no clue to its owner, neither inscription, nor name, nor date. The box, it is true, was in the style of the 13th century; but it seemed doutful, that, had the heart been S. Louis', such an important relic should have been lost sight of, and no record of it given by the Benedictines at S. Denis in their inventory of the treasures which they had received from the Sainte-Chapelle. The matter was referred to the Academie des Inscriptions et Belles Lettres, and fully discussed; but the members could arrive at no decision, and consequently the box was replaced where it had been found.

While the kings resided in the old Cité, the most brilliant ceremonies succeeded one another at the Sainte-Chapelle; it was, in fact, the chapel belonging to the adjoining palace, now the Palais de Justice. The Queens, Marie de Brabant, second wife of Philippe le Hardi; Marie de Luxembourg, second wife of Charles le Bel; Jeanne d'Evreux, third wife of the same Prince; and Isabelle de Bavière, wife of Charles VI., were all crowned there. The marriage of the Emperor, Henri VII. and Marguerite de Brabant, and the betrothal of Isabeau, eldest daughter of Charles VI. with Richard II. of England, were also solemnised in the chapel. There, in 1332, Philippe de Valois held a great assembly of prelates and barons, to announce his project of another crusade against the Infidels—a project which was never carried out. On the feast of the Epiphany, 1378, King Charles V., the Emperor Charles IV., and his son Wenceslas, King of the Romans, offered gold, frankincense and myrrh, after the manner of the three holy Magi. Every time that the sovereigns convoked an assemblage of the clergy in the palace, the prelates first went to the chapel and asked the blessing of the Holy Spirit, while prostrated before the relics. In 1483, when Louis XI. was lying ill at Tours, he hoped to prolong his life by surrounding himself with the most sacred relics of his kingdom—so reluctant was this *devôt* to depart from our wicked world. The Sainte Ampoule was brought by the religious of S. Remi from Reims; the canons of the Sainte-Chapelle took the Cross of Victory and the Rod of Moses out of their treasury, and a grand procession of clergy and laity was formed on the 1st of August to carry them from Paris to Plessis-les-Tours. But, alas! to no end; for on the 30th of the same month the poor creature finished his earthly career of hypocrisy.

Boileau, in his *Lutrin*, gives an amusing account of an unseemly squabble which took place between the canons of the chapel, and which was in this wise. On a certain Sunday in 1667, one of the precentors named Barrin found a huge lectern placed in front of his stall. He protested against the intruder, and the other canons taking his part, it was ordered to be removed. But here the treasurer stepped in with objections, and a whole month was passed in discussions, orders, and counter-orders; the dispute only being ended through the mediation of the first president, Guillaume de Lamoignon, who decreed that the precentor should remain imprisoned behind the lectern an entire morning, until the end of the High Mass, the treasurer undertaking to remove the offending piece of furniture before the hour of vespers.

It was the president who suggested this subject to the poet. Boileau had remarked to M. de Lamoignon that an epic poem could be written upon the most trivial incident, if only a poet had sufficient imagination to work it out. "*Faites donc un poème sur le débat de la Sainte-Chapelle. Vous pourrez l'intituler 'Le Lutrin enlevé,' ou 'La Conquête du Lutrin.*"

"*Pourquoi non,*" replied Boileau. "*Il ne faut jamais défier un fou; et je le suis assez, non seulement pour entreprendre ce poème, mais encore pour le dédier à Monsieur le premier président.*"

The result of defying the "fool," who was withal a wit, is a series of portraits in verse, of the canons, the singers, the precentor, and the treasurer. The latter was not spared, as may be seen by the following lines:—

> "Dans le réduit obscur d'une alcove enfoncée,
> S'élève un lit de plume à grands frais amassée.
> Quatre rideaux pompeux, par un double contour,
> En défendent l'entrée à la clarté du jour.

> "Là, parmi les douceurs d'un tranquille silence,
> Règne sur le duvet une heureuse indolence.
> C'est là que le prélat, muni d'un déjeuner,
> Dormant d'un léger sommeil, attendait le dîner.
> La jeunesse en sa fleur brille sur son visage ;
> Son menton sur son sein descend à double étage,
> Et son corps, ramassé dans sa courte grosseur,
> Fait gémir les coussins sous sa molle épaisseur."

The canons are touched off with an equal vivacity; all their failings and follies, their idleness and their gluttony, brought into the pure light of day:

> "Parmi les doux plaisirs d'une paix fraternelle,
> Paris voyait fleurir son antique chapelle ;
> Ses chanoines vermeils et brillants de santé
> S'engraissaient d'une longue et sainte oisiveté ;
> Sans sortir de leurs lits, plus doux que leurs hermines,
> Ces pieux fainéants faisaient chanter matines,
> Veillaient à bien dîner, et laissaient en leur lieu
> A des chantres gagés le soin de leur Dieu."

And then the "machine" itself, the offending *lutrin*, is described:

> "Aussitôt dans le chœur la machine emportée,
> Est sur le banc du chantre à grand bruit remontée,
> Ses ais demi-pourris, que l'âge a relâchés,
> Sont à coups de maillet unis et rapprochés ;
> Sous les coups redoublés tous les bancs retentissent
> Les murs en sont émus, les voûtes en mugissent,
> Et l'orgue même en pousse un long gemissement."

The dream of the *Chantre*, perhaps the indirect cause of all the trouble, in making the man cantankerous, and extra liable to be rubbed up the wrong way, is no less worth quoting:

> "Les cloches dans les airs, de leurs voix argentines,
> Appelaient à grand bruit les chantres à matines,
> Quand leur chef, agité d'un sommeil effrayant,
> Encor tout en sueur, se réveille en criant :
> ' Pour la seconde fois (dit-il) un sommeil gracieux
> Avait sous ses pavots appesenti mes yeux ;
> Quand, l'esprit agité d'une douce fumée,
> J'ai cru remplir au chœur ma place accoutumée.
> Là, triomphant aux yeux des chantres impuissants,
> Je bénissais le peuple, et j'avalais l'encens :
> Lorsque, du fond caché de notre sacristie,
> Une épaisse nuée à grands flots est sortie,
> Que s'ouvrant à mes yeux, dans son bleuâtre éclat
> M'a fait voir un serpent conduit par le prélat.

> Du corps de ce dragon plein de soufre et de nitre,
> Une tête sortait en forme de pupitre,
> Dont le triangle affreux, tout hérissé de crins,
> Surpassait en grosseur nos plus épais lutrins :
> Animé par son guide, en sifflant il s'élance.
> J'ai crié, mais en vain ; et, fuyant sa fureur
> Je me suis réveillé plein de trouble et d'horreur."

An order of the Conseil d'Etat, dated March 11, 1787, sequestered all the goods of the chapel, suppressed the chaplaincies and canonries, and ordained that the services should be continued by the king's ordinary chaplains. Three years later, the chapel shared the fate of all the abbeys, chapters, and religious foundations; and soon after, S. Louis' beautiful oratory was closed. The relics were sent to S. Denis, and the other objects were dispersed to the National museums. *Propriété Nationale à Vendre* was written upon the building, a piece of information which has only disappeared in our own time. Under the Directoire a club held its meetings there; and later, it was converted into a warehouse for corn and flour. Towards 1800, certain ecclesiastics hired the lower chapel and celebrated mass there, but in 1803 it was further profaned; the upper chapel was turned into a depository for judicial documents, and the lower one was given for the same purpose to the Cour des Comptes. In vain Louis XVIII. and Charles X. endeavoured to restore the building to its proper use ; and it was only in 1837, in the reign of Louis Philippe, that its restoration was decided upon. MM. Duban, Lassus, Viollet-le-Duc, and Boeswillwald were commissioned to undertake the work at a cost of 2,000,000 francs, a sum nearly equal to the original value of the relics and reliquaries (2,800,000 francs), while it exceeded by nearly two millions the original cost of the building, 800,000 francs. The 3rd November, 1849, the work was sufficiently advanced for the ceremony of the Institution of the Judicature, when the ancient chants were sung as in former times. Since then, until quite recently, a mass has always been celebrated in the chapel, upon the opening of the Law Courts, in the presence of the judges, barristers, and others who could gain admission. But this function has lately been abolished, and the keeper now impresses upon visitors (rather eagerly and unnecessarily), the permission to keep on their hats. "*Mais couvrez vous, messieurs, ce n'est plus une chapelle, ce n'est qu'un monument*"!

INTERIOR OF THE CHAPEL.

The celebration of the *Fête des Fous* was one of the customs of the Middle Ages which was very tenacious of life. Although forbidden by the legate in 1198, it flourished for another 250 years. The Council of Paris, held in 1212, endeavoured to put it down; but it was only in 1435 that the Council of Basle succeeded in suppressing it, together with stage plays and other profanities. It was the custom at the Sainte-Chapelle, upon the Holy Innocents' day, for the boy acolytes* to deck themselves in the canons' copes and vestments, and to sit in their stalls, one boy bearing the mace carried by the precentor as an attribute of his dignity. They were also exempted, during a certain time, from doing homage to anyone. A curious custom prevailed at Easter. At three o'clock in the morning, the clergy, carrying the Host, went in procession round the interior of the palace; and by reason of a foundation of one of the canons, Eustache Picot, under-master of music during the reigns of Louis XIII. and XIV., only his own compositions could be sung on the occasion. On Easter day a chronological table of the principal events and festivals connected with the chapel, with the date and the age of the King, was attached to the Paschal candle. Other customs were peculiar to the chapel, as, for instance, on Whit Sunday, when, during mass, while the Gospel was chanted, an Angel descended from the vault, holding a silver cruet, from which he poured water upon the hands of the celebrant. Flowers, roses, wafers, a white pigeon, a quantity of small birds, and flax for burning, had to be provided by the Chevecier† in memory of the tongues of fire which descended upon the apostles at Pentecost.

On the Good Fridays of each year the chapel scarcely sufficed to contain the crowds of sick persons who flocked to it from all parts of the city. All maladies were supposed to be curable through the virtues of the holy relics, but specially that known formerly as *le mal caduc*. At midnight the relic of the True Cross was exposed, and at the same moment the chapel was

---

* The *enfants de chœur* of the S. Chapelle seem to have been employed in singing elsewhere for the *divertissement* of the King : " Les Enfans de Chœur de la Sainte-Chapelle illec disoient de beaux virelets, Chansons et autres Bergerettes, moult mélodieusement."

† The *Chevecier*, or *Chefcier*, was the official who had charge of the altar, the linen, the vases, the ornaments, &c., and who took care of the sacristy and its contents. The treasurer usually held the two offices.

filled by the most fearful shrieks of these poor epileptics. The afflicted threw themselves about, foamed at the mouth, and fell into convulsions, invoking the aid especially of S. John the Baptist and S. Spire. The people were convinced every year that some wondrous miracle had been wrought; but the abuses connected with this nocturnal exposition were so great that, in 1781, Louis XVI. ordered it to be discontinued. The relics now shown in the Treasury of Notre-Dame, and exposed there during Holy Week, are said to be the veritable ones belonging to the Sainte-Chapelle; but the account of their preservation after the desecration of S. Denis is so miraculous (almost as much so as the original finding of the True Cross by S. Helena) that it requires a large amount of faith to believe in them. The reliquaries were of course all melted up, even Alexandre Lenoir could not save them. Those at Notre-Dame are quite modern, although somewhat of the same form.

Another custom peculiar to the chapel was the singing upon Christmas-day of the hymn "*Noël*," in place of "*O Salutaris Hostia*." The former had been originally a joy-song, welcoming the kings upon their entry into Paris; and thus, when our Henry V. entered the capital in 1420, and likewise Henry VI. in 1431, they were greeted with this exclamation.

The kings were not the only persons who profited by the virtues of the relics; the first president of the *parlement* was so far privileged that he could have them brought to him on his death-bed; and on Quinquagesima Sunday they were exposed at the central window of the *chevet* for the good of the public in the street. The *châsse* containing the relics had no less than ten locks, the keys thereof being in the custody of the kings until the reign of Louis XIII.; but while that monarch was at Lyons, a fire broke out in the chapel (26th July, 1630), and the doors of the *châsse* had to be broken open, a disaster which led to a change in the custodian, the president of the Chambre des Comptes being substituted for the sovereign. This worthy lived opposite; and it was also his duty to keep the relics clean, assisted of course by a vast number of other presidents and officials. It was the duty, or the privilege, of the kings to mount the little winding staircase at the side of the altar, and to exhibit the relics to the people gathered in the chapel below. S. Louis probably ofttimes walked up the steps on the left for this purpose (the right-hand staircase is modern); and on Good Friday, 1423, the Duke of Bedford, as regent of France for Henry VI., gave the blessing with the relics. In 1575, on the 10th July, a great theft took place of a portion of the cross which was frequently shown to the

INTERIOR OF THE RELIQUARY.

people (not the piece in the principal *châsse*), and this in spite of six guards who "*allans et venans toute nuict par icelle, tant pour la garde des sainctes reliques comme du lieu.*" This was looked upon as a great calamity by many people; but by some of the incredulous was thought to be a feint of Henri III., who had permitted the relic to be sent to Italy as security for some money borrowed by that good daughter of the Church, the Queen-mother, Catherine de' Medici. In 1793 the destruction of the *châsses* and the dispersion of the relics was ordered by the Convention, and carried out by the notorious constitutional bishop Gobel. We cannot but lament the loss to art of these reliquaries; whether, reading over the list in full of the relics given by Canon Morand, we need sigh over their destruction, is another matter. They had swollen in number since S. Louis' time, and besides a portion of the true cross, the crown of thorns, and the lance, there was the rod of Moses, the cross of victory borne by the Emperors of the East, part of the purple mantle, the reed, and other instruments of the Passion, the linen with which Our Lord wiped the Apostles' feet, the sponge, the handcuffs, the holy blood, the Virgin's veil and a piece of her hair, an imprint of the face of Our Lord, a piece of the Holy Sepulchre, and the upper part of the head of S. John Baptist. All these objects, and one or two others which it is needless to mention, were enclosed in the reliquaries which either stood or hung in the great *châsse*. But other valuables were kept elsewhere. There existed up to the reign of Louis XVI. an elegant little sacristy upon the north-east side, having two storeys, in which were deposited deeds, charters, and gold and silver vessels for the use of the altar. In it was kept the splendid agate, now in the Bibliothèque Nationale, representing the Apotheosis of Augustus, which was absolutely presented to the people as a *pax* upon great festivals, until de Peiresc, Councillor of the Parlement of Provence, about 1619, discovered the mistake, and the so-called "Triumph of Joseph" became acknowledged to be the "Apotheosis of Augustus." A careful drawing of the cameo was made by de Peiresc's friend Rubens, which was engraved by Luc Vosterman of Antwerpen. It was called in the inventory of the chapel *le Grand Camahieu* and the *Agate de Tibère;* it is, indeed, the largest known, and is of most exquisite workmanship. The whole family of the Cæsars is represented; some on earth, some in Heaven. The cracks in it are mentioned in the inventory of 1480, and it is described as: *Item unum pulcherrimum camaut in cujus circuitu sunt plures reliquiæ.* The cameo is supposed to have been one of the treasures brought by S. Louis from Constantinople. In 1343, Philippe VI. sent it to the Pope who had desired to see it, but Charles V. restored it to the chapel in 1379, and then the chapter made their possession certain, by engraving upon the socle: *ce camaieu bailla à la Sainte-Chapelle du Palais, Charles cinquième de ce nom, roi de France, qui fut fils du roi Jean, l'an MCCCLXXIX.* The Byzantine mounting, described by Tristan de Saint-Amant, was melted up when the cameo was stolen, in 1804: *Car les quatres évangélistes sont représentés de part et d'autre du châssis ou tableau d'or, dans lequel cette pierre est enchâssée.*

Another antique, an agate bust of Valentinian III.,* was metamorphosed into a S. Louis, and formed the crowning point of the precentor's mace. The clothing of this bust in silver-gilt drapery, the placing of a crown of thorns in the right-hand and a cross in the left, show the manner in which objects of Pagan art were adapted to Christian uses. That S. Louis should appear as a fat middle-aged man with a clean shaven face and cropped hair, was an anomaly of no consequence to the Mediæval artists. Another instance of the same *naïveté* is the bust of Caracalla which formerly figured as a S. Peter upon the cover of a book of the Gospels, now in the department of manuscripts. The cover is of silver-gilt, Christ crucified with the Virgin and S. John upon either side, the amethyst bust

---

* It has also been designated as Titus, and Constantine the Great. It is without doubt of the 4th century (Chabouillet).

being placed at the foot of the cross. Upon the other side is Christ enthroned, and an imitation emerald which no doubt represents some precious gem that has since disappeared.

THE CHAPEL IN THE SIXTEENTH CENTURY.

Some idea of the richness of the contents of the treasury may be formed by stating that the list of the images, vessels, reliquaries, crosses, &c., in the last inventory, taken in 1784, occupies twenty pages of Morand's book. Besides the objects already mentioned we read of a silver-gilt statue of S. Louis d'Anjou; a fragment of the cup of S. Martin; a portion of the tunic of S. Louis; an ivory Virgin, and thirty reliquaries of the 13th and 14th centuries. These were all conveyed to S. Denis on the 12th March, 1791, in a coach drawn by eight horses, and guarded by a chaplain and an officer of the king's household, who gave them over to the Benedictines, then still at the Abbey. In 1793 the relics trundled back to Paris in a procession which mimicked the former one, and after being taken to the Convention, they were melted up at the mint.

The Royal archives were stowed away in two great rooms above the sacristy of the upper church. When they were first installed there, is not known; but in 1615, when an inventory was drawn up by Pierre Dupuy and Theodore Godefroy, there were three hundred and fifty drawers, two hundred and sixty registers, fifty-two sacks, forty-two shelves, and fifteen coffers. This inventory consists of eight volumes of manuscripts in folio. In 1783 the sacristy was sacrificed to the love of symmetry in the new Cour d'honneur, and the archives were removed to the Chancellerie du Palais. At the present time some of them are in the Bibliothèque, but the greater part are at the Archives Nationale in the Rue Rambuteau.

The state of dilapidation into which the chapel had fallen when the restoration was commenced, was terrible. The tracery of the windows was destroyed, the glass was broken and filled up with plaster, the *flèche* and gargoyles had disappeared, and the interior was filled with shelves and woodwork for the storage of the archives. But the beautiful Renaissance staircase of forty-four steps (the scene of Boileau's poem, the *Lutrin*) had disappeared long before.

The dimensions of the building are as follow :—

Length of exterior	36 mètres.
Length of interior	33 ,,
Width of exterior	17 ,,
Width of interior	10.70 ,,
Height of exterior from the ground of the lower chapel to the point of the gable of the *façade*	42.50 ,,
Height of the *flèche* to the summit	33.25 ,,
Height of the vault of the lower chapel under the key-stone	6.50 ,,
Height of the vault of the upper-chapel	20.50 ,,

M. Viollet-le-Duc, in his "Dictionnaire Raisonné de l'Architecture," thus describes the building : " De la base au faîte, l'edifice est entièrement construit en pierre dure de choix, connue sous le nom de liais cliquart (Portland stone) chaque assise est cramponnée par des agrafes de fer coulées en plomb, les tailles et la pose sont exécutées avec une précision rare ; la sculpture en est composée et ciselée avec un soin particulier. Sur aucun point on ne peut constater ces négligences qui ne sont que trop souvent le résultat de la précipitation." At page 401 of the above work is an explanation of the system of courses employed by Pierre de Montereau—a manner of strengthening masonry which was in use before this period (13th century), but which was improved upon by the great architect of the Sainte-Chapelle. It is very similar to the system now in use.

The only communication between the lower and upper chapels at the present time is by means of the small turret staircase, but formerly the upper church was approached by a wide exterior flight of forty-four steps. It was reconstructed many times, and the last one, in the Egyptian style, was dated 1811. The demolition of this is no loss ; but it seems a pity it should not have been replaced by one in better taste, as the only approach to the upper chapel (except the turret stairs) is through the corridors of the Palais de Justice.

The first thing that strikes the visitor upon entering is the enormous size of the windows, which occupy the entire space between the buttresses, and rise to the base of the roof. All the weight of the vaulting rests, therefore, upon the exterior buttresses, but not the slightest inflection has ever taken place. The church is built truly east and west, the entrance to each chapel being by separate portals. The only modification the exterior of the building has sustained since S. Louis' time is the addition of a little oratory attributed to Louis XI., and the rebuilding of a part of the *façade* in the 15th century.

The porch of the lower chapel is divided into two bays by a pier, on which is a statue of the Blessed Virgin, while above, in the tympanum, is a representation of the *Coronation of the Virgin*. The restoration of this and the entire ornament of the doorway is the work of M. Geoffroy-Dechaume. The original statue had the reputation of working miracles ; and it is related that when, towards 1304, Jean Duns Scotus, a celebrated theologian of the University of Paris, was praying at its feet, it bent its head in approval of the doctrine of the Immaculate Conception, which that learned doctor was teaching. It has since always remained in the same position. The portal of the upper chapel is of the same character as the lower one, but richer in its decoration. It is nearly all new, for the old ornament had not only been mutilated, but had been completely chiselled off. The *voussure* is a mass of sculptures—single figures, groups, and ornament. The figures are forty-four in number: Angels carrying the elect to heaven, Angels censing and bearing crowns, martyrs with the instruments of their sufferings, and the lost souls surrounded by the flames of hell, the whole forming a framework to the central subject in the tympanum, the *Last Judgement*; the work is a marvel of patient study, modelled upon the portals of Notre-Dame and S. Ger-

main l'Auxerrois, each figure having been fitted into its place upon the lines of the original wherever any traces of the old sculptures had been preserved.

The plan of the church is a parallelogram, terminating in a polygonal apse. The buttresses reach to the parapet, and terminate in pinnacles surrounded by gargoyles ornamented with the most grotesque birds and beasts. The windows of the nave are divided into four lights, with foliated circles in the heads very similar to those of the Chapter House at Salisbury. Several *flèches* have preceded the present one; the first fell in the reign of Charles VI., the second was burnt in the great fire of 16th July, 1630; the third was erected by Louis XIII. in the ogival style of that period, and remained until the 17th century. When it was destroyed, in 1791, it contained five bells, which had been cast in 1738; the Dauphin, the Duc d'Orléans, the Duc de Chartres, and the first President of the Chambre des Comptes being their sponsors. The present *flèche* was erected in 1853, and is in the style of the 15th century. It is of wood, covered with lead, and consists of three octagonal storeys supporting the spire.

On the lower storey are colossal statues of the twelve Apostles, most of them portraits, the S. Thomas being that of the sculptor Lassus. The gables of the upper storey support Angels with the instruments of the Passion. The crockets of the spire are *fleurs-de-lys*, and the whole is resplendent with gilding. The summit of the *chevet* is surmounted by a huge Angel, in lead, holding a processional cross. There was an idea, never carried out, of making this statue turn round mechanically upon a pivot during the twenty-four hours, that it might present the symbol of salvation successively to all quarters of the city. The masks upon the pedestal of this figure are all portraits of the artists and workmen engaged upon the restoration of the chapel, posing as the Kings of France. The oratory, erected by Louis XI., between the two buttresses of the fourth bay, upon the south side, is decorated with niches and corbels of human heads.

The vaulting of the lower chapel is supported by fourteen single-shaft pillars, surrounded by foliated capitals of various designs. The walls are decorated with arcading, terminated at the east end by an apse. The two columns without capitals were added at the same time as the apsidal tribune in the upper chapel. The decoration is in imitation of the original 13th century work, some of which, a fragment of an *Annunciation*, was discovered in removing the remains of some later work in a style utterly at variance with the architecture, by Martin Fréminet, painter to Henri IV. and Louis XIII. In 1691 the tracery of the windows and the stained glass were destroyed and replaced by white in order to give extra light. Formerly there were seven altars and a font in the lower chapel, Boileau, whose father had a house in the court of the palace, being amongst those who were baptised there.

The upper chapel is one of those buildings which one never tires of admiring. When we wend our way up the turret stairs, and enter it from the semi-darkness of the crypt, it strikes us as the most exquisite scheme of colour imaginable. Add to the beauty of the chapel all the associations which crowd upon the memory—S. Louis' beautiful faith and noble life, his enthusiasm for God's work and man's welfare; all the ceremonies and the processions which have taken place there, with the lights, the flowers, and the incense, and our imagination forms a picture that no hand could adequately paint. The chapel is composed of four bays for the nave, and seven smaller for the apse. The vault is groined and is supported by clustered columns and capitals ornamented with foliage. The windows occupy the entire space between the supporting pillars, and are filled with most beautiful stained glass;* while below is an

---

* "Vin de la couleur des vitres de la Sainte-Chapelle."—(*Old proverb*.)

arcade rising from a stone seat. The capitals of the columns are most exquisitely carved in imitation of the flora of France, and the quatrefoils between the arches are filled with a kind of decoration which is as rare as it is effective. The designs were drawn upon the stone, and the backgrounds filled in with incrustations of blue glass and gold, the subjects being taken from the lives of the martyrs. Most of them have been restored; but, very wisely, two or three have been left in the state in which they were discovered. Between the arches of the arcades are Angels with outstretched arms, who seem to be crowning the martyrs in the quatrefoils. At the third bay of the nave on each side are recesses which formed reserved places for some privileged persons during Mass; and it is thought that they were probably occupied by the king and queen, the former on the Gospel, the latter on the Epistle side. On the south wall is a slanting recess, which formerly must have served as a chapel, as there was an altar at the end of it having a painted reredos representing the interior of the great *châsse*, with all its contents ranged in proper order, and S. Louis praying before it. It is supposed that Louis XI. may have used this niche as a place where he could pray without being seen, but in sight of the altar and the relics.

It has always been the custom at the consecration of a church to place a cross wherever the sign of the cross had been made by the bishop. The architect of the Sainte-Chapelle conceived the happy idea of placing the twelve Apostles as pillars of the Church, supporting these crosses, which are in the form of monstrances. The pedestals on which the figures stand are affixed to the pillars, and the statues, like the rest of the church, are painted and gilt, those of the 13th century being marvellous examples of the sculpture of that period. After the closing of the chapel these statues were sent to the Musée des Monuments Français; but when the Museum was suppressed they were dispersed or broken up. S. Peter was discovered in fragments at S. Denis, another was given to the church at Creteil, where it passed as S. Louis, and four were given to the missionaries for their Calvary at Mt. Valerien. The latter were in perfect preservation, and the colour had not disappeared. They remained at the entrance of one of the chapels of the Way of the Cross until 1830, when some senseless vandals threw them down and broke them; but the fragments were preserved, and are now in the garden of the Hôtel Cluny, a museum of fragments. The rest were replaced in the chapel, and are the fourth and fifth on each side facing the altar; all the others are new.

The pavement is modern incised stone, with incrustations of colour, representing geometrical patterns, animals, and flowers. In the apse are subjects—the *Four rivers of Paradise*, and the *Seven Sacraments* in the form of rivers. The altar is an exact copy of the original one. Above it is the tribune and canopy where the relics were exposed, with a spiral staircase leading up to it;* the northern one is ancient, and was found by Alexandre Lenoir, in the Musée des Petits-Augustins, where for half a century it had been attached to the *façade* of the Château de Gaillon, a 16th century work, now in the court of the Ecole des Beaux-Arts. On one side of the apse is a very beautiful *piscina*. Part of the *baldachino* is ancient, and the rest has been restored from old drawings.

Formerly several statues occupied places in the chapel; one, a terra-cotta Notre-Dame de Pitié, by Germain Pilon, which is now in the chapel of the military school of St. Cyr. A 16th century *jubé*, with altars attached to it, marked the nave from the chancel. The retables of these altars (now in the Louvre) were in enamel, signed and dated Léonard Limousin, 1533, and contain portraits of François I. and his second wife, Eléonore d'Autriche, sister of Charles V. and of Henri II. and Catherine de'Medici, all kneeling. The choir was filled with carved stalls of the time of Henri II. At the four corners of the altar pavement, Henri III. elevated bronze Angels upon black marble pillars. On the *retro*-altar was a silver-gilt model of the chapel, three or four feet high, executed in 1631 by Pijard, goldsmith, and guardian of the relics. This contained some of the treasures, and was considered a very fine work of art, costing some 13,000 *livres*. There is an excellent drawing of the original altar in Viollet-le-Duc's dictionary. Canon Morand tells us, in his history of the chapel, that the *ciborium*, which is usually placed in the tabernacle, was here suspended in front of the altar—probably the *retro*-altar, as in the engraving of the High Altar in the Canon's book, there is no representation of it. All the old furniture of the church has

---

* *Pour deniers paiés à Jehan de Lille, orfèvre, pour j siège qu'il fist du commandement du Roy pour séoir de lez les saintes reliques en la Saincte Chapelle de Paris—iiij escus.* (*Comptes royaux.*)

disappeared, the carved stalls, the *jubé*, the altars, and the pulpit. Upon the subject of letting, or taking money for seats or chairs in church, the Abbé waxes wrathful. Nothing is more "indécent que de vendre ou de louer des places à l'Eglise. En Angleterre et en Hollande on est assis dans les Temples sans aucun frais, et sans être interrompu par les Mandians, par les quêteurs, ou par les loueurs de chaises; en quoi les non-Catholiques nous donnent un bel exemple à suivre, si nous étions assez raisonables et assez désinterressés

THE JUBÉ, SIXTEENTH CENTURY.

pour cela." This is a proof that the letting of pews which prevailed in this country some years ago was a bad departure from the free-and-open seat system of the last century; and the picture drawn of the restlessness of a French church, from the incessant perambulating of the *Suisses*, the *quêteurs*, and the chair-owners, is as true now as it was in the time of Morand.

The Canon then goes on to record the want of reverence of the congregation, how they just *half* kneel when the bell rings; how they must needs sit, and even gossip, during the short quarter of an hour occupied by a low mass; how they take snuff and bear themselves generally, and then go out and stand about for the greater part of the day at their business.

S. Louis ordained, in his foundation charters, that the offerings received by the priests at the altar should be devoted to the reparation of the glass, and that if it should be insufficient, the necessary funds should be taken from the Royal Treasury deposited at the Temple. The restoration of the windows is now complete, this being the work of MM. Steinheil and Lusson. These artists have done their work so well, and matched the colours so perfectly, that it is difficult to distinguish the new from the old. The rose-window is of the 15th century, the others of the 13th century. The subjects are from the Old and New Testament, and from the life of S. Louis. Some of these latter are original, and, as it is probable that the artists assisted at the ceremonies held in the chapel, it is also probable that the pictures may be true portraits of the personages represented. The subjects of the rose-window are all taken from the Apocalypse.

Such is the chapel which was so dear to the King that he felt a "*malaise*" when he heard divine service elsewhere, and of which the troubadour Rutebeuf sings the praises in a poem written after the death of the Saint, entitled, *Les Regrès au roys Loeys:*

> Chapèle de Paris ! bien èrves maintenue
> La mort, ce m'est aduis, t'a fet desconvenue
> Du miex de tes amys, t'a laissée toute nue
> De la mort, sont plaintifs et grant gent et menue."—
> (*MS. Bibliothèque Nationale.*)

SAINT-DENIS.

Although the Benedictine abbey church of S. Denis is some miles from Paris, it is so mixed up with the history of the capital that it ought not to be omitted in a series of "Paris Churches." Moreover, as it is by far the finest church in, or near, the metropolis, and one of the grandest examples of French 13th century architecture, no one ought to grudge the tiresome journey by train or tram in order to see it, even if his stay in Paris be limited to a few days. The only thing required to make it perfectly beautiful is new stained glass in the windows of the clerestory to replace that put up during the early years of this century, a horrible example of the execrable taste of the period.

SAINT-DENIS.

S. Denis was one of the sacred spots of mediæval Europe—a species of Christian Mecca. "Si les lieux sont reputez aincts," says one of its children, Dom Millet,* "à cause des

THE ABBEY CHURCH FROM THE GRANDE PLACE.

choses sainctes faictes ou aduenuës en iceux, comme ont esté est sont encores, les montagnes de Thabor et de Caluaire, ou

* Religious, Benedictine of the convent (congregation) of S. Maur, Order of S. Benedict.

bien à cause des choses sainctes qu'ils contiennent, comme estoit l'Arche d'Alliance, et le Sancta Sanctorum des Juifs ; je croy qu'il n'y a personne qui n'aduoüe que l'Eglise de S. Denys en France ne soit vn lieu tres-sainct en toutes ces considerations, puis qu'elle a esté dediée des propres mains de nostre Sauueur Jesus-Christ, descendu exprés du Ciel auec vne grande multitude d'Anges et de Saincts, et qu'elle contient en soy tant des choses sainctes, et des Reliques si precieuses et rares." It was a poor but worthy leper who saw this strange vision. He had been left shut up in the church, when in the dead of night he was startled by a dazzling light; and then he beheld the Saviour, His Apostles, multitudes of Angels, and S. Denis and his companions. Our Lord sprinkled the church with holy water, and S. Denis and his companions served Him; and then He said to the leper: "*Go and tell le bon roy Dagobort what thou hast seen.*" "*But how can a poor leper penetrate the presence of the King?*" said he. Then a wondrous miracle was performed; the Saviour touching him with his finger, made the leper clean. Then he went to the King, and they all believed.

Not only was S. Denis specially favoured by this miraculous dedication, but it was privileged by Charlemagne in a charter, as the chief and mistress of all the churches in the kingdom; and its abbot as the Primate of all the prelates of France. This great man was allowed to have six deacons vested in dalmatics whenever he officiated, an honour conferred upon him by Pope Stephen III. when he consecrated the High Altar in 753, and at the same time anointed and crowned King Pépin and Queen Bertrade, and their two sons Charles and Carloman. People, high and low, from all the ends of the earth, flocked to the famous abbey as we now rush to the World's Fairs; and the great ones of the earth, princes, nobles, and ambassadors, considered that they had seen nought of the civilised world if they had not paid their respects to the relics at S. Denis. Some went for love, some out of sheer curiosity to see the riches of the treasury: divers crosses, reliquaries, statues, vases, chalices, and other vessels for the altars; S. Denis' mitre, chalice, and rings; the famous head of solid silver gilt, containing his skull, and presented to the abbey by Marguerite de France in 1360; a wonderful golden cup enriched with precious stones which had belonged to King Solomon, and a rock crystal vase from the Temple of the wise man—both the gift of Charles the Bald. He, being abbot, made it his custom to attend "the duties of his station at the Abbaye, on the solemn festivals, passing the day in pious conversation with the monks and in religious observances." He also made considerable donations,* added to the many lamps which are kept continually burning before the shrines, and increased the number of wax tapers employed in the services of the church. Then further, amongst the curiosities, were the nail of a griffin upon a silver-gilt animal; a unicorn's horn six feet high, sent by Aaron King of Persia to Charlemagne; the hunting horn of Roland, nephew of Charlemagne; and the lantern which was used at the betrayal of our Lord in the Garden, called the Lantern of Judas. The latter was of copper, embellished by rock crystal, through which the light shone. (This was also the gift of Charles the Bald). The mirror of the prince of poets, Virgil, which was of jet; the sword of the *genereuse Amazone, Jeanne la Pucelle*. Of the beauty of the croziers and pastoral crosses, the mitres and episcopal rings, Dom Millet's description leaves no doubt; and of the magnificence of the abbots, and the splendour of their monastery, we have more than ample evidence. As an old epigram puts it:

> Au tems passé du siècle d'or,
> Crosse de *bois*, Evêque d'or,
> Maintenant changent les lois,
> Crosse d'or, Evêque de *bois*.

The Huguenots destroyed many of the church ornaments, ruined chapels, and worse still, "ces impies la pillerent (S. Denis) et dissiperent entierement, sans y laisser aucune chose, sinon ce qu'ils ne voulutent point. Ils ne pouuoient faire pis, sinon mettre le feu par tout le Monastere, comme ils firent en tant d'autres par la France." It was supposed that the "Prince de Condé, leur chef," was not present at these little pastimes of his valiant soldiers, for when he heard what had been done "il fit pendre vne douzaine, pour monstrer comment il detestoit leur sacrilege: mais pour cela les pertes ne furent pas reconnettes."

In a *History of the Royal Abbaye of Saint Denis*, published in London in 1795, we have some curious details connected with the church. "Every Sunday and Holy Day at mass, the Deacons and Sub-deacons, after having received the 'precious

* All the river Seine from the *ru de Sève* (Sèvres) near S. Cloud, to S. Germain-en-Laye.

body of Our Lord,' repaired to a side altar to suck up through a reed, enclosed in a tube of enamelled gold, the 'precious blood,' according to a very ancient custom adopted in the church of S. Denis, which is retained without any variation to this day." Whether this was so, or whether it was the result of the anonymous writer's imagination, I cannot say, as I find nothing about it in other books that I have studied.

The same author speaks of the "miraculous silver keys of S. Denis which they apply to the faces of those persons who have been so unfortunate as to be bitten by mad dogs, and who receive a certain and immediate relief by only touching them." Alas, that these keys should have been melted up; for here was a cure for hydrophobia without any of the vicarious suffering which M. Pasteur's discovery has caused.

The legend of S. Denis, the patron of France, is exceedingly picturesque. By some ecclesiastical authorities he is said to have lived in the 1st century, by others in the 2nd or 4th, but by most he is one and the same person as Dionysius the Areopagite. Hilduin, abbot of S. Denis at the beginning of the 9th century, seems to have had no doubt upon the subject, and in art the Saint and the disciple of S. Paul have always been looked upon as the self-same personage, although tradition records the existence of another S. Denis, a bishop of Paris, in the 3rd century. Dionysius was an Athenian philosopher named Theosophus. Travelling in Egypt to study astrology with a companion named Apollophanes, they were surprised by a strange darkness that came over the heavens, and were naturally much troubled thereby. Returning to Athens, Dionysius heard S. Paul preach, and thereupon being converted to Christianity, he understood that the darkness which he had seen at Heliopolis was none other than that which fell upon the earth for the space of three hours when the Blessed Redeemer was crucified. Baptised and ordained priest, Dionysius subsequently became bishop of Athens; and in some of the writings attributed to him he relates that he travelled to Jerusalem to see the Blessed Virgin, whom he found continually surrounded by a dazzling light, and attended by a company of Angels. He also gives an account of her death at which he was present with certain of the Apostles. After this, he returned to Athens and was subsequently present at S. Paul's martyrdom in Rome. Thence he was sent by S. Clement to preach the Gospel, together with a priest named Rusticus, and a deacon Eleutherius.

Arrived at Paris, an exceeding great city full of people and provided with all the good things of the earth, they found it so attractive that it seemed to them another Athens, and so they sojourned there, teaching the people, who were learned in all things but the way of truth. S. Denis then sent missionaries into other parts of Gaul, and into Germany. But these successes were not pleasing unto Satan, and so he stirred up the nobles against the good bishop, who was accused before the Emperor Trajan. Some say it was Domitian, but in either case the result was the despatch of one Frescennius, a pro-consul, from Rome, with orders to throw Denis and his companions into prison. This was done, and finding that they would not retract, they were put to death upon the Hill of Mercury (who was so much honoured by the Gauls), and which was subsequently called Montmartre (*Mons Martyrum*).

"Le Saint evêque Denis, et ses deux compagnons, le prêtre Rustique et le diacre Eleuthère, souffrirent leur mémorable et très-glorieuse passion, à la vue de la cité des Parisiens, sur la colline qui se nommait auparavant Mont de Mercure, parce que cette idole y était particulièrement honorée de Gaulois, et qu'on appelle aujourd'hui le Mont des Martyrs en mémoire des saints du Seigneur qui accomplirent en ce lieu même leur martyre triomphal."*

Then a stupendous miracle took place. S. Denis not desiring, or not being permitted, to become food for wolves, took up his decapitated head in his hands, and walked for the space of two miles, Angels singing by the way. Accompanied by this celestial body-guard, the Saint marched over the plains beyond the city, and signified, in some way unrecorded, that he desired burial where now stands the church dedicated to his memory. This was accomplished by a pious woman named Catulla, who had ministered unto the three blessed martyrs in their prison, and who now laid their mutilated remains in her own field.

Paris formerly, even as late as the last century, contained many spots sacred to the memory of S. Denis and his three companions. At Notre-Dame-des-Champs a crypt used to be shown where they preached to their first disciples. At S. Benoît, now destroyed, there was formerly an oratory, on the wall of which was an inscription recording that S. Denis first

* Hulduin, abbot of S. Denis, commencement of 9th century, who took possession the same day as that upon which Charlemagne died.—*Les Areopagitiques.*

invoked the name of the Most High on that spot. At S. Denis-de-la-Chartre was the prison where the martyrs were visited by our Lord, and where He administered His Blessed Body and Blood to them. At S. Denis-du-Pas was the ground upon which they suffered their first tortures; and upon Montmartre the church of S. Pierre records the spot upon which they were decapitated. The way across the plain from Montmartre to the place of burial was marked by a succession of crosses, and the field where the Saint's remains were laid subsequently became the precincts of the famous abbey.

SILVER STATUETTE FORMERLY IN THE TREASURY.

The first church is said to have been erected before the invasion of the Franks, but this had fallen into ruins in the 5th century, and it was through the piety of S. Geneviève and the people of Paris that it was rebuilt. This Saint, like all good Parisians, held S. Denis in great esteem; and it was during a visit paid to his shrine that her taper, maliciously blown out by the arch-enemy, was successfully relighted through the fervour of her prayers. Gregoire de Tours relates many wondrous miracles which took place in the new church for the benefit of the faithful and the chastisement of the wicked.

But the magnificence with which Dagobert rebuilt and endowed S. Denis completely eclipsed the work of the maid of Nanterre; and so effectually was the king looked upon as the founder of the abbey that, up to the dissolution of the monasteries, the monks celebrated his festival upon the 19th of January with great solemnity and splendour. It was about the year 630 that Dagobert undertook the rebuilding of the church, which is said to have been decorated with precious marbles, magnificent bronze doors, and gold and silver vessels enriched with precious stones. These latter, and the shrine of the Saint, as well as the great cross at the entrance of the choir, were the work of the famous artificer in metals, S. Eloy, who was also the maker of the shrines of SS. Martin, Germain, and Geneviève. These, and, in fact, all this great smith's works (as far as is known) have perished; but his memory is still preserved by pictures and sculptures representing some of the legendary incidents of his life. In the Firenze Academy is a picture by Botticelli, and at the church of Or San Michele is a statue and a bas-relief, both of which represent one of the great events of the Saint's life. A horse having been brought to him to be shod, the animal proved restive, and the Saint being exercised in his mind as to how he should keep the beast still, bethought him of an excellent plan. He calmly cut off the leg, and placing it upon his anvil, fastened on the shoe; this done, he replaced the leg upon the horse, to the amazement of the beast and the edification of his owner. Another picture, painted for the Company of the Goldsmiths, represents S. Eloy under the form of Benvenuto Cellini, presenting a shrine to King Dagobert, who figures in the costume of François I$^{er.}$ In 754, Pépin and his queen Berthe, after being anointed at S. Denis by Pope Stephen II., began the reconstruction of the Merovingian church which Charlemagne finished and dedicated in 775. From that year until the 12th century, little is known of the history of the abbey. Like all churches and monasteries in the north of France, it was probably destroyed, and its lands laid waste by the invasions of the Northmen and the disastrous civil wars which characterised the end of the Carlovingian dynasty, for nothing remains of the magnificence of the churches of Dagobert and of Charlemagne but a few columns and marble capitals in the crypt.

The third and present church was commenced by the great Abbot Suger, and is considered by many French architects to be the earliest example of Pointed architecture. Suger erected the tower, the portals, the nave, and the choir in rapid succession, and subsequently the *chevet* and chapels; he filled the windows with the most exquisite jewel-like stained glass, and loaded the shrines and altars with precious stones. Some of the sacred vessels formerly belonging to the church are now in the Salle d'Apollon of the Louvre, and testify to the exquisite artistic taste as well as to the religious enthusiasm of the good abbot. "*As it is our duty to present unto God oblations*

TOMB OF HENRI II. IN THE VALOIS CHAPEL BUILT BY PHILIBERT DELORME.

of gems and of gold, I, Suger, offer this vase unto the Lord," is the inscription upon an antique sardonyx amphora which he converted into a vessel for the altar. The dedication of this church took place twice, in 1140 and 1144, but it was only to remain intact some 70 years. In 1219, the day after the feast of the nativity of the Virgin, its *flèche* was struck by lightning, and a few years after, the church itself was partially destroyed. Abbot Eudes Clément replaced the wooden *flèche* by a stone one, and raised the interior of the apse; and his third successor, Matthieu de Vendôme, finished the transept and the nave. The chapels of the nave upon the north side were built in the 14th century, and a few unimportant additions were made in the succeeding century. Of the magnificent circular chapel of the Valois erected for Henri II. and Catherine de'Medici, nothing remains but a beautiful colonnade, now forming a sham ruin in the Parc Monceau. The chapel was situated upon the north of the apse, near the steps, and was destroyed during the regency of Philippe d'Orléans, in 1719.

It is generally supposed that the destruction of churches and the despoiling of monasteries in France were the work of the enemies of religion in the form of the "people." But the kings did not hesitate to rob the church when they could drain no more money out of their long-suffering subjects. To Francis I.* and Louis XIV. the eighth commandment was no more binding than the seventh; laws, divine or otherwise, were made for the vulgar herd, not for their most Christian Majesties; and so, when the "Grand Monarque" saw fit to please Mme. de Maintenon by founding St. Cyr, he suppressed the abbacy of S. Denis, and relieved the monastery of the abbot's revenues for an endowment. This was the beginning of the downfall, and in 1791, the Benedictines were dispersed after an occupation of twelve centuries. In the memoirs of the organist attached to the abbey at the time, there is a touching account of the last mass celebrated by the prior upon the day of departure. But the church remained intact, and

* See the Inventory of the Treasury of Laon, from which we cull the following: In 1523, when François I. wanted money to carry on his war against Charles V. and Henry VIII., we read in the *Journal d'un Bourgeois de Paris*, his manner of getting it. "Le roy envoya aussi quérir trois ou quatre appostres d'or qui estoient ès-reliques en l'église épiscopale à Laon, en Picardie, dont il y en avoit douze, mais les aultres n'estoient que d'argent, parquoy furent délaissez; et valloient iceux III. ou IIII. appostres environ quatre mille escus; et fit ce le roy pour subvenir et ayder en ses guerres de Picardie qu'il avoit contres les Anglais." Louis XIV. also, when his star had paled a little, put various cathedral chapters under contribution; the church of Notre-Dame de Liesse sending silver to the royal treasury to the amount of 28,600 livres.

was even made the *dépôt* of the relics of the Sainte-Chapelle,* after the suppression of the chaplains belonging to the latter. The *Moniteur* of 3rd September, 1791, gives an account of the sittings of the commission of *savants*, established at the Bibliothèque des Quatre-Nations, for the consideration of the preservation of works of art. This commission was appointed by the National Assembly after the passing of the law for the appropriation of the property of the clergy by *la chose publique*. M. De Larochefoucauld was the president of this "Commission des Monuments," assisted by many artists and *connoisseurs*. They first of all chose certain places as receptacles for the works of art, and then decided what to keep and what to destroy. The former quarters of the Petits-Augustins became the museum of tombs and sepulchral sculptures; and to the Capucins, the Grands-Jésuites, and the Cordeliers were sent the books and manuscripts. A descriptive catalogue was drawn up by Alexandre Lenoir,† who was appointed curator in 1790. Unfortunately, much was destroyed, as, for instance, at the abbey of Royaumont, where two Benedictines, Poirier and Puthod, were sent by the commission to superintend matters. The mausoleum of the princes of S. Louis' family was "*démoli avec adresse*," says the *Moniteur;* the coffins were opened "*avec circonspection*," the ashes taken up with care, and then, ticketed and sealed, sent to S. Denis. Les sieurs Puthod and Poirier carried off the remains of seven princes and six monuments, which arrived just in time to be packed off to the museum of the Petits-Augustins.

Many of the seventy-three abbots, from Dodon, the first (living in 637), to the last, Jean-François-Paul de Gondi, Cardinal de Retz, were distinguished for their piety, for their learning, their greed, or their vices. Amongst them we find the names of Fulrad, Hilduin, Suger, Mathieu de Vendôme, the Emperor Charles the Bald, the Kings Eudes, Robert and Hugues Capet,‡ the Cardinals de Bourbon, de Lorraine, de Guise, and Mazarin. The conventual buildings were all de-

---

* See pages 18, 19.

† *Musée des Monuments Français*.

‡ It seems that one object in electing the king as abbot was to have some lay element in the chapter, and thus disarm the enemies of the Church. Charles le Chauve was abbot for about sixteen years; he chose his provost, treasurer, and dean, and gave into their keeping all the working of the monastery, with the exception of the military contingent, which was given over to the *maire* or *avoué*. Adjoining the abbey was a palace for the use of the kings.

stroyed in the reign of Louis XV., and during the Revolution the church suffered in the same way as Notre-Dame and S. Eustache, by being secularized in the most revolting manner. But if the Revolutionists destroyed and carried away monuments, the Imperial architects did worse, for they began a restoration in their own hideous taste and "style"; and it was not until a few years ago that the old church was restored to its pristine beauty.

Perhaps few churches have seen more changes than the silent walls of S. Denis have witnessed. The burial place of most of the kings of France, it was also upon its High Altar that Louis le Gros deposited the *oriflamme*, the famous standard of France,* while some seven centuries later, its tombs were only preserved from utter ruin by the wit of Alexandre Lenoir. Even the church itself was threatened with destruction, and was only saved by an architect seriously suggesting that it should be turned into a market, the side chapels forming shops. By turns a Temple of Reason, a *dépôt* of artillery, a theatre of acrobats, a flour warehouse, and a granary, its desecration was not consummated until the glass was removed, and the leaden covering of its roof converted into bullets. Napoleon saved what remained, and began restoring it as a resting-place for the defunct members of his dynasty. The Concordat guaranteed it a chapter, and religious services were restored.† But the 19th century proved as disastrous as wars

---

* The *oriflamme*, or *enseigne*, derived its name from being made of scarlet silk, and covered with flames of gold. When it was to be taken from its depository, the king and princes first went to Notre-Dame and offered up some prayers to the Blessed Virgin; then they proceeded to the abbey, where, after being solemnly received by the religious, they descended ("*sans chaperon et sans ceinture*") into the crypt, where the bodies of the holy martyrs lay, and where the *oriflamme* was kept. The abbot then delivered the flag into the king's own hands, and the king presented it to the Count de Vesin, who carried it to the altar. The standard-bearer was always a *Chevalier* of undoubted loyalty, courage, and piety. Previously to receiving the charge, he confessed his sins, obtained absolution, received the Holy Eucharist, and took a solemn oath to be faithful to his trust, and never to suffer the flag to be torn from his hands, except at the cost of his life. But at the battle of Rosbec it mysteriously disappeared. And to think that the red flag is now the emblem of all that is Revolutionary, Communistic, and Anarchist! Perhaps if the Government gave it the old name, we might see it burnt in the Place de la République.

† The Chapter formerly consisted of a *Primicier*, *Chanoines évêques*, non-resident; and Canons residentiary. The office of *Primicier* was, I think, abolished only a few years ago, and now the chapter simply consists of canons in residence.

THE NORTH-WEST DOORWAY.

and revolutions. Lightning once more brought down the *flèche* in 1837, and again in 1846; and scrapings and cleanings carried away all the old surfaces of the walls. Still, through the talent and learning of Viollet-le-Duc, it is one of the finest of 13th century churches, and now that the tombs have all been replaced in their former positions, one of the most interesting.

The *façade* has three doorways, which are rich in the somewhat rude sculpture of the time of Suger. The subject of the central tympanum and *voussure* is The Last Judgment. Christ is pronouncing the last sentence, surrounded by the dead who are rising from their graves. His Blessed Mother is interceding for sinners, and Abraham is receiving the elect into his bosom. The Apostles, and the four-and-twenty elders, holding musical instruments, and vases for the reception of the prayers of the just as a sweet-smelling incense, are there, looking on at the damned tossed into hell. Upon the stylobate of the portal we read the parable of the Wise and foolish Virgins.

The southern doorway is decorated with the Martyrdom of S. Denis, and the appearance of our Blessed Lord to the holy martyrs while in prison. Unfortunately, much of these bas-reliefs is modern.

Some statues on one of the transept doorways are curious examples of how a fraud may be perpetuated. They represent, without doubt, some members of the royal house of David, but at some period they were said to be kings of the Capétien line, and as such, casts were taken and sent to Versailles, where they figured as portrait statues of Hugues Capet, Robert, Henri, Philippe, Louis VI., and Louis VII. The capitals of the columns and the foliage ornament of these portals are vastly superior in style to the figures.

On each side of the western rose-window are some bands of black and white marble, after the manner of the churches of Pisa and Genoa, *souvenirs*, probably, of Suger's travels in Italy. Indeed, he tells us in the account of his administration that he took much trouble in preserving a mosaic which he had brought home and placed in the tympanum of one of the doors. This was unfortunately replaced, in 1774, by a bas-relief of the meanest possible workmanship.

The interior consists of a nave and two aisles, with a *chevet* of seven chapels at the east end, considerably raised above the level of the nave. Access to these chapels is gained by a flight of steps on each side of the High Altar, and under them is the royal crypt. The whole of the east end of the church, the double aisles, with their single-shaft pillars, the chapels, the vaulting, and the glass, form a mass of colour, and a most beautiful *coup d'œil*;* indeed, there is but one eyesore in the whole building, the aforesaid series of windows representing Louis Philippe's heroic deeds. Blue swallow-tailed coats and white trousers scarcely form a costume which is either effective or appropriate as designs for church windows.

The wood carving of the stalls is of the 15th century, and was brought from the abbey of S. Lucien-lez-Beauvais; the inlaid marquetry work at the backs of the seats is from the Château de Gaillon, built by Cardinal d'Amboise. Many of the *miséréres* have the usual quaint conceits which one sees everywhere. Portions of the old glass were preserved by Lenoir in the museum of the Petits-Augustins during the stormy period, and were afterwards replaced in the windows of the apse. They consist mainly of fragments of a tree of Jesse, and may be found in the chapel of the Virgin. There are in all eleven lozenge-shaped medallions representing scenes in the life of Moses, and mystical subjects from the Apocalypse, bearing inscriptions by Suger. Upon the medallion of the Annunciation, the good abbot himself is portrayed prostrate before the Blessed Virgin. In one or two of the other chapels there are a few fragments of the legend of S. Laurence.

THE LADY CHAPEL.

Of the early kings of France Dagobert was the first to be buried at S. Denis, and his memorial tomb (much restored) still stands on the right of the High Altar. Clovis and Clotilde were buried in the crypt of the first church erected upon

---

* How fine the effect must have been when the great cross of S. Eloy stood upon the *grille*, shutting off the nave from the choir! It was of gold, enriched with precious stones and pearls.

the site of S. Geneviève, then called the Church of the Holy
Apostles. Childebert was laid in the church of the Abbey of S.
Vincent (founded by him), afterwards called S. Germain-des-
Près. Chlodoald was buried at S. Cloud; S. Radegonde, wife
of Clotaire I., at Poitiers; Chilpéric and Frédégonde laid the
body of one of their children in the first church of S. Denis.
Besides Dagobert I., his queen, Nanthilde, and their sons,
Sigebert II. and Clovis II. were buried at S. Denis; and although
it is thought that other Merovingian princes also received burial
there, many repose at Chelles, S. Waast d'Arras, S. Bertin,
S. Etienne de Choisy, Metz, Angoulême, S. Romain de
Blaye, Jumièges, and S. Crépin de Soissons. The monuments
of Charles-Martel, Pépin and Berthe, Carloman, Charles the
Bald, Ermentrude, Louis, Carloman, and Eudes were all at S.
Denis. Charlemagne was buried at Aix-la-Chapelle, where
the magnificent *châsses* containing his skull and some of his
bones may still be seen. His descendants were distributed all
over Europe: at Köln, Mainz, Prüm, Regensburg, Loresheim,
Oettinghen, Reichenau, Audlau, Verona, Milan, and Piacenza;
those in France, at Metz, Sens, Bourges, S. Laurent, S. Sulpice,
Tours, Angers, Lyon, Portiers, Compiègne, Reims, Péronne,
and Soissons.

From Hugues Capet to Louis XV. most of the kings were
interred at S. Denis; but it must be borne in mind that
almost all the tombs of the earlier sovereigns are modern,
either wholly or in part. In the 13th century the strange custom came into fashion of dividing the bodies of royal personages, and burying the parts in different places. The Benedictine monks of S. Denis protested against this division of
valuable property, asserting their right to possess the entire remains of the kings; but the Dominicans and the Cordeliers
contested these claims, and subsequently gained permission for
their own churches to share in the spoil. Later on, other religious orders obtained the same privileges; and the ladies of
Val-de-Grâce were distinguished by the possession of the hearts
of nearly all the royal princes and princesses from Anne
d'Autriche, the founder of the monastery. Naturally, when
each defunct sovereign was divided into three portions—the
body, the heart, and the intestines—great opportunties were
afforded to architects and sculptors; and we thus find three
marble monuments with recumbent figures erected for the
remains of Charles V., that at S. Denis containing his body,

URN SCULPTURED FOR THE HEART OF FRANÇOIS Ier.

while Rouen and Maubuisson respectively possessed his heart and his *et ceteras*.* Francis I.'s heart was placed in an exquisite urn in the church of the nuns of Haute-Bruyère; while his body was buried in the grand monument at S. Denis. The urn was the work of Pierre Bontems, and is now in the same chapel as the tomb, which was the joint work of Philibert Delorme and Bontems. The beautiful group of the *Three Graces*, by Germain Pilon, formerly in the church of the Célestins, and now in the Renaissance Museum of the Louvre, supported an urn containing the heart of Henri II.;† the hearts of the 13th and 14th Louis, enveloped in shrines in the form of silver Angels, being the property of the church of the Jesuits. The number of monuments erected at S. Denis to the memory of the families of the sovereigns was small; and none of them were to be compared, as works of art, to the beautiful tombs of the Dukes of Bourgogne and of Brétagne at Dijon, at Bruges, and at Nantes. Most of the princes of the different families, the Condés, the Contis, the Valois, the Bourbons, &c., had founded chapels or monasteries where they were afterwards buried; as, for instance, the Orléans chapel at the Célestins, which was celebrated for its magnificence.‡

* This custom of dividing bodies is of very ancient date, and was sanctioned by the Church in order that the remains might benefit, by their miraculous powers, as many places as possible. Sometimes the superiors of divers monasteries agreed to exchange "a rib of one saint for a cubit bone of another, an eye for an eye, a tooth for a tooth, &c." At other times these fragments had to be purchased for very considerable sums.—*History of S. Denis.*

† The original urn was cast in bronze by Benoist Boucher from the design of Domenico da Firenze, who also designed the relief on the pedestal.

‡ Some of its sculptures are now in the Renaissance Museum of the Louvre. The recumbent alabaster statue of Philippe de Chabot, by Jean Cousin; a white marble column and three Genii, by Etienne Lehongre, from the tomb of Louis de Cossé, duc de Brissac, and of his brother, J. A. de Cossé; a column with allegorical statues, &c., in bas relief, by Prieur Barthélemy, from the monument erected for the reception of the heart of Anne de Montmorency; sepulchral Genii, by Jean Cousin, from the tomb of Philippe de Chabot; a Fortune, by the same sculptor and from the same tomb; sepulchral monument of the Ducs de Longueville, by François Anguier; and the recumbent statue of Anne de Bourgogne, daughter of Jean-sans-Peur, wife of the Duke of Bedford. In the same museum of the Louvre is a bas-relief from S. Denis of the 14th century with traces of colour, the subject being the three martyrs, SS. Denis, Rusticus, and Eleutherius.

None of the monuments of the early kings are anterior to the 13th century; consequently, even the original portions of the effigies which remain cannot be looked upon as in the slightest degree portrait statues. On the other hand, the magnificent

THE CHOIR AND SANCTUARY.

tombs in bronze, and the brasses which adorned them, erected to the memory of Philippe Auguste, S. Louis, and his father, and which were destroyed centuries ago, were most probably as valuable as contemporary portraits as they were for their workmanship; likewise the 13th century effigies which remain are remarkable for the beauty of their workmanship. Louis IV. was the last prince who was laid under a simple stone monument. The last tomb erected was that of Henri II., the sovereigns who followed him having had no memorials. They were laid together in one great crypt, and when disturbed by the Revolutionists for the sake of the lead of their coffins ("of the coffins of our old tyrants let us make bullets to hurl at our enemies"), there were fifty-four bodies arranged upon iron trestles side by side, Henri IV.* heading the list, and the Dauphin, elder son of Louis XVI., ending it. The monuments now occupy the same position that they did before the Revolution; and if we stand upon the raised platform of the apse behind the High Altar we can gaze down upon what may be called the history of France, from the artistic point of view, during four or five centuries. On the left, the 13th century tomb of Dagobert stands erect; beyond it, the Renaissance mausoleum of Francis I., one of the *chefs-d'œuvres* of that grand sculptor, Philibert Delorme. On the right, the enamelled brasses of the children of S. Louis and the tomb of Henri II. A mosaic effigy of Frédégonde, the Orléans monument, and the tomb of Louis XII. by the brothers Juste, of Tours, complete the list of important works, while all about are recumbent figures upon arcaded monuments. The resting-places of the abbots were simply marked by inscriptions or flat slabs. The historian of the Abbey, Dom Michel Félibien, records the number of thirteen stones of grand priors with effigies, besides the abbots' tombs.

Among the distinguished men buried at S. Denis were the following:—

Pierre Chambellan, of whom Joinville writes, "Messire Pierre Chambellan fut le plus loial homme et le plus droicturier que je veisse oncques en la maision du roi . . . . l'homme du monde en qui le roy croirit plus"; and Alphonse, son of Jean de Brienne, King of Jerusalem and uncle of S. Louis, whose epitaph designates him as "moult saige et moult loial chevaliers." Both of them died "au service de Dieu et de Monsieur Loys, roy de France, dessous Cartaige l'an de l'incarnation de Nostre-Seigneur MCCLXX," and were "enterrés en l'église Monsieur Saint Denis" in the year MCCLXXI, "le vendredi devant la Penthecoste le jour et l'heure quand Monsieur le roy

---

* Henri IV. also abjured "his accursed heresy" at S. Denis.

Loys fut enterré"; indeed, the old chronicler says, "aus pieds du bon roys tout en la manière qu'il gisoit à ses pieds quand il estoit en vie." Pierre accompanied S. Louis in the disastrous crusade which terminated his reign. No doubt his tomb was of metal, destroyed with many others long before the Revolution, as for example, that of the Comte d'Eu, in gilt copper, enriched with enamels, which succumbed to the greed of the Huguenots.

Close to the tomb of Charles V. were those of Duguesclin, Louis de Sancerre, Bureau de la Rivière, Arnaud de Guilhem seigneur de Barbazan, who, before Bayard, was called *le chevalier sans reproche*, and who, with six others, was victorious over seven English knights in 1404. Near Duguesclin Charles V. had marked the spot for the burial place of Jean Pastourel, one of his principal councillors, whose wife was laid at S. Denis in 1380, but having, sick of the world, retired to the Abbey of S. Victor towards the end of his life, he desired to be buried there rather than amidst the splendours of the royal tombs. He was the only civilian who was offered this much-coveted privilege.

Guillaume de Chastel was another non-royal personage whom it pleased his master, Charles VII., *pour sa grande vaillance et les services qui lui avoit faiz en maintes manières*, to bury at S. Denis. The warrior held the town of Pontoise against the English, and died during the siege, 20th July, 1441. Another *vaillant capitaine de gendarmes*, the chevalier Louis de Pontoise, fell by the side of Louis XI. at the assault of the town of Crotoy, and was rewarded by being laid to rest amongst the Royalties.

Louis XIV. of course accorded burial at S. Denis to his great commanders. First, the Duc de Châtillon, for his magnificent services. *Feu nostre très-cher cousin* was killed at the taking, in 1649, of Charenton, that peaceful suburb of Paris just outside the Bois de Vincennes; and the King, wishing to *tesmoigner le ressentiment que nous avons d'une si grande perte*, honoured the valiant *Duc* with burial at S. Denis. The service was to be at the King's expense, which looks as if the honour were sometimes a costly one to the relatives; and no pomp or ceremony was to be omitted—such were the instructions of his most glorious majesty.

The Marquis de Saint Maigrin seems, according to the King's epistle, to have been of a *valeur extraordinaire, dans toutes les occasions où il s'est trouvé;* his majesty felt *avec beaucoup de douleur la perte que nous en avons faite au dernier combat qui s'est fait dans les fauxbourgs de nostre bonne **ville de Paris**;* and so he, too, was to rest with the great ones, socially, of the earth.

Louis seems to have been a sort of complete letter writer; the note in which he eulogises Turenne might serve as a model for those masters of style amongst us who delight in long sentences and a scarcity of full-stops; but, unlike the moderns, "la grande monarque" never gets involved, he only causes a slight shortness of breath to his readers. Witness the following page: "Chers et bien amez, les grands et signalez services qui ont esté rendus à cet Estat par feu nostre cousin, le vicomte de Turenne, et les preuves éclatantes qu'il a données de son zèle, de son affection à nostre service, et de sa capacité dans le commandement de nos armées que nous luy avons confiées avec une espérance certaine des heureux et grands succès que sa prudence consommée et sa valeur extraordinaire ont procuré à nos armes, nous ayant fait ressentir avec beaucoup de douleur la perte d'un aussi grand homme et d'un sujet aussi nécessaire et aussi distingué par sa vertu et par sa mérite, nous avons voulu donner un tesmoignage public digne de nostre estime et de ses grandes actions, en ordonnant qu'il fust rendu à sa mémoire tous les honneurs qui peuvent marquer à la postérité l'extrême satisfaction qui nous reste, et le souvenir que nous voulons conserver de tout ce qu'il a faict pour la gloire de nos armes et pour le soutien de nostre Estat ; et comme nous ne pouvons en donner des marques plus publiques et plus certaines qu'en prenant soin de sa sépulture, nous avons voulu y pourvoir en telle sorte que le lieu où elle séroit, fust un tesmoignage de la grandeur de ses services et de nostre reconnoissance ; c'est pourquoy, ayant résolu de faire bastir dans l'église de Saint-Denys une chapelle pour la sépulture des rois et des princes de la branche royale de Bourbon, nous voulons que, lorsqu'elle sera achevée, le corps de nostredit cousin y soit transféré, pour y estre mis en lieu honorable, suivant l'ordre que nous en donnerons ; et cependant nous avons permis à nos cousins le cardinal et le duc de Bouillon, ses neveux, de mettre son corps en dépost dans la chapelle de Saint-Eustache de ladite église de Saint-Denys, et d'y eslever un monument à la mémoire de leur oncle, suivant les desseins qui en ont esté arrestez ; c'est de quoy nous avons bien voulu vous donner avis, et vous dire en mesme temps que nous voulons que vous exécutiez ce qui est en cela de nostre volonté, en faisant mettre ledit corps dans la cave de ladite chapelle et en laissant la liberté aux ouvriers de travailler audit monument jusqu'à son entière perfection. Si n'y faictes fautes ; car tel est nostre plaisir. Donné à Saint-Germain en Laye, le xxii⁰ jour de Novembre 1675. *Signé*, Louis. Et plus bas, Colbert, Et sur le reply : A nos chers et amez les abbé, prieur et religieux de l'abbaye royale de Saint-Denys, en France."

The projected Bourbon chapel was never built, and the Revolution found the monument of Turenne in the same chapel, that of S. Eustache, whence it was trundled out as late as April, 1796, and transported to the Petits-Augustins ; for up to that time Turenne, not being a royal person, had been left in peace. The demolition of the tombs seems to have gone on fitfully from 1793 to 1795, as a little diversion between more exciting events. After the emigration of the nobility in 1790 ; the flight of the King to Varennes, and his false swearing to uphold the constitution in 1792 ; and his treachery in carrying on a correspondence with the enemies at the frontier ; the popular anger waxed strong, and led to the storming of the Tuileries on the 10th August,* which event was to be celebrated the next year by the demolition of the tombs of S. Denis. Louis XVI. had paid the penalty of his crimes ; and like his forerunner, Charles I., had shown that if he did not know how to live, he at least had learnt how to die ; but his ancestors had got off scot-free. Why should they be allowed to rest peacefully, what remained of them ? Besides, lead was wanted for ammunition ; and, just as the church bells were in requisition for guns, and gold and silver vessels for coinage, so the leaden coffins and roofs of churches could be melted up into cannon balls. Imagine the stampede of Parisians along that paved road that led from Paris to S. Denis. Only the other day, when the trams were instituted, were those great rough stones taken up. At Versailles you may still see the like ; the paved

---

* That Louis XVI. was not simply weak-minded and vacillating, but treacherous and double-faced, there can be little doubt. A print exhibited at the Exposition Historique de la Révolution, held in the Salle des Etats of the Tuileries in 1889, represents the opening of an iron closet after the slaughter of the 10th of August, and the display of numberless documents —letters to Pitt, asking for help to reinstate the monarchy; plans and projects for a counter-revolution ; and correspondence to and from the *emigrés* and foreign princes.

part of the road very much curved, with mud paths on each side—side walks for the people, while the centre pavement was reserved for the quality. They radiate from the palace, and enabled the "Roi Soleil" to visit his satellites at Bellevue, the Trianon, Meudon, and S. Germain, without danger of his lumbering coach sticking in the mire, to which he and his belonged. Many must have been the journeys from the capital to S. Denis, which the decree of the Convention sanctioned—journeys accompanied by crowbars and pickaxes for the better destruction of the tombs. It was a ghastly idea, but in no wise an exaggerated revenge for the kingly brutalities perpetrated upon the living bodies of Ravaillac, Damiens, and such like *canaille*.* We have a full account of the whole affair from the pen of an eye-witness, one Dom Poirier, the custodian of the archives of the monastery, who was present when the commission carried out the decree of the Convention of the 31st July, 1793. The report of this commission is so curious that I will quote it in full. After assigning to the children of *Louis le conspirateur*† the portion of simple citizens, Barrère continued as to the proposed arrangements to be carried out at "la Franciade": "Enfin, le comité a pensé que, pour célébrer la journée du 10 août, qui a abattu le trône, il fallait, dans son anniversaire, détruire les mausolées fastueux qui sont à Saint-Denis. Dans la monarchie, les tombeaux même avaient appris à flatter les rois. L'orgueil et le faste royal ne pouvaient s'adoucir sur ce théâtre de la mort; et les porte-sceptre qui ont fait tant de maux à la France et a l'humanité semblent encore, même dans la tombe, s'enorgueillir d'une grandeur évanouie. La main puissante de la république doit effacer impitoyablement ces épitaphes superbes et démolir ces mausolées qui rappeleraient des rois l'effrayant souvenir." Thereupon a discussion ensued. One member suggested that the nation being in peril, and wanting guns to carry on its defence, a commission should proceed to Franciade, otherwise S. Denis, in order to commence "l'exhumation

---

* The *procès verbal* of these villanies, giving the most hideous and disgusting details, and the names of the distinguished persons who were present at the entertainments, were to be seen and read in the prison department of the Centenary Exhibition of 1889, together with accounts of some of the doings within the walls of the Bastille in the happy days when *lettres de cachet* were kept ready signed for distribution.

† See note, page 52.

des ci-devant rois et reines, princes et princesses, dont les corps étaient renfermés dans les caveaux de cette église." Their coffins were to be broken, the lead and the bronze to be melted up, and sent to the arsenals for conversion into arms and munitions of war. The former Benedictine Dom Poirier was nominated commissioner for the Institut, and ordered to be present at the performance. Some days after, the *Moniteur* triumphantly records the commencement of the business. Then there must have been a lull, for on the 7th September the Conventionnel Lequinio cried from the Tribune: " Je dénonce l'inexécution du décret qui ordonne l'entière démolition des tombeaux de nos anciens tyrans à Saint-Denis. Sans doute, en détruisant ces restes du despotisme, il faut conserver les monuments des arts; mais il faut qu'au lieu d'être des objets d'idolâtrie, il ne servent plus qu'à nourrir l'admiration des amis des arts, l'émulation et le génie des artistes."

The notes taken by Dom Poirier are full of interesting details, told with a certain *naïveté;* as, for instance, " in the morning, after dinner, they descended into the tomb." Or "early in the morning they began the work, but left off while they went to *déjeûner.*" It must be remembered, also (to quote M. Guilhermy), that the destruction "des tombeaux et l'extraction des corps ont été deux opérations distinctes. Au mois d'août, 1793, pour célébrer l'anniversaire *de la victoire du peuple* (10 août), on fit disparaître de l'église la plupart des tombeaux et des statues; mais le temps pressait, on ne profana que les restes déposés dans les massifs des monuments. Au mois d'octobre, on acheva l'œuvre commencée, en fouillant toutes les fosses et tous les caveaux qu'il fut possible de retrouver. On n'épargna ni le temps ni les recherches."

The work went on merrily. Marble tombs were smashed up as effectually as the bodies, which were thrown into a pit dug upon the site of the demolished Orléans chapel. Quick-lime helped the business as far as the kings were concerned, but to the assistants it was of no use; and so they had recourse to the burning of strong smelling powders, and the firing of guns, in order to purify the air. Here is one of Dom Poirier's notes:—

" *Nota.*—Rièn n'a été remarquable dans l'extraction des cercueils faite dans la journée du mardi 15 Oct^{bre,} 1793 : la plupart de ces corps étaient en putréfaction ; il en sortait une vapeur noire et épaisse, d'une odeur infecte, qu'on chassait à force de vinaigre et de poudre qu'on eut la précaution de brûler; ce qui n'empêcha pas les ouvriers de gagner des dévoiements et des fièvres, *qui n'ont pas eu de mauvaises suites.*"

What say the modern sanitary authorities to that!

The body of Henri IV. was found in a perfect state of preservation; and he was kept some time in the church lying-in-state, as it were, while a cast was taken of his face; but it may be noted that Dom Poirier makes no allusion to the story of a soldier cutting off his beard and sticking it on his own face.

The names of the princes and princesses were engraved upon little brass plates attached to the covers of the coffins; and a few years ago three or four of these brasses were found in the shop of a coppersmith, that of Louis XIV. having served as the bottom of a stewpan. How are the mighty fallen!

Let me quote some more of Dom Poirier's jottings :—

Remarques.—In Charles V.'s coffin they found a crown in silver, gilt, in a good state of preservation, a hand of justice of silver, a sceptre 5 feet in length surmounted with acanthus leaves in silver, exquisitely gilt, the gold possessing all its freshness and brilliancy. "Ce sceptre était surmonté d'un bouquet en feuillage, an milieu duquel s'élevait une grappe de corymbe, ce qui lui donne à peu près la forme d'un thyrse, tel qu'on en voit dans Monfaucon, article de *sceptres;* morceau d'orfèvrerie assez bien travaillé pour son époque." (Alexandre Lenoir, *Musée des Monuments français.*

"Remarque. Une singularité de l'embaumement du corps de Charles VII., c'est qu'on y avait parsemé du vif-argent, qui avait conservé toute sa fluidité. On a observé la même singularité dans quelques autres embaumements de corps du XIVe et du XVe siècles."

The following may interest some persons :—

"Le mercredi, 16 Octobre, 1793.

"Towards 7 o'clock in the morning the work was continued in the vault of the Bourbons. They began with the coffin of Henriette Marie, daughter of Henri IV. and wife of the unfortunate Charles I., King of England, d. in 1669, aged 60;[*] and continued with Anne Stuart, her daughter, the wife of *Monsieur,* only brother of Louis XIV. d. in 1670, aged 26."

The body of Louis VIII., the father of S. Louis, had almost disappeared. A cross was sculptured upon the lid of the stone coffin; in it was found a sceptre of rotten wood, and

[*] Bossuet's panegyric upon the queen reads like a satiric ode: "Elle va descendre à ces sombres lieux, à ces demeures souterraines pour y dormir dans la poussière avec les grands de la terre, comme parle Job; avec ces rois et ces princes anéantis, parmi lesquels à peine peut on la placer, tant les rangs y sont pressés, tant la mort est prompte à remplir ces places."

a skull-cap of satin surrounded by a band of gold woven stuff, forming a diadem. The body had been enveloped in a winding sheet of gold tissue, some pieces of which were in a good state of preservation.

Remarques.—His body thus enveloped had been sewn up in a strong leather covering.* "Il est vraisemblable qu'on ne l'a fait pour lui que pour que son cadavre n'exhalât pas au dehors de mauvaise odeur, dans le transport qu'on en fit de Montpensier en Auvergne, où il mourut à son retour de la guerre contre les Albigeois."

"Ce cuir avait conservé toute son élasticité. . . Dans les fouilles de Saint-Germain-des-Prés, on trouva un corps également enveloppé dans un cuir. (Alexandre Lenoir, *Musée des Monuments Français*.) Nous pourrions citer quelques autres exemples. Les corps de plusieurs princes de la maison des Plantagenets, au douzième siècle, furent apportés à Rouen, cousus dans une enveloppe de cuir; c'étaient ceux de Henry I., de Henry-le-Jeune, de Richard-Cœur-de-Lion. Hugues de Grantemaisnil, mort à Londres en 1098, ayant demandé à être inhumé à l'abbaye de Saint-Évrould, en Normandie, son corps y fut transféré salé, et cousu dans une peau de bœuf. Enfin on sait que saint Bernard fut enseveli dans un sac de cuir" (v. B. de Peterborough; Orderic Vital; *Histoire de Saint Bernard*, &c.) (Guilhermy).

There are notes upon the height of François I., by Alexandre Lenoir:—

"Le corps de François Ier. portait une taille extraordinaire et une structure très-forte; l'un des fémurs de ce prince que j'ai mesuré portait 53^c (20 pouces) des condiles à la tête de l'os." And upon the beauty of another gentleman's locks: "Le connétable Louis de Sancerre avait de forts beaux cheveux; lors de l'exhumation des corps à St. Denis, il fut trouvé ayant encore trois longues tresses d'environ 40 centimètres" (Alex. Lenoir).

The *procès-verbal* makes no mention of the heart of Cardinal de Bourbon, nor of the graves of Châtillon and the Marquis de Saint-Maigrin, nor of the abbots, and grand priors; their remains probably still rest in the soil under the church, for vaults have several times been discovered in all parts during the restorations of the building. It will be seen that the amount of valuables found was not great: Five silver-gilt and

---

* Alexandre Lenoir made a coloured drawing of the body at the time, representing the entire skeleton wrapped up in white stuff embroidered in gold.

five copper-gilt crowns, two silver-gilt sceptres, four of copper-gilt, and three of wood; one silver hand of justice, one silver-gilt, and one broken; (the *bâton d'ebêne* was possibly the stem of a hand of justice belonging to Charles le Bel); the upper part of a crozier; four rings, two silver and two gold; the silver seal of Constance of Castille bearing the effigy of the princess and an inscription (now in the Bibliothèque); remains of spindles and distaffs; four chains of bracelets; two clasps and a silver buckle; a good many fragments of stuffs, tissues, and embroideries; a winding-sheet of gold tissue, a silver one; a chasuble; a satin belt; shoes; a Carmelite habit, and some gold thread. What became of these things, many of them of no value but for a museum, is not known.

Such was the result of this disgusting entertainment, which was principally a search for valuables to keep up the struggle for life. Empty coffers, starving multitudes, an enemy crying at the frontier; such was the legacy left by the wanton waste of a profligate court, and a debased race of kings. The terrible revenge which followed did them little harm; could they have been made to suffer in their life-time, it would have been better than mauling about their dead bodies and rummaging in their tombs; but unfortunately the last of the race was the least guilty, although he had much heartlessness and treachery to answer for; and had he felt the storm which had been threatening for some time, the hurricane might have passed over. But selfishness is always blind; and so the flood carried the poor thing away; and the skeletons, the lead, the gold and the silver, were all swept into their respective lime-strewn pits and melting pots. Here is the epilogue. In 1815 the "Sous-préfet et le maire de Saint-Denis firent élever un tertre couvert de gazon, de lis et de cyprès sur les deux fosses dans lesquelles avaient été jetés les restes des rois et des princes." (Gilbert, *Description historique de l'église de Saint-Denis*.) "On se proposait d'ériger en ce lieu un monument expiatoire; mais il parut plus convenable de réintègrer dans l'église les ossements que les deux fosses contenaient encore." (Guilhermy.)

The metal of the monuments, with the exception of two enamelled brass slabs which came from Royaumont, was all melted up. In the *Moniteur* of 14th August, 1792, may be read a list of the tombs destroyed, furnished by the town of S. Denis. The monument of Charles le Chauve must have been magnificent. The effigy of the emperor reposed on a slab supported by four lions. Two Angels censed the defunct; and four bishops sat at the corners. We know the style of tomb from the description given by Richer, a monk of Sénone, who wrote a chronicle during the reign of S. Louis, and who saw it soon after it was set up. Charles had been a great patron of the abbey and had given it the Holy Nail and a thorn from the Holy Crown, besides part of the course of the Seine and the domain of Ruel.

The tomb of "la noble royne de france Marguerite qui fu fame monseigneur Sainct Loys, jadis roy de France" is engraved in Montfaucon's *Monuments de la Monarchie française.* The tomb of Arnaud de Guilhem, seigneur de Barbazan, was canopied, the warrior being represented in full armour. The whole was in bronze, with an inscription, at the end of which was the name of the artist: *fait à paris par Jehan Morant.*

The monument of Charles VIII. was of gilt copper. The king's effigy, praying, was upon the platform, with little Angels at the corners also kneeling and holding shields. Charles VIII. died of apoplexy, at Amboise, praying, "*Mon Dieu et la glorieuse Vierge, Monseigneur saint Claude, et Monseigneur saint Blaise me soient en ayde.*" He was a pious king and had been holding "quelques discours spirituels avec la reyne et autres assistans," when he was struck down, being only twenty-eight years of age. His tomb was said to be the finest in the choir. He was regretted by all his subjects "spécialement de ses domestiques," for he was generous, magnanimous, and decorated with all kingly virtues. The queen was much afflicted, and thought she would die of grief, "demeurant deux jours et deux nuicts sans reposer ny prendre aucun aliment." Thus Dom Millet. Philippe de Commynes says the chamberlains "le feirent ensevelir fort richement, et sur l'heure luy commencea le service, qui jamais ne failloit ne jour ne nuict." For a whole month the chamberlains and others watched the corpse, the entire expense amounting to "quarante-cinq mil francs." The tomb was the work of Paganini of Modena, no doubt one of the "ouvriers excellens en plusieurs ouvraiges comme tailleurs et painctres" whom the king brought from Naples,[*] together with a large collection

[*] Philippe de Commynes.

SAINT-DENIS.

of works of art, for the carriage of which, and for "la nourriture de XXII. hommes de mestier, de XXXIII. jours à la raison de XL. sous par jour," the king had to pay his tapissier ordinaire 1594 livres; the collection weighing 87,000 livres.

Many marble tombs were also destroyed, some canopied, some resting upon columns, others recumbent, the fragments of which were built up into a pedestal for a figure of Liberty in the Place d'armes opposite the church, a barbarous proceeding, surely; but forget not that the slabs and broken tombs in our old burial grounds are treated much in the same fashion, and piled up into pyramids to ornament the gardens. The transportation of what was saved from the wreck to Paris was no mean work. Think of the huge monument of François I., and about

MONUMENT OF FRANÇOIS Ier.

eighty statues! The Convention had no cash to spend upon art; with its fourteen armies defending the frontiers, it had enough expense without paying for the carriage of monuments and such like. And so Lenoir conceived the idea of stopping the military as they returned with empty waggons. Arrived in Paris the difficulties did not end. Statues were chopped about to enable them to fill certain spaces in the museum of the Petits-Augustins, recumbent figures found themselves standing upright; fragments of one tomb were taken to decorate another. But taking it all in all, the museum arranged by Lenoir must have been very imposing. The magnificent tomb of François I. stood in a chapel of the church, now occupied by casts of the works of Michael-Angelo. Louis XII. had a place of honour in another *salle*. But no sooner was all arranged, indeed before the huge Henri II. monument had been set up, a royal decree of 16th December, 1816, ordered the museum to be closed, the building to be turned into the École des Beaux-Arts, and all the kings and queens to be marched back to S. Denis and the other churches whence they came. So swiftly was the order carried out, that the poor old sovereigns became still more mutilated; some were stowed away in the cellars, others were re-erected upon principles of the greatest economy. If the revolutionists tore down the monuments, the restored monarchists did not take the trouble to set them up again; and those who went to study art in the new schools were enabled to see the respect with which Mediæval art was treated. Statues, canopies, columns, were tossed about anywhere; until Louis XVIII. decided that they should be reinstated at S. Denis. Then strange things occurred. The effigies were matched indiscriminately, and every king was placed by the side of a queen, whether his own or another's. Hence "singuliers incestes de pierre, et des adultères de marbre de la pire espèce. On n'imaginerait jamais ce qui se commit d'immoralités archéologiques sous les voutes obscures de Saint-Denis."* The monuments were all arranged, museum fashion, in the crypt until our own day, when they were once again removed, and replaced in their old positions in the church, to be left, let us hope, at last in peace.

The following is a list of the monuments returned to S. Denis:

* Guilhermy.

Monuments formerly at S. Denis		...	...	...	52
,,	from S. Germain-des-Prés	...	...	...	6
,,	,, Notre-Dame de Corbeil	...	...	...	2
,,	,, S. Geneviève	...	...	...	1
,,	,, S. Catherine-du-Val	...	..	...	2
,,	,, des Cordeliers	...	...	...	3
,,	,, des Jacobins	...	...	...	7
,,	,, des Célestins	...	...	...	12
,,	,, des Minimes	...	...	...	2
,,	,, des Grands-Jésuites	...	...	...	1
,,	,, l'abbaye de Royaumont	...	...	...	6
,,	,, l'abbaye de Maubuisson	...	...	...	2
,,	,, l'abbaye de Poissy	...	...	...	1
,,	,, l'abbaye de Notre-Dame à Soissons	...	...		1
,,	,, l'abbaye de Haute Bruyère	...	...	...	1
,,	,, la collégiale de Saint-Cloud	...	...	...	2
,,	of origin unknown	...	...	...	13
,,	new or made up of fragments	...	...	...	53
					167

By far the most beautiful tomb is that of Louis XII. "Sur le lieu de la sépulture de Louis XII. et de la reyne Anne, le roy François leur gendre et successeur à la couronne, leur à fait dresser un très-somptueux mausolée de fin marbre blanc, à deux estages, qui est une des belles pièces de l'Europe, pour ne pas dire la plus belle."* Dom Jacques Doublet and Germain Millet both attributed the work to Ponzio; but Félibien, reading a passage in a Latin commentary printed by Jean Brèche in 1550, discovered the true author: "Voyez le monument" (says Brèche) "de marbre consacré à Louis XII., travaillé avec un artifice admirable et plein d'élégance, dans notre très-illustre cité de Tours, par Jean Juste, statuaire du plus grand talent." The discovery of an order for payment of 400 écus to Juste in a letter from the king to Cardinal Duprat, sets the matter at rest if the date of Ponzio's arrival did not also do so.† The tomb was taken to S. Denis in 1527; whereas Ponzio did not arrive in France until about 1530. This way of attributing all that is good in art to Italy was formerly very common. Even in our own time all branches of French art were looked upon by our fathers as frivolous and trivial. Italian Renaissance was trivial enough, but French

* G. Millet.
† In the Cathedral of Dol the remains of a monument by Juste are signed: *Magister Johannes cujus cognomen est Justus et Florentinus*, possibly indicating that the Justes were of Italian origin (Giusto).

TOMB OF LOUIS XII., AND COLUMN OF FRANCOIS II.

Renaissance utterly meretricious. To the insane worshippers of the "Gothic style," it alone was pure. The sumptuous grandiosities of Louis XIV. were tolerable, because they aimed at being Classic. The portico of the Panthéon or the colonnade of the Louvre were considered fine; but the elegancies of Jean Goujon were wanting in severity. Even Watteau, though admitted to be graceful, was "meretricious"; Berlioz amongst musicians was only "noisy and claptrap;" and sculpture and architecture were criticised in like manner. And yet the designs upon the tomb of Louis XII., especially the pilasters which support the canopy, could not be surpassed in beauty by the artists of any country. Jean Juste, Philibert Delorme, Jean Goujon, Michel Colomb, Jean Cousin, and Germain Pilon formed a group of men scarcely surpassed by Sansovino, Riccio, Desiderio da Settignano and the Rossellini. The Italians led the way, but the French proved themselves very apt pupils.

It is not my intention to describe the tomb of Louis XII., or, indeed, any of the others, minutely. Descriptions without illustrations are mostly dry and dreary. Nor have I tried to illustrate the details of ornament in the churches or their contents—in a book of this size it would be impossible; my aim has rather been to give the general effect of their styles; of their everyday appearance; of the life which goes on in and around them; and of the position, especially in the case of S. Denis, of their tombs and furniture. A large photograph and a manifying glass will show the beauty of the sculpture of the tombs far better than any drawing of mine; for such subjects photography is unique. But for artistic effect, for general impressions of buildings it mostly fails, and all artists will agree with me that, for some reason or other, photographs of buildings seem generally to have been taken from the worst point of view, and are nearly always wanting in impressiveness.

Jean Juste had a brother Antoine, and they seem together to have been the authors of the beautiful tomb of the children of Charles VIII. at Tours; of the fountain called de Beaune, also at Tours; of the two monuments of the *famille* Gaudin; and the tomb of the *général des finances*, Thomas Bohier. In 1530, one Juste de Just, *tailleur en marbre*, living at Tours received 102 *livres* 10 *sous* from the king for a Hercules and a Leda. This Juste was probably the same as Jean. The bas-reliefs round the base of Louis XII.'s tomb

TOMB OF HENRI II. AND CATHERINE DE MEDICI.

represent various campaigns of the king; the figures at the four corners are the Cardinal Virtues, those within the arcades are the twelve Apostles. Within are the king and queen, entirely nude, lying upon a mattress in the last agony of death; while above, upon the platform, they are praying before a cushioned faldstool, for their own departed souls. Such is the motive of this and the other two tombs of the same character, those of Henri II. and François Ier.

The former of these is the work of Germain Pilon, and was originally placed under the dome of Philibert Delorme's magnificent chapel erected for the Valois family. It is of marble with bronze figures. The king and queen pray upon the housetop; at each end are openings through which are to be seen the figures of the defunct in the sleep of death. The terrible side of death, which is prominent in the expression on the faces of Louis XII. and his queen, is here absent; and Catherine is represented young and beautiful as she appeared at the death of her husband, whom she survived thirty years. At the four corners are bronze figures of the Cardinal Virtues; and the kneeling figures of the sovereigns upon the canopy are also in bronze. The tomb has always been justly esteemed as a magnificent work, and even Bernini admired it. "*Le cavalier Bernin,*" says Sauval, "*a admiré le tombeau de Valois, qui voulait ne rien trouver de passable en France.*" The Virtues ornament this tomb also, and present a noteworthy point for Total Abstainers, the figure of Temperance bears *two* cups; can this be meant for wine as well as water? or for two sorts of water, aërated and mineral?

When the tomb was reconstructed it was found that many of the marbles had antique sculptures upon the back, showing that they had been taken from works of Classic origin.

The monument of François Ier. and Claude de France is the largest of these splendid tombs. It was erected about 1552 by Philibert Delorme with the assistance of several sculptors. Pierre Bontems was the author of the bas-reliefs upon the stylobate and some of the kneeling figures upon the canopy; Germain Pilon sculptured the statues of children under the canopy, allegorically representing Fortune, and Ambroise Perret, the Four Evangelists; while the details of ornament were the work of Jacques Chantrel, Bastien Galles, Pierre Bigoigne, and Jean de Bourges. The recumbent figures have been attributed to Jean Goujon, from the exceptional beauty

F

of the workmanship, but without any positive proof. The tomb is of white marble, with a little black and grey introduced for some of the mouldings; the bas-reliefs represent the king's campaigns in Italy. In the bas-reliefs of the Louis XII. monument many of the costumes are more Roman than French; but those upon the tomb of François I$^{er.}$ are treated with more historical truth, and represent the fashion of the day. The faces of the recumbent statues are beautifully modelled; that of the queen bearing an expression of the sanctity with which she was accredited.

S. Denis is rich in columns erected as memorials, often bearing urns upon the top containing some worthy heart. That of François II. was formerly at the church of the Célestins. It is the work of Germain Pilon, and was considered by Sauval and *"les habiles gens"* to be as beautiful as the "Three Graces" or "Charités" which bore the urn containing the heart of Henri II. The pedestal is triangular, of white marble; so, too, are the three little Genii who guard the corners. One weeps for the defunct; the other two seem to take the matter philosophically. The shaft of the column is

COLUMN OF HENRI III.

dotted over with flames, said to be symbolic of the pillar of fire which marched before the Hebrews; may they not rather mean the flames of purgatory?* The gilt bronze urn which formerly surmounted it, and the winged child holding a crown, were both consigned to the melting pot. This column was an act of fraternal homage on the part of Charles IX.

The column of Henri III. was originally erected in the church of S. Cloud by the secretary of Henri III., Charles Benoise. The shaft is of red marble, twisted, with ivy twirling round it—the work of Barthélemy Prieur.

The column of the Cardinal Louis de Bourbon formerly bore the effigy of the great man, if honours and emoluments can make a man great. He was naturally a peer; bishop of Laon, of Saintes, of Mans, of Luçon, and of Tréguier; archbishop of Sens; abbot of S. Denis, of Corbie, of Saint-Vincent-de-Laon, of Saint-Faron-de-Meaux, of Ainay, of Saint-Amand, of Saint-Crépin-le-Grand, of Soissons, and of Saint-Serge. And yet some people profess to be scandalised at the excesses of the unprivileged classes!

The cardinal was, however, a great patron of art; at Sens and at Laon, monuments testify to this and all his other magnificences. His body was buried in the cathedral of Laon; the Benedictines of S. Denis only having succeeded in obtaining his heart. The column, like many other beautiful works of art, is by an unknown artist. It is of red marble with a white alabaster base and capital, which is exquisitely sculptured with little figures of children bathed in foliage.

The history of some of the recumbent statues of the kings is curious. Having been made to lie down, they were, after the dispersal of the Musée des Monuments Français, stuck up against the wall of the crypt; and others were rebaptised and renamed. Thus, at the museum, Charles V. and Jeanne de Bourbon became S. Louis and Marguerite de Provence; and so named, when they were trotted back to S. Denis, they received the homage of the faithful. To make matters worse, a copy of S. Louis' statue was sent to Tunis for the church which was built in memory of the saint, and the head became the authentic type for his portraits. The same may be said

---

* Through the flames of purgatory, we attain the crown. See page 62.

of the false Marguerite; she wears a costume more than a hundred years too late.

The elaborately enamelled brass slabs of the children of S. Louis, Jean and Blanche, came from Royaument. The design is rude, but the colouring good; the figures are in relief upon a ground incrusted in enamel; the heads and hands, the lions at the feet, and the Angels swinging censers are of polished brass; while the feet and the draperies are in coloured enamel. To see these brasses, permission must be obtained from the architect of the church, as they are upon one side of the High Altar, a part which is not generally shown to ordinary visitors. The motto upon the tomb of Jean is as follows:

HIC JACET: IOANNES: EXCELLENTISSIMI LVD
ovici regis francorvm filivs qui in etate infancie migra
VIT AD XPM ANNO GRACIE: MILLESI
MO: DVCENTESSIMO: QVADRAGESIMO: SEPTIMO: SEXTO: IDVS: MARTII

The body of Turenne did not have much peace after it was routed out of its tomb. Not being royal, it was put aside in a chapel until the Convention should decide its fate; when thinking so great a man a worthy object as a specimen of natural history, and deeming it profitable for students of various "ologies," it was put into a glass case by the side of stuffed birds, bottled snakes, criminal curiosities, and monstrosities. Then it was transferred to the Petits-Augustins, where it found a niche to repose in; but when Consuls reigned supreme, it was marched with great pomp, with drums and guns and all the paraphernalia of a military funeral, to the church of the Invalides, where it was placed in its old house or the remains of it rebuilt—the S. Denis tomb. The epitaphs of some of the Kings remain, or have been restored:—

ICY GIST LE ROY CHARLES LE QUINT SAGES
ET ELOQUENT FILS DU ROY IEHAN QUI REGNA SEIZE ANS CINQ MOIS ET SEPT JOURS ET TRESPASSA L'AN DE GRACE MCCCLXXX LE XVIe JOUR DE SEPTEMBRE.

ICI GIST LE ROY CHARLES SIXIESME TRES AME LARGE ET DEBONNAIRE FILS DU ROY CHARLES LE QUINT QUI REGNA QUARANTE ET II ANS UNG MOIS ET SIX JOURS ET TRESPASSA LE XXIe JOUR DOCTOBRE LAN MIL CCCC VINGT ET DEUX: PRIES DIEU QUEN PARADIX SOIT SON AME:

CY GIST LA ROYNE ISABEL DE BAUIERE ESPOUSE DU ROY CHARLES VIe
ET FILLE DE TRES PUISSANT PNCE. ESTIENNE DUC DE BAUIERE COTE

PALATIN DU RIN QUI REGNA AUEC SOND ESPOUS ET TRESPASSA LAN M : CCCC ET XXXV LE DERNIER JOUR DE SEPTEMBRE : PRIES DIEU POUR ELLE :

CY GIST LE ROY CHARLES SEPTIESME TRES GLORIEUX VICTORIEUX ET BIEN SERUY FILS DU ROY CHARLES SIXIESMES : QUI REGNA TRENTE NEUF ANS NEUF MOIS ET I JOUR ET TRESPASSA LE JOUR DE LA MAGDELAINE XXVIIe JOUR DE JUILLET LA M : CCCCLXI : PRIES POUR LUY :

ICY GIST LA ROYNE JEHANNE DE BOURBON ESPOUSE DU ROY CHARLES LE QUINT ET FILLE DE TRES NOBLE PRINCE MONS^r PIERRE DUC DE BOURBON QUI REGNA AUECQS SONE ESPOUS XIII ANS ET DIX MOIS ET TSPASSA LA M : CCCLXXVII LE DERN JOUR DE FEUER

CY GIST LA ROYNE MARIE FILLE DU ROY DE SICILE DUC DANIOU ESPOUSE DU ROY CHARLES VIIe QUI REGNA AUECQS SOND ESPX ET TRESPASSA LE PENULTIESME JOUR DE NOUEMBRE LAN MIL : CCCCLXIII : PRIES DIEU POUR ELLE.

After the restoration of the tombs a tablet was set up to the memory of Jeanne-d'Arc, bearing the representation of some armour of the 16th century, and the following epitaph :—

CE QUE ESTAIT LE HARNAIS DE JEHANNE PAR ELLE BAILLE EN HOMMAGE A MONSEIGNEUR SAINCT DENIS.

Several portraits of the great Abbot Suger existed in Dom Millet's time : " On voit encores aujourd'huy en la partie supérieure de l'église Saint-Denis que nous nommons le chevet, une vieille tapisserie où le roy Louis VII. est représenté avec les habits royaux, et la couronne en teste, qui donne son sceptre et sa main de justice au susdit abbé Sugere représenté en habit pontifical, et au-dessus y a une inscription contenant ceste escriture : Lud. rex franc Suggerium abbatem et reaedificatorem hujus templi, viceregem constituit, anno 1140. Mais le tapissier, ou ceux qui ont fourny le mémoire se sont trompez ; car ceste commission ne fut donnée à Sugère que l'an 1147, auquel an le roy partit de France, au mois d'aoust, pour un voyage de la Terre-Sainte."

"Il y a en ceste royale abbaye plusieurs figures de l'abbé Sugère, deux desquelles sont en veue à toutes personnes. L'un est sur l'un des battans de la grande porte de l'église,[*] l'autre en une vitre de la Chapelle Notre-Dame, en la partie supérieure que nous nommons le chevet[†] Il est représenté en tous les deux endroits, non revestu d'un rochet ou d'un camail, non avec la perruque ou le bonnet carré sur la teste,

[*] Unfortunately, this being metal, was melted up in 1793.
[†] This still exists.

mais au plus simple habit et en la plus humble posture, qu'on puisse représenter un pauvre religieux, scavoir est avec un froc plissé* (approchant fort de celuy dont nous usons maintenant) et la tonsure monacale, couché à plate terre; en la vitre, devant une image de la sacrée Vierge, avec ces mots: Suggerius abbas; sur la porte, devant l'image de Notre-Sauveur, assis à table avec les pélerins d'Emmaüs. Il n'a en l'une ny en l'autre figure aucune marque qui le puisse distinguer d'avec le moindre novice de son monastère, sinon la crosse abbatiale qu'il tient d'une main, pour marque de sa dignité, et pour monstrer que c'est luy qui est là représenté."

"Or, comme il est très-certain que c'est luy-mesme qui a fait faire ces figures, aussi est-il très-asseuré qu'il n'avoit garde de les faire représenter en autre habit que celuy qu'il portoit publiquement et continuellement, spécialement depuis la réformation; car autrement c'eust par une hypocrisie trop grossière se sacrifier à la risée de tout le monde." This description of the portrait is most interesting; we can see the great abbot as Dom Millet paints him upon the glass which he himself devised, if he did not absolutely design it.

The tomb of Dagobert is an enormous canopied structure, originally of the 13th century, but so much restored that it is practically modern. Dagobert died in 638, and was embalmed and buried in the church of his foundation; but of the style of this first tomb we have no knowledge whatever. Of the existing tomb, the principal part is the legendary history of the king taken from the "*Gesta Dagoberti*," told in three alto-reliefs. Below these, the king sleeps upon his left side in a rather uncomfortable fashion; standing on one side is his wife Nantilde, or Nantechilde; on the other, one of his sons, Clovis II. or Sigebert. At the apex of the arch is Our Lord giving the benediction, with SS. Martin and Denis on each side. These two saints, with S. Maurice, had the kindness to hear the prayers of Dagobert, when he was held in bondage by devils, during a voyage in a boat, on the waters of the great gulf fixed between Abraham and Hades. The story was told by a hermit to Ansoald, on his way back from Sicily, and by the 9th century had been worked up into a fact, as it is mentioned in a letter from Louis le Débonnaire to

---

* This is curious as showing the antiquity of the fashion of plaiting surplices which is customary in France.

Hilduin, abbot of S. Denis. May it not have been originally a dovetailing together of the story of Charon and *le bon roy Dagobert*, a *mélange* of Classic myth and Christian legend which was very common in the early centuries of the Christian era? The sculptures, although, as regards the drapery, sufficiently graceful, are very curious and quaint, especially the boat and its contents. The three saints coming to the rescue, Dagobert pressing the hand of the foremost, the discomforted demons, and the soul of the king standing upon a napkin held by S. Denis and S. Martin, are all vigorous to a degree, if somewhat rude; but the Angels round the *voussure* carrying censers, are charming. In the account of the legend given by Guillaume de Nangis, quoted by Alexandre Lenoir, we seem to have another reading of the opening part of the story of Job. " Mais monseigneur sainct Denis, qui n'oblia mie son bon amy le roy Dagobert, requist à Nostre Seigneur Jesus-Crist qui luy donast congié d'aler secourre la dicte ame; laquelle chose comme Nostre Seigneur luy eust ottroié, sainct Denis s'en ala et mena avecques luy Sainct Morise et aultres amys que le roy Dagobert avoit moult honorés en sa vie, et avecques eulx orent des anges qui les conduirent jusques en la mer, et quant ils vindrent là où les deables tenoient et ammenoient à grant feste l'ame du roy Dagobert, si le misrent entre eulx et se

TOMB OF DAGOBERT.

combattirent encontre les deables." It was all done because of *Monseigneur S. Denis'* love of "*le bon roy*," who had founded the abbey in honour of the martyr; and if you doubt these facts, and "ne me croyez, alez à Sainct-Denis en France, en l'église, et regardez devant l'autel où l'en chante tous les jours la grant messe, là où le roy Dagobert gist. La verrez vous audessus de luy ce que vous ay dit, pourtrait et de noble euvre richement enluminée." From this, there can be no doubt that the whole mass of sculpture was originally coloured; indeed, a close inspection shows a little still visible in the folds of the drapery. Lenoir, whose depreciation of Mediæval sculpture as compared to that of the Renaissance was considerable, speaks of the draped figures as *pour le style comme pour le goût, comparable aux belles inventions de Raphaël.*

Upon the platform of the apse is the mosaic effigy of Frédégonde, not earlier than the 12th century. It is composed of a stone slab of the form of the early stone coffins. The design is marked out by thin bands of metal between which are incrustations of very small pieces of porphyry, serpentine, and white marble. This, like several of the early tombs, was originally in the abbey of S. Germain-des-Près.

The central part of the crypt was formerly the depository for the relics—a sort of sanctuary dedicated to S. Démètre. Another part of the crypt became the burial place of the Bourbon family. All the princes were buried in vaults underneath their tombs. "Tous le roys, reynes et autres ensépulturez à Saint-Denys reposent dans les caveaux qui sont sous leurs tombeaux, sans qu'il y en ait aucun ailleurs, ce que je dis pour désabuser plusieurs personnes (mesmes des gens de qualité) qui s'imaginent qu'il y ait une grande cave dans laquelle sont tous les roys, en chair et en os, et demandent qu'on la leur monstre, dont je me suis souventefois estonné, veu mesme que plusieurs qui vivent encores ont peu voir mettre les cinq derniers roys décédéz non en ceste cave imaginaire, mais dans le tombeau des Vallois, sçavoir, Henry II. et ces trois fils, et Henry IV., dans le caveau commun des rois, où il est encore. On en peut dire autant de François Ier et de Louis XII., et de tous les autres; car quant à la grotte qui est sous le chevet, il n'y a, ny eut jamais, corps ny sépulture d'aucune personne.* The day of the funeral the body was placed in the vault, "sur des barres de fer, devant une statue en marbre de Nostre-Dame."

* Dom Millet.

There it remained for a year, after which it was deposited in the tomb of the sovereign's ancestors. This curious arrangement became a custom by pure accident. Henri IV. not having signified any desire as to his place of burial, was left in this vault, "*le caveau des cérémonies*," while his widow and *les Etats* discussed the question of erecting a monument; and thus, by force of habit, the succeeding Bourbons being placed by the side of Henri, the "caveau" became the mausoleum of the family. But the Bourbons were a prolific race, and before very long the overcrowding became too great to admit of any more inhabitants; so upon the burial of Marie-Thérèse, the wife of Louis XIV., it was decided to tunnel a long passage to connect it with the central part of the crypt. It was a difficult and dangerous proceeding: "On perça," says Félibien, "par-dessous le chevet, à l'endroit où estoit une ancienne chapelle de Saint-Démètre, un petit corridor de la largeur de trois pieds sur sept de haut. Les ouvriers voûtoient à mesure qu'ils avançoient; et dans le poursuite de leur ouvrage, ils découvrirent quelques tombeaux dont on ne reconnut que celui de l'abbé Antoine de La Haye, par une inscription qu'on y trouva. Enfin, après avoir poussé environ sept toises et demie, les ouvriers arrivèrent à l'ancien caveau; de sorte qu'il a été aisé d'y joindre, par ce corridor de communication, un caveau specieux qui occupe aujourd'huy, dessous le chevet, l'ancienne crypte où estoient autrefois les corps des saints martyrs. La place est de neuf toises de long sur environ deux toises et demi dans sa plus grande largeur." The new vault was consecrated the 31st August, 1683. This accounts for the apparent want of an entrance to the centre of the crypt; as all visitors to the church are aware, you look through little apertures to the place where a few post-revolution burials have taken place. I commend all these particulars, which exemplify the horrors of burial above ground, with the rifling of tombs and coffins perpetrated by the officers of the Convention, to the opposers of cremation. Had all these poor royalties been converted into ashes, no such doings could have taken place. The entrance to the Bourbon vaults still exists, close to the altar of S. Maurice, to the right of the High Altar looking eastwards; but visitors enter by some steps farther east, by the side of the ascent to the apse. It is a miserably gloomy hole, with a few coffins upon trestles, shedding their violet coverings. Can any sort of burial equal in horror this of open vaults?

The statues of the early kings were erected by S. Louis. Ordered by him as commemorative effigies of his ancestors, it does not seem to have been within the wit of the 13th century sculptors to vary the physiognomy of the early sovereigns. Thus there is a strong likeness between Charles Martel* and Pépin, and Louis and Carloman. There is a curious divergence in the opinions passed upon Louis III. The chronicle of S. Denis calls him a "*homs plains de toutes ordures et toutes vanitez;*" whereas the annals of Metz say, "*Tous les peuples des Gaules pleurèrent sa mort avec une extrême douleur. Il fut en effet homme de rare mérite, et défendit courageusement et virilement contre les incursions des payens le royaume qui lui était soumis.*" So we see that it is not only the 19th century which vaunts and cries down a man, according as he belongs to the political sheep or the goats.

Carloman, at his eighteen years, has the appearance of a man of forty, and many years older than his brother. The statue of Charlemagne's brother Carloman has had a queer history.

* "Ensépouturé fut en l'église Saint-Denis en France à cui il avoit donnez maint biau don, mis fu en costé le mestre autel en un riche sarcu d'alebastre." (Chronicle of S. Denis.) And yet, soon after Charles's death, S. Eucher is supposed to have seen, by revelation, the sufferings of the Maire du Palais in Hell, where for his sins he was precipitated before the Day of Judgment. The tomb was opened in the presence of Bishop Eucher, Boniface the legate, and Fulrad, abbot of S. Denis, when behold! a great dragon jumped out, and the coffin had the appearance of having been burned.

It was marched to the Petits-Augustins with the rest, and there christened Charles le Chauve, but when sent back to S. Denis it was rebaptised Henri I.

Hugues Capet was buried at S. Denis close to his father, the great Hugues; his last words addressed to his son Robert prove him to have been possessed of piety, a proper notion of justice, and a large amount of common sense. "Bon fils, je t'adjure, au nom de la sainte et indivisible Trinité, de ne pas livrer ton âme aux conseils des flatteurs et de ne pas écouter les voeux de leur ambition, en leur faisant un don empoisonné de ces abbayes que je te confie pour toujours. Je désire également qu'il ne t'arrive point, conduit par la légèreté d'esprit ou ému par la colère, de distraire ou enlever quelque chose de leurs biens. Je te recommande surtout de veiller à ce que, pour aucune raison, tu ne déplaises jamais à leur chef commun, le grand saint Benoit, qui est un accès certain auprès du souverain juge, un port de tranquillité et un asile de sûreté après la sortie de la chair."* His particular friends to whom he commends his son are the Blessed Virgin, S. Benedict, S. Martin, S. Aignan, and SS. Cornelius and Cyprian, and above all S. Geneviève. Queen Adélaïde, like most Middle-Age ladies, did much embroidering as she sat up in her tower, and naturally S. Denis was her first thought. She gave the great statue of S. Martin (I do not know in what part of the church this was placed) a wondrous cope, embroidered between the shoulders with a "*Pontife éternel*" and adoring Cherubim and Seraphim. In the front was the "Lamb of God" and the Four Beasts of the Apocalypse.†

Robert must have profited by the good advice given him by his father, for we find the monk Helgand giving him a tremendous panegyric in the account of his death. "Peu de temps après avoir reçu le saint et salutaire viatique du corps vivifiant de notre Seigneur Jésus-Christ, Robert alla au Roi des rois, au Seigneur des seigneurs, et entra heureux dans les célestes royaumes. Il mourut le vingtième jour de juillet (1031) au commencement de la journée du mardi, au château de Melun, et il fut porté à Paris, puis enseveli à Saint-Denis, près de son père. Il y eut là un grand deuil, une douleur intolérable ; car la foule de moines gémissait sur la perte d'un tel père,‡ et une

---

* Helgaud, *Vie de Robert le Pieux*.
† Idem.
‡ Robert was abbot of S. Denis.

multitude innombrable de clercs se plaignait de leur misère que soulageait avec tant de piété ce saint homme. Un nombre infini de veuves et d'orphelins regrettait tant de bienfaits reçus de lui. Tous poussaient de grands cris jusqu'au ciel, disant d'une commune voix : 'Grand Roi, Dieu bon, pourquoi nous tuer ainsi en nous ôtant ce bon père et l'unissant à toi !' Ils se frappaient avec les poings la poitrine, allaient et venaient au saint tombeau, répétaient encore les paroles marquées plus haut et se joinaient aux prières des saints afin que Dieu eût pitié de lui dans le siècle éternel. Dieu ! quelle douleur causa cette mort. Tous s'écriaient avec des clameurs redoublées : 'Tant que Robert a régné et commandé, nous avons vécu tranquilles, nous n'avons rien craint ; que l'âme de ce père pieux, ce père du sénat, ce père de tout bien, soit heureuse et sauvée ! qu'elle monte et habite pour toujours avec Jésus-Christ, Roi des rois !' . . . . Dans tout cela, nous avons un grand sujet de douleur, en voyant qu'un tel et si grand homme repose sans une pierre ornée d'inscriptions, sans monument, sans épitaphe, lui dont la gloire et la mémoire ont été en bénédiction à toute la terre." As late as the 16th century Robert's tomb was enriched with colour, and even now a small amount remains.

Another king's death, that of Louis le Gros, is recorded by Suger : "Après avoir reçu en communion le corps et le sang de Jésus-Christ, le roi rejetant loin de lui toutes les pompes de l'orgueil du siècle, s'étendit sur un lit de simple toile. M'ayant vu pleurer sur lui qui, par le sort commun aux hommes, était devenu si petit et si humble de si grand et si élevé qu'il était, il me dit : 'Ne pleure pas sur moi, très-cher ami, mais plutôt triomphe et réjouis-toi de ce que Dieu, dans sa miséricorde, m'a donné, comme tu le vois, les moyens de me préparer à paraître devant lui.' . . . Un peu avant de mourir, il ordonna qu'on étendit un tapis par terre, et que sur ce tapis on jetât des cendres en forme de croix ; puis il s'y fit porter et déposer par ses serviteurs, et fortifiant toute sa personne par le signe de la croix, il rendit l'âme le jour les calendes d'août (Ier août 1137), dans la trentième année de son règne et presque la soixantième de son âge. Son corps fut à l'heure même enveloppé de riches étoffes pour être transporté et enterré dans l'église des saints martyrs."

Suger mentions the finding of the remains of Carloman when they were about to bury Louis VI., and how the former were removed to a spot between the altar of the Holy Trinity and that of the Martyrs: "On l'y déposa donc avec le cérémonial d'usage pour les rois, au milieu de chants nombreux, d'hymnes et de prières, après lui avoir fait de pieuses et solennelles funérailles. C'est là qu'il attend d'être admis à jouer de sa résurrection future, et qu'il est d'autant plus près de se réunir en esprit à la troupe des esprits célestes, que son corps est plus voisin des corps des saints martyrs et plus à portée d'en être protégé."

"Felix qui potuit mundi nutante ruina
Quo jaceat præscisse loco . . "

"Puisse le Rédempteur ressusciter l'âme de ce roi à l'intercession des saintes martyrs pour lesquels il avait un si pieux dévouement ! puisse cette âme être placée au rang des saints par celui qui a donné la sienne pour le salut du monde, notre seigneur Jésus-Christ qui vit et règne, Roi des rois, et maître des puissances, aux siècles des siècles. Amen."*

Of the burial of Louis VII. the monk Rigord gives some interesting details : "L'année 1181, le jeudi dix-huitième jour de septembre, mourut à Paris Louis, roi des Français. Son corps fut honorablement enseveli et couvert d'aromates dans l'église de Sainte-Marie de Barbeau, qu'il avait fondée. C'est là qu'en l'honneur de notre seigneur Jésus-Christ et de la bienheureuse mère de Dieu, Marie toujours vierge, de saints religieux célèbrent jour et nuit les offices divins pour l'âme du défunt roi, pour celles de tous ses prédécesseurs et pour le salut du royaume de France. C'est aussi dans cette église, et sur le lieu même de la sépulture du roi, que l'illustre reine des Français, Adèle† son épouse et mère de Phillippe-Auguste, roi des Français, fit construire un tombeau où l'art le plus exquis avait fait un heureux mélange des matières les plus brillantes, d'or et d'argent, d'airain et de pierres précieuses. Jamais chef-d'œuvre aussi étonnant n'avait paru dans aucun royaume depuis le règne de Salomon." In 1182 Philippe Auguste decreed that a taper should always be kept alight before the tomb of his father. What became of the monument is not known. At the Revolution it consisted of a sarcophagus which had been renovated in 1695 by the Cardinal de Furstemberg, abbot of Barbeau ‡ and prince bishop of Strasburg. When Charles IX.

---

* Suger, *Vie de Louis-le-Gros.*
† Adèle ou Alix, daughter of Thibaut le Grand, comte de Champagne, third wife of Louis VII.
‡ Near Melun.

was at Fontainebleau he had the curiosity to open this latter tomb of Louis. The body was nearly entire; but the sceptre, some silver seals and ornaments, were partially destroyed. The king had rings on his fingers and a gold cross on his neck; "le roi et les princes du sang qui se trouvèrent là présents, les prirent pour les porter en mémoire d'un si bon est religieux prédécesseur."* One would like to know why ignorant, poverty-stricken fisher and peasant folk should be anathematized for robbing the dead after a wreck or a battle, when such a pious prince as the author of the massacre of S. Bartholomew pilfered the rings from his ancestor without a word of protest—on the contrary, his relations and friends " du sang " aided and abetted him. But then, of course, a few centuries had elapsed in the latter case, and poor Louis was reduced to a state of dry bones; it was robbing a skeleton, not a body. In the reign of Napoléon the abbey of Barbeau was converted into a school for the daughters of members of the Legion of Honour, and in 1817 the remains of Louis VII. were transported to S. Denis.

Why does it happen that children who die young seem to be so superior to those who survive? Would the Duc de Bourgogne, Philippe, son of Louis VI., Edward V., or Prince Arthur have made better sovereigns than their relations who reigned in their stead? Suger gives a picturesque account of the death of Philippe, " un enfant dans la fleur de l'âge." This "malheur étrange" happened on the 13th October, 1131. " Le fils aîné du roi Louis Philippe, d'une grande douceur, l'espoir des bons et la terreur des méchants, se promenait un jour à cheval dans un faubourg de la cité de Paris ; un détestable porc se jette dans le chemin du cheval ; celui-ci tombe rudement, renverse, écrase contre une pierre le noble enfant qui le montait, et l'étouffe sous le poids de son corps. Ce jour-là même on avait convoqué l'armée pour une expédition ; aussi les habitants de la ville et tout les autres qui apprennent cet événement, consternés de douleur, crient, pleurent, poussent des sanglots, s'empressent à relever le tendre enfant presque mort, et le portent dans une maison voisine. O douleur ! à l'entrée de la nuit il rendit l'âme. Quelle tristesse et quel désespoir accablèrent son père, sa mère et les grands du royaume ! Homère lui-même ne pourrait l'exprimer. On l'enterra dans l'église du bienheureux Denis, dans le lieu resérvé

* Mézeray.

à la sépulture des rois et à la gauche de l'autel de la Sainte-Trinité, avec tout le cérémonial usité pour les rois, en présence d'une foule d'évêques et de grands de l'Etat."* Philippe's was the last statue that S. Louis gave to the church, and the crown and sceptre show that the young prince had been crowned by his father at Reims during the latter's life—probably in order to share the duties of kingship.

Although three abbeys were the happy possessors of the remains of Blanche of Castille (Maubuisson, Lys, and Saint-Corentin-lez-Mantes), no tomb exists of the sweet mother of S. Louis.† Upon the monument at Maubuisson the queen was attired in the habit of the Cistercian order, which she assumed in her last moments; the crown was placed over the veil, the royal robes over the nun's habit, and so she passed away, and was thus buried. In 1793 various tombs, armorial bearings, and the like *aliments de l'orgueil*, were transported from Maubuisson to Pontoise; some were broken, some burnt; golden vessels and silver saints were thrust into the melting-pot; and Blanche of Castille, with the help of a prince perhaps, or a warrior, became transformed into an instrument of war. But the museum of the Petits-Augustins wanted an effigy of the mother of Monsieur Saint Louis; and so they set up a black marble image of Catherine de Courtenay, empress of Constantinople and wife of Charles of Valois, who had lately, and all alone, journeyed from Maubuisson; and, thinking it a joke to turn a black empress into a white queen, they wrote upon the slab, in 13th century characters, that it was the true monument of *Madame la royne Blanche mere de Monsieur Saint Loys*. After twenty years Madame Catherine-Blanche became divorced from her other half, and the white queen faded away in favour of the black empress.

One of the most beautiful tombs is that of Philippe, the brother of S. Louis, which was formerly at Royaumont. The prince lies upon a sarcophagus, round which are niches filled with little figures of monks, bishops, and angels, full of charac-

---

* *Vie de Louis-le-Gros.*

† " If zealous love should go in search of virtue,
  Where should he find it purer than in Blanche?
  . . . . .
  Such as she is, in beauty, virtue, birth,
  Is the young Dauphin every way complete."
                              Shakespeare. King John.

ter and expression. One of these represents a king: "On y voyait le cercueil de Louis porté par les barons de France et par le roi d'Angleterre.* Une figure couronnée porte sur l'épaule un des bâtons; c'est le roi anglais "†—proving the sovereignty of France over England. There is a curious engraving by Boulogne representing this procession. The church is in the distance; a string of monks are zigzagging across the plain, and in the foreground we see this crowned head and others bearing the reliquary; behind are bishops; the whole in the grandiose style of the 17th and 18th centuries—drapery flying in the wind, bishops and monks prancing, and all the faces turned to the spectator. S. Louis had always held the abbey in most respectful esteem. He visited it before he started upon his various expeditions; and in 1267, when he had conferred the order of chivalry upon his son Philippe and sixty other young noblemen, he rode to S. Denis on horseback to implore the blessing of God, accompanied by a large concourse of courtiers and princes.

The monuments of the battle of Bouvines came from the church of S. Catherine-du-Val-des-Écoliers. They are incised stones, coloured and gilt, bearing the following inscriptions:—

A LA PRIERE DES SERGENS DARMES MONS^r SAINT LOYS FONDA CESTE EGLISE ET Y MIST LA PREMIERE
PIERRE ET FU POUR LA JOIE DE LA VITTOIRE QUE FU AU PONT DE BOUINES LAN MIL. CC. ET. XIIII.
LES SERGENS DARMES POUR LE TEMPS GARDOIENT LEDIT PONT ET VOUERENT QUE SE DIEU LEUR
DONNOIT VITTOIRE ILS FONDEROIENT VNE EGLISE EN LONNEUR DE MADAME SAINTE KATHERINE ET AINSI FU IL.

Another epitaph to Blanche de France came from the Cordeliers:

ICY GIST MADAME BLANCHE FILLE DE MONSEIGNEUR SANCT LOYS ET FEME DE MONS. FERDINAND DE LACERDE ROY DE CASTILLE QUI TRESPASSA DU CEST SIECLE LAN DE GCE

* Millin, *Antiquités Nationales*.
† Le corps de Saint-Louis fut porté une partie du chemin depuis Saint-Denis par Henri III., roi d'Angleterre, et par les barons de France et d'Angleterre sur leurs épaules, cérémonie qui est représentée sur le tombeau, où le prince est couvert d'un drap d'or bordé d'une bande d'étoffe bleue, semée de fleurs de lis d'or, la tête soutenue par le roi saint Louis, et les pieds par le roi d'Angleterre.'—P. Anselme, *Histoire de la Maison de France*.

MCCCXX LE DIX SEPTIESME JOUR DE JUN
PRIES POUR LAME DELLE Q. DEU BONNE MERCI LI FACE, AMEN.

When Isabelle d'Aragon died at Cosenza, in Calabria, her husband, Philippe le Hardi, wrote to the abbot and religious of S. Denis to commend her soul to their prayers, for her life *était aimable à Dieu et aux hommes*. Her epitaph begins:

DYSABEL. LAME. AIT. PARADYS, *etc.*

Louis XI. was not buried at S. Denis; he desired to be laid in the church of Our Lady of Cléry, "for which the Heretics (meaning the Huguenots and Calvinists) had not the same respect which they inviolably entertained for the holy and royal tombs of S. Denis.* But inspired by the Devil, with an abominable and hellish spirit of rage and profanation, they tore the king's remains from the tomb, and, together with the queen's, burnt them and scattered their ashes to the winds. Thus he who would not let his body rest under the protection of the Holy Martyers found no rest in the grave."†

This monument was of bronze, but another was erected in 1622 by an Orléans sculptor, Michel Bourdin. La Fontaine described the latter as follows, in a letter to his wife, dated 1633: "Nous nous arrêtâmes à Cléry. J'allai aussitôt visiter l'église; c'est une collégiale assez bien rentée pour un bourg. Louis XI. y est enterré. On le voit à genoux sur son tombeau, quatre enfants aux coins; ce seraient quatre anges, si on ne leur avait pas arraché les ailes. Le bon apôtre du roi fait là le saint homme, et il est bien mieux pris que lorsque le Bourguignon le mena à Liége.

> Je lui trouvai la mine d'un matois :
> Ainsi l'étoit ce prince dont la vie
> Doit rarement servir d'exemple aux rois,
> Mais pourroit être en quelques points suivie.

"À ses genoux sont ses heures et son chapelet, la main de justice, son sceptre, son chapeau et sa Notre-Dame. Je ne

---

* This does not quite agree with Dom Millet's account of the Huguenot depredations already given upon page 33.

† He could not have found much more rest at S. Denis, for which he had a great respect, although he desired to be buried at Cléry. Many a time this king perambulated from Paris to S. Denis barefooted, for he held the Saint to be the "Holy Protector of his dominions, the Guide of his councils, and the Guardian of his soul."

sais comment le statuaire n'y a pas mis le prévôt Tristan; le tout est en marbre blanc et m'a paru d'assez bonne main."

This monument suffered some mutilations during the Revolution, the head being chopped into three pieces[*]; but in 1817 it was repaired. It is, in style, very similar to the descriptions of the bronze monument of Charles VIII.

TOMB OF THE HOUSE OF ORLÉANS.

The tomb of the house of Orléans was erected by Louis XII. in the centre of the magnificent chapel of the family, in the church of the Célestins. It contained besides, the statue

[*] This was a sort of posthumous decapitation. Cardinal Richelieu's statue at the Sorbonne was treated in the same way.

of Philippe de Chabot, by Jean Cousin; Germain Pilon's Three Graces; the columns of Anne de Montmorency, of François II., and of Timoléon de Brissac; the obelisk of the Longuevilles; the tombs of Rénée d'Orléans, and of the duc de Rohan, by Michel Anguier. The destruction of this chapel and the dispersal of its contents was one of the greatest acts of vandalism of modern times; although a good deal has been preserved, the loss of the rest cannot but be bewailed.

Charles, duc d'Orléans, was a lettered man and given to verse writing; he was made prisoner at the battle of Agincourt, and passed more than twenty years of his life in England. The little porcupine at the king's feet (upon the tomb) symbolized the order of chivalry which he founded, and which adopted that animal as its emblem.

The beautiful marble monument of Rénée d'Orléans recalls those of Santa Croce, and other Italian churches, and it is a magnificent example of French Renaissance sculpture.

The epitaph to Marguerite de Valois, first wife of Henri IV., attributed to the queen's authorship, is taken from a manuscript in the Bibliothèque:

> Ceste brillante fleur de l'arbre des Valoys
> En qui mourust le nom de tant de puissans Roys,
> Marguerite, pour qui tant de lauriers fleurirent,
> Pour qui tant de bouquets chez les Muses se firent.
> A vu fleurs et lauriers, sur sa tête sécher,
> Et par un coup fatal, les lys s'en détacher.
> Las! le cercle Royal dont l'avoit couronnée
> En tumulte et sans ordre un trop prompt himénée,
> Rompu du même coup devant ses pieds tombant
> La laissa comme un tronc dégradé par les vents.
> Epouse sans espoux, et Royne sans royaume,
> Vaine ombre du passé, grand et noble fantosme
> Elle traisna depuis les restes de son sort,
> Et vist jusqu'a son nom mourir avant sa mort.

The epitaph upon Henri's second wife, Marie de' Medici, is in a very different style. Marie, after having built the splendid Luxembourg palace, and filled it with Rubens' sparkling magnificences of colour, died in exile at Köln:

> Le Louvre de Paris vit éclater ma gloire;
> Le nom de mon époux, d'immortelle mémoire,
> Est placé dans le ciel comme un astre nouveau.
> Pour gendres j'eus deux rois, pour fils ce clair flambeau,
> Qui par mille rayons brillera dans l'histoire.
> Parmi tant de grandeur (le pourra-t-on bien croire?)

TOMB OF RÉNÉE D'ORLÉANS-LONGUEVILLE.

Je suis morte en exil ; Cologne est mon tombeau !
Cologne, œil des cités de la terre Allemande,
Si jamais un passant curieux te demande
Le funeste récit des maux que j'ai soufferts,
Dis : ce triste cercueil chétivement enserre
La reine dont le sang coule en tout l'univers,
Qui n'eut pas en mourant un seul pouce de terre.*

Louis XIII., or rather, part of him, was buried at the Jesuits' church; and Anne d'Autriche erected therein a fine monument sculptured by Jacques Sarrazin. Two colossal angels in bronze and silver supported a silver-gilt heart; but its magnificence only made it of greater use to the mint for coinage.

This good king, the thirteenth of his name, was a great devotee of S. Denis. He had instituted reform in the abbey by introducing the congregation of S. Maur ; and we are told that he acquired "strength and spirits in his last illness, as he lay languishing upon his bed, as often as he thought of S. Denis. At such times he would remark to his attendants, with a smile of pious serenity, how much he felt himself reconciled to his near approaching dissolution, and fortified against all the usual desires of life or dread of death; in a sweet anticipation of the happiness he should enjoy by reposing near the tombs of the Holy Martyrs, in whom he placed the most sacred and unbounded confidence."

There is one more exquisite work of art which ought to be mentioned, the beautiful urn from the abbey of Haute-Bruyère, which contained the heart of that magnificent profligate, François I$^{er.}$ It is of white marble, of perfect form, with the most delicious little Genii sitting on the top. The bas reliefs represent the Arts and Sciences, Faith, and the Church. It is the work of Pierre Bontems.

Some of the kings were crowned at S. Denis after having been anointed and consecrated at Reims; some, like Philippe Auguste, were re-invested at the abbey. Philippe le Hardi,

* There is a queer story told by Félibien of Marie's desire to possess some marbles left at S. Denis, after the building of the Henri II. tomb by Catherine de' Medici. Marie was about to build her a house, and she demanded of her son permission to carry off the marbles; but the monks objected, and appealed to the Parliament. The king, however, having quarrelled with his mother, was not sorry to make peace at another's cost, so he commanded the monks to deliver the marbles; but the latter were not to be conquered so easily, and another appeal was made which ended as fruitlessly as the first, and the poor convent eventually lost its marbles.

Charles VIII., Louis XII., François Ier., and Louis XIII., were all anointed at Reims and crowned at S. Denis. An account in an old book of the coronation of Louis XIII. is so quaint, and gives so graphic a picture of some of the manners and customs of the period, that it is, I think, worth quoting in full.*

The description of the magnificent ceremony was extracted from a chronicle of the reign of Louis XIII., and translated into English a hundred and fifty years ago :—

"The royall ornaments, which are kept in the *Abbey of* Saint Denis, being caryed to Rheims, on the 14th October, 1610, the King made his entrie into the towne, where his Maiestie was received with greate pompe and magnificence ; the particularities whereof I am forced, for brevities sake, to omit. The day before **the ceremonie**, the King went vnto the Cathedrall, to assist at Euensong, and to heare a sermon made by Father Coton, vpon the *diuine* institution of **the *unction of the Kings of France*,** and of confirmation, which he received from the hands of the Cardinall of Joyeuse, to whom he was presented by Queen Marguerite and the Prince of Condé.

"On Sunday, the 17th of October, the King sent foure Barons vnto the Abbey of Saint Remy, to fetch the *holie oyle*. They parted earlie in the morning, with their Esquires and Gentlemen ; either of them having a banner, with his armes, caried before him, causing a *white hackney* to be led, for the Prior of Saint Remy, who was to carry the said *holie oyle*.

"The Cardinal of Joyeuse, who was to represent **the Archbishop of** Rheims, and to doe the office, at the ceremonie, came soone after into the church, with eight Bishops to assist him, where, attending the comming of the Peeres, he sat him downe in his pontificall robes. Two of these Bishops were attired like Deacons, with mitres ; two like Sub-Deacons, with mitres ; and foure with copes and mitres. Soon after arrived the ecclesiasticall Peeres, in their pontificall robes. . . . . At the same instant there came, from the King's lodging, the Princes of Condé and Conty . . . . who were deputed by the King **to** hold **the** places of . . . . attyred in their **robes and coronets, according to** their qualities. Having done their **devotions, and saluted one another, they** sent the bishops of Laon and Beauuais **to fetch the King, in their pontificall** habits (*having certaine reliques of the holie Saintes* hanging *about their neckes*), conducted by the Master of the Ceremonies ; all the Prebendes of oure Ladies church marching in goodlie procession before them. Being come to the King's chamber, and finding it shut, **the** Bishop of Laon knocked three several times, to either of which the greate Chamberlaine demanded, '*What would ye?*' The Bishop answered, '*Lewis the Thirteenth, son to Henrie the Greate*'; whereunto the Chamberlaine replied, '*He sleepeth*'; then knocking againe, he had the like answere. But at the third time the Bishop answered, '*Lewis the Thirteenth, which God hath given us for King*'; then the door was opened, and the Bishops entered with the

---

* "History and description of the Royal Abbaye of St. Denis, and of the vast riches which have been accumulating for ages in the celebrated abbaye. Extracted from the records of S. Denis," London, 1795.

cheife chaunter of Rheims, &c., where they found the King laid on his bed, *having his shirt slit before and behind,* to receive the holie Vnction, and uppon it a waistecoat of crimson sattin, *slitted in like maner,* and thereon a long robe of cloth-of-*siluer*. The Bishop of Laon having finished a prayer, kissing their hands, they lifted the King from his bed, with all *shewes of honour,* and then led him, *singing,* to the church doore. Before him, there marched, first the greate Prouost, with his archeres; then the Clergie which had accompanied the two Prelates; the hundrede tall Swissers of his guard: the drummes, haultbois, and herauldes; the nobilitie; the great Master of the Ceremonies; the Knights of the Holie Ghoste, with their great order hong about their neckes, in the middest of two hundred Gentlemen of the King's house; and *the Scottish Guards, in their own proper* habiliments. Before his Maiestie went the Mareschall la Chastre, *representinge the Constable,* carying a naked sworde, &c. &c. After some ceremonies at the church doore, the King approacheth neare untoe the high altar, where he was presented, by the Bishops of Laon and Chalons, untoe the Cardinal Joyeuse, who said many prayers, whilest the King was at his deuotions. After this he was led untoe his seate, with his Noblemen and officers about him. In the meane tyme, all the religious men of Saint Remy came solemnlie in procession, being accompanied by the cheife of the towne, caryinge torches of virgines waxe in their hands: Their Prior was mounted upon the *white hackney,* having a foote-cloath of cloath-of-silver, caryinge the *violl of holie oyle, in a pixe,* hanginge about his necke, being under a canopie of cloath-of-silver, borne by foure Monkes. The Cardinall being advertised of the arrivall of *the said oyle,* hee went, in his pontificalibus, to meet it, with the eight Bishops which assisted him, and all the singinge men and quiristeres. But before they would deliver it unto the Cardinall, they made him (according to the custome) binde himself to restore it untoe them againe. After saying a praier, hee shewed the *holie oyle* untoe the people; and then set it down vpon the high altar, *with all the Godlie reuerence.* (The coronation oath and some ceremonies are here omitted for brevity). The King having taken the oathes, with inuocation of the name of God, laying his handes vpon the Gospel, which he kist with greate reuerence. The King's ornaments . . . were layd upon the altar; and on the left hande side, neere vnto them, stoode the *Prior of Saint Denis,* who hath the keeping of them; and on the right side stoode the Prior of Saint Remy, *looking sharplie to the holie oyle.** The Bishops of Laon and Beauvais, hauing conducted him vnto the altar, Mons. de Belgarde tooke off his roabe of cloath-of-silver. Being in his waistecoate of sattin, when the Cardinall had made certaine prayers and blessings, the Duke of Esguillon put on his buskins, and the Prince of Condé put on his spurres (in the place of the Duke of Bourgundie) and presentlie took them off againe. After this, the Cardinall blessed the royale sworde, it being in the scabberd, and girt the King therewith, and presentlie ungirted him againe. Then he drew it out of the scabberd, and kissed it, saying manie praiers, whilest that the Quier sang certaine anthems. The King kist the sworde also; and layd it upon the altar, in testimonie of his zeale and affection to the defence of the holie church. The Cardinall delivered it

---

* The holy oil was brought from heaven by a dove, in the very same phial in which it is kept. It has continued unwasted and unimpaired from the time of Clovis, for whose use it was sent, A.D. 500.

into his hande againe; which his Maiestie tooke reuerentlie vpon his knee, and gave it to the *Mareschall la Chastre*. The Cardinall returning to the altar, to prepare the sacred vnction, after this manner: '*Hee drewe out of the forenamed holie violl, with a needell of gold, a small quantitie of liquor, of the bignesse of a pease, and mingled it, with his finger, with the holie creme prepared in the couer of the chalice.*

" This vnction being thus ordered, the tyinges of the King's garments *were let loose both before and behinde*, by the Cardinall and the two Bishops; after which his Maiestie kneeled down in his oratorie, and the Cardinall with him, to crave the assistance of God for the preseruation of France. The Lettanie being sung, the Cardinall stoode up, to saye certaine praiers ouer the King, who was yet kneeling. Then the Cardinall sett him downe, as in the consecration of a Bishop, and holding in his hand *the patenne* whereon the *heavenlie oyle* was layd, he beganne, with his right *thumbe*, to anoynte the King, in divers places, *viz.*, on the crowne of the head, on the stomacke, betwixte his shouldere blades, on bothe shoulderes, and on the bendinges of his armes. The consecration praiers being ended, the Cardinall, with the two Bishops, closed vp his shirte, waistecoate, and other garmentes, in reverence of the sacred Vnction. Then the high Chamberlaine presented the three habitts accustomed to be worne, in the lyke ceremonies, viz., a long jackett, representinge a Sub-Deacon, a surplis for a Deacon, and a *royall cloake*, insteade of a coape, representinge a Prieste; which ended, the Cardinall *anoynted the palmes of his handes*, and then put him on *thin* gloues, lest, peradventure, hee should touche anie thinge with his bare handes, for reverence of the vnction, which gloues he blest, and sprinkled with holie water; the royall ringe being alsoe blest by the Cardinall (a symbole of loue, whereby the King was wedded untoe his realme), he put it on the fourthe fingere of his Maiesties right hande, with all the accustomed ceremonie. This done, hee tooke the sceptere from the altar, and put it intoe his right hande, for a mark of the Soueraigne power: then he tooke the hande of Justice, which hee put into his lefte hande, it being a wande, hauing, on the top thereof, a hande of mylke white iuorie.

"Then the Chancelloure of France came vp, with his face towarde the King, and, with a stoute voyce, did call vp the Peeres, according to their dignities, to assist at the coronation. When as, this ceremonie being ended, the Cardinall took *the great crowne* from the altar, and lifting it with bothe his handes, did poise it over the King's heade; the Peeres did then come to support them, and the Cardinall blest it; and then he alone sett the crowne upon the King's heade, whereuntoe all the Peeres did incontinentlie put their handes. The Cardinall then said manie praiers, and blest the King; the which being ended, *hee took him bie the right sleeve*, and conducted him to his royall throne, the which was builded on high at the bottome of the quier, forasmuch as that he might be seene of all the people, holdinge still in his handes the royall sceptere and rod of Justice. The Queen Regent, the whilst she beheld all these ceremonies, was sorely disquieted, not being able to endure, with patience, to see his Maiestie *bare headed*, vnder the crowne, havinge his capp taken from him; which shewes that crownes and greatness have their discomodities, as well as the most ordinarie thinges, and the poorest cottages. The King being come to his royall throwne, attended bie the Princes, Peeres, and Officers, according to their degrees, the Cardinall, holding him by the hande. caused him to sit downe, and praied untoe God to confirme him in his throne, and to make him invincible and inexpugnable against his enemies. After which, having sayd a praier, being bare-headed, he made a low obeysance untoe the King, and kissed him, saying thrice, with a loude voyce, '*God save the King*'; and at the laste, he added, '*God save the King eternallie.*' All the Peeres did the lyke obeysance, one after the other, and *kist* him, with the lyke acclamation, and then returned untoe the seates that were prepared for them on either hand."

The treasury of S. Denis was one of the richest in Europe. Commenced by the religious enthusiasts of the time of Charlemagne, it increased year by year, through the donations of the

RELIQUARY CONTAINING THE HEAD OF S. DENIS.

grateful patients who had been cured, or whose sufferings had been relieved, by the intercession of S. Denis and his companions. For every wax arm or leg, which we see hanging up in bunches at the side of a shrine in these days, the ages of Faith could have produced a valuable plaque, gem, cross, reliquary, or altar vessel. Thankfulness was then more costly in its expression. Doubtless poor offerings were also made, but the richness of the churches and their contents, as compared with the difficulty of obtaining a few thousands at the present day, shows that gratitude was more practical than in modern times. Charles le Chauve was a great donor to the monastery. It was he who gave the magnificent *ante-pendium*, besides some jewelled Gospels and altar-vessels. Philippe-Auguste bequeathed all his jewels to the abbey, including a cross of gold valued at 400 livres, this benefaction being for the maintenance of twenty additional monks; but his son, Louis, repurchased some of the valuables at the estimated price of 11,600 *livres*, a little business transaction which was not unprofitable to the convent. Louis le Gros established the custom of leaving the royal ornaments to the abbey at the decease of the kings. Matthieu de Vendôme, one of the regular abbots, gave the marvellous *chef* of S. Denis, a gold reliquary in the form of a head, with a jewelled mitre, and silver-gilt supporting Angels, and a young Child-angel holding another reliquary containing a portion of the Saint's shoulder-blade. Gilles de Pontoise, another abbot, presented a beautiful reliquary, containing the under-jaw of S. Louis—a marvel of goldsmithy in the form of statuettes of gold, jewelled and enamelled. The great Suger gave a number of magnificent objects of all kinds; the huge gold cross, six feet in height, placed over the altar, and another which stood upon the *grille* dividing the choir from the nave. These probably were made at S. Denis, as Suger set up a great school for the fashioning of gold and silver, as well as for writing and painting; and so famous did it become, that brethren from other monasteries flocked to the monks of S. Denis to perfect themselves in these arts.

There is a representation of Charles le Chauve's *ante-pendium* in the picture formerly in the Dudley collection, and now in the possession of Mr. Edward Steinkopff, and generally known as the "Mass of S. Giles." The altar stands as at present; on the right we see a portion of the tomb of Dagobert; and behind are the windows of the apsidal clerestory. The only difference in the sculptures, as represented in the picture, and the actual monument, is that the head of Nantilde is bent in the modern statue, but is erect in the old one; and the feet of Dagobert seem to have nothing to rest upon. A priest is before the altar; on his left is a king; behind are some assistants, one holding a tall candle; and above is an Angel bearing a paper, alluding to the legend, that as S. Giles was once saying mass before a king with some hidden sin he dare not confess, an Angel descended with a written pardon. The

THE "MASS OF S. GILES" (FRAGMENT).

question is, Who is the king? May it not be Charles le Chauve, the donor of the retable? Charles was abbot of S. Denis; and his devotion to the Saint was so great that he attended the offices of the church on all solemn days, and passed the rest of the time in pious conversation with the monks. The crown the king wears is of the time of Charles V., but it has upon it the Imperial circle, which seems to point to Charles the Bald; and the later style of the crown may be accounted for, as it has evidently been copied from one in the treasury of S. Denis (see Félibien). Moreover, it very much resembles the one worn by Charles le Chauve in a miniature of a Latin Bible in the Bibliothèque; on the other hand, the king wears a moustache in the latter, whereas in the picture he is bearded.

Another question is this, Does the picture represent a mass? It probably has gained its title as much from being the companion *volet* to Lord Northbrook's S. Giles as to the incident of the scroll-bearing Angel. But there is not the slightest resemblance between the hunting personage in Lord Northbrook's picture and the king in the "Mass." In the former, the kneeling hunter appears in a cap, and has no beard; may not this be Charles Martel? We are told in the legend of S. Giles that the king of France was one day hunting in the South, near Nismes, when, in the pursuit of a hind, the hunters came upon S. Giles living hermit-wise in a cave. Charles Martel was never actually sovereign, although governing the kingdom; therefore a cap would be an appropriate head covering for the Maire du Palais. And the dates correspond. S. Giles died in 725; Charles Martel in 741. Is there any evidence that the S. Denis picture represents the S. Giles legend? There is no reason why each *volet* of a triptich should be decorated with incidents in the life of the same saint. Again, does the picture represent a mass? There are no lights upon the altar, which is contrary to the almost invariable custom of the church from all time. Two lights were used from the earliest period; whereas a single light, either taper, torch, or lantern, borne by an assistant kneeling behind the celebrant, generally denotes a communion of the faithful, after, or out of, mass. It is true there is a picture by van der Weyden in the National Gallery of the "Mass of S. Hubert," with no lights, and there is no doubt about the subject, as the vessels requisite for a mass are visible upon the altar; but in the "Mass of S. Giles" there are no evidences of the celebration of mass, except that the priest is elevating the Host while facing the altar, and reading from a book placed thereon; whereas at a communion the celebrant turns his back to the altar when elevating the consecrated wafer. Now may not the picture represent either the communion of Charles le Chauve, or his induction as abbot, or his presentation of the retable? I have not lost sight of the difficulty of the Angel. But if it be really the sin-forgiven scroll which he holds, there is no reason why this particular king should not have had a hidden sin, pious man though he may have been; indeed, that would be a reason for his thinking ill of himself. And must the subject be necessarily that incident, when we know that in Mediæval times Angels were constantly in the habit of flying about with all kinds of objects of celestial manufacture—stoles, girdles, chalices, crowns, palms, &c. (In van der Weyden's picture, mentioned above, an Angel is descending with a stole).

These are merely suggestions of a theory, which others, more qualified than myself, may be able to solve. Suger is said to have added to the *ante-pendium* given by Charles le Chauve, and placed it over the altar as a retable;* therefore there would be nothing extraordinary in the 15th-century artist placing Charles kneeling as the original donor, and Suger celebrating, as the founder of the new altar, or reredos. Has the abbot Giles de Pontoise, who died in 1325, caused any confusion in naming this picture? There is another curious resemblance in the crowns borne by the Angels upon the retable, and the crowns of Guarrazar in the Hôtel Cluny. The latter are supposed to be of Byzantine workmanship, the largest bearing the name of Reccesvinthus, king of the Visigoths, who reigned from 649 to 672. Charles le Chauve died in 823; but, according to Grégoire de Tours, when Childebert returned from a campaign against the Visigoths in Spain, he brought away divers gold and silver treasures, including a gold cross from Toledo; therefore there must have been an extensive school of goldsmithy in Spain at that time, and Toledo is the very spot near which the Guarrazar spoils were discovered. Were they made there some 100 years or so after Childebert's death? Grégoire de Tours also speaks of the king setting up

---

* Viollet le Duc, who attributes the picture to van Eyck, states that the cross was given by Suger (it is engraved in Félibien). In the *Dictionnaire raisonné d'Architecture*, le Duc has engraved the altar. Dom Doublet also gives a minute description of the gold retable with its ornaments of precious stones. The reliquary behind was destroyed by the Huguenots.

workshops in the Parvis Notre-Dame, doubtless in imitation of the Spanish school; and in his *Notice de l'Orfèvrerie*, M. Alfred Darcel points out a similarity between the Merovingian and the Spanish style of work. "Ce qui ressort de la plupart des passages que nous venons de citer, c'est que l'orfévrerie mérovingienne a pour principal caractère l'alliance des pierreries aux métaux précieux. Ce caractère se retrouve dans l'ornementation des couronnes de Guarrazar . . . et dans l'orfévrerie Byzantine." Is it possible, then, that the *ante-pendium* presented by Charles le Chauve to S. Denis was made at the workshops set up by Childebert in the Parvis Notre-Dame, in imitation of those he had seen at Toledo; and that the workmanship was also an imitation of the Spanish goldsmithy of a hundred years earlier?

But of all this beauty, of all this wealth, what have we now? Marvellously little; still, considering the robbers, royal and plebeian, the fires, the wars, and the undisciplined mobs, we ought to be thankful that so much has been preserved. That even the great churchmen were not above suspicion we see by the account of the coronation of Louis XIII.; the cardinal being obliged "to binde himself" to restore the "holy oyle" before the monks would let him take it into his hands; and the Prior of S. Remy, who had the custody of it, standing by and "looking sharplie to the holie oyle."

Of the few things which remain from the wreck, the following will be found in the Louvre and the Bibliothèque Nationale, commencing with the former.*

The beautiful Egyptian Amphora of porphyry transformed by Abbot Suger† into an eagle for service as an altar vessel. It is silver-gilt, and bears an inscription round the bird's neck: *Incldudi Gemmis lapis ista meretur et auro—marmor erat sed in his marmore carior est.*‡ Suger himself thus describes it: "Un vase de porphyre, chef-d'œuvre de taille et de sculpture; depuis longues années il était sans emploi dans l'écrin; d'amphore qu'il était, nous l'avons transformé en un aigle, au moyen de l'or et de l'argent, nous l'avons adapté au service de l'autel, et sur ce vase nous avons fait inscrire les vers qui suivent."

* See *Notice de Émaux et de l'Orfèvrerie*, by Alfred Darcel. *Gemmes et Joyaux*, by Barbet de Jouy. *Handbook of the Louvre*; S. Beale.
† In the Salle d'Apollon; one of the centre cases.
‡ Suger was abbot from 1122 to 1151.

Another antique sardonyx[*] set by Suger, with a mounting of silver-gilt filagree and precious stones ornamenting it. Suger's account of this vase is as follows: "Nous avons acheté, pour le service du même autel, un calice précieux de sardonyx ; nous y avons joint, en guise d'amphore, un autre vase de la même matière, mais de forme différente, sur lequel sont ces vers : *Dum libare Deo gemmis debemus et auro—Hoc ego Sugerius offero vas Domino.*" . . . "Il était de ce sentiment que l'on doit employer à la décoration des autels tout ce que l'on a de plus précieux ; il disait que si les juifs se sont servis dans l'ancienne loi de vases et de fioles d'or, pour ramasser le sang des animaux, à plus forte raison doit-on moins épargner, dans la nouvelle, l'or et les pierreries pour tout ce qui a rapport au saint sacrifice du corps et du sang de Jésus Christ." Twenty-four *plaques* which decorated a book of the Gospels, in *cloisonné* enamel, are of the 9th century. Some of them are ornamented with foliage, others with the four Evangelists. They belonged to the gold book-cover bearing the legend : *Beatrix me in honore Dei omnipotentis et omnium sanctorum eius fieri precepit ;* which probably refers to Beatrix, grand-daughter of Hugues Capet and sister of Robert, king of France, wife of Ebles I., count of Reims.

VASE DE SUGER.

A 13th century reliquary in *champlevé* enamel.

The psalter of Charles le Chauve.

The beautiful antique rock-crystal vase, bearing the name of Aliénor d'Aquitaine. It was given by her to Louis VII., who presented it to Suger, who, in his turn, offered it to the Saints, as saith the inscription upon the foot: "*This vase was given by Aliénor to Louis, her husband. Mitadol gave it to her grandfather, and the King to me, Suger ; and I, Suger, to SS. Rusticus and Eleutherius.*"

The paten belonging to Suger's lost chalice. It is a serpentine disc incrusted with golden fishes.

[*] Salle d'Apollon, centre case.

A rectangular plaque of gold, *repoussée* and gilt, bearing inscriptions in Greek.

A statuette of the Blessed Virgin, in silver, *repoussée*, chased, and parcel gilt and enamelled. The Virgin holds a *fleur-de-lys*, enriched with precious stones, in her right hand. It was given to the abbey by Jehanne d'Evreux, in 1334.

A sceptre with a statuette of Charlemagne upon a lily, of the reign of Charles V.

Another statuette of the Blessed Virgin in silver *repoussée* and parcel gilt; with a little rock-crystal reliquary enclosing a piece of the swaddling clothes.

In the Bibliothèque:

A cameo (sardonyx) head of Augustus, formerly one of the gems of the reliquary containing the skull of S. Hilary. The reliquary was in the form of a mitred head, after the manner of that of S. Denis. The shoulders were vested in a cope, and this cameo set in the centre of the orphrey. The reliquary was made during the administration of Jérôme de Chambellan, grand prior from 1583 to 1606, but part of the mounting holding the pearls and stones seems to be of earlier date. There are three sapphires and three imitation rubies, separated by six bouquets composed of three pearls.*

A little chalcedony bust of Annius Verus as Bacchus, inscribed: *Verinus consulis probat tempora.* The bust bears a striking likeness to some medals and coins of the little son of Marcus Aurelius. It was the custom of the Roman consuls to send presents upon their appointments; thus, in sending this bust to a friend, some consul engraved the inscription, which signifies: *The little Verus will remind you of my consulate.* In the list by Dom Félibien of the treasury at S. Denis, this is called: *Tête d'un enfant faite d'une agate orientale.*

One of the most precious of the treasures was the Bacchic cantharus, called the Cup of the Ptolomies. It is a sardonyx cup upon a pedestal, with handles of vine stalks, and covered with bas-reliefs. It is supposed to have gained its name from having belonged to Ptolomy XI., the husband of Cleopatra, who bore the surname of Dionysos or Bacchus. From the subjects of the bas-reliefs, it was undoubtedly consecrated to Bacchus. It has also been called the Cup of Mithridates, as having perhaps belonged to the celebrated collection of vases

---

* *Catalogue des Camées*, by M. Chabouillet.

formed by the famous King. Singular though it may appear, this cup dedicated to Bacchus was given to S. Denis by one of the Carlovingian Kings; was it some blundering over the names, Dionysos and Dionysius? The gold foot was added to give it the form of a chalice, says Tristran de Saint-Amant, and the "grossier distique latin," placed upon this foot, "était profondément gravé sur l'or et la gravure remplie d'émail de couleur d'acier braze." The following inscription is easily read in the engraving in Félibien's history, but not the date: *Hoc vas Christe tibi mente dicavit tertius in Francos regmine Karlus.**

It has been thought that it was Charles the Simple who made the donation, but Félibien remarks that Charles le Gros as well as Charles le Chauve were also designated Charles III. In any case, it is known to have been in the treasury as early as the 9th century. In 1790, it was placed in the Cabinet de Médailles, but some years after it was stolen with the great cameo and other valuables. The thieves were arrested in Holland, and the cup and the cameo restored to the Bibliothèque; but the mounting of the latter and the foot of the cup had been melted up. According to a tradition referred to by Marion de Mersan, the queens of France drank consecrated wine from this cup upon their coronation day. Another tradition asserts that Henri III., in direful need of money, borrowed the cup, and pawned it to the Jews of Metz for a million of *livres tournois*.

A beautiful aqua-marine bust is the authentic portrait of the daughter of Titus, wife of Flavius Sabinus. It is signed Evodus, the name of a Greek artist known by two other signed gems. It formed part of the reliquary known as *escrain* or *oratoire de Charlemagne*. Félibien speaks of it thus: "Ce reliquaire n'est qu'or, perles et pierreries. Sur le haut est réprésentée une princesse que quelques uns estiment être ou Cléopâtre, ou Julie, fille de l'empereur Titus." Some of the stones are gone, but one of the remaining sapphires is an antique intaglio representing upon one side a dauphin, and upon the other a monogram surmounted by a cross of the 5th or 6th century. The letters of the monogram are MAΘY, possibly the initials of the owner, or the designation of the Virgin: ΜΑΡΙΛ ΜΗΤΗΡ ΘΕΟΥ (*Marie, mère de Dieu*).

---

* O Christ, Charles III. of the name upon the throne of France consecrates this cup to thee!

The Coupe de Chrosroës I., King of Persia, of the dynasty of the Sassanides (531-579) is of transparent rock-crystal, engraved with a representation of the King sitting upon his throne. In the history of the abbey, published in 1625, by F. I. Doublet, we find this cup mentioned as having been in the treasury, under the name of Solomon's cup, for more than

STEPS LEADING TO THE APSE.

ten centuries, "et donnée par l'Empereur et Roy de France Charles le Chauve." How it got into the hands of the King is not known. Chrosroës was defeated by Justinian, general of Tiberius Constantine, Emperor of the East; so that possibly the cup found its way to Constantinople after the battle. Félibien's description of it is: "Espèce de sous-couppe d'or ornée de crystaux de différentes sortes de couleurs. Au milieu l'on y voit un Roy assis dans son trône."

Such are a few of the treasures formerly at S. Denis. The church is lovely now, garnished only with its tombs and glass; what it must have been upon a great festival a couple of hundred years ago, or still farther back, imagination must be left to picture to itself. Even now, upon the fête of the Saint (October 9th), the effect of the procession, as it winds up and down the aisles and steps, is very fine, and quaint, too; for the Suisses wear black hats and feathers, cloaks, breeches, and stockings, after the style of Lawrence's "Kemble as Hamlet"; indeed, they seem to be the Dane, according to the courtly painter, personified. The costume of the boys, also, is different to that of the other churches. They wear violet cassocks, white cottas, scarlet capes with yellow edges, and red skull caps. The whole affair, the old canons bearing the relics, the boys in their quaint attire, the old-world vergers and beadles, the lights few and far between in the great dim church, the vistas of arched aisles ending in darkness, and the sparse congregation, give the impression of some period long before the end of this prosaic 19th century. The *châsses* are in their old places upon the raised apse behind the altar; but they are of no artistic value. The setting of the jewels is there, but the jewels are gone. The church remains one of the grandest of its date, but its contents have been mended, patched, and re-made. Still, it is an exquisitely beautiful relic, left us by the ages of Faith.

S. Denis still goes barefoot, but not for love. Stern necessity keeps it so, or thrusts its cold feet into wooden shoes. It carries its red flag also, and waves it menacingly at all who love peace and quiet. Likewise, it perambulates in processions; but its relics are rags and hungry children. From a haven of rest, raised up with perhaps some grains of foolish superstition; from an artistic centre of all that was beautiful; from the trysting place of enthusiasts, diluted probably with a certain amount of bigotry, S. Denis has become faithless, hopeless, and restless; bigoted in its excessive Communism, unjust in its perversion of true Socialism, flaunting its Anarchic *oriflamme* in the face of law and order. It is a strange contrast; but perhaps the cause and effect are nearer allied than is generally supposed.

SAINTE-ELIZABETH.

Situated in the Rue du Temple, the church dedicated to the great Hungarian princess formerly faced the entrance to the grim fortress of the Templars, where the poor little Dauphin sighed out his infant life. The church was built for the nuns of the third order of S. Francis, of which S. Elizabeth was a member; and the first stone was laid in 1628 by a very different sort of Queen, Marie de' Medici. The exterior, with its Doric pilastered doorway, and the interior, with its poor glass and indifferent sculptures, are alike utterly uninteresting; but the white marble font, bearing the date of 1654, and the woodwork which ornaments the aisle of the sanctuary, are worth a visit. The latter consists of a series of little panels representing scenes from the Old and New Testament in bas-relief, of the end of the 16th century, and are said to have been originally in a church at Arras. There is nothing in the building worthy of its patron, that most perfect of saints, whether we think of her as woman, as queen, or as mother.

> "AVE GEMMA SPECIOSA!
> MULIERUM SYDUS, ROSA!
> EX REGALI STIRPE NATA,
> MUNDO LICET VIRO DATA
> NUNC IN COELIS CORONATA;
> CHRISTO TAMEN DESPONSATA.
> UTRIUSQUE SPONSALIA,
> SIMUL SERVANS ILLIBATA;
> SARAM SEQUENS FIDE PIA,
> ET REBECCAM PRUDENTIA,
> O DILECTA! O BEATA!
> NOSTRA ESTO ADVOCATA,
> ELIZABETH EGREGIA!" *

SAINT-ÉTIENNE DU MONT.

Upon the summit of the hill which rises up from the Seine, opposite and on the south side of Notre-Dame, is the church of S. Étienne du Mont. Some few years ago this "mountain" was an interesting hunting ground to the archæological explorer and the collector of *bric-à-brac;* but it has been so cut through by new streets and boulevards that it has almost been improved out of existence. At the foot of it, in a little street turning on

---

* From a German breviary, printed at Nürnberg, 1515, quoted by Mrs. Jameson: *Sacred and Legendary Art.*

from the Quai de la Tourelle, is all that remains of the famous college of the Bernardins, now used by the *sapeurs-pompiers*. The college was founded by an Englishman, Stephen of Lexington, Abbot of Clairvaux, in 1244, upon some ground belong-

SAINT-ÉTIENNE DU MONT.

ing to the rich abbey of S. Victor; Alphonse, the brother of S. Louis, being the titular founder and protector of the establishment. The great church, begun in 1338 by Pope Benedict XII. and Cardinal Curti, to replace the one built by Stephen

Lexington, was never finished, but was considered, in the 14th century, to be of great beauty. (Pope Benedict, as Jacques Fournier, was professor of theology in the college.) But more fortunate than the church, the refectory has remained intact in all its beauty until our own time, though unfortunately, in 1845, it was sadly mutilated in order to adapt it for use as a barrack. A portion of the cloister may still be seen in the Rue de Poissy, a pointed arch built into the modern wall of a house with square windows in between. It is time the municipality of Paris or the Society for the Preservation of Ancient Buildings bestirred itself to restore the few fragments of old Paris which yet remain. The Revolution did much damage, but often it only put the conventual buildings to secular uses without destroying them, leaving for later governments, and those moreover professedly religious, to utterly demolish the mutilated monasteries and churches, in order to make straight streets and spacious boulevards, which, beautiful as they are, do not prevent us from regretting the past.

The convent of S. Geneviève was founded by Clovis, and so extensive were its lands and dependencies that ere long it drew to it a large population of workmen and labourers for the cultivation of its land. A priest, one of the monks of the abbey, was appointed to take spiritual charge of these people; and from this commencement grew the parish of S. Étienne. Originally the congregation met and worshipped in the crypt of the abbey church, which was dedicated to Our Lady; then the chapel was placed under the protection of S. John the Evangelist, and called St. Jean-du-Mont. But at the beginning of the 13th century the congregation outgrew its chapel, and in 1224 the Bishop of Paris authorised the building of a church by the side of the abbey, to be consecrated to the memory of S. Étienne, the proto-martyr. This first church, in fact, was only a part of the abbey; having had no separate entrance of its own, it could only be entered by a doorway from the choir of S. Geneviève. The reason for changing its name for the third time was probably the demolition of a church dedicated to S. Stephen to make space for Notre-Dame. The memory of the first of martyrs being dear to the citizens, nothing would be more appropriate than the naming of a new church to take the place of the old one, although upon a different site. The first mention of S. Étienne is in the History of Guillaume le Breton, in the year 1221.

This first church lasted three hundred years, and then again, the population having increased enormously, S. Étienne was found to be too small for its congregation, and another and finer church was projected. In 1491 it was deemed better to rebuild than to patch up and enlarge the church; but many years passed in projects and delays, and it was only in 1517 that the work was actually commenced. Abbot Philippe Lebel finished the choir in 1537, and in 1541 the Bishop of Mégare consecrated the altars in the name of the Bishop of Paris; but that the church was not finished in 1552, or even in 1563, the diocesan permission to apply the Lenten offerings to the work is sufficient proof. The *jubé* was commenced in 1600, the porches nine years later, and the chapel of the Virgin (rebuilt) was only finished in 1661. It was Queen Marguerite de Valois, the lady who so strangely prances about Paris upon a white palfrey at dead of night in the much-admired controversial opera, who laid the first stone of the great portal in 1610; and, moreover, she gave a sum of three thousand *livres* to aid the work; but what was this when so much was wanted? All was not complete until 1626, and meanwhile the alms during Lent were appropriated to the building fund. However, a glance at a slab of black marble on the north wall of the nave will tell us that on the 25th February, 1626, the Sunday called Sexagesime, under the pontificate of Urban VIII., and in the reign of Louis XIII. of gracious memory, the church and the high altar were dedicated to the glory of God and of the Virgin Mary by the "*révérendissime messire Jean-François de Gondi,*" archbishop of Paris. Another inscription informs the reader of a wonderful accident which took place on this occasion :—

"Et pendant les cérimonies de la dédicace, devs filles de la paroisse tombèrent dv havvlt des galleries du cœvr, avec l'appvy et devx des ballvstres, qui fvrent miracvlevsement préservées, comme les assistants; ne s'étant rencontré personne sovbs les rvines, vev l'afflvence dv pevple qvi assistaient avs dites cérimonies."

Before the Revolution the *curé* was always one of the regular canons of S. Geneviève. At the end of the 16th century he was assisted in his duties by a community consisting of twenty-four priests. In 1791, when the parishes of the city were reorganized, it was determined to remove the relics, the ornaments, and the monuments of the abbey church to S. Étienne, and to re-name the latter after the maid of Nanterre; but the decree was never carried out. Reforms and resolutions followed each other so rapidly that there was no time to put them into execution.

S. Étienne is a cruciform building, very much leaning to the right (as is so common in old churches), with a nave, two aisles, and nineteen chapels. The transepts scarcely project beyond the nave. The exterior is a mass of elegant ornamentation, and on the north side, under the windows, is a passage which connects the porch of the second bay with the *charnier*, a sort of cloister, built at the end of the Lady Chapel, exterior to the church. The enclosure within this cloister was formerly the little burial ground; the great cemetery being situated in the square which fronts the church.

There is something extremely coquettish and fascinating about the building, with its high-pitched roof, springing from a

SAINT-ÉTIENNE AND THE OLD CHURCH OF SAINTE-GENEVIÈVE.

Renaissance façade, and its 15th century tower surmounted by a pepper-box lantern.

The old church of the abbey, which completely joined S. Étienne, has been entirely swept away to make room for the Rue Clovis; but the refectory and the tower still form a part of the Lycée Henri IV., a little turret at the easternmost angle of S. Étienne indicating the extremity of the monastery's domains.

Above the great doorway is a bas-relief of the stoning of S. Stephen and the legend: *Lapis templum Domini destruit, lapis astruit.* Right and left are statues of S. Étienne and S. Geneviève, the two patrons; above are Angels bearing torches. Upon the pediment is the Resurrection, and under the lintel we read: *Stephano archimartyro sacrum.* Two Angels above

SAINT-ÉTIENNE DU MONT. 105

the great rose window bear the arms of Marguerite de Valois, and at the summit are the statues of S. Hilary and S. Benedict, patrons of two churches in the parish, now demolished.

The interior of S. Étienne is no less singular than the ex-

THE SCREEN LOOKING TOWARDS THE CHOIR.

terior. The side aisles are nearly as high as the nave, and have enormous windows. The shafts which support the vault of the nave are of great height, and the bays are of the same elevation as the side aisles. Above these bays is a clerestory, the windows of which are as broad as they are high, with depressed pointed arches. In order to diminish the enormous height of the bays, the architect conceived a curious device. At about one-third of the height of the shafts he has thrown a depressed arch from pillar to pillar, which forms an elevated passage round the church. It is arrested at the transepts, but taken up again round the choir. The passage encircling each pillar is just wide enough to enable a person to walk. These *tournées*, as the old records call the gallery, and the splendid *jubé* form a distinctive feature of the church. On the side of the nave the *tournée* has an open pilaster balustrade, and at the entrance of the choir it joins the *jubé*. On each side of this is a spiral staircase leading up first to the *jubé*, and then, a second flight to the choir gallery, the former being formed of a single flying-arch supported by two pilasters. The whole screen is ornamented with rich carving; an Angel with palm leaves is in each spandrel, and above all is a huge crucifix, completing this beautiful and original specimen of French Renaissance, the only *jubé* which has survived the 17th century restorations. It was the work of a celebrated sculptor named Biart *(père)*. Upon each side of it is a doorway, surmounted by a sitting figure, listening to the chanting of the Gospel. *Ascende qui evangelizas Sion. Audiam quid loquatur Dominus meus*, are the words upon the right. At the left: *Quam dulcia faucibus meis eloquia tua. Levavi manus meas ad mandata tua.*

The pendant bosses of the nave and crossing are exceedingly rich in ornament—garlands of flowers, Angels' heads, the Symbols of the Evangelists, rosettes, and armorial bearings. The central boss of the transept falls 18ft., and has for ornament Angels playing instruments, the emblems of the Four Evangelists, and a Lamb encircled with thorns and bearing a crown.

The pulpit was designed by Laurent de la Hire, the painter, and sculptured by Claude Lestocard. It is a mass of rich carving. A huge Samson supports the lower part, while upon the canopy are little Angels of the winged-Cupid tribe, and at the summit a draped Angel with a trumpet. Samson is sitting upon the lion he tamed with the jawbone of an ass, and holds the strange weapon in his hand. Sauval remarked that *il la porte bien* (the pulpit), and certainly he appears to be doing so without much effort. The medallions upon the staircase and round the pulpit represent Evangelists and Doctors, among

DOORWAY OF THE SCREEN.

them Augustin and Jerome, and scenes from the life of S. Stephen, in which he figures as a preacher. The Cardinal Virtues go hand in hand in a becoming fashion with the Theological Ladies: Prudence bearing her mirror, which reflects the wisdom of the serpent hard by; Justice has her sword; Faith a heart as well as her cross; Hope leans upon her anchor; Temperance pours out water from an *amphora*; Courage holds a dangerous weapon of the mallet order; Charity is surrounded by the most charming of children. All these statuettes are exquisitely carved. Behind the preacher the Word of God, bearing the world, blesses those who preach the Gospel in His name; upon His head the Holy Spirit spreads His wings. Upon the edge of the canopy little Angels are playing with the crowns destined for the elect; and at the summit is a larger Angel bearing a trumpet to awake them from their long sleep. The organ is also a mass of fine carving: S. Stephen stoned; S. Geneviève and her sheep; the Elders of the Apocalypse; the "Jewish ladies of the Bible," as a German kindly interpreted, and the Passage of the Red Sea; above all, our Blessed Lord ascending to Heaven.

When the Abbey of Port-Royal was destroyed in 1710, the body of Racine was transferred to S. Étienne and placed in the crypt of the Lady Chapel by the side of Pascal; and in 1808 a Latin epitaph, composed by Boileau, which was discovered in the pavement of the church of Magny-les-Hameaux, was also transferred. Ten years later, on April 21st, 1818, a great function was held in honour of the poet and the author of those much-loved *Pensées*; the Academy sent a deputation, and one of their members, the Abbé Sicard, officiated.

Epitaph on Pascal.
pro columna superiori,
sub tumulo marmoreo.

JACET BLASIUS PASCAL CLAROMONTA-
NUS STEPHANI PASCAL IN SUPREMA APUD
AVERNOS SUBSIDIORUM CURIA PRAESI-
DIS * FILIUS, POST ALIQUOT ANNOS IN SEVE-
RIORI SECESSU ET DIVINAE LEGIS MEDI-
TATIONE TRANSACTOS, FAELICITER ET
RELIGIOSE IN PACE CHRISTI VITA FUNC-
TUS, ANNO 1662, AETATIS 39°, DIE 19ª
AUGUSTI, OPTASSET ILLE QUIDEM

* President of the court of Clermont. He gave up his appointment to devote himself to the education of his son.

PRAE PAUPERTATIS ET HUMILITATIS
STUDIO ETIAM HIS SEPULCHRI HONO-
RIBUS CARERE, MORTUUSQUE ETIAM-
NUM LATERE QUI VIVUS SEMPER LATERE
VOLUERAT. VERUM EJUS IN HAC PARTE
VOTIS CUM CEDERE NON POSSET
FLORINUS PERIER IN EADEM SUBSIDIO-
RUM CURIA CONSILIARIUS, GILBERTAE
PASCAL BLASII PASCAL SORORIS CONJUX
AMANTISSIMUS, HANC TABULAM POSUIT
QUA ET SUAM IN ILLUM PIETATEM
SIGNIFICARET, ET CHRISTIANOS AD
CHRISTIANA PRECUM OFFICIA SIBI AC
DEFUNCTO PROFUTURA COHORTARETUR.

Another epitaph in the North aisle of the nave records the virtues and wisdom of Jacques-Bénigne Winslow, the anatomist and member of the Academy of Sciences, brought back from his evil and heretical ways by the preaching of Bossuet. Eustache Lesueur, the somewhat feeble painter of the Life of S. Bruno, was also buried at S. Étienne. Many other names adorn the list of those laid to rest in the churches or burial grounds of the parish: Vigenère, secretary to Henri III., 1598; the surgeon, Thognet, 1642; Antoine Lemaistre, and Lemaistre de Sacy, brought from Port Royal in 1710; the botanist, de Tournefort, 1708; Rollin, rector of the University, who died in 1741, in the Rue Neuve de Saint-Étienne du Mont, which was re-named after him.

But it is the glass of S. Étienne which is perhaps its chief glory. Although a great deal has been destroyed and patched up, much remains which is quite worthy of study, being, as it is, in the best style of the 16th and 17th centuries, and the work of Jean Cousin, Claude Henriet, d'Enguerrand Leprince, Pinaigrier, Michu, François Périez, Nicolas Desengives, Nicolas Lavasseur, and Jean Mounier. But, unhappily, mendings and patchings have quite destroyed our power of discovering to which artist the different windows are due. In the *charnier* there is a very curious composition, illustrating the allegory of the wine-press; our Lord lies upon the press in the presence of the Father and the Holy Spirit, bathed in a sea of blood, which flows from His side, His hands, and His feet. Underneath, the blood pours down through an opening into a large cask. Prelates and kings * carry to a cellar those barrels which have been

* Sauval professed to see the portraits of Pope Paul III., of Charles V., of François Ier., and of Henry VIII., in some of the numerous worthies.

filled with the Sacred Blood by the Doctors of the Church; while, from under a rich Classic portico, we see the faithful flocking to confess their sins, and to receive the Holy Eucharist. In the distance, the Patriarchs are digging the ground and pruning the vines, while the Apostles gather in the vintage. S. Peter throws the grapes into a vat, and a chariot drawn by the Ox, the Lion, and the Eagle of the Apocalypse, and guided by the Angel of S. Matthew, carries the Divine vintage to the four quarters of the earth. Such is the allegory of the wine-press, the *Pressoir mystique*, the outcome of the verse of Isaiah: "I have trodden the wine-press alone, and of the people there was none with me"; but, unfortunately for the correctness of the illustration, there is, in this window, a large concourse of people, great and small in worldly means and wisdom. The window is attributed to the Pinaigriers. Robert Pinaigrier had painted the subject for the church of S. Hilaire, at Chartres in 1530; and about a century later Nicolas Pinaigrier reproduced his father's design, with some modifications, at S. Étienne.

The emblem of the Precious Blood was adopted by many confraternities of wine merchants, which led Leveil to think that this window was given to the church by Jean le Juge, a very rich wine merchant. Sauval speaks of this subject being represented at S. Sauveur, at S. Jacques de la Boucherie, at the hospital of S. Gervais, and in the sacristy of the Célestins; and l'abbé Lebeuf notes a window in S. André des Arcs, representing Christ crushed like the grapes in a wine-press. The cathedral of Troyes and the church of S. Foy at Conches still possess windows of the same character.

The following verses describe this subject in quaint old French :—

> "Heureux homme Chrestien si fermement tu crois
> Que Dieu pour te sauuer a souffert a la croix,
> Et que les Sacrements retenus à l'Eglise.
> De Son sang precieux ont eu commencement;
> Qu'en les bien receuant toute offence est remise,
> Et qu'on ne peut sans eux auoir son sauuement."

In te Domine Speravi non confundar in aeternum.—PSAL. xxx.
Non nob s Domine, non nobis sed nomini tuo da gloriam.—PSAL. cxiii.

> "Les anciens patriarches
> Qui le futur ont sceu
> Pour leur Salut ne fu
> A cultiuer le Vigne.

"Ce pressoir fut la Venerable croix
 Ou le sang fut le Nectar de la Vie;
 Quel sang celuy par qui le roy des Rois
 Rachepta lhomme et sa race asseruie.

"Tous urais Chrestiens le doiuent receuoir
 Auec respect des Prebtres de l'Eglise,
 Mais il conuient premierement auoir
 L'ame constriste, et la coulpe remise.

"Tous les cantons de ce large Vniuers
 En ont gusté par les Evangelistes
 Edifies ont esté les peruers
 Laissant d'Adam les anciennes pistes.

"Dans les Vaisseaus en reserue il fut mis.
 Par les docteurs de l'Eglise, pour estre
 Le lauement de nos peches commis,
 Mesme de ceux qu'on a Venant a naitre.

"Papes, Prelats, Princes, Rois, Empereurs
 L'ont au cellier mis avec reuerence,
 Ce Vin de vie efface les erreurs,
 Et donne a l'Ame une saincte esperance."

This strange design reminds one somewhat of a little chapel near Partenkirchen, Tyrol. Up the hill is a Way of the Cross and at the summit a tiny chapel containing a life-size figure of our Lord, behind a grating. At his feet is a pool of water—I imagine with some miraculous powers; a cup fastened by a chain allows the passer-by to drink thereof. But the strange part is the supply of water which comes from our Lord's wounds, and fills the pool—symbolic of His being the living water, the well from which whosoever drinketh obtaineth everlasting life. The idea is somewhat materialistic and startling to the mundane dweller in cities, but to the simple-minded inhabitants of Tyrol it is full of poetry.

The oldest glass in S. Étienne is in the upper windows of the apse, representing the apparitions of Christ, to the disciples on the road to Emmäus, to the Magdalen, to S. Peter, and to the three Maries. In the western rose window the Eternal Father is vested in the insignia of the Pope, that common device of 16th century Ultramontanism. Far better is the design of a window on the north side of the nave: the Eternal Father seated in glory, with the book of the seven seals on His knees; the Lamb opens it, the four-and-twenty

Elders sit around, and Angels pour the Divine anger from chalices upon the earth. The donors were evidently a large family, for they fill up all the lower part of the window, one behind the other, devoutly kneeling upon their knees. Some little scenes from the legend of S. Claude are charming in colour and design; so, too, are those from the life of the Virgin.

In one of the chapels of the nave we see a family repast, symbolising the wedding feast of the Gospel. The banquet is prepared, but the guests are not ready; one is going to fetch his wife, another takes an excursion to his country house, a third is inspecting a couple of oxen—but all beg to be excused.

The glass of S. Étienne was given by enthusiastic parishioners; indeed, so much rivalry took place amongst them, to fill the church with richly coloured windows, that the authorities were obliged to restrain their eagerness, and to point out that the bells, the porch, and other parts of the building required their aid.

It was at S. Étienne that Monseigneur Sibour, archbishop of Paris, was assassinated in 1857, during the *neuvaine** of S. Geneviève. The procession had travelled round the church, and was re-entering the nave, when the assassin, a discontented priest, rushed at the prelate and stabbed him. He was carried into the presbytery, but died soon after.

The main attraction of S. Étienne is the tomb of S. Geneviève. Long before the Panthéon ceased to be the church of the maid of Nanterre, it was to S. Étienne that the faithful journeyed to pray for her intercession, and to have their belongings laid upon her coffin. Here, any day, but especially during the octave of her *fête*, you may see people bringing handkerchiefs, rosaries, crosses, towels, etc., to be placed in the shrine, in order to carry the Saint's blessing and help to the sick and the suffering at home. The stone coffin is said to have been found in the crypt of the abbey church during its demolition in 1801, but whether it be the original one in which Saint Geneviève was buried in 511 it is impossible to say, as it is so surrounded by ornamental ironwork that its workmanship cannot be studied; but the effect of the little chapel containing this *tombeau*, with its lights and flowers and

---

* The eight days (octave) devoted to her festival.

stained-glass, is very charming, and during the *neuvaine,* when the church is ablaze with candles, and hundreds of people *font queue* to the shrine, it is a sight not easily forgotten.

The history of this *culte* is elaborately worked out. S. Geneviève was buried, it is asserted upon pretty good authority, in the crypt of the old abbey church of the Holy Apostles.

TOMB OF SAINTE-GENEVIÈVE.

When the Normans overran the country, the monks took up the body of their patroness, and carried it off to distant parts in a wooden box. Peace being restored, the religious went back to their abbey and repaired the various tombs, among others those of S. Prudence and S. Céran, Bishop of Paris; but the remains of S. Geneviève were not replaced in the stone coffin in which they had previously been laid. A splendid *châsse* was made for their reception, and until the Revolution, upon every occasion that the good citizens of Paris fell into any grievous trouble, the reliquary was carried about, up and down the "mountain," in and out of the tortuous streets, as a means of gaining the intercession of the patron Saint. And no less honoured was the empty tomb; the faithful paid their respects to that, after having visited the *châsse*.

In 1628, when Cardinal de La Rochefoucault began to restore the church, he covered the crypt with costly marbles. In the centre was the stone coffin of the Saint raised upon a few steps, enclosed by four columns and an iron *grille*. Right and left were the tombs of S. Prudence and S. Céran.

At the Revolution all was dispersed or destroyed, the *châsse* was turned into coin, the Saint's bones were burnt on the Place de Grève, and the tomb broken; but in 1802, when Amable de Voisins became *curé* of S. Étienne, he obtained permission from the archbishop, M. de Belloy, to translate the fragments of the stone coffin to S. Étienne, and to hold the festivals in the Saint's honour in that church.

During the *Neuvaine* thousands of persons crowd into the church to visit the shrine, a few in honour, many more in the dishonour of mere curiosity; and all round the church are to be seen the same class of itinerant vendors of goods as at the various *fêtes* and fairs. At some, they sell gingerbread, pop-guns, and penny trumpets; at others, and particularly at S. Étienne, their merchandise consists of rosaries, pious books, medals, and the like; it is a curious combination of the world and heaven—the flesh in the way of comfits, *vin ordinaire* and the devil—religious exercises and *le bon Dieu*. "Vous avez reçu le bon Dieu, Madame?" "Mais oui, Mademoiselle; et après, nous sommes allés, mon fils et moi, déjeûner au restaurant Voltaire," is the edifying conversation one hears in the omnibus. It is all on a par with the midnight mass and the *Réveillon*; Salvation Army drills, Mr. Howler's tabernacle, and the popular preacher over the wine vaults. Extremes meet, and people are much the same all the world over; for one earnest man or woman, you get a crowd of curiositymongers, whether the excitement be in Paris, or London, or Trèves, or Ober-Ammergau; unfortunately, there is not much salt in the earth, either Protestant, Catholic, or Agnostic. But if the salt is wanting, the waxen arms and legs and crutches are numerous enough. If you glance at S. Geneviève's shrine you will see bundles and bundles; and then we scoff. Are not they evidence that there is some faith left in the world, real earnest, trustful faith which believes all things, and hopes all things. And why not? Can anyone say whether it be more silly to take a journey, long or short, say some prayers, set up some tapers, present some flowers and a few pence, than to pin your faith upon pills and potions? In the one case the power of healing is believed to be in the hands of an all-merciful God who has promised to answer our prayers when so doing will be good for us; and in the other, it is thought to reside in pills which are worth twenty times their price, in nostrums which cure and prevent all the ills to which man is subjected, and in belts and bands and other such contrivances. The intercession of those who have gone before is asked by one set of believers; while the others pray Dr. Faith-Healer to cure them by letter, or Dr. Bread-and-Senna by his precious compound pills.

But how can S. Geneviève's bones be at S. Étienne when we know they were burnt on the Place de Grève? is a question answered by the *Moniteur* of 3 and 4 Frimaire, in the year II. (23rd and 24th November, 1793), which declares that the body was not entire; and we further know that previously, in olden time, relics of the Saint were distributed to many churches, the abbey of Chelles amongst others.

The ordinary offices at S. Étienne are in no way remarkable for splendour of ritual or of music, but one is worthy of notice— the Washing of the Feet in Holy Week. In spite of so-called uniformity, certain functions have a totally different aspect at the various churches. Take, for instance, the ceremonies of Holy Thursday, the Washing of the Feet, and the Distribution of the Bread and Wine. At many churches the priest who performs this function generally passes down in front of an array of old men and women; each receives a loaf and a bottle of wine, and that is all. But at S. Étienne it is a very quaint affair. A square portion of the nave is railed off; within sit the boys whose feet are to be washed, and upon a table are rows of loaves and bottles of wine. Then comes the *curé*, a tall, elegant-mannered man, and kneeling to each, he washes and wipes their feet, and then distributes the wine and bread. It is a very curious function; seeing all those boys taking off their boots in the middle of a church is most extraordinary; and then the quaint expressions, the keen curiosity or stupid dull gaze, the costumes and the surrounding audience, form a picture which is eminently quaint and queer.

SAINT-EUSTACHE.

S. Eustache, often called by the ancestors of *les dames de la Halle* Notre-Dame des Halles, though by no means one of the oldest of Parisian churches, is, after the cathedral, the largest.

THE OLD FAÇADE.

In plan and arrangement it is Gothic, while its decorations and details are in the Renaissance style It has double aisles, octagonal shafts, round-headed arches, and curvilinear tracery. It was finished in 1641, having been more than a century in building; but in spite of this, the original plan was carried out, and few churches that were so long in course of construction present so harmonious an appearance. Unfortunately, the west end, the towers of which were left unfinished, was sacrificed to the stupid taste of the 18th century; Mansard de Jouy and Moreau being allowed to replace what an old print shows to have been an interesting façade, in keeping with the rest of the church, by the heavy structure we all know, because, forsooth, the artistic gentlemen of the day found the original to be in a "*goût barbare qui choquait les yeux !*"

Père Du Breul (one of the Benedictines of S. Germain des Prés), writing in 1612 in his *Théâtre des Antiquités de Paris*, speaks of the church as follows : " Ce sera un des plus beaux bâtiments de l'Europe, s'il peut être parfait comme il a été commencé ; car rien n'y manque pour ce qui est de la perfection de l'architecture, soit pour le haut exhaussement, les fenêtres et ouvertures, et aussi l'enrichissement des diverses frises et moulures de toutes sortes et façons. Toutefois, pour la grande dépense qu'il y conviendrait faire, il est demeuré imparfait jusques à présent." To meet this *grande dépense*, the chancellor Séquier, and the *Surintendant de finance*, Claude de Bullion, supplied a considerable sum.

But a church existed upon the same site long before the foundation stone of the present building was laid by Jean de La Barre in 1532. Whether there is any truth in the tradition that the Romans erected a temple dedicated to Cybele upon the spot during the reign of Julian the Apostate, based probably upon the discovery of a large bronze head of the goddess at the entrance to the Rue Coquillière, there is no doubt that a chapel under the patronage of S. Agnes was built in the early ages of Christianity, for an account of its foundation is given by Gilles Corrozet, the first of the historians of Paris. It appears that a certain citizen named Jean Alais, in consideration of his help in financial matters, obtained from the king the right to levy a tax of a penny upon every basket of fish sold in the market. Remorse overtaking this modern publican, he begged his sovereign to revoke the tax ; but the victims gained nothing by the repentance, as the privilege was accorded to another citizen, with an augmentation of the tax. Thereupon Alais, dying of remorse, was buried near the chapel he had founded in expiation of his sins, at the spot where a stream passed through the market. A large stone was placed hard by, which served as a bridge in time of rain and flood—hence, *Pont Alais*.

Thus the legend. But the chapel is mentioned for the first time in authentic documents of the year 1213, when it is described as situated on the vast territory belonging to S. Germain l'Auxerrois (the eldest daughter of Notre-Dame), at a little distance from the cemetery of the Holy Innocents, upon the road leading from the capital to Montmartre. Whoever may have been the founder, it is mentioned in this same year (1213) as a parish, for the *curé* appealed to the abbot of S. Geneviève, and the dean of Notre-Dame de Chartres, in the matter of a squabble between himself and the dean of S. Germain l'Auxerrois. Ten years later, it is called the church of S. Eustache, in a charter giving the sentence delivered by the bishop of Paris and two of his canons in another squabble between Simon, *prestre de l'église Saint-Eustache*, and the dean of S. Germain, who seems to have been of a combative temperament. This *curé's* name figures at the head of the list of rectors of the church, which ends with another of the same name, the grand abbé Simon who was seized by the Communists, and all but received martyrdom with Archbishop Darboy and the *curé* of the Madeleine, Duguerry. L'abbé Le Beuf records the increase of population, and the necessary want of a larger church; consequently some relics of S. Eustache preserved at S. Denis were brought to Paris, and became the reason for the substitution of the Roman warrior for the gentle maiden Agnes as patron of the church. But later, the two Saints were combined in the patronage, probably from the crypt under the Lady Chapel bearing Agnes' name—a crypt that would be more truthfully called a cellar, from the use it is, or was, put to by a neighbouring fruiterer. The lease may have run out lately, in which case it now belongs to the church; as the clergy had determined to regain possession as soon as possible.

What appearance the first church presented, we know not, but in 1429 the high altar was advanced a foot into the chancel, and the altar of S. Gregory destroyed, to make a passage to the crypt of S. Agnes. In 1434, the church was enlarged "*pour la multiplication du peuple*"; and again in 1466, an addition required the demolition of the greater part of a house in the Rue de Séjour (now Rue du Jour), next to the Hôtel de Royaumont. Thirty years later the bishop gave the churchwardens a little piece of ground situated at the corner of Pont-Alais, in the Rue Montmartre, in order to extend the building still farther.

Here a slight digression may not be out of place to relate the legend of S. Eustache, whose *fête* day occurs on September 20th, a day, among several others, when the church is visited by crowds, some of whom go to pray, and others to hear the exquisite music for which S. Eustache is famous. When the 20th falls on a weekday, the festival is transferred to the following Sunday.

S. Eustache was a Roman soldier and captain of the guards of the Emperor Trajan. His name in early life was Placidus, and he had a beautiful wife and two fine sons. He lived in great style, practised all the heathen virtues, notably those of charity and loyalty, and was not only a brave warrior, but withal, a great huntsman. Now it happened one day, while sporting in the forest, that a beautiful white stag appeared before him, having a cross of radiant light between its horns, and on the cross an image of the Redeemer. Being astonished and dazzled by the vision, he fell upon his knees, and lo! a voice came from the crucifix and cried to him : " Placidus, why pursuest thou Me? I am Christ, whom thou hast hitherto served without knowing Me ? Dost thou now believe ? " And Placidus fell with his face upon the ground and said, " Lord, I believe ! " And the voice said : " Thou shalt suffer many tribulations for my sake, and shalt be tried by many temptations ; but be strong and of good courage, I will not forsake thee." To which Placidus replied, " Lord, I am content. Give thou me but patience to suffer ! " And when he looked up again, the wondrous vision had faded away. Then he arose and returned to his wife, and the next day the whole family was baptised, Placidus adopting the name of Eustatius.

But it came about as was foretold by the vision. All his possessions were spoiled by robbers, and his beautiful and loving wife was taken away by pirates ; poverty stared him in the face, and affliction pursued him. Then one day, as he wandered forth with his children, he came to a swollen river which he was obliged to cross ; and being troubled as to his means of fording the torrent, he took one child in his arms and swam across, leaving the other on the bank. Having placed the little one in a safe nook, he returned for the other; but when in mid-stream he saw a wolf come out of the forest, and carry off one child, while a lion appeared upon the opposite bank, and seizing the other babe, carried it off and made away with it! Then the wretched father tore his hair and gave way to weeping and lamentations; but remembering his promise to suffer for Christ's sake, he dried his tears and prayed for patience and resignation. So he came to a village where he lived peacefully for fifteen years by the labour of his hands ; but at the end of that time, the Emperor Adrian being on the throne, sent out messengers to all parts of the Empire to seek for Placidus, as he had need of him ; and at length they found him, and he was restored to his former position, and led his troops to victory. But although the Emperor loaded him with honours and wealth, his heart was sad for the loss of his wife and children. Meanwhile the latter had been rescued from the jaws of the wolf and the lion, and his wife had escaped from the hands of the pirates; so it came about, after many years, that they all met again and were re-united; and Eustace said in his heart: "Surely all my sorrows are now at an end." But it was not so; for the Emperor desiring to celebrate a mighty victory over the Barbarians by a great sacrifice to the gods, and Eustace and his family refusing to offer incense, they were shut up in a brazen bull, and a fire being kindled under it, they all perished together. Such is the legend, which, like all the stories of the lives of Saints and early martyrs, shows forth the steadfastness with which they clung to their faith, and the simplicity with which they practised the virtues of fortitude, patience, resignation, and courage. There is a certain similarity between the legend of S. Eustace and that of S. Hubert; but in art they are easily distinguished, as the former is in Classic or warrior costume, and the latter is represented either as a huntsman or a priest. Pictures of S. Eustace are not uncommon; in the Pitti Palace there is one by Soggi; and somewhere I have seen one by Domenichino. The traditional date of the martyrdom of S. Eustace is 118, which is much earlier than that of the other patron of the church, the simple maiden Agnes, who suffered in 304, and whose *fête* day is January 21st. The legend of this Saint is one of the most authentic, and one of the oldest, being mentioned by S. Jerome, in the 4th century, as popular throughout the world. Hymns and homilies had been written in her honour from the earliest times; and her youth and beauty, added to her innocence, had combined to invest her person with a charm and a fascination which few of the Saints possess.

Agnes was a Roman maiden of thirteen, filled with all the good gifts of the Holy Spirit, having loved and followed Christ from her infancy, and being withal most beautiful, when the son of the Prefect passed her way. Whether the name was given to her because of her lamblike innocence or otherwise, is not recorded. The young man no sooner beheld her than he loved her passionately, and asked her in marriage. But Agnes repelled him, even though he came laden with gold and gems, and costly ornaments; and, unlike poor Gretchen, she cried: "Away from me, tempter! for I am already betrothed to a lover who is greater and fairer than any earthly suitor. To him I have pledged my faith, and he will crown me with jewels compared to which thy gifts are dross . . . . The music of His divine voice has sounded in mine ears; He is so fair that the sun and moon are ravished by His beauty, and so mighty is He that the Angels are but His servants."

Hearing these words the youth naturally felt consumed by jealousy and rage; and he went home, only to fall ill of a fever, and to be sick almost unto death. The wise medicine men immediately discovered the cause, and told the Prefect that the illness being unrequited love, their potions could avail nothing. Then the great man questioned his son, who replied: "My father, unless I can take me Agnes to wife, I die." Now the Prefect, Sempronius, loved his son tenderly, and so he went weeping to Agnes' parents, and besought them to intercede for the youth. But Agnes made the same answer, and Sempronius was much angered that she should prefer another to his son, and asked who this great prince might be to whom Agnes was betrothed. And some one said: "Knowest thou not that the maiden hath been a Christian from her infancy; and her husband of whom she speaks is none other than Jesus Christ?" When the Prefect heard this, he rejoiced greatly, for he knew he could force Agnes to marry his son, by threats of imprisonment; for an edict had gone forth against the Christians. And so he sent for Agnes, and told her that since she was resolved not to marry, she must enter the service of the goddess Vesta. But Agnes replied: "Thinkest thou that I, who would not listen to thy son, who is yet a man and can hear and see and move and speak, will bow down to vain images, which are but senseless wood and stone; or, what is worse, to the demons who inhabit them?"

When Sempronius heard this he fell into a fury; he loaded Agnes' limbs with chains, and threatened her with death; and as nothing would prevail, he ordered her to be exposed to the most degrading outrages; but being stripped of her garments, she fell on her knees and prayed, and immediately her hair became so thick and long that it formed a complete covering. Then, although the onlookers were dismayed, they shut her up in a chamber, and left her. And suddenly she saw a bright and glistening garment, with which she clothed herself, praising God and saying: "I thank thee, O Lord, that I am found worthy to put on the garment of Thine elect!" And the whole place was filled with miraculous light, brighter than the sun at noonday.

Then the young man thought that if he visited her, Agnes would give way; but as soon as he entered her chamber he was struck blind, and fell into convulsions. And the mother and father appearing, and falling into lamentations and weeping, Agnes was moved with compassion, and prayed that their son might be restored to health; and her prayer was granted. Then Sempronius would have saved Agnes; but the people caused a tumult, and cried out that the maid was a witch and a sorceress, and therefore worthy of death. And so she was judged and thrown into the fire; but the flames, refusing to touch her, severely scorched the executioners, which still more irritated Sempronius and the people. Then the wicked Prefect commanded the executioners to slay her; and she, looking up to Heaven, yielded up her pure spirit to her God. And it happened that when her friends were one day praying at her tomb, in the cemetery on the Via Nomentana, she appeared unto them arrayed in white, with a lamb whiter than snow. And she said: "Weep not, dry your tears, and rejoice with exceeding joy; for me a throne is prepared by the side of Him who on earth I preferred to all others, and to whom I am united for ever in Heaven." And having thus spoken, she vanished.

As we have seen, the devotion paid to S. Agnes is of so early a period that it is quite possible the first chapel in the Halles dedicated to her memory may date back to the 8th or 9th century; but nothing authentic is recorded before the 13th century, and no part of the present church of S. Eustache and S. Agnes is earlier than the 16th century, when it was commenced during the reign of François I$^{er.}$ L'abbé Le Beuf gives the name of the architect as Charles David, and undoubtedly one of that name was attached to the church, as the fact is recorded upon an epitaph. But as he died in 1650, at the age of ninety-eight, he must have been born in 1552; and, the church having been commenced in 1532, this David could only have been a master of the works, carrying out the design of some predecessor. A theory has been propounded that this may have been Dominico da Cortona (Boccadoro), the architect of the Hôtel de Ville, or one of his pupils, who followed him from Italy; the evidence brought forward being the similarity of some of the details of the two buildings. S.

Eustache was commenced, as we have seen, in 1532, the Hôtel de Ville in the following year; but beyond this and a resemblance between the niches for statues of the two edifices, there is absolutely no evidence for the supposition, and the name of the architect of S. Eustache remains a hidden mystery. That he was an accomplished artist, a man having an eye for great effects, with a first-rate sense of proportion, the church bears witness, although it has had its detractors ever since it was finished. Too Gothic for the men patronized by Louis XIV., its Renaissance element shocked the artistic taste of their successors; called a *barbarous style* by the first, because of its Gothic plan, its Renaissance detail was *pernicious* to the æsthetic instincts of the latter. It is amusing to read Mr. Dibden's opinion of the church in his *Picturesque Tour*,* as it is that of a cultured traveller, and probably is an example of the judgment passed upon S. Eustache by the artists of his day. "Next in importance to S. Gervais is the Gothic church of S. Eustache; a perfect specimen, throughout, of that adulterated style of Gothic architecture (called its restoration!) which prevailed at the commencement of the reign of Francis I. Faulty, and even meretricious, as is the whole of the interior, the choir will not fail to strike you with surprise and gratification. It is light, rich, and lofty. This church is very large, but not so capacious as S. Gervais, while its situation is, if possible, still more objectionable." How the good parson could compare the two churches, apparently to the advantage of S. Gervais, seems extraordinary; for no unbiassed person can fail to be impressed by the beauty of the proportions of S. Eustache, its length and height, its effective choir, and its grand, but simple, altar. With the exception of its glass chandeliers, all the furniture and accessories are in keeping with the building; there is nothing tawdry, nor in bad taste; and it lends itself more effectively than even Notre-Dame to processions and grand ceremonials.

After its commencement the building seems to have struggled on for eight years; when, for want of funds, it remained stationary until 1552, although some of the altars had been consecrated by the Bishop of Mégare sixteen years previously. In 1552 it was helped on again by Lenten offerings, in return for dispensations to consume butter and milk. How much

* Thomas Frognall **Dibden, F.R.S., S.A.**: *Picturesque Tour in France and Germany*, 1821.

these dispensations produced, and how long the funds lasted, we are not informed; but civil war and religious troubles stopped the works again, and it was not until 1624 that they were resumed. Both Sauval and du Breul speak of the choir having been commenced in that year, and the latter's description of it is interesting as showing its original form. "Le chœur est un des plus beaux et un des plus grands de Paris

SAINT-EUSTACHE FROM THE HALLES CENTRALES.

après celui de Notre-Dame, large, spacieux, garni de quatre rangées de chaises; l'autel est fort haut en forme de frontispice, enrichi de six colonnes de marbre, d'un riche tableau au fond et d'un tabernacle ample et grand de bois ciselé et doré. Toute la clôture de ce chœur est composée de piliers de cuivre et de marbre. Au derrière est un autre autel de bois où l'art de la menuiserie n'est pas épargné, non plus que l'or et le marbre, et dans cet autel est le sainct ciboire où repose le saint Sacrement." Of the west front, the destruction of which, with two chapels erected by Colbert and decorated by Mignard, is the cause of the disproportion of length to height, Du Breul thus speaks: "Le portail est fort massif, illustré d'ouvrages et ciselures de pierre. Au-dessus de la grande porte par dehors est une galerie environnée de balustres; au deux coings de ce portail sont commencées deux grosses tours. En celle de main droicte sont les cloches. Aux deux costés de devant sont les images de pierre de Saint Eustache et de Sainte Agnès, patrons de la dite église et au dehors un assez ample parvis entouré de piliers." Writing a century later Piganiol de la Force only speaks of this part of the church. "Il était formé par six piliers buttants d'environ trente pieds de saillie au delà du pignon, dont deux aux encoignures de dix pieds d'épaisseur; deux autres de treize pieds servaient à soutenir la poussée des arcades intérieures qui exigeait une grande solidité. Ces quatre piliers formaient trois travées; dans celle du milieu était la porte d'entrée; les deux autres avaient été construites pour porter deux tours, et dans leur intérieur M. Colbert avait fait construire deux chapelles, l'une pour les mariages et l'autre pour les fonts."

The church was finished and consecrated by Jean de Gondy, first archbishop of Paris, on the 26th April, 1637. Round the altar were ten statues, which, according to the taste of the day, were portraits of contemporaries, although representing sacred personages. They were by Jacques Sarrazin. Louis XIII. was the embodiment of S. Louis; Anne d'Autriche and the future *Grande monarque* were allowed to represent the Blessed Virgin and her Child. Above these were the patron saints.

It must be remembered by critics who find fault with the disproportion between length and height of S. Eustache, that an entire bay of the nave and two chapels were demolished with the west front, thus reducing the length. One of the chapels, erected at Colbert's expense, must have been of value artistically, certainly more so than the present west front which was substituted; for Mignard's frescoes are immortalised by Molière in his *Gloire du Val-de-Grâce*. They represented the Heavens with the Almighty surrounded by Angels, the Circumcision, and the Baptism of Christ:

> "Colbert, dont le bon goût suit celui de son maître,
> A senti même charme et nous le fait paraître.
> Ce vigoureux génie au travail si constant,
> Dont la vaste prudence à tous emplois s'étend,
> Qui du choix souverain tient par son haut mérite
> Du commerce et des arts la suprême conduite,
> A d'une noble idée enfanté le dessein,
> Qu'il confie au talent de cette docte main,
> Et dont il veut par elle attacher la richesse
> Aux sacrés murs du temple où son cœur s'intéresse (St-Eust.).
> La voilà cette main qui se met en chaleur ;
> Elle prend les pinceaux, trace, étend la couleur ;
> Empâte, adoucit, touche et ne fait nulle pose.
> Voilà qu'elle a fini : l'ouvrage aux yeux s'expose,
> Et nous y découvrons aux yeux des grands experts
> Trois miracles de l'art en trois tableaux divers."

The other chapel was decorated by Charles de Lafosse, a pupil of Lebrun, and the painter of the dome of the Invalides. The subjects were God, surrounded by the four Evangelists, blessing Adam and Eve, and the marriage of the Virgin and S. Joseph. These chapels were erected respectively for baptisms and marriages.

The present west front, ugly and lumbering though it be, with its Doric portal and Corinthian gallery, had a royal prince to usher it into the world, no less a personage than the Duc de Chartres, Philippe-Egalité. Had it been built up in front of S. Nicholas du Chardonnet, or any church of that period, it might have passed muster; but tacked on to S. Eustache, it is completely out of place. Were the *curé* privileged to give the Papal benediction, said an 18th century critic, this porch might have some use; but its only merit is that it was built upon a sufficiently large scale to save it from insignificance. Let us turn to the south door, constructed under François I^{er,} but much restored since the last siege. Never completely finished, as regards statues and other ornament, it was so terribly knocked about by the Communists, that niches, tracery, corbels, and glass had to be renewed; but perhaps, had it not suffered so much destruction in 1871, we should never have had the opportunity of admiring it in its completed beauty.

The doors are divided by a pier surmounted by a figure of the Virgin and Child under an elaborately carved canopy, which stands out upon the plain, undecorated lintel. In three little niches under these figures are statuettes representing Faith, Hope, and Charity. In the *voussure* above the window are niches for some fifty statuettes, which are still wanting; on either side are statues of Joachim, S. Anne and two Angels bearing censers. The niches are formed of pilasters with a pediment, and capitals composed of little canopies mixed with acanthus leaves. All the details, the fantastic figures upon the stylobate, the ornament of the pilasters, and the canopies, are in the best style of the Renaissance. Two rows of arcades lead up to the rose window, flanked on each side by graceful turrets. In the centre of the gable is a smaller rose, surmounted by a stag's head with a crucifix between the horns, emblem of the conversion of the warrior Saint. A curious sundial is fixed to the wall between the two arcades; and at the intersection of the transepts and nave is an open-work turret. Between the chapels are Com-

PART OF THE SOUTH DOOR.

posite pilasters supporting the cornice; the capitals are enriched with masks, Angel's heads, monograms, and divers emblems; in one case the double L L crowned, in another, foliage, animals, and Genii. Flying buttresses support the nave, choir, and transepts; and a multitude of gargoyles, fantastic in design, representing men, women, and children, with foliage terminations, and mostly winged, surround the pilasters of the aisles. On one of these is the date 1629.

The building, which blocks up a part of the chapel of Our Lady, was another excrescence of the reign of Louis XIV., and the work of Moreaux; it is used as a treasury and vestry. Above the chapel of the Virgin is a belfry erected in the 17th century, surmounted by a cross and the ship of the city of Paris. The bell weighs 2,500 kilogrammes. It was preserved by the Revolutionists in consequence of its usefulness; but a shell from Montmartre on the 25th of May, 1871 (during the Commune), set fire to the steeple. The blaze was soon extinguished, but not before it had done a considerable amount of harm. The north door is of later date, 1640. It has two turrets, in one of which is a staircase leading up to the presbytery. S. Eustache, costumed as a Roman warrior, guards the doorway upon the central pillar; while S. Denis bearing a palm, and S. Geneviève with a lamb at her feet, keep watch upon each side. The socles are ornamented with the Cardinal Virtues of Prudence, Courage, Justice, and Temperance, which were discovered some years ago, hidden behind a shop for the sale of religious books and images which obstructed the entrance to the passage. The capital of one of the pilasters upon this side of the church is well worth attentive study. In the midst of some foliage is a child bearing a basket of fruit, and on each side are two young and beautiful Genii forming a sort of buttress to the abacus.

On entering the church the effect is most impressive, and upon any great festival, or during the evening services of the Adoration Perpétuelle, when the whole east end is ablaze with candles, few churches can compare with it in grandeur. Nowhere else is to be found such a curious combination of styles, with a more harmonious result. The architect's ambition must have been to prove that two styles so opposed to each other in every respect were capable of being united with the best effect. The Renaissance of S. Eustache seems to give new life to the dying Gothic, by marrying its pilasters, its columns, and its Greek pediments to the pointed groining and arches.

Like the generality of early churches, S. Eustache leans a little to the right; whether in consequence of some peculiarity of the ground, or symbolically of the drooping of the head of the Saviour upon the cross, we cannot tell. There are double aisles on each side, and adjoining them a series of chapels, the depth of which varies, as the church is wider at one end than at the other. All the arches are round with the exception of those of the apse, which are pointed. The entire church is 88 *mètres* 48^c in length, and 42 *mètres* 74^c in width. The height of the nave is 33 *mètres* 46^c. The clerestory is filled with stained glass by Cartaux, of elegant design and harmonious colouring. In some of the details, as for instance the corbels, we see the same ideas that flitted across the brains of the Mediæval sculptors—namely, that of carving masks representing heads of devils and monsters, some grinning, some scowling, all more or less hideous and *bizarre*.

The *banc d'œuvre*, a sort of pew erected opposite the pulpit for the clergy and Monsieur le Maire and his assistants during sermon, is a *chef-d'œuvre* of Renaissance sculpture in wood. Its design is the glory of S. Agnes, the young martyr being represented kneeling upon the summit of the entablature, with outstretched arms; Angels descend with palms in their hands to give her the crown of life. Below, between the Ionic columns, two other Angels support a medallion, which a third hangs to the roof of the arch. Upon this medallion a crucifix is carved, the figure of which is in plaster; for, unfortunately, time and wanton destruction have done their work upon the ornament, a good deal of it being now only of stucco. Upon the side panels were the monograms of the two patrons interlaced (if I remember aright); these were taken down, or covered up, some few years ago, to give place to marble slabs recording the names of all the *curés* of the parish, from Simon, *prestre de l'église* in 1223, to l'abbé Simon, one of the actors in the tragedy of the Commune, which he survived only a few years. Owing to the luck of the back of the pew being decorated with a medallion upon which are the Roman *fasces* crowned with laurel leaves, the men of the First Revolution left it intact—the emblems were Republican; that was enough. The *banc*, which cost the Regent Orléans 20,000 *livres*, was executed by Lepautre from the drawings of Cartaux. One would imagine, thereby, that the Duke was a benefactor to the church; but if he gave with one hand, he took away with the other, and being a great connoisseur in matters artistic, he determined to get possession of a picture belonging to the church, painted by Valentin, of S. James kneeling. Being unable to persuade the *curé* to give it up, we may infer he sent his emissaries (in other words, hired thieves) to carry it off, and put a copy in its place. The whole affair was studiously planned and carried out; but the church authorities compelled the royal pirate to pay them 20,000 *livres* in compensation.

The pulpit, with its canopy, is a handsome specimen of carving, with figures of Faith, Hope, and Charity on three medallions. It replaces the old pulpit which was executed from drawings by Lebrun. The organ case is as beautiful as the instrument it encloses. Put up in 1854, architecturally, it is in the style of the church itself. The lower part consists of a gallery of Corinthian columns and arcades, united by a balustrade which follows the curves of the stone tribune upon which it rests. The case is ornamented at the top with figures of Saul brandishing a javelin and David holding his harp, with which he hopes to calm the King's anger—emblem of the power of music to humanise evil men's passions. In the centre stands S. Cecilia, with her organ and palm—the martyred patroness of the divine art. These statues are by the eminent sculptor, M. Guillaume. The frieze is a series of winged Cherubim; and in various parts are griffins, harpies, birds, chimeras, swans, spitting serpents, and little birds and lizards—a whole army of strange creatures, subdued by the sweet strains of the *Voix céleste*.

The great boss which descends from the centre of the transept is nine *mètres* long, composed of colossal Angels holding the cross; other bosses are also remarkable, having emblems of the Holy Spirit, monograms, little Angels, and heads of Seraphim. The rose of the south transept is the older of the two; the window below it has for subject the Birth of Christ, which occupies the five upright divisions and the six hexagons of which the window is composed. Upon the pier, between the two parts of the south door, stands a Gothic statue which belonged to the earlier church, the pedestal being ornamented with charming little statuettes. On each side of the transept are figures of the Apostles, and bas-reliefs in enamelled terra-cotta of the patrons of music, S. Ambrose and S. Gregory the Great. Here, too, are frescoes painted by Signol of The Entombment; with the Four Evangelists, and the Cardinal Virtues. In the north transept is a statue by Delaplace of the patroness, and wall paintings by Signol, to correspond with those of the south transept, the principal subject being The Way of the Cross.

One remarkable feature of the church is the placing of a corbel under the capitals of the pilasters. Those in the choir are of winged Cherubim, while in the rest of the church various grotesque monsters, human and animal, figure in their stead. The glass in the east end bears the date 1631 and the name of Solignac, a *verrier* totally unknown to fame, but an "*artiste distingué*," as our neighbours say, when nothing more flattering suggests itself to their minds and lips. S. Eustache figures upon the central light, under a colonnade in perspective, and upon each side of him are the four Latin Fathers and the twelve Apostles. Above our heads we see a rich groined roof, and a boss which is more wonderful than beautiful. Groups of Angels' heads and numberless Cherubim sitting upon clouds are interlaced with a large crown; the whole being about ten *mètres* in length.

In 1795, upon the suppression of the convent of the Canonesses of Picpus, S. Eustache, for a consideration of 5,000 *francs*, gained possession of the nuns' beautiful stalls, which have since been a notable part of the church, especially the *misereres* and the curious little stools upon which the *enfants de chœur* sit.

The pavement and the altar are modern; the former, of various coloured marbles, having been laid in 1869. The altar is raised upon five steps; in the centre is the tabernacle under a domed *baldachino*, the whole being in white Paros marble, designed by M. Baltard. All the sculptures are enriched by gilding. In the centre is the *Sacrifice of the Lamb*, with grapes and corn encircling it. On each side, the symbols of the four Evangelists—the Angel, the Lion, the Ox, and the Eagle; the bull in which S. Eustache was immolated; the ropes and chains, a sword, some palms and lilies, all suggestive of S. Agnes. The *baldachino* having been found to be out of proportion to the rest of the altar, a pilaster, destined to hold pans for burning incense, was placed at each extremity; but the effect of the whole is good, nay, even beautiful, in spite of

K 2

the want of proportion. The doors of the tabernacle, in gilt bronze, are chased with great care and elegance. Before the Revolution, a bas-relief said to have been sculptured by Daniele da Volterra,* representing *The Entombment*, formed the reredos. The gates of the choir are composed of modern ironwork, by M. Calla, of excellent design.

Under the west door is a white marble bust of Chevert, a warrior whose deeds and virtues may be read upon his epitaph, composed by d'Alembert :

CY-GIT
FRANÇOIS CHEVERT
COMMANDEUR, GRAND'CROIX DE L'ORDRE DE SAINT-LOUIS,
CHEVALIER DE L'AIGLE BLANC DE POLOGNE,
GOUVERNEUR DE GIVET ET DE CHARLEMONT,
LIEUTENANT GENERAL DES ARMÉES DU ROY.

SANS AYEUX, SANS FORTUNE, SANS APPUY,
ORPHELIN DÈS L'ENFANCE,
IL ENTRA AU SERVICE A L'AGE DE XI ANS,
IL S'ÉLEVA A FORCE DE MÉRITE,
ET CHAQUE GRADE FUT LE PRIX D'UNE ACTION D'ÉCLAT.
LE SEUL TITRE DE MARÉCHAL DE FRANCE
A MANQUÉ NON PAS A SA GLOIRE
MAIS A L'EXEMPLE DE CEUX QUI LE
PRENDRONT POUR MODÈLE
IL ÉTAIT NÉ A VERDUN SUR MEUSE, LE 2
FÉVRIER 1695. IL MOURUT A PARIS,
LE 24 JANVIER 1769.

PRIEZ DIEU POUR LE REPOS DE SON AME

The picture of the Martyrdom of S. Eustache, hard by, is by Simon Vouet, and was the gift of Louis XIV. Sold during the Revolution, it was bought by Cardinal Fesch, at whose death it was purchased by M. Moret, for presentation to the church.

It will be seen that the outer wall of the church is oblique, and, consequently, that the first two chapels are not deep enough even to contain an altar. In 1849, when some repairs were going on, it was discovered that the chapels had all been painted and gilt, and duly smeared over, after the fashion of our forefathers, with sundry coats of whitewash. These being removed, enough of the original decoration remained to restore it to its former splendour, which was done under the super-

---

* This is now in the Renaissance Museum of the Louvre, but it is no longer attributed to D. da Volterra.

intendence of M. Baltard. The chapel of the Virgin was painted by M. Dénuel, the others by M. Séchaut, while the renewing of the sculpture was the work of MM. Gallois and Poignant.

The first chapel, called that of the City of Paris, being too shallow for an altar, has the following inscription engraved in golden letters upon a black marble slab:—

"L'an mil six cent trente sept, le vingt-sixième jour d'avril, deuxième dimanche d'après Pasques, cette église, ayant été rebastie de fonds en comble, a été de nouveau desdiée et consacrée avec le maistre autel d'icelle, à l'honneur de Dieu, soubs l'invocation de la bienheureuse Vierge Marie et des bienheureux martyrs sainct Eustache et saincte Agnès et de sainct Louis, confesseur, jadis roy de France, par révérendissime père en Dieu, messire Jean-François de Gondi, premier archevêque de Paris, conseiller du Roi en ses conseils, commandeur de ses ordres et grand maistre de chapelle de sa Majesté. Ce requérant, vénérable et discrète personne maistre Estienne Tonnelier, presbstre, docteur en théologie et curé de la dicte église, avec haut et puissant seigneur Mons. P. Séguier, chevalier, chancelier de France, M. Maistre Gratien Menardeau, conseiller du roi en la cour du Parlement, honorable Jean Bachelier et Charles Gourlin, marchands bourgeois de Paris, au nom et comme Marguilliers de l'œuvre et fabrique d'icelle église. Et a ledit sieur Archevêque donné indulgence en la forme ordinaire de l'église à tous ceulx et celles qui visiteront annuellement la dicte église, le deuxième dimanche d'après Pasques, jour et feste de la dédicace d'icelle."

This chapel is decorated with the arms of the city of Paris, the ship*; and upon each of the others will be found the arms of the founders.

The chapel of Calvary was founded by the Counts of Castille, and was originally dedicated to S. Peter. It contains a crucifix, *souvenir* of a mission preached in 1825, and was the burial place of François and Nicolas de Castille, *conseillers du roi*, who died in 1630 and 1634 respectively. In the chapel of S. Cecilia may be seen a little fresco in a very good state of preservation, representing the titular Saint holding the sword of her martyrdom, and S. Leonard. Sold in 1604 to Claude de Montescot, treasurer *des parties casuelles*, it was originally known by the name of S. Claude. Buying a chapel seems to have

---

* See page vii.

been the custom; and we find that of the Holy Innocents costing 1,100 *livres* to the Chantereau-Lestang family. The fresco was painted in 1850 by M. Barre, and relates to S. Joseph, to whom the chapel was dedicated some twenty years ago. The sculptures are of the time of Louis XIII.

In the chapel Des Ames du Purgatoire, founded by the Gentian family in honour of the Holy Sepulchre, reliquaries may be seen containing a portion of the Sepulchre, and of the column upon which Our Lord was bound during the flagellation —so said Cardinal Patrizzi, who has authenticated the relics. More beautiful, and at least as authentic, are the frescoes by M. Margimel, representing the *Descent into Hades*. Moses and David are seen with other Old Testament worthies, the group of Adam and Eve with their children being particularly happy in its treatment. Below, of course, are purgatorial flames and a bruised serpent, with the inscription *Ecce agnus Dei, qui tollit peccatum mundi*. The opposite picture is less satisfactory, it is a conventional reading of the Eternal Father pitying the sufferings of the Son, who is attached to the pillar between weeping Angels. The elegant Renaissance re-table, and a statue by Chartrousse of a mother clasping a cross, with the text: *Bienheureux ceux qui pleurent, parce qu'ils seront consolés*, complete the contents of this chapel. The vaulting is very graceful, and is supported by corbels. The altar is a carved wood representation of *Christ upon the Mount of Olives*. The founder of this chapel or chantry was a descendant of Jean-Jacques Gentian, who saved the life of Philippe le Bel at the battle of Mons in 1304, for which act Gentian was allowed to incorporate the lilies into his arms. He died in 1305, and was buried on this spot in the old church; his descendant, a master merchant, was buried in the chapel in 1578.

It is curious to see how these chapels have changed names, and the why and wherefore. For instance, the first one in the *chevet* was consecrated in 1608 to the Three Kings, the original founder being Guillaume Morot, one of the king's councillors and *contrôleur des finances*. Then it passed into the hands of the Puysieux family. In 1780 it was called the chapel of S. John the Baptist, in memory of Jean-Baptiste Fleuriau, chevalier d'Armenonville, keeper of the seals, who died at Madrid, and was transported to S. Eustache for burial. Charles Fleuriau, count de Morville, a minister, was buried here in 1732. These d'Armenonvilles inhabited an hotel in the Rue Jean-Jacques

Rousseau, which has been swallowed up by the post office. The hide merchants held the meetings of their guild in this chapel. In 1843 it was dedicated to the Sacred Heart, and is decorated by M. de Larivière to celebrate that article of faith, the four personages who accompany Our Lord being Pope Clement XIII., the zealous devotee of the *Sacré Cœur;* the blessed Marie-Marguerite Alacoque, of the order of the Visitation, and the discoverer of the miracle at Paray-le-Monial; the reverend father La Colombière, who defended the apparition against the unbelievers; and Monseigneur de Belzunce, bishop of Marseilles, who, in putting the city under the protection of the new dogma, saved it from the effects of a grievous pestilence, by causing the immediate retreat thereof to less favoured purlieus. In the next chapel we come upon more relics. The Rouillé family, and the Lecouteulx de Canteleu, founded it, and dedicated it to S. Margaret; but after the Revolution, S. Joseph was called in as patron, and as S. Agnes required a special altar, this was once more changed in name, and made over to her good protection in 1850. Or possibly the acquisition of her relics required a resting-place fitted specially for them. They consist of three fingers of the Saint from the abbey of S. Corentin, near Septeuil, and a pretty large portion of one of her ribs from the cemetery of S. Priscilla at Rome, given by Marie-Félix des Ursins, Duchesse de Montmorency, Supérieure de la Visitation de Moulins. The picture over the altar is attributed to Titian or Giordano; the modern frescoes are by M. Vauchelet: the *Martyrdom of S. Agnes,* in which one executioner is thrown down by the rush of flames, while the other, avenging himself upon the innocent victim, cleaves her head asunder with a sword.

When Archbishop Sibour verified the relics of S. Anne, in 1853, a chapel was dedicated to her, displacing Notre-Dame de Pitié, S. Adrien, S. Hubert, and S. Jacques. One would imagine, that is, the blasphemer might imagine, that saints would not take it well when they are deposed and supplanted, but possibly, being in higher realms than ours, they see the insignificance of such proceedings. The frescoes are by Lazerges.

It was in the west chapel, that of the Holy Angels, that the 17th century mural paintings were discovered. So completely were they enveloped in whitewash, that they escaped the vandalism of the last century. The Duval family founded the chantry. They seem to have had various posts under the government. Nicolas was a councillor in 1542; Jérôme in 1543; Jean was a receiver of taxes and the payer of members of Parliament, besides being a councillor in 1584; another Nicolas was councillor in 1585; Tristan was lord of Fontenay; François, ambassador at Rome; and Catherine's husband, Christophe Harlay, was Seigneur de Beaumont, président of the parliament, and father of the président Harlay. The fresco representing the *Triumph of S. Michael over the revolting Angels*

THE CROSS BEARER OF S. EUSTACHE.

is by M. Cornu. Above the altar is another fresco of *Christ in Glory*, with S. Lucretia and S. Radegonde, queen of France, and afterwards a nun at Poitiers, kneeling at His feet. The Saints appear with the donors, aforesaid, clad respectively as *chevalier*, priest, and *bourgeois*. Here were buried Marguerite Duval, Jean Lesecq, and a Seigneur de Bridevalles, Nicolas Lesecq, who was the king's chafe-wax, and sealer of the chancellery, and who, worthy man, left twelve *sous* to the organist, and three to the bellows blower. Françoise-Madeleine Lesecq, who lived in the Hôtel de Gesvres, Rue Coq-Héron, since incorporated into the Caisse d'Épargne, was also buried here.

Formerly, before Louis XIV. admitted them to the Louvre, the Guild of Painters and Sculptors held its meetings in the Rue Trainée, and its *fêtes* and funeral masses in the chapel of S. André in S. Eustache; in consequence of which the king, to do honour to the Academy, allowed its rector, Antoine Coysevox, to add the royal lily to his arms, and to place them in this chapel, thus honouring Coysevox at the same time as his fellow sculptors and painters. The guild was founded by Lebrun, and held its meetings at the Sieur Martin de Charmois' house. This

Seigneur de Lauré was secretary to Marshal Schomberg; and full of zeal for art and artists, was the author of the scheme of a guild. Signed by Lebrun, Sarazin, Perrier, Bourdon, de la Hire Corneille, Juste d'Egmont, Vanolstat, Hause, de Guernier, Errard, Van-Mol, Guillier, and Eustace Lesueur, the petition was presented to the king, and supported by chancellor Séguier and de la Veillière, it obtained the royal assent. Like our later foundation, the Academy made several moves before it was finally settled. First in Charmois' house, it migrated to the Hôtel Clisson, Rue des Deux-Boules, where it held its meetings until the squabbles of the rival artists subsided, and accommodation was found for the members at the Louvre. Most appropriately, the decoration of this chapel was given in 1850 to Isidore Pils, one of the great painters of the latter part of this century, so well known by his *Battle of the Alma*, the *Mort d'une Sœur de Charité*, and *La Prière à l'Hospice*. The subjects are from the life and death of the titular saint, Andrew; on one side, his crucifixion upon the transverse cross which bears his name; upon the other, Angels bearing him to heaven. In the latter, a more delicious little group of children, *soi-disant* Angels, has rarely been painted, even by that master of chubby and graceful babies, Prud'hon. Pils, says M. l'abbé Koeneg* loved children, and he certainly painted them as none but a lover of childhood could have done. The chapel Richelieu was founded by the great cardinal, and is the burial place of the Vrillière family, whose hotel is now the Banque de France. The door close by is called the *Porte de la Miséricorde* by reason of its paintings, which represent the *Seven Works of Mercy*. They are by M. Biennourry.

The Chapelle des Catéchismes is a very ancient foundation, having been erected in the old church by Louis d'Orléans, the brother of Charles VI., in honour of S. Michael. Two centuries later, the Orléans family sold it to Président Forget, and a chapel was built out of it to serve, first as a sacristy, and then as a room for confraternities to hold their meetings in. The staircase is very elegant, with its handsome wrought-iron *grille* and balustrade of the time of Louis XVI. The chapel seems to be used now as a boys' vestry, and the effect of the acolytes in their red cassocks and white albs passing up or down this beautiful flight of steps is picturesque in the extreme.

* *Histoire de Saint-Eustache.*

S. Eustache is one of the few churches in Paris which has not adopted the Roman use as regards the dress of the acolytes, who still wear the long alb plaited or trimmed with lace, and the sash, red, white, or pale blue, according to the season. Years ago, before the Parisian rite was superseded by the Roman, there were many little differences in the ritual; to wit, the two precentors sitting near the chancel *grille*, vested in copes, and at certain times during mass marching up and down the choir. Then again, on great festivals, six men holding censers stood in a row, and throwing them up, knelt upon one knee to catch them. The effect of this during Benediction was grand in the extreme; the Roman practice of two boys gently swinging the censers bearing no comparison to the Parisian. The Lady chapel, known as Notre-Dame de Bon-Secours, served in the 17th century as the assembling place of various charitable societies, and notably of the Société de Bons-Secours, which was so much patronised by the *noblesse* and the rich tradespeople. The chapel is in the same style as the side ones, and is a mass of colour, the decorations being by M. Dénuel. The frescoes were originally undertaken by Ary Scheffer, who, perhaps fortuntately for posterity, was so long working out his subject that he gave the matter up, Couture taking his place. But great artist as he was, Couture was hardly the man to decorate a church; his work and his sympathies were so eminently Classic in style, that it is difficult to feel that his paintings illustrate pages of Gospel history and legendary lore. There is no more religious sentiment in Couture's work than in the Eclectic decadence of Italy, or the 18th century French school. Many persons object to our latest group of religious painters; but the feeling expressed in the pictures of M. Lhermitte, of Bastien-Lepage, of Mr. C. Pierce, of M. Dagnan-Bouveret, and even in M. Béraud's *Crucifixion*, to say nothing of Herr Uhde's work, is far more religious than in many, one might almost say, in most of the frescoes and pictures by modern artists in the various churches. Sentimentality is not religious sentiment, and cast-up eyes do not necessarily express devotion. Again, the light is so bad in this chapel that it is very difficult to judge of Couture's work, even from the æsthetic point of view; and therefore we cannot think this picture equal to the grand *Romains de la Décadence* in the Louvre. The altar is a handsome specimen of the reign of Louis XIII., but the statue which surmounts it, by Pigalle, has the usual sentimental character of 18th century sculpture. A *plaque* informs the faithful that it was blessed by Pius VII. in 1804; but, unfortunately, a pope's blessing will not turn a piece of marble into a fine work of art.

The chapel of S. Louis de Gonzague was the property of the Colbert family, and contains the tomb of the great minister. The monument was executed from a design by Lebrun, and, although of the usual type of that period, it is not without a certain grandeur. A black marble sarcophagus supports the kneeling figure of Colbert, arrayed in the robes of the order of the Saint-Esprit. The hands, joined in prayer, are exquisitely modelled. The expression of the face is fine, and the flow of the draperies is well executed. At the foot of the monument are figures of Religion by Tubi and Abundance by Coysevox; the latter a good example of the sculptor's style. This was one of the monuments saved from the Vandal mob in 1792, by Lenoir, who marched it off to the museum of the Petits-Augustins, where it remained until 1801, when it was returned to S. Eustache.

More relics are to be seen in the next chapel, those of S. Pierre l'Exorciste, a saint who suffered in the neighbourhood of Rome, having obligingly dug his own grave previously to being beheaded. The authenticity of the relics are vouched for by the sign manual of Cardinal Caprara. One requires faith to believe in the authenticity of these, or any other relics; not that one doubts their preservation by loving hands after the martyrdoms, but there is a great gulf of time which is not easily bridged over. Take, for instance, the relic of the True Cross kept at Notre-Dame. It is not at all improbable that the cross might have been preserved by the friends of Our Lord; and the same remark applies to many of the other relics with which S. Louis and others adorned the Sainte-Chapelle—the Spear, the Handcuffs, the Crown of Thorns, even the linen stained by the precious blood. That the Apostles, or S. Joseph of Arimathea, or Nicodemus, or S. Mary and her sister Martha, would have done their best to gain possession of these relics of their dear Master, is not only possible, but probable. We are all relic-mongers at heart; our forefathers gathered together the remains of saints and martyrs; we ourselves keep locks and curls of hair, babies' teeth, bits of clothing, rings, and photographs. Where is the difference?

If the lost first-born's only tooth is precious to its mother, why should not S. Holocaustus' toe-nail be equally so to those who live in the Saint's parish or commune? We have Charles I.'s hair, and Queen Elizabeth's stockings; and there is no reason why a thousand years hence they should not still be in their cases. But if a great upheavement took place, such as the siege of Jerusalem, or the first French Revolution, the saving of such relics would be difficult, although not by any means impossible. Take the finding of the True Cross by S. Helena early in the 4th century. If this be true, it is by no means impossible that it was preserved up to the time of S. Louis. Nor is it impossible that someone connected with the church of S. Denis should have secreted the relic before the desecration of the tombs in 1793. Rumours precede acts; and having a valuable relic, why not hide it away when dangers lurk in the distance? But if so, why did not this person preserve the vessels in which the relics were kept? Why not have buried all those costly chalices, crosses and reliquaries? Why have left them to be seized upon by profane hands and melted up, if there were time to save their contents? But the chief difficulty is to account reasonably for the gap between the Crucifixion and the finding of the Cross; and it requires such a long bridge of faith to traverse this space of three hundred years that one feels reluctantly obliged to take the "Invention" of the Cross in its most literal sense.

The arms over the chapel of the Sainte-Madeleine are those of France *barré*, commemorating the foundation (in the old church) by Charles, Comte de Valois, duc d'Angoulême, a natural son of Charles IX., that most excellent Christian king and zealous son of the Church, who persecuted and slaughtered heretics for the good of their souls, thereby converting them (in the next world) from the error of their ways, and so covering his own multitudinous sins and wickednesses. There is a handsome confessional of carved wood, period Louis XV., in this chapel; and in the next, the relics of S. Vincent de Paul are enclosed in a fine Louis XIV. *châsse.* Lest any reader doubts the correctness of my translation, let me give the list of these relics in the original. " Les reliques de St. Vincent de Paul se composent d'une image teinte du sang du saint prêtre retrouvée légèrement coagulé quand on a ouvert son tombeau, de deux médailles formées de sa chair et de ses os mis en pâte, d'une parcelle de sa chair, de fragments de son suaire, de la soutane qu'il portait de son vivant, de la soutane dont il a été retrouvé vêtu dans sa bière, enfin d'un morceau de cette bière. Le tout est muni du cachet de la Mission et accompagné de quatres authentiques signés par MM. les supérieurs de Saint-Lazare." This and the S. Madeleine are the oldest of the chapels, and are both architecturally fine, with wrought-iron *grilles* of elegant and cunning workmanship. The paintings (1634), attributed to Simon Vouët or his Italian pupils, represent scenes in the life of S. Anne, to whom the chapel was originally dedicated by Anne de Monsigot, dame de Bourlon, who may be seen humbly sitting upon the stairs of the temple, with her two children standing by her side; while above, the high priest Zachariah is receiving the Blessed Virgin, who is presented by her mother and father. Very beautiful are the Angels bearing the instruments of the Passion, which are painted upon the eight compartments of the ceiling.

The founder of the chapel of S. Geneviève was one Jehan Brice, a merchant, whose desire that it should be richly decorated was carried out by the widow, Guillemette de l'Arche, in 1546, who is said to have been the heroine of a tale, which has been made familiar to us through the Italian opera of *La Gazza Ladra*. It appears that an old MS. in the possession of M. Boblet gives the list of foundation masses in the parish, and amongst them is one entitled *La Pie Voleuse*, which was said daily for the poor servant unjustly accused of stealing the spoon, found later on in the roof of the church. But the unwonted hour fixed for the mass, 4 a.m., and the name thereof, seem rather to point to the magpie than to the maid. May not the mass have been for the thief rather than for the innocent damsel? And was it not made thus early to assure the attendance of all the feathered tribes (who are wont to rise betimes), and to be unto them at once a warning and a duty paid to their cousin-german, the mean and wicked magpie? A *Tobias and the Angel*, by Santi di Tito, belonging originally to Louis XV., and ascribed to Andrea del Sarto, is of a certain interest. The frescoes, taken from the life of S. Louis in the chapel bearing his name, are amongst the best in the church. M. Barrias has thrown much grandeur into his subject, *S. Louis carrying the Crown of Thorns to the Sainte-Chapelle ;* but no one has so thoroughly depicted the ascetic beauty of the King, his true piety and unflinching faith, as M. Olivier-Merson in the wall-paintings of the corridor of the Cour de Cassation, in the Palais de Justice. In all the works of the latter painter the truest religious sentiment is invariably to be found; and if he errs upon the side of ugliness, is it not an infinitely smaller fault than the sentimental upturned eyes and radiant beauty of the German religious painters of the Cornelius and Hesse schools?

The tribune over the sacristy door was put up by the Duchesse d'Orléans, Adélaïde, the mother of Louis Philippe, in 1778, that she might enjoy privacy when she was present at the offices. It is a noble example of the finished style of Louis XVI.

Amongst the treasures of S. Eustache are an ivory crucifix in the sacristy: a bone of the patron Saint, from the cemetery of S. Priscilla, given in 1660 by Pope Alexander VII. to Sieur Chauvin; a tooth, formerly in the church of S. Jacques-l'Hôpital; and some bones of S. Eustache and his wife and children, said to have been formerly amongst the treasures of S. Denis; but I find no record of them in Dom Millet. The frescoes in the chapel of the patron Saint were painted by M. le Hénaff, in imitation of those found in the catacombs of Rome, the painter having copied the incorrect drawing as well as the fervent feeling of the early painters.

One or two more pictures by Vouët may be seen; and in the chapel of the Redemption are the frescoes of M. Glaize, one of the few painters who seems to have understood the spirit in which a church should be decorated.

S. Eustache was a royal parish up to the great crash at the end of the last century; its domain extended from the Chaussée des Gaillons to the Rue S. Denis, and being in the centre of the great world, it was very fashionable. Hard by were the royal palaces, and the new and "magnifique bastiment de l'hostel royal dit des Tuileries lez Paris, pour ce qu'il y avoit anciennement une tuilerie audict lieu," the *chef-d'œuvre* of Philibert Delorme, built by order of Catherine de' Medici to outrival the Château d'Anet, erected by the same great artist for the irregular queen, the lovely Diane. Not far from the Place Royale, and in the centre of a nest of hotels belonging to great and noble personages, S. Eustache became the praying-place of the living and the burial-place of the defunct notabilities. The great ministers of Henri III., Louis XIII., and Louis XIV. lived in the parish: the Duc d'Epernon, in the Rue Platrière (now Jean-Jacques-Rousseau, by reason of the sage having occupied the 4th *étage* of No. 49, in the year 1770); Cardinal Richelieu, in the Rue St.-Honoré, au

L'ADORATION PERPÉTUELLE AT SAINT-EUSTACHE.

Palais-Cardinal, otherwise the modern tourist's hunting-ground, the Palais-Royal; and Mazarin, the Rue Neuve-des-Petits-

Champs. The *curés* were naturally much in vogue as confessors and directors to these high personages and their swarms of followers and appendages—men and women. One of the rectors, preaching in 1537, before the King (François I.), the Cardinal de Lorraine, brother of the Duc de Guise, the Cardinal de Tournon, and ladies and gentlemen of the court, seems to have been shaky in his theology, according to some of his hearers, but *estonnant de vérité*, quoth others. Even the royal mind itself was unquiet for several days, but upon persuasion by the Cardinals it became reassured.

It was a time of troubles, civil and religious. The church work was stopped, and horrors were around, for in 1558 a poor student, denounced as a Lutheran by an old zealot of the weaker sex, was dragged out of the church and massacred upon the steps. But to return to Messire Jean Lecoq, the aforesaid *curé*. In the choir is his tomb, where he was buried with several of his relatives. His epitaph, bearing his arms *d'azur au coq d'or*, is as follows:

Nobilis venerabilis D. Magister Joannes Lecoq.
Hujus ecclesiæ pastor—1568.

ANT. LECOQ, SEIG. D'ESGRENAY ET DE CORBEUIL (frère du curé), 1566.
F. PAJOT, SEIGNEUR DE BURY, mari D'ESTIENNETTE LECOQ, 1563
F. PAJOT, SEIG. D'AUTEUIL, LEUR FILS, 1583.

A story is told of this reverend *curé* by Bonaventure Déperriers, in his *Joyeux Devis*, which, if not authentic, is characteristic of the times. A certain popular actor and head of a wandering dramatic company, one Jean de l'Espine, called *Pont-Allais*, was one day beating his drum near the church, to announce the commencement of his entertainment. Within the church the *curé* was preaching, but alas, his voice could not be heard above the rattle outside. Exit the preacher from his pulpit. He hurries out, and addresses the comedian upon the stage of his booth: "How can you dare to strum while I am preaching?" "And how can you dare to preach while I am drumming?" retorted the actor. The *curé*, enraged at this impudent reply, broke the drum; but Jean *Pont-Allais*, with the swiftness of a man of action, seized the priest, and popping the drum upon his head, pushed him into the church. Whether the discourse was continued, with or without the *coiffure*, history does not relate. Jean Lecoq died in 1568.

René Benoist, born at Angers, and a member of the school of theologians calling itself the Société Royale de Navarre, was, when quite young, the confessor of **Marie** Stuart, whom he followed to Scotland. Upon the death of the queen he became *curé* of St. Pierre-des-Arcis, and afterwards of S. Eustache. At the commencement of his career he was a *Ligueur*, and by reason of his great influence was nicknamed *le roi des Halles*. In 1588 he pronounced a funeral oration upon the assassinated Guises at Blois:

> Escouté, peuple, dit-il, par Isaïe: *Auferam a vobis fortem et virum bellatorem, judicem et prophetam.* Quand Dieu veut punir un peuple, il oste les personnes généreux et le conseil, car comme disait Cicéron en son premier des Offices: *Non valent arma foris nisi sit consilium domi.* Nous avions tous les deux en ce bon prince le duc de Guise: il était fort comme un Samson, prudent et advisé comme un Salomon. . . . Les anciens disaient un exercite estre plus fort quand le chef est lion que quand les soldats sont lions et le chef cerf. . . . Cette balafre qu'il portait, c'était en conservant la religion et l'état en France qu'il l'avait endurée. Cela devait faire peur aux méchants, *non est vulnus aversum sed adversum.* Faut des hommes vaillants, balafrés, qui ne fuient pas et ainsi que Notre Seigneur a porté ses cicatrices au ciel pour montrer ce qu'il avait enduré ainsi il a porté sa balafre pour le témoignage de sa vertu. Il ne faut pas perdre courage, la maison en est seulement escornée. (Then he concluded thus:) Prions Dieu pour les échevins d'icelle, qu'ils aient la crainte de Dieu et une bonne prudence. Ce mot d'échevins veut dire chefs de la ville, *sicut capita Urbis.* Je les compare aux quatre parties qui conservent la santé de l'homme et aux quatre éléments qui sont les choses les plus nécessaires au monde. Paris a pour ses armes un navire qu'est *Mare populi*, ceux là sont les pilotes; ils quéront à Dieu qu'il leur donne son saint Spérit, mais surtout à eux et à nous l'union, faut que Civitas soit Civium unitas.

However, going over to the enemy, like many a better man, Benoist became the butt of l'Estoile:

> *De trois B B B garder se doit on,*
> *De Bourges, Benoist et Bourbon.*
> *Bourges croit Dieu piteusement,*
> *Benoist le prêche finement,*
> *Mais Dieu nous gard' de la finesse*
> *Et de Bourbon et de sa messe.*

Another preacher of the time, Master Rose, gave Benoist the nickname of *le Diable des Halles;* but nevertheless he remained faithful to the king's party, and controverted those who refused to receive the royal heretic, even if he were to be converted. These views of the *curé*, coming to the ears of the Duc de Mayenne, caused Benoist to be sent for when the time came for Henri to abjure Protestantism, and he was present at S. Denis on the memorable 25th of July, 1592, when the king heard the mass which he bargained for the city of Paris.

This, of course, angered the Ligueurs yet more, and one said publicly that Benoist deserved to be hanged; and a poor woman of the parish (one of the forerunners of the celebrated "Dames de la Halle" who more than once defended their *curés* at all costs) was mauled and mangled by a Spanish soldier for having stood up for her parish priest and pronounced him a worthy man. Later on, being named bishop of Troyes by the king (whose confessor he became), the Ligue refused him obedience. Benoist was not only a fervent politician; he was also a writer of no mean merit, a learned preacher, an erudite theologian, and, above all, a friend beloved of his parishioners. He left his mark upon the church, embellishing the great door with a representation of his patron S. René, and composing an anthem, which was performed upon his *fête* day. Some authorities, Launoy to wit, give the number of his works as 154, Niceron 159. He was forty years at S. Eustache, and ten years dean of the Faculty of Theology. He died on the 7th March, 1608, at the ripe old age of eighty-seven, and just two years before the assassination of Henri, which took place at the very doors, one may say, of S. Eustache, in the Rue de la Ferronnerie.

After the death of René, Benoist's successor, we find the "Dames de la Halle" coming to the fore and asserting their importance. It appears that the appointment by the archbishop of a new curate (I use this term in its proper sense: the occupier of a cure) to succeed M. Tonnellier, led to a three day's revolt. The nephew of the latter, having been promised the cure by his uncle, opposed the new appointment, and, assisted by the market women, repulsed the soldiers—sent them flying, says tradition. However that may be, there was a vast commotion, which lasted three days, and was only ended by a species of armistice. "Les Dames de la Halle" consented to send a deputation to the queen (although it is not very apparent what her majesty could do in the matter), and after giving an account of the cause of the trouble, the envoy went on as follows:—

Notre curé qui est mort était si bon, si humain que nous l'avons tous pleuré. En mourant il a désigné son neveu pour son successeur et l'on a voulu nous en donner un autre. Ce n'est pas juste, n'est-ce pas, madame la Reine? Les Marlin, voyez-vous, depuis bien longtemps, sont curés de Saint-Eustache, *de père en fils*, et les paroissiens n'en souffriront pas d'autre.

The curious argument advanced by the deputy in favour of Marlin no doubt amused the queen, and she promised to do what she could. But "Les Dames" would have no evasive answers; they wanted their curate and intended to have him; and so, on their return, chains were put across the streets barricades were commenced, and the revolt waxed stronger. At this juncture, the archbishop gave way, and the nephew was installed amidst enthusiastic cries of *Vive l'archevêque! Vive la reine!* While upon the church some wag placarded a notice: *Avis. Le curé de Saint-Eustache est à la nomination des Dames de la Halle.*

This little tale seems to have been the origin of the romantic story trumped up in 1783, in which Marie Antoinette is said to have given a flower-girl her bracelet in recognition of some interview between them; which story was added to and amended later on, to the effect that the queen, upon her way to the guillotine, recognising the girl by her bracelet, betrayed her, and thus inadvertently caused her arrest and execution.

This Marlin was curate when Louis XIV. made his first communion at S. Eustache, that being his parish church at the time he was living in the Palais-Royal with his mother. Louis' last wife was also a parishioner of S. Eustache before her marriage with Scarron. As Frances d'Aubigné she seems to have been as much of a *dévote* as in her later days, for she arose at midnight, and attended matins at two of the clock. At that time was in receipt of alms from a charitable lady of the parish, and her extraordinary career had scarcely commenced.

Funeral orations abounded at S. Eustache. In 1666 Anne of Austria was eulogised by a celebrated preacher, père Sénault, in no mild terms:—

Souffrez que je vous dise que si elle a vaincu la douleur et la mort, si elle a procuré la paix à l'Europe, si elle a heureusement gouverné l'Etat pendant sa régence, si elle a obtenu des enfants du Ciel, ce n'a été que parce qu'elle se confiait en Dieu et qu'elle l'a obligé de faire cent miracles en sa faveur parce qu'elle espérait en sa bonté, *spera in eo et ipse faciet.*

Ten years later a greater preacher, the eloquent Fléchier, was called upon to sing the praises of Turenne, all the world following in the train of the king to hear him:

Quelle matière fut jamais plus disposée à recevoir tous les ornements d'une grave et solide éloquence, que la vie et la mort de très-haut et très-puissant Prince Henri de la Tour d'Auvergne, vicomte de Turenne, maréchal général des camps et armées du roi et colonel général de la cavalerie légère ? Où brillent avec plus d'éclat les effets glorieux de la vertu militaire: conduite d'armées, sièges de places, prises de villes, passages de rivières, attaques hardies, retraites honorables, campements bien ordonnés, combats soutenus, batailles gagnées, ennemis vaincus par la force, dissipés par l'adresse, lassés et consumés par une sage patience ; où peut-on trouver tant et de si puissants exemples que dans les actions d'un homme sage, modeste, libéral, désintéressé, dévoué au service du prince et de la patrie, grand dans l'adversité par son courage, dans la prospérité par sa modestie, dans les difficultés par sa prudence, dans les périls par sa valeur, dans la religion par sa piété.

Yet another celebrated orator, Massillon, was often heard at S. Eustache, and in 1704, preaching upon the small number of the elect, so terrified were his hearers that they all rose as one man, when he pronounced the words of the Supreme Judge. A lesser man, who rose to be a Cardinal, perhaps more by intrigues than anything else, was Guillaume Dubois. He was born at Brives-la-Gaillarde in 1657, and coming to Paris, he entered, while still quite young, the service of the *curé* of S. Eustache. Thence he obtained engagements as tutor to the great personages of the neighbourhood ; entering the house of the Duc de Chartres, he managed to obtain the abbey of Saint-Just, in the diocese of Beauvais. A grand monument by Coustou was erected to his memory in the church of S. Honoré, with an epitaph composed by Couture, which seems to be a slight satire upon the worldly-minded who love the rich things of this nether world. After giving the titles of the defunct, the lines go on : " *Quid autem hi titulis nisi arcus coloratus et fumus ad modicum parens Viator, stabiliora, solidioraque bona mortuo apprecare, etc., et:. Mais que sont ces dignités? nuages brillants, fumée qui s'évapore. Passant, demande à Dieu pour ce mort des biens plus stables et plus solides.*"

S. Eustache is still famous for its processions, and few churches are so fitted for grand ceremonial ; but what are the functions of to-day compared with those of the 18th century ? Here is an extract from the archives giving an outline of the procession upon the Fête Dieu, 20th June, 1716, during the minority of Louis XV. :—

Several lacqueys bearing torches.
Footmen of M. le duc de Charot with lights at the top of their weapons.
Sixteen footmen of M. le Comte de Toulouse.
Six pages of my lord count.
The preceptor of the pages of M. the duc d'Orléans, the Regent, in long

SAINT-EUSTACHE.   149

cassock and surplice; their tutor bearing a taper; twelve pages of His
Royal Highness, and two sub-tutors.
  The banner of the confraternity of the Holy Sacrament.
  The cross of the clergy of S. Eustache.
  An officer bearing a cushion for His Royal Highness.
  The *Suisses* armed, carrying halbards upon their shoulders and torches
in their hands, the officers at their head accompanied by drums and fifes.
  The dais of the Holy Sacrament, borne by high personages.
  The *curé* under the dais.
  Monseigneur le duc d'Orléans carrying a taper, preceded by several
officers of his house, and two chaplains in surplices.
  An officer bearing a bouquet of His Royal Highness.
  Forty of the body-guard, the councillor of Parliament, and the church-wardens.
  A coach belonging to His Royal Highness, followed by eight guards on
horseback.
  The archers of the town bringing up the rear.
  The watchmen of Paris arranged in a line from the church door to the
Hôtel de Soissons, on both sides of the Rue Coquillière, with flags and
officers at their head; drums to be beaten when His Royal Highness
arrives at the church in his coach, and on his return.

  In 1736 the *reposoir** in the Palais-Royal was constructed
from the design of Servandoni, the architect of S. Sulpice; and
its importance attracted multitudes of curiosity-hunters from
all parts of the town.
  In 1729 Jean-François-Robert Secousse succeeded his uncle,
and was the author of a pamphlet which he gave away
to his parishioners entitled: *Lettre d'un Curé à N—— au sujet
des Spectacles*. His successor, Jean-Jacques Poupart, was for
some time confessor to Louis XVI and Marie Antoinette.
When the storm arose, he took the oath to the Constitution;
but, finding the lengths to which it carried him, he retracted,
went into hiding, and administered to his flock in secret.
During the early years of the Revolution, no church suffered
more than S. Eustache. Situated in the midst of a populous
district, it became the scene of untold horrors. But it was
also the resting place for Mirabeau's body on its way to the
Panthéon, on the 4th April, 1791; and had nothing worse than
the funeral oration by Cerutti, pronounced from the *banc-
d'œuvre*,† taken place, the sacrilege would have been but
small. Trouble was looked for in the following May, when

---
  * An altar erected at various points along the route taken by the
procession, at which a pause is made for prayer, and the benediction
given.
  † The pew for clergy and officials during sermon.

the hairdressers' assistants caused a service to be said for the great orator; but instead of the church being invaded by 10,000 persons, as was expected, a poor 600 were all that put in an appearance, and these were well conducted. Not so the Women's Club which was held in the building, if Lamartine's *Histoire des Girondins* * is to be trusted:

> La société révolutionnaire siégeait à Saint-Eustache; elle était composée de femmes perdues, aventurières de leur sexe, recrutées dans le vice, où dans les réduits de la misère, ou dans les cabanons de la démence. Le scandale de leurs séances, le tumulte de leurs motions, la bizarrerie de leur éloquence, l'audace de leurs pétitions importuna le Comité de Salut Public, qui ferma le club. On peut juger par là ce qu'il devait en être de la pauvre église. Près de là siégeait aussi le fameux club de la rue Mauconseil.

Another club for women, founded by an actress named Lacombe, was dissolved after a speech of Robespierre's, in which we find that "Cette réunion de vraies sans-culottes ne saurait durer plus long-temps, parce qu'elle prête au ridicule et aux propos malins."

In 1793 the Feast of Reason was celebrated with as much profanity and indecency here as at Notre-Dame, as witness Mercier's account, told in the forcible language of Carlyle:

> The corresponding festival in the church of S. Eustache offered the spectacle of a great tavern. The interior of the choir represented a landscape decorated with cottages and boskets of trees. Round the choir stood tables overloaded with bottles, with sausages, pork-puddings, pasties, and other meats. The guests flowed in and out through all doors; whosoever presented himself took part of the good things; children of eight, girls as well as boys, put hand to plate, in sign of Liberty; they drank also of the bottles, and their prompt intoxication created laughter. Reason sat in azure mantle aloft, in a serene manner; cannoneers, pipe in mouth, serving her as acolytes. And out of doors (continues the exaggerative man) were mad multitudes dancing round the bonfire of chapel-balustrades, of priests' and canons' stalls; and the dancers—I exaggerate nothing—the dancers nigh bare of breeches, neck and breast naked, stockings down, went whirling and spinning, like those Dust-vortexes, forerunners of Tempest and Destruction. †

S. Eustache was re-opened for divine service sooner than many of the other churches, M. Poupart coming out of his hiding in June, 1795; but he had to share his church for some time with the philanthropists and the municipal coun-

---

* Vol. vii p. 35.
† Carlyle, *French Revolution*, vol. III. p. 194.

cillors, who held their meetings there upon certain days. And the church was, moreover, but four walls and a roof; nearly all the contents had vanished. The altars, the bronze statues, the pulpit, the pictures, the tombs, the slabs and epitaphs, all but the *banc-d'œuvre*, had gone to the museum of the Petits-Augustins; happily, for otherwise they would have gone into the fire.

In 1804, Pius VII., dragged to Paris by Napoleon to perform the coronation ceremony, was invited to visit S. Eustache and bless a statue of the Blessed Virgin; which he did with "*une bonté paternelle.*" The occasion naturally called forth all the ceremonial of which the church was capable: *Suisses* (beadles), vergers, *MM. les maires*, and *MM. les marguilliers*, magistrates, *juges de paix*, clergy, M. le curé Bossic, and his eminence the cardinal archbishop. His Holiness was received at the church door by the archbishop, M. de Belloy, and divers other bishops and dignitaries of church and state; who had to submit to hearing a Latin oration by the *curé*. The music was brilliantly executed by a large choir, and the ceremonial of an imposing character; peculiarly touching was the moment when the archbishop, an old man of ninety-six, who had to be supported by two prelates, mounted the steps of the altar, and presented the linen cloth to his Holiness for wiping his hands. After mass a reception took place in one of the chapels, and a number of the faithful had the honour of "kissing the papal slipper," says the account of the ceremony signed by a number of the dignitaries present.

Among the celebrities buried in the church or the burial-ground hard by are the following: Bernard de Girard, Seigneur du Haillan, historian, who died in 1610; Marie Jars de Gournay, the adopted daughter of Montaigne, and the editress of his essays; Vincent Voiture, poet and wit, who died in 1650; the Academician François de la Motte-le-Vayer; the poet Isaac Benserade; another Academician Furetière; the graceful music-maker, Rameau; the painter, Lafosse; a superintendent of finance, Claude de Bullion (a curiously appropriate name); Phélippeau, duke of la Vrillière; the chancellor d'Amenonville; a peer and marshal, François d'Aubusson de la Feuillade, who worshipped his king, the fourteenth Louis, and elevated a wondrous monument to his glory, the prancing steed and man in the Place des Victoires; and a medicine man of the same king a member, too, of the Academy,

Martin Cureau de la Chambre, aged seventy-five when he died in 1669. The physician is said to have been the consulter-general of the king, and they carried on a secret correspondence, in which the former thought that the sovereign would "*court grand risque de faire à l'avenir de mauvais choix de ministres,*" if he survived Cureau. The last curate buried in the church was Poupart, in 1796.

What is now the market of S. Joseph was formerly the burial-ground dedicated to that Saint. It belonged to the parish of S. Eustache, and in 1630 Chancellor Séguier built a chapel therein at his own expense. Here Molière and La Fontaine were buried, but the monuments were carried off to the museum of the Petits-Augustins, where they remained until 1818, when they were re-erected at Père-la-Chaise. Molière was also born in the parish, at a house, since pulled down, which occupied the site of the corner of the rue St. Honoré and the rue du Pont Neuf, formerly de la Tonnellerie.

The following epitaphs used to be in the church, and are interesting; the two first for their quaintness; the last as a record of an architect of S. Eustache, if not the original builder:

BARTHÉLÉMI TREMBLET, SCULPTEUR DU ROY, DÉCÉDÉ A L'AGE DE 61 ANS, EN 1629.

Louvre me donna l'être et Paris la fortune.
J'eus l'honneur d être au roy, St. Eustache a mes os ;
Passant, au nom de Dieu, si je ne t'importune,
Durant ce mien sommeil, priés pour mon repos.

Le monde n'a ésté à *Françoise*
Gallois que passage à l'éternité ;
Elle y a demeuré comme toujours
Preste d'en sortir, Les XXIII années
De son âge, n'ont estées qu'innocence,
Les quarte de son mariage, que paix
Et concorde, les vertus furent ses
Exercices, la piété son contentement,
La crainte de Dieu la conduite de
Sa vie qu'elle finit le XXVIIe Aoust
MDCXVI. Si chrestiennement,
Que *Richard Petit*, son mary,
Cons^{er} secrét. du roy, M. et C. de
Fr. ne console l'affliction de son
Absence que par la souvenance
De sa mort.

Cy-devant gît le corps
D'honorable homme *Charles David*, vivant sujet du Roy
Es-œuvres de maçonnerie, doyen des jurés et bourgeois

De Paris, architecte et conducteur du bâtiment de l'Eglise
De céans, lequel après avoir vescu avec *Anne Lemercier*
Sa femme l'espace de 53 ans, il décéda le quatrième jour
De décembre 1650 âgé de 98 ans.

S. Eustache has suffered much of late years by fire and the doings of wicked men. In 1844 fire attacked the organ, and smoke and water destroyed a great portion of the church. L'abbé Duguerry, who was shot in 1871 by the Communists, was *curé* at the time of the conflagration; and in order to rebuild the organ, he instituted a lottery, and appealed for aid to the whole country. Ten years later the new organ was built, and inaugurated under a new *curé*, Gaudereau, Duguerry having been appointed to the Madeleine. It was an exquisite instrument, of delicious tone and with a large number of stops. But alas! during the Commune it suffered again, several bombs having exploded in the church. Glass was smashed, organ pipes pierced, and a great deal of damage done to the roof; and it was several years before the church was restored to its pristine beauty. In 1879 the organ was finished, having been reconstructed and very much enlarged by J. Merklin, under a committee of organists and musicians; other instruments may be larger, but few are so beautiful in tone. Several of the Paris organs are fine, and the French school of organists is of all the least conventional. One is not bored by Rinck and his fellows; one does not hear choruses by Handel intended to be sung, or solos by the same master upon flute and clarinet stops with a poor tum-tum accompaniment, or sonatas written for the pianoforte or violin. That, to some of us, peculiarly irritating form of composition, the fugue, is rarely heard (except at the Madeleine), and Batiste, I think, must have held them in holy horror as did Berlioz, and, was it Chopin? Many a time for years I heard Batiste "touch" the S. Eustache organ, and surely no more divine sounds (if organ notes can be divine?) have ever been drawn from an instrument than when he played some soft, tender, pathetic melody upon the *voix celeste* or *vox humana* with accompaniment upon the far-off stops and tremolo; it was, in effect, what one might conceive a chorus of Angels accompanying some beautiful human voice. I know all the principal Paris organs, and most of them have been played upon by distinguished musicians; I also heard Lefebure-Wély frequently in former days; but no one seemed to equal or to excel Batiste in taste. His soft passages were perfection; and when he made the instrument thunder forth in all its *fortissimo*, it was grand in the extreme. Such an admiration had I for the musician, that I looked upon him as an invisible master, and my enthusiasm led me one day to waylay him as he came down the stairs. Query, if one admires an artist or an author, a poet or a musician, is it wise to see him in the flesh? Some painters and pianists, some violinists or singers, have been appropriately built, so to speak. Nature, sometimes unassisted, more often aided and pruned, has turned out bodies which are fitted to become the cases of distinguished minds. But everyone knows instances of actors and actresses who are nought minus their war-paint; of painters who might be grocers, and of poets as un-ideal in appearance as any publican or butterman. On the other hand, there are exquisites behind the counters, ethereal-looking butchers, and poetic vendors of cooked ham and beef. It is as if nature had made a number of bodies and minds, and shuffling them like a pack of cards, had tossed them together without any thought or heeding. Such seemed to have been the case with Batiste, for he was the exact model of the French Mossoo so dear to *Punch*—the Mossoo one so rarely sees out of that sportive periodical. Nevertheless, the soul within that commonplace body was able to peal forth in most sublime sounds which touched the hearts of all who heard them. Batiste's was essentially emotional playing of the highest order. Never shall I forget the thrill which went through the crowd when he played Chopin's "Funeral March" at the funeral of the dear old *curé*, l'abbé Simon—the very type of the courteous, fine-gentleman priests of other days, without their vices. When, years ago, the abbé Simon and Duguerry his friend, sat side by side, their finely chiselled features and longish hair, their elegant manner, and courteous bearing, reminded one of the portraits of Fléchier, Massillon and Bossuet.

It may interest musicians to know the composition of the S. Eustache organ, and as many of the stops are French, I may as well give them in their original names. It has four manuals, and 72 stops; 4356 pipes and 20 pedals.

Grand Orgue....................................	54 notes,	16 stops.
Positif...	5¼ ,,	14 ,,
Récit expressif	54 .,	16 ,,
Clavier Bombarde	54 ,,	11 ,,
Pédales	30 ,,	15 ,,

TOTAL............... 72

SAINT-EUSTACHE.

1ST MANUAL.—GREAT ORGAN.

	ft.			ft.
1	Montre 16	10	Nasard	2
2	Montre 8	11	Doublette............	2
3	Flûte à pavillon 8		COMBINATION STOPS.	
4	Bourdon 8	12	Furniture et Cymbale .	3
5	Flûte harmonique ... 8	13	Cornet	8
6	Viole de Gambe 8	14	Trompette	8
7	Gemshorn 8	15	Clarinette	8
8	Rohrflûte 4	16	Clairon	4
9	Prestant 4			

2ND MANUAL.—CHOIR ORGAN.

	ft.			ft.
1	Montre............... 8	9	Clochette	1
2	Bourdon 8		COMBINATION STOPS.	
3	Keraulophone......... 8	10	Plein jeu	2
4	Flûte harmonique ... 8	11	Clarinette............	16
5	Bourdon 16	12	Cromhorn	8
6	Flûte harmonique ... 4	13	Trompette	8
7	Fugara............... 4	14	Clairon...............	4
8	Doublette............ 2			

3RD MANUAL.—SWELL ORGAN.

SOLO STOPS.

	ft.			ft.
1	Viole de Gambe...... 8	9	Trompette harmonique.	8
2	Voix céleste 8	10	Clairon	4
3	Bourdon 8		JEUX DE FOND.	
4	Piccolo............... 1	11	Bourdon	16
5	Basson-Hautbois..... 8	12	Principal	8
6	Voix humaine 8	13	Flûte harmonique	8
	COMBINATION STOPS.	14	Flûte octaviante	4
7	Cornet 8	15	Prestant	4
8	Trombone 16	16	Flageolet.............	2

4TH MANUAL.—SOLO ORGAN.

	ft.		COMBINATION STOPS.	
1	Bourdon 16			ft.
2	Gambe................ 16	7	Cornet	16
3	Gambe................ 8	8	Bombarde	16
4	Salicional............ 8	9	Trompette	8
5°	Quintaton 8	10	Cor anglais	8
6°	Dulciana............. 4	11	Clairon...............	4

PEDALS.

	ft.			ft.
1	Principal 32	9	Flûte	4
2	Flûte 16		COMBINATION STOPS.	
3	Sous-Basse 16	10	Bombarde	32
4	Contrebasse.......... 16	11	Bombarde	16
5	Grosse Flûte 8	12	Basson...............	16
6	Quinte 12	13	Basson...............	8
7°	Violoncelle 8	14	Trompette	8
8°	Bourdon 8	15	Clairon...............	4

COMBINATION STOPS FOR THE SWELL.

SOLO	ANCHES	FONDS
TREMOLO	TREMOLO	TREMOLO

COMBINATION PEDALS.

1. Tonnerre.
2. Tirasse du 1er clavier sur le pédalier.
3. Tirasse du 2me clavier sur le pédalier.
4. Tirasse du 3me clavier sur le pédalier.
5. Tirasse du 4me clavier sur le pédalier.
6. Réunion du mécanisme des jeux du 1er clavier sur le levier pneumatique.
7. Accouplement du 2me clavier sur le 1er.
8. Accouplement du 3me clavier sur le 1er, à l'unisson.
9. Accouplement du 4me clavier sur le 1er.
10. Accouplement du 4me clavier sur le 3me.
11. Accouplement du 3me clavier à l'octave grave sur le 1er clavier.
12. Forte général.
13. Introduction des jeux de combinaisons du pédalier.
14. Introduction des jeux de combinaisons du 1er clavier.
15. Introduction des jeux de combinaisons du 2me clavier.
16. Introduction des jeux de combinasions du 4me clavier.
17. Expression sur le 3me clavier récit.

No one should omit visiting S. Eustache on S. Cecilia's day (November 22), when a grand mass is always performed, with full orchestra, in aid of the Society of Musicians; and indeed, any Sunday the music is quite well worth hearing, and the ceremonial is the finest in Paris. At the same time much has been lost by the substitution of the Roman for the Parisian rite, which took place in 1876. In the former, two acolytes swing the censers; in the latter, four or six acolytes standing in a row threw them up on high six times, the last time catching them while kneeling on one knee. As has been said, the grand effect of this use can never be forgotten by those who saw it.

The church owes the new marble pavement to its good *curé* l'abbé Simon, one of the heroes of the Commune, and, almost, one of its victims. So much has been related (and with justice) against the *Communards*, that an incident connected with S. Eustache ought not to be forgotten. The day the abbé Simon was arrested he had three thousand *francs* in his pocket, which were destined to pay for the pavement of the choir. Of course upon his arrival at the prison they were given up to the police, and were not restored when the *curé* was released through the intervention of his *chères paroissiennes, les Dames de la Halle*, who went *en masse* to demand his freedom. On Easter Monday, however, Raoul Rigault's secretary went to the sacristy, asked M. Simon if the money had been returned, and finding that it had not, he left the church, to return in an hour's time, with the three thousand *francs* intact.

In the south transept is a little Gothic statue of S. John, and on the wall is a sad memorial of the names of all the hostages who suffered death under the Commune, headed by the archbishop (Darboy) and the *curé* of the Madeleine, Duguerry, who was formerly *curé* of S. Eustache.

S. Eustache, like most large churches, looks grandest in the evening, when the altar is ablaze with lights, and long vistas fade away into the darkness; but under all conditions it is a splendid church, a mass of harmonious colouring from floor to ceiling. At the evening services during Lent, it is seen to advantage; or again on Christmas Day at vespers, when it is resplendent with lights; those curious and unchurchlike glass chandeliers filled with candles, and clusters of gas jets round the walls.

Another great day is Good Friday, when Rossini's "Stabat Mater" is performed. It is always beautifully rendered, but for three-fourths of the crowd which assembles—and the church is always crammed—for most of the people it is a mere performance. So is the midnight mass on Christmas Day. Religious enthusiasm carries one away upon one or two occasions; the sentiment is exquisite; the emotions which are aroused are of the purest, and we feel almost that we are by the veritable manger listening to the heavenly Host: "Glory to God in the Highest." But alas! human beings are but mortal; and so upon experience we find that the crowds who attend the mass do so mainly as a pastime before the *réveillon*; that is the function of the night; eating and drinking, junkettings and merrymakings; and just a little church-going to fill up the time until the hour of feasting commences. Cardinal Manning in his wisdom saw this many years ago, and stopped the practice of saying midnight mass, a measure he probably regretted as much as any of us; for apart from its being a very ancient custom, it is a most poetic idea, appealing strongly to our best emotions and our most vivid imagination.

SAINT-FRANÇOIS XAVIER.

Until quite lately, the only church in Paris dedicated to the memory of the great Jesuit was the little chapel belonging to the Missions Étrangères in the Rue de Bac. The first stone was laid in 1683 by the archbishop of Paris, in the name of the king. It is a double chapel with a flight of steps leading from the lower to the upper church.

SAINTE-GENEVIÈVE (LE PANTHÉON).

As we walk up the Rue Soufflot and see the great domed Panthéon facing us in its Classic glory, it is difficult to realise that the space occupied by the modern building is but a small portion of what was formerly the domain of the important abbey of S. Geneviève belonging to the Augustinian canons. When the religious orders were suppressed in France, Paris contained nine abbeys: S. Geneviève, S. Victor, belonging to the Augustins; S. Germain des Prés to the Benedictines; Val des Grâce to the nuns of S. Benedict; Port-Royal, Pantemont, l'Abbaye aux Bois, and S. Antoine to the Cistercian nuns; and the Cordelières to the order of the Poor Clares. An inspection of a pre-Revolution map of the city shows us that a large part of it was swallowed up by these abbeys and other monastic lands and properties.

The foundation of the abbey of S. Geneviève was due to the desire of Clovis to celebrate his victory over the Visigoths in the plains of Vouillé. Having overrun a great part of Gaul, and annexed it to the kingdom of the Franks, what was more natural than that he should offer his thanks for robbery, violence, and slaughter, by the building of a church upon the hill overshadowing his Palais des Thermes? He dedicated it to S. Peter and S. Paul, and put it under the charge of some monks who were succeeded later on by secular canons, and eventually in the 12th century, by regular canons of S. Augustin. Clovis died ere the church was terminated, but Queen Clotilde was able to carry the work on, and it became the resting place of both sovereigns, as well as of the children of Clodomir, who were done to death by their loving relatives after the manner of some modern Africans. In the 11th century, the church was put under the patronage of S. Geneviève in consequence of the numberless miracles performed at her tomb, for the maid of Nanterre had been laid to rest in this church. The legend of S. Geneviève is picturesque in the extreme, affording endless subjects for the artist, as witness the wall paintings in the modern church. Born in 421 at Nanterre, a little village situated upon the plain over which the fort of Mt. Valérien now frowns, she was employed, as are many of her compatriots of the present day, in tending sheep. A graceful, if somewhat affected picture by Guérin, represents her with a

SAINTE-GENEVIÈVE FROM THE RUE SOUFFLOT.

distaff in her hands. When about seven years old, S. Germain, bishop of Auxerre, passed through Nanterre on his way to Britain. A crowd assembled to receive the good bishop's blessing, and among them were S. Geneviève and her parents. *La pucelette* was already famed for her piety and humility, and S. Germain, wise man, had no sooner cast his eyes upon her than he became aware of her future glory ; and finding that she desired to be a handmaiden of Christ, he hung round her neck a small coin marked with the symbol of the cross, thus con secrating her to God's service. Many were the miracles which she wrought by prayer, even in her childhood; as for instance, when her mother, being struck blind for boxing her little Saintship's ears, recovered her sight through the prayers of the daughter. Some say that Geneviève prayed for her hasty parent after a year and nine months had elapsed; but surely it is better to believe that the prayers were unanswered for that length of time, than that the daughter, whose intercession was so efficacious, should have omitted to help her mother for so many months.

At fifteen, Geneviève renewed her vows, but remained with her parents until their death. She then took up her abode with an old kinswoman in Paris, where, from her piety and devotion, she became the subject of disputes between those who venerated her as a saint, and others who considered her sanctity and benevolence mere hypocrisy and sham piety. And so it came about that at night, when she kept her vigils, the arch enemy, not content with putting into the hearts of men the desire to slander and vilify the godly maiden, set himself to worry her, by extinguishing her candle. But she had a tinder-box in her faith and prayer, and so she was never left in darkness. This is a favourite subject of the old artists; one frequently sees the Saint holding her taper, while a demon is blowing it out, sometimes using a pair of bellows, as at the doorway of S. Germain l'Auxerrois, S. Nicholas, and other French churches; and it is obvious that the legend grew out of the promise that God never leaves those in darkness who pray for light. So, too, the holding up of the re-kindled taper in the face of the fiend, and his consequent flight, symbolises the Light of the World chasing away evil. Another legend relates that when a storm overtook her and some friends on their way to S. Denis, and blew out their tapers, an Angel descended to relight them in answer to Geneviève's prayers.

The Saint was a sort of early Jeanne d'Arc, inasmuch as she delivered the city from its enemies; but Geneviève depended only upon her prayers; and yet, simply by these means, she caused the Huns, who were besieging Paris under Attila, to flee. On another occasion, when the city was invested by Childéric, she took command of some boats which were sent up the river to Troyes for succour, and brought them back laden with provisions. When the city was taken, Geneviève was treated with great respect by Childéric, and it was through her influence

SAINTE-GENEVIÈVE.

that Clovis and his wife, Clotilde, were converted to Christianity, and the first Christian church was erected in Paris.* Geneviève died at the ripe old age of eighty-nine, and was buried in what was then called the church of SS. Peter and Paul; and it was in consequence of her miracle-working tomb that the patronage of the church was given over to her, the Apostles falling into complete oblivion. Among these miracles was a cessation of a terrible visitation of the plague called the *mal ardent*, which raged in Paris in the reign of Louis le Gros; hence the dedication of a church to S. Geneviève-des-Ardents, situated near the cathedral, and long since destroyed.

Most painters of modern times have depicted the Saint as a shepherdess, somewhat after the Chelsea china pattern, and a few have given her the suggestiveness of the nymphs of Boucher. Watteau's is a charming picture, but the graceful maiden scarcely comes up to our ideal of the pious little peasant girl of Nanterre. Guérin's is pure and refined, if somewhat affected, but one feels inclined to hail our old friend with the fiend behind her puffing or blowing the bellows as a more worthy reading of the character of S. Geneviève. In the church of S. Merri there is a very curious picture representing the maid surrounded by her sheep, and enclosed by a circle of huge stones after the manner of those at Stonehenge.

The legend of feeding the besieged Parisians is said to be the origin of the *pain bénit* of the Paris churches, a custom peculiar to the old Parisian rite, and almost the only one kept up since that use was superseded by the Roman, some few years since. This blessed bread is a large *brioche* offered by some of

---

* Hincmar (Archbishop of Reims, 9th century) tells us that S. Remy, who was at Reims at the time, received a spiritual revelation from the Holy Spirit, at the very moment of Clovis' death.

Many early sculptures and frescoes commemorate the life and deeds of Clovis, at Reims, at Rome, and at Siena, but they are all of much later date than the king.

Grégoire of Tours gives a picturesque account of the last days of Clotilde: "La reine Chrotechilde après la mort de son mari, vint à Tours: et là servant Dieu dans la basilique de Saint-Martin, avec une grande chasteté et une extrême bonté, elle demeura en ce lieu tous le jours de sa vie, et visita rarement Paris. . . . Pleine de jours et riche en bonnes œuvres, elle mourut à Tours du temps de l'évêque Injuriosus. Elle fut transportée à Paris, suivie d'un choeur nombreaux qui chantait des hymnes, et ensevelie par ses fils, les rois Childebert et Clotaire, dans le sanctuaire de la basilique de Saint-Pierre, à côté du roi Clovis. Elle avait construit cette basilique où repose aussi la très bienheureuse Geneviève."

M

the parishioners, and brought into church in procession during the offertory. It is usually piled up on a stage and decorated with flowers and lights, the whole being carried on the shoulders of acolytes. Preceded by the beadle and donor, it is taken to the altar and sprinkled with holy water; some prayers are said, the donor is presented with a pax to kiss, and the procession then returns to the sacristy, where the bread is cut up and put into baskets, which are then carried round the church, and the *brioche* distributed among the congregation. One often sees strangers refuse this, thinking it something peculiarly popish; indeed, I was once assured by a friend that he had been offered the Sacrament, "which of course he had refused." But we may be certain that if the *pain bénit* were considered so exceedingly holy, promiscuous strangers would not get the chance of partaking of it. It rather figures a sort of amicable meal after the manner of the early Agapæ, and is a very pretty ceremony; besides, it is always refreshing to witness any little peculiarity in ritual, instead of the dull uniformity which recent papal decrees have enforced over western Europe.

In the 9th century S. Geneviève became the patron of the abbey; and some of the capitals of the church of that period are now in the court of the École de Beaux-Arts. In the 13th century the church was rebuilt, but gradually falling into decay, it was condemned in the reign of Louis XV., and demolished in 1801-7 to make way for the Rue Clovis. When the crypt was destroyed a large quantity of stone coffins, medals, pottery, shields and lances of Gallo-Roman and Mérovingian workmanship were found.

The early capitals mentioned above are rude in treatment, and the personages, Adam and Eve, and other Old Testament worthies, are coarse, but the scraps of ornament are quaint, and the carving of the foliage is vastly superior to that of the figures. The crypt of the church was the largest of any in Paris, and being the burial place of so many holy and regal persons, was interesting in the extreme; but to the men of the 18th century what mattered it that 13th century work should be swept away? The street was required as a short cut, a deviation of five minutes more or less had to be rectified; and so all that remains of the abbey church is its tower. But from the ruins many precious fragments were saved. The stone coffin of S. Geneviève was carried off to S. Étienne hard by, and there enveloped in a gorgeous shrine; which, besides being a work of art, had the advantage of being portative, and so could be marched about when processioning was resorted to as a remedy for city troubles. In the *Statistique Monumentale de Paris*, published by Albert Lenoir, may be seen some plates representing this motley crew of fragments. Portions of stone coffins, sculptured with crosses and monograms, were sent to the museum of the Petits-Augustins, but do not seem to have survived the dissolution of the collection; they were similar to those at the Hôtels de Cluny and Carnavalet.

The reliquary of the Saint was in the form of a church, and was executed by order of the abbot, Robert de la Ferté-Milon, in 1242. The craftsman was one of the most cunning goldsmiths of the city, Bonnard. It contained 193 marks of silver and 7½ marks of gold; and kings, queens, and commoners vied with each other to cover it with precious stones. Marie de' Medici crowned the front with a mass of diamonds; and Germain Pilon was engaged to sculp a group of four women standing upon a marble pedestal to support the *châsse*. This graceful work of art was all that was saved in 1793: being of wood it was of little value to a starving and poverty-stricken mob. Or, had the municipality any reverence for it as an art treasure? Certain it is that, whereas the reliquary was melted up into coin, and the jewels sold, the part which was really the most precious was saved, and is now in the Renaissance Museum of the Louvre. But in spite of the value and beauty of the *châsse*, the *Conventionel* Grégoire, in his report, gives 21,000 *livres* only as the sum obtained by its destruction.

Some of the monuments of the church were saved; that of the Cardinal François de la Rochefoucault, abbot of S. Geneviève, and High Almoner of France, who died in 1645, sculptured by Philippe Buister, being placed in the chapel of the Hospital for Incurable Women, of which he was the founder. The statue of Clovis, renewed in the 12th century, is now at S. Denis, owing to the accident of its having been replaced in the 17th century by a superior one in white marble, which was destroyed in 1793.* Another tomb, that of a chancellor of

---

* The finding of the statue of Clovis was the reward of well-doing. The Cardinal de la Rochefoucault, desiring to honour the old king and the founder of the abbey, set up a fine marble image in the place of the old stone one "*mangé et difformé d'antiquité.*" This the Revolution destroyed;

Notre-Dame de Noyon, who died in 1350, is now in the École des Beaux-Arts. The monument of René Descartes was less fortunate, for, after having been transferred to the museum of the Petits-Augustins, it was dismembered, and dispersed or destroyed; but the remains of the great philosopher were reburied at S. Germain des Prés.

Some of the conventual buildings remain and form part of the Lycée Henri IV. The tower is Romanesque at the base and pointed at the upper stories—14th and 15th century respectively. The cloisters and refectory form part of the school buildings, but they have been much modernized. The latter is an elegant structure of the 13th century, and now serves as the school chapel. In the sacristy is a large stone statue of the patroness (13th century) which formerly formed part of the central pillar of the principal doorway of the abbey church; it represents her with a demon on one shoulder blowing out her candle, and an Angel on the other relighting

but the old stone statue, which was shunted to the crypt, was found later on, and sent to S. Denis—an illustration of the exaltation of the humble; in this case, a clumsy gentleman with long hair, with his feet upon a feeble-looking lion. Although not contemporary with Clovis, the work and design prove it to be not later than the 12th century. A Latin epitaph once accompanied the statue in its old resting-place:

> Hic est illustrissimus rex Ludovicus qui et Clodoveus ante baptismum est dictus
> Francorum rex quintus sed verus christianus qui ab Anastasio imperatore consul et Augustus est creatus
> Hunc sanctus Remigius baptisavit et in baptismate ejus angelus ampullam sacri chrismatis detulit
> Vi Aquitania arianos expulit et totam illam terram usque ad montes Pirenaeos subjugavit
> Huic per Viennam fluvium cervus miræ magnitudinis viam ostendit
> Post quem rex ac milites vadum transierunt et in ejus adventu muri Angolismae civitatis corruerunt
> Alamanniam Tornigiam et Burgundiam tributarias fecit et terram adjacentem transivit
> Parisiis sedem regni constituit ecclesiam istam fundavit in honore apostolorum Petri et Pauli
> monitis sanctissimae et non satis commendandae Clotildis uxoris suae et beatae Genovefae
> quam sanctus Remigius dedicavit in qua post laudabilia opera Rex sepultus est
> A quatuor filiis suis regibus Theodorico Clodomiro Childeberto et Clotario
> Anno Domini V. XIII regni sui XXX.

it. What was formerly the library is a series of galleries upon the plan of a cross, with a cupola at the intersections. It is no longer used for this purpose, all the books having been placed in the new building on the other side of the square.

"Contiguous to the Sorbonne church there stands, raising its neatly-constructed dome aloft in air, the Nouvelle Eglise Ste. Geneviève, better known by the name of the Panthéon. The interior presents, to my eye, the most beautiful and perfect specimen of Grecian architecture with which I am acquainted. In the crypt are the tombs of the French warriors. From the gallery running along the bottom of the dome, the whole a miniature representation of our S. Paul's, you have a sort of panorama of Paris, but not a favourable one. The absence of sea-coal fume strikes you very agreeably, but I could not help thinking of the superior beauty of the panorama of Rouen from the heights of St. Catherine."* This "perfect specimen of Grecian architecture" owes its birth, it is said, to Madame de Pompadour; and if this be so, it must have been one of the last of that lady's contributions to art, as she died in April, 1764, the foundation stone being laid in the following September. It is curious how artistic the French kings' handmaidens were, and, with the exception of the daughters of the house of Medici, how little we owe to the queens in the way of fine works of art. Whether this particular handmaiden obliged the king to decide upon the rebuilding of the old church, which had been tumbling into decay for a long period, or whether it was the king's fright lest he should fall ill again if he did not propitiate the Saint who had cured him of a sinking fever, it is impossible to decide. Very likely it was the king's own fears. He had all but died at Metz; he had appealed to the patroness of Paris; she had answered his prayers, somewhat unwisely perhaps, in the interest of his hapless subjects; and in sheer gratitude, thus proving himself far more honest than many a holier and more godly man, he decided that the much-talked-of church should be set going, and that it should be worthy of the maid of Nanterre. And so it is. Soufflot was the architect, and his design is one of the happiest of its class. But what a strange life the church has had! And what an extraordinary jumble of Christianity and philosophy the great dome has witnessed! Emblems of the Roman Republic and the religion of Christ stand side-by-side. Cardinals

* Dibden.

repose in the crypt by the side of Voltaire and Jean-Jacques. At one time masses are said for the repose of the souls of defunct Christians; at another, funeral allocutions are delivered by laymen. And the chopping and changing about! Scarcely finished in 1791, the Constitutional Assembly decreed that the new church should become a Temple of Fame, and be known as the Panthéon. The cross was taken down from the summit of the dome, the inscription, *Aux grands hommes, la Patrie reconnaissante*, was substituted for *D.O.M. Sub invocatione sanctae Genovefae sacrum;* and under the peristyle was written: *Panthéon français, l'an III. de la Liberté.* The words of the report issued, describing the changes to be adopted in the building, are in the accustomed grandiloquent language of the First Republic: . . . "en un moment où tout doit contribuer à renforcer dans l'ame des citoyens toutes les sensations que l'enthousiasme de la liberté fait puiser dans l'amour de la Patrie, &c." Mirabeau, Marat, and Lepelletier Saint-Fargeau were laid to rest in the crypt.

One of Napoleon's first acts was to decide that "l'église Sainte-Geneviève serait rendue au culte, conformément à l'intention de son fondateur, sous l'invocation de Sainte Geneviève, patronne de Paris." But it was also to preserve the destination ascribed to it by the Constituante, that of being the burial-place of senators, officers of state, dignitaries, officers of the Legion of Honour, and of citizens who had rendered eminent service to their country. The divine offices were to be conducted by the canons of Notre-Dame, and to this end they were increased by six members. With the restoration of Louis XVIII. all homage to "great men" disappeared, and the old inscription was restored. Baron Gros was commissioned to paint the dome with the Apotheosis of S. Geneviève, a work described by an old writer in not over flattering terms: "On one of the cupolas of the dome, which is surrounded by a colonnade of Corinthian pillars, is painted the Apotheosis of St. Geneviève. Her saintship is in the costume of a shepherdess, breathing all peace, all happiness, all immortality. Nothing of earth is in her composition. Beside her is Louis XVIII. and little winged angels. They are very busy—the angels—in scattering flowers about the saint. Above her is Louis XVI. and his queen, as elegant as she was upon the threshold of Versailles, and Louis XVII., all surrounded by celestial glory. Before her are the persons the most illustrious of each race;

Clovis, who looks very savage; St. Clotilde, very pretty; Charlemagne, very heroic; and St. Louis and Queen Margarite, who look very pious. . . . The floor of this temple, incrusted with various-coloured marble, is very remarkable and very beautiful. It is exclusively occupied by Voltaire and Rousseau, at opposite extremities. Who would have thought that these two champions of Infidelity, who were refused Christian burial, would one day have assigned to their remains the first church of France, and one of the first in Christendom, as their mausoleum? I wonder if Jean-Jacques, in his prophetic visions, foresaw this? Why did they not lay them at the side of each other, that we might all learn how vain are the jealousies, the petty competitions and animosities of men so soon to come to this appointed and unavoidable term of all human contentions? It was once the custom of these old countries to multiply a man by burying him piecemeal, — his heart at Rouen and his legs in Kent,—because the world was then on short allowance of heroes; but modern times have reversed this practice; and Bonaparte has laid up together a whole batch of them in the basement of this church, for eternity, as you lay up potatoes in your cellar for winter. Here are the names graven overhead in a catalogue, on the marble,

THE PANTHÉON FROM CHARENTON.

of men famous for giving counsel to the Emperor (who never took any) in the Senate, and of men who gained a great deal of celebrity by having their brains knocked out on the fields of Austerlitz and Marengo. When Marat was deified by the Convention he was interred here in 1793, and in 1794 he was disinterred and undeified, and then thrown into his native element, the common sewer, in the Rue Montmartre—to purify him."*

In 1830 another *bouleversement* took place, and the law of the Constituante was promulgated once more; but inasmuch as some former heroes had found their way, through change of opinion, into the sewers, it was decreed that nobody's ashes should be considered worthy of burial in the national Walhalla until ten years had elapsed from the time of death. Thus citizens could be turned into *les grands hommes* in a comparatively short period, as compared to the years often required for beatification or canonization. The second Republic also busied itself with lowering the cross, and replacing the inscription *Aux grands hommes, la Patrie reconnaissante*. It was used as an ambulance during the 1848 troubles, but restored to divine service by that devoted son of the Church, Louis-Napoléon, soon after his iniquitous massacre of the people in the streets of the city; and then, having endowed himself with Imperial honours, he obtained the aid of the archbishop to create a number of chaplains to serve at the altar of S. Geneviève. The decree of 1851, which took "ultérieurement des mesures pour régler l'exercise permanent de culte catholique," only lasted nineteen years. When the city was besieged, the permanency of the services exploded like the bombs from Mont Valérien, and the crypt became a powder-magazine. The church was shored up, the windows were bricked, and the interior was filled with some 30,000 bundles of straw, as a precaution against the enemy's artillery. But the German invasion left the building as it found it, and the troubles in the immediate future were the work of the Comité central. The soldiers were replaced by National Guards, who began their occupation by industriously sawing off the arms of the crosses upon the pediment, and at the summit of the dome, and converting the emblems of Christianity into flagstaffs for the red flag of the Commune. From the 26th March until the 24th May it waved aloft in all its pride; but upon the latter

* *The American in Paris, 1838.*

day it saw the church occupied by the Versaillais, who entered just in time to save the building from the vengeance of the Fédérés, who had threatened it with fire. Like all the other churches and public buildings, the Panthéon suffered far more from the shells of the Communists than from those of the enemy; and it took some years before all the repairs were executed, and "*le plus beau gâteau de Savoie qu'on est jamais fait en pierre*"* was restored to its former condition. Some few years ago the Republic suppressed the chaplains, and reconverted the church into what the Parisian press fondly calls "their Westminster"; and the next *grand homme* who was laid in "the most lovely *gâteau de Savoie*" was, oddly enough, Victor Hugo himself. He was buried there immediately after his death; but it is not likely that posterity will ever wish to reverse our judgment of the poet's greatness, or look upon him as anything but one of France's noblest sons.

The sculptures of the pediment, representing that sentimental personage La Patrie accompanied by Liberty and History, are by David d'Angers. La Patrie is throwing crowns about to its great men; Liberty is fabricating the crowns, and History is religiously writing up the names, that there may be no mistake. Civilians stand on the right, *messieurs les militaires* are relegated to the left, while several young men and youths are labouring vigorously in order to attain in the future their right to be amongst the elect. It is no case of Angels and scales, no weighing of good and bad deeds; the services of Madame la Justice are not even required; it is simply Patriotism which selects and serves up for glory those who have deserved well of their country. The bas-reliefs of the peristyle are by Nanteuil. Here La Patrie, holding a palm in one hand, is guiding with the other one of her sons who has died in her service; while Renown is puffing away at a trumpet to herald forth the deeds of this devoted hero. In another bas-relief Art and Science are honouring the country by their works; a warrior is, one knows not why, refusing the crown tendered to him; and a woman, representing Study and Intellect, is propounding the advantages of Education to the mothers who have brought their children to Madame la Patrie. The bronze doors are the work of Destouches, and recall, in style of ornamentation, those of Ghiberti at Florence.

The interior is, no doubt, grand. Originally lighted by

* Victor Hugo.

windows in the walls, it is now somewhat dark and sombre, suitable to a temple for the repose of the dead. The walls have been covered with paintings, which partially relieve the dull monotony of the stone; but a building devoid of sunlight must of necessity be gloomy in a city the sky over which is, for half the year, grey and colourless.

Although the first of the 425 steps leading to the summit of the dome is upon the level of the top of the towers of Notre-Dame, the view is not nearly so interesting as from the latter. There is no river winding at our feet, and none of those guardian monsters who gaze at the city from the heights of the cathedral.

The decoration of the interior is now almost completed, and, whether for good or for evil, it is irrevocable. It was not probable that so artistic a nation as the French would allow such a building to remain in an incomplete state; they would rather run the risk of perpetuating failure than leave the work undone. We English are different. S. Paul's is double the age of the Panthéon, and we are still squabbling over its decoration; we hang up designs and drag them down again, we lay out enormous sums in the embellishment of the altar, and then we spend ever so much more in trying to circumvent our neighbours, and get rid of the ornament. It is a fate not necessarily peculiar to our country or this city, because at Brompton a magnificent church has been designed, built, and decorated in a few years, a model of refinement, beauty, and grandeur. But the embellishment of S. Paul's is attempted by spurts only, and up to the present time has left much to be desired.* That may perhaps be an advantage; if nothing is done, there can be nothing to regret. But the French have acted otherwise, and the Panthéon embellishment is almost an accomplished fact.

With one or two exceptions, the painting of the church has been confided to artists with reputations, wearers of the palm-embroidered coats; the procession of decorators being led by Baron Gros and Gérard, who covered the dome with pictures in the false, pretentious style of the First Empire, leaving it a glowing mass of bad taste, as a warning to their successors. Baron Gros was a great painter, an early naturalist, as witness his *Battlefield of Eylau*, in the Salle des Sept Cheminées of the Louvre. There is an amount of realism in the painting of

---

* Of Mr. W. B. Richmond's work, undertaken since the above was written, it is as yet impossible to form an opinion.

the dying and the dead, of the snow and the "man of bronze," that is not surpassed by the realists of the day. But when he set to work upon Saints and Angels, he must fain idealise and sentimentalise; and so, instead of having a S. Geneviève in modest dress as befits a village maiden, we see a sprawling lady in flowing garments of silk and satin, receiving her guests of kings and queens in a cloudy apartment of the seventh heaven.

The first, or one of the first walls attacked by the decorator was Alexander Cabanel's. Here we have the *Great works of S. Louis* treated in the academic fashion. Learned in composition and refined in style, with a good deal of historical truth in costume and character, it is nevertheless crude and harsh in colour, unharmonious, stagey, and completely undecorative. The best of the panels is *S. Louis learning to read at his mother's knee*, which has a certain pathos in the fair child's expression.

The Coronation of Charlemagne by Leo III. in the old basilica of S. Peter, by Henri Lévy, looks as if it had lost its way, or had been taken to the Panthéon until a suitable dwelling could be found elsewhere. Like Cabanel's *S. Louis*, it is neither Classic, nor Mediæval, nor Modern—simply weak and smooth, respectable and historic, after the manner of the Delaroche school. It is a pity, for, in other hands, these subjects would have been a treasure. Think of the charming frescoes by Olivier-Merson in the gallery of the Cour de Cassation of the Palais de Justice, how exquisite is the simplicity of the boy king, and the grave beauty of his mother. The *Coronation of Charlemagne* is composed as an academician would be sure to conceive the subject. A flight of steps, with the emperor sitting at the top; churchmen and laymen adoring, and an Angel swooping down with a crown. At the bottom of the steps, a warrior standing with sword and shield, and a sitting monk instructing some children from an open book.

Completely opposed to these works are the panels of Puvis de Chavannes, one of the first decorative artists of our time. His painting is vague, and somewhat foggy; his figures are clumsy, thick of ankle, neck, and wrist, but otherwise attenuated to the last degree; and were it not that the far-off people are smaller than those near the spectator, no one would know that they are on different planes, for of aërial perspective there is none. Yet there is a certain purity of sentiment about this, as in all M. de Chavannes' work, which is almost Archaic. The very dulness of the surface and the opacity of the medium employed render these pictures a suitable wall covering for Soufflot's grandiose classicality. The treatment is dignified, poetic, refined, but at the same time intensely modern and realistic—witness a hen and chickens picking up some grain in the foreground, and the charming vistas of landscape background. The colour is tame, and all the members of the Geneviève family are remarkable for plainness, not to say ugliness of face and clumsiness of figure; but the feeling which pervades the whole work is that of a sort of Pagan Renaissance, suitable to Soufflot's "*gâteau de Savoie.*"

The first of the series, properly entitled *La jeunesse et la vie pastorale de Sainte-Geneviève* represents the maiden praying, while a woodcutter and his wife are looking on. The centre and principal compartment is occupied with the discovery by S. Germain of her little saintship, surrounded by her father and mother and a small and admiring crowd. On the left, boatmen are contemplating the scene from the river bank, while upon the right is an old man trying to bend his knee to receive the good bishop's blessing. A youth, sick unto death, and a poor little beggar are being led to the man of God, and two women hurry up from milking to see what is going on. The Seine flows through the pastures of Nanterre, and Mont Valérien smiles down upon the company, not having yet learned the art of war. This is all delightfully pastoral and *naïve.*

PUVIS DE CHAVANNES (FRAGMENT).

The little maid's face, as she looks up at the good bishop, is sweetness itself; the parents bend their heads, and a neighbour holds up her wee swaddled babe; but the *ensemble* is marred by the parrot-like profile of S. Germain and the general ugliness of the company. Ugliness is a veritable passion with Puvis de Chavannes, a gospel which he never loses faith in, a partner allied to eccentricity in all his works.

In another panel we see Faith, Hope, and Charity watching over the child's cradle, by which is a lamb, the emblem of innocence, purity, and the pastoral life. Above is a frieze of saints, illustrating the national religious history of France; SS. Paterne of Vannes, Clément of Metz, Firmin of Amiens, Lucien of Beauvais, Lucain of Beauce, Martail of Limoges, Solange of Berry, Madeleine and Marthe of Provence, Colombe of Sens, Crépin and Crépinien of Soissons, Saturnin of Toulouse, Julien of Brioude, Austremoine of Clermont, Trophime of Arles, and Paul of Narbonne.

The picture by Th. Maillot is equally wanting in aërial perspective, but instead of an obscuring fog overwhelming the good citizens of Paris who are pouring down the "mountain" with S. Geneviève's *châsse*, a glaring sun cuts out the figures from the background. The scene represents a procession through what is now the market of the Place Maubert. It was the 12th of January, 1496; so says a manuscript in the Bibliothèque Nationale. Rain had been pouring down incessantly for an unnatural period, although there was then no Eiffel tower upon which to lay the blame. What was to be done? Clearly an appeal must be made to the patron Saint, and her intercession supplicated to stay the flood. And so the bishop, the abbot, and the canons regular and secular, trudged barefooted down the *montagne*, bearing the *châsse* containing the relics of the maid of Nanterre. An account of the event is given in a letter from Erasmus to his friend Nicholas Werner. The sage was ill of a fever at the time, but that did not prevent him from taking part in the procession, and we easily recognise his familiar physiognomy in the foreground of M. Maillot's work. "Il y a trois mois qu'il pleut ici, sans cesse. La Seine étant sortie de son lit, a inondé la campagne et la ville. La châsse de Sainte Geneviève a été descendue et portée en procession à Notre-Dame. L'évêque, accompagné de son clergé et du peuple, est venu au-devant. Dans cette auguste cérémonie, les chanoines réguliers, précédés de leur abbé marchant nu-pieds, conduisaient les reliques et quatre porteurs en chemise étaient chargés de ce précieux fardeau. Depuis ce temps le ciel est si serein qu'il ne peut l'être davantage."

The bishop is represented with a gilt mitre, the abbot wears a white one. Behind them are the provosts, the military, the magistrates, the canons, and the people, the procession terminating with the king's drummers and trumpeters. The crowd of people seem to be walking, or rather tripping down a very perpendicular street, to cross a zigzag wooden bridge with no side rails. The horizon is close to the top of the frame, so that the *châsse* appears to be falling off the shoulders of the men who are carrying it, and the people seem to be stepping down a steep incline. The colour is bright, and the costumes are picturesque, the whole picture having the effect of an early Flemish work, or of a page torn out of an old manuscript; so early is it in style that it is as incongruous in its place as would be a van Eyck, or a van der Weyden. Imagine Raffaello and Michael Angelo decorating S. Peter's after the manner of Giotto, Botticelli, or Ghirlandajo, and you have no greater incongruity than Maillot's fresco in S. Geneviève. Placed in S. Germain l'Auxerrois, or Notre-Dame, the picture would be in keeping with the architecture; in the Panthéon one feels that the decoration preceded the building.

Totally different in style, but equally out of keeping with the building, are the noble pictures of J. P. Laurens, *The last moments and the funeral of the Saint*. The artist has endeavoured to depict the semi-barbarous Gallo-Roman period. S. Geneviève, old and dying, is surrounded by women who are bringing their children to receive her last blessing. Rich and poor, nobles and serfs, old men and children, matrons and young girls, priests and soldiers—all are tearful at their approaching loss. Splendidly drawn and full of vigour and dramatic power (which are the characteristics of all M. Laurens' works) the pictures are somewhat black in colour; and, by reason of their very strength, they look completely out of harmony with the cold, grey purity of this Classic temple. M. J.-P. Laurens is a grand artist, a lover of dramatic effect and movement, but in the *Death of S. Geneviève* he is subdued and reposeful. The grouping of the figures round the bed of the Saint, the wistful gaze of the children, and the prayerful expression of the mothers, are all most truthfully rendered; but might not the Saint have had a little more beauty; might she not have been a little idealised?

M. Bonnat's *Martyrdom of S. Denis* is well known. The Saint, just decapitated, clutches at his head; upon the block blazes a nimbus of the sun tribe; above is an Angel, hurrying down with a palm and crown; general consternation is depicted upon the faces of the assistants, as might be expected. It is a masculine work, full of power, but over dramatic and heavy in colour.

Of J. E. Delaunay's work we can form no idea yet awhile; he began it, but death cut him off too soon, and another must finish it. One of France's greatest artists, the painter of the *Peste à Rom* in the Louvre, is not likely to have failed in his designs for the Panthéon. Baudry was also commissioned, but he, too, went all too soon, or we might have had some panels which would have been fit *pendants* to those of Puvis de Chavannes.

The *Return of Clovis from Tolbiac*, by M. Joseph Blanc, is also academic and correct; superb in drawing, and sober of colour, its chief interest is in the fact that it contains contemporary portraits—Gambetta, Arago, Lockroy; and Coquelin figuring as a monk.

Jeanne d'Arc is no more fortunate here than elsewhere; it seems as if she were an impossibility in art. When one contemplates the number of painters, sculptors, poets, and musicians who have essayed her history and sung her praises, one is appalled by the results. One of the most sublime pages of history; the finest character among heroines; the grandest of women, of patriots, and of dreamers; the most modest, the most saint-like, the most unselfish of warriors, *la Pucelle* seems to oppress everyone who tries to depict any scene from her life. Perhaps the greatest success of modern times is Frémiet's fine Renaissance statue in the Place des Pyramids. Very beautiful also is Bastien-Lepage's *Jeanne* as a whole; but the figure does not possess the nobleness which one attaches to the militant maiden. Certainly M. Lenepveu's compositions form no exception to the general failure of Jeannes d'Arc. The maid is tied to the stake surrounded by a goodly assemblage of faggots; one monk reads, another flings a cross into her hands—as if the poor maid had objected to the cross! Soldiers are all about, and old Rouen at the back is picturesque with its gabled houses, and the cathedral in the distance. A man is just seizing a torch, and you know the end is near; but you are not impressed; you either do not care, or you do not realise the horror. But it is popular with the populace, and so serves one purpose for which it was painted—that of pointing a moral of patriotism and unselfish devotion almost unique but for the recent example of Garibaldi.

Last, but not least, charming in design, refined, and quite in harmony with the style of the building, are the mosaics of A. E. Hébert, which are among the best works of the artist, and quite exempt from the affectation and sentimentality which, somewhat too often, mar his pictures. These compositions occupy the apse. In the centre *Le Christ montre à l'ange de la France les grandes destinées du peuple dont il lui confia la garde.* Below this are the words: *Christus vincit, Christus regnat, Christus imperat.* At the side of the Saviour is the Blessed Virgin interceding for France; near her, the patroness, clad as a shepherdess, with a lamb under her arm, is praying for the city under the symbol of a ship. Above are the following subjects, *The baptism of Clovis by S. Remi in the presence of S. Clotilde; S. Louis seated between Justice and Power; Jeanne d'Arc listening to the voices.*

LA JEUNESSE DE SAINTE-GENEVIÈVE, PUVIS DE CHAVANNES.

The ornamental framing of the several pictures has been executed by a master of decorative art, the late V. Galland. The borders are formed of garlands of flowers in a low scale of colour, which are divided at regular intervals by tablets bearing inscriptions and monograms. On the whole, the decoration of the Panthéon gives little encouragement to other nations who are desirous of covering large surfaces of wall in their public buildings. The art seems to be lost; for if the greatest of the French painters have, from one reason and another, failed to produce an harmonious scheme of decoration, who is likely to succeed? At best, the church presents a sort of *pot-pourri*. No schools are so dramatic as the French; and yet these wall paintings fail to impress us in the same way as do those, for example, of the Riccardi Palace, by Benozzo Gozzoli. It is probably the religious spirit which is wanting. We can draw better and paint better than the early Italian or Flemish artists—but the sentiment is lacking; and thus, whether we turn to Paris or München, to Berlin or London, we find the decoration of large buildings, and particularly of churches, more or less a failure. Perhaps the worst examples are the terribly dismal, cold, maudlin Nibelung series at München, compared to which the Panthéon is Raffaelesque. Had Puvis de Chavannes been allowed to do the whole church, the result would have been certainly more harmonious, and possibly more edifying; but though gaining in harmony, the frescoes might possibly have lost in variety. Sometimes too much of a good thing results in a wearisome monotony.

Sculpture will also be represented later on by a group of the Revolution, by Falguière; and doubtless we shall have monuments to Victor Hugo, Rénan, and other *grands hommes*, from their grateful country. Let us hope the decoration may always be as Catholic as heretofore; for S. Louis, Clovis, Geneviève and Jeanne d'Arc form as much a part of the history of France as do Voltaire, Mirabeau, Danton, and Dumouriez. We may not care to sing the "Marseillaise" with Camille Desmoulins, and we may wish we could forget the fourteenth Louis and all the Napoléons; but it is as foolish to deny their influence upon the nation as to sponge out the fact recorded on a door-head that Louis-Napoleon joined the Louvre and the Tuileries.

SAINT-GERMAIN L'AUXERROIS.

Between the years 420 and 430, the ancient British church became infected with the heresy of Pelagianism, "which budded forth afresh into this island," as Camden says; and the orthodox clergy, being unable to stay its progress, sent to Gaul desiring assistance. Thereupon a synod of the Gallican church was held, and it was determined to send Germanus, bishop of Auxerre, and Lupus, bishop of Troyes, to confute the heretics. The date assigned to this event by Prosper, a contemporary writer (and also Camden), is 429; but he makes no allusion to Lupus, whose participation in the mission rests upon the evidence of Constantius of Lyons, the biographer of S. Germanus. This Lupus was a brother of Vincent of Lerins, a famous teacher, and the author of *A Defence of the Catholic Faith*, a book which was of much use to Cranmer and Ridley at the time of the Reformation. The meeting appointed for the public disputation with the Pelagians is supposed to have taken place at Verulam, now S. Albans, Hertfordshire, in 429; and according to the Venerable Bede's account, the heretics came to the council in great pomp, and advocated their cause with much "inflated rhetoric." But to no end. Germanus and Lupus silenced them with overwhelming arguments, and they were utterly discomfited. Bede's account is so quaint, and shows so great a difference between a 5th and a 19th century council that it is worth while to quote it in full: "An immense multitude was there assembled with their wives and children. The people stood round as spectators and judges; but the parties present differed much in appearance. On the one side was divine faith, on the other human presumption; on the one side piety, on the other pride; on the one side Pelagius, on the other Christ. The most holy priests Germanus and Lupus permitted their adversaries to speak first, who long took up the time and filled the ears with empty words. Then the venerable prelates poured forth the torrent of their apostolical and evangelical eloquence. Their discourse was interspersed with scriptural sentences, and they supported their most weighty assertions by reading the written testimonies of famous writers. Vanity was convinced, and perfidiousness confuted; so that at every objection made against them, not being able to reply, they confessed their errors. The people, who were judges, could scarce refrain from violence, but signified their judgment by their acclamations."

It is worth noting that at this time the *people were the judges in matters theological.* Rather a different state of things from that which now prevails at Rome and other places; but perhaps a return to primitive custom might not tend to increase peace, or help us out of our theological troubles.

When the meeting of the synod was over, Germanus and his companion seemed to have helped the Britons in a war against a wandering contingent of Pagan Saxons and Picts, and by a simple stratagem, worthy a better cause, routed the enemy. Germanus assembled the British troops in a hollow surrounded by hills, and enjoined his followers to shout "Alleluia" three times. This they did, and the echo taking up the sound, produced such an effect upon the enemy that they took flight for

SAINT-GERMAIN AND THE MAIRIE.

fear of the multitude which they thought had come out against them. The battle took place, as Constantius relates, "when the sacred days of Lent were at hand, which the presence of the divines rendered more solemn, insomuch that those instructed by their daily preaching flocked eagerly to the grace of baptism. For the great multitude of the army was desirous of the water of the laver of salvation. A church formed of interwoven branches of trees is prepared against the day of the resurrection of our Lord, and though the expedition was encamped in the field, is fitted up like that of a city. The army wet with baptism advances, the people are fervent in faith, and neglecting the protection of arms, they await the assistance of the Deity. In the meantime, this plan of proceeding, or state of the camp, is reported to the enemy, who, anticipating a victory over an unarmed multitude, hastened with alacrity. But their approach is discovered by the scouts; and when, after concluding the solemnities of Easter, the greater part of the army, fresh from their baptism, were preparing to take up arms and give battle, Germanus offers himself as the leader of the war." Such is Constantius' account of the opening of the battle, which may be completed with Fuller's: "God sent a hollowness into the hearts of the Pagans; so that their apprehensions added to their ears, and cowardice often resounded the same shout in their breasts, till beaten with the reverberation thereof, without striking a blow, they confusedly ran away; and many were drowned for speed in the river Alen, lately the Christians' font, now the Pagans' grave. Thus a bloodless victory was gotten, without sword drawn, consisting of no fight, but a fright and a flight; and that 'Alleluia,' the song of the saints after conquest achieved, was here the forerunner and procurer of victory; so good a *grace* it is to be said both before and after a battle."

Although this "Alleluiatic victory," as we have seen, is related by Bede (who copied it from Constantius) and Fuller, it does not appear that the Welsh MSS. take any notice of it, and its truth is doubted by Dr. Whitaker in his *Ancient Cathedral of Cornwall*; but, says Mr. Yeowell, "that a battle was fought at Maesgarmon, in the parish of Mold, Flintshire, under circumstances which were afterwards improved into a miracle, is not improbable; and there are names of places in that neighbourhood which show that the district has, for some reason or other, been tenacious of the memory of S. Germain."[*] Pelagius himself was a Welshman given to travel—he visited Italy, Africa, and even Palestine; and it was at Rome that the evil communications of one Rufinus, a man deeply imbued with the principles of Origen, corrupted his good faith in regard

---

[*] *Chronicles of the Ancient British Church.* James Yeowell.

to the doctrine of original sin. But the heresy appears to have been introduced into Britain by Agricola, a Gallic bishop, and Celestius.

After this victory the good bishop returned to his own country; but in 447, the Pelagians again becoming aggressive, he took a second journey to Britain, and this time not only baffled the heretics, but banished them. "News is brought out of Britain," says Constantius, "that the Pelagians' perverseness is again diffused by a few preachers. The supplications of all are once more conveyed to this most blessed man that he would come and preserve the cause of God, which he had formerly won. With this petition he hastily complies, being delighted with the labour, and willingly spending himself for Christ." This time Germanus was attended by one of Lupus' scholars, "a man of all sanctity, who, being then consecrated bishop of Trèves, was preaching the word of life to the inhabitants of Germania Prima." On their arrival, they were again met by a great multitude, whom they blessed; and then preaching the word of God, discomfited the heretics and banished them from the island.

Germanus seems to have reformed the British Church, and modelled it upon the Gallican; for it was about his time, and no doubt through his influence, that parochial churches were founded in country places; the rural populations having previously depended upon missionaries from the towns and monasteries for their spiritual teaching. But in 442, the council of Vaison, in Gaul, decreed that presbyters should be attached to country parishes as well as to the city churches.

Germanus is thought by some authorities to have introduced the Gallican liturgy into Britain; he certainly established schools of learning, colleges and monasteries, where study was the principal work accomplished. During the Roman occupation of the country, there were no doubt professors of Greek and Latin in all the chief cities, possibly at London, York, and Caerleon; for it is not probable that the edict of Gratian, which required all the chief cities of the Empire to maintain such professorships, should not have been in force in Britain. But after the withdrawal of the Roman legions, it became difficult to keep up these professorships; and hence the foundation of monasteries, as schools of learning for the training of youths for the service of the Church, was suggested by Germanus; and to this end he consecrated Dubricius archbishop of

Llandaff, and Daniel bishop of Bangor, besides appointing Iltutus to a place which took his name—Llan Iltut. The former founded colleges at Hentland-on-the-Wye (where he had a thousand pupils), and Llancarfan, or Llanfeithin, Caerworgorn, and Caerleon. The word *bangor* in Welsh is simply a name for any college; and towards the end of the 5th century all Christian societies began to assume that epithet, *ban*, high; *côr*, circle or congregation. The word is written variously (in MSS.), "Ban Cor," "Banchor," and "Bangor." Bangor Garmon, or the College of Germanus, at Llanveiltrin, in Glamorgan, was founded by him in 460. The congregation instituted by the Emperor Theodosius in Caer Worgorn having been destroyed by the Irish in the middle of the 5th century, was restored by Germanus, who placed Iltutus over it. This is now called in Welsh, "Llanilltyd Vawr," in Glamorganshire. According to the Triads, it contained no less than two thousand four hundred members, one hundred being employed every hour in order that the praise and service of God might be continued day and night without intermission. Gildas, the historian, and Talhaiarn, the bard, are said to have been educated there; and S. Cadvan and S. Padarn, the companions of S. Germanus, were among the members of the college until their appointment to similar work elsewhere. The College of S. Cadoc was also founded under the direction of Germanus and Catog, who preferred a life of study and religion to succession to his father's principality.

Little is known of the internal regulations of these colleges, but the dicipline instituted by S. Columba, about a hundred years later, was very severe. Religious offices were held three times during the day, and as often during the night. Each day office consisted of prayers and three psalms, and in the night ones, from October to February, the monks were to chant thirty-six psalms and twelve anthems at three different times; but on Saturday and Lord's Day nights, twenty-five psalms and as many anthems. That such training raised up a set of men who went by the names of "*Ordo Apostolicus*," "*Ordo Divi Colombæ*," is not astonishing, although by themselves they were called "*Famuli Dei*," the servants of God.

That S. Germanus was a remarkable man there is no doubt, as we also owe the discovery of S. Geneviève to his foresight; for when he saw her at Nanterre, on his way to Britain, he was so impressed by her piety that he consecrated her to the service of God.

SAINT-GERMAIN L'AUXERROIS.

The church in Paris was probably founded in commemoration of some miracle performed by the bishop during his sojourn in that city, perhaps by his namesake S. Germain of Paris, who held the memory of his brother of Auxerre in great esteem and veneration. That its origin was very ancient is shown by the record of certain gifts from King Childebert and Queen Ultrogothe. It was probably a round church in its early days, as in 866, when it was pillaged and destroyed by the Normans, it was called S. Germain-le-Rond, and it must have been in that edifice that S. Landry, bishop of Paris, was buried. Formerly a chapter composed of a dean, a precentor, thirteen canons, and eleven chaplains, served the church, and it ranked

SAINT-GERMAIN, FROM AN OLD ENGRAVING.

immediately after the cathedral; but in 1744, its chapter was merged into that of Notre-Dame, and it became a simple parish church.

The Quai and Place de l'École, situated near S. Germain, owed their names, as early as the 13th century, to a public school of great celebrity, which was established about, or soon after, the time of Charlemagne. S. Germain was rebuilt by King Robert, and again in the 12th century, to which period the tower belongs. The principal door, the choir, and the apse are of the 13th century; the porch, the greater part of the *façade*, the nave and aisles, and the chapels of the *chevet*, are of the 15th and 16th centuries. The cloister which surrounded the church has disappeared, as also the dean's house which stood in the space between the church and the Louvre. It was in traversing the cloisters of S. Germain that Admiral Coligny was shot, and it was the great bell of this church which gave the signal for the massacre of S. Bartholomew. S. Germain was the parish church of the Louvre and the Tuileries, and some of the royal children were baptised there; and many a time the kings went there in great state to perform their paschal duties.

The portico projects in front of the three principal West doors, and is the work of Master Jean Gaussel. It was constructed in 1435, and is a mass of very beautiful carving. Some of the corbels are examples of the grotesque imagery of the period. The interior was decorated with frescoes some years ago, but they are in a parlous, peeling, condition. Two of the statues are old, S. Francis of Assisi, and S. Mary of Egypt holding the three little loaves which nourished her in the desert. The central doorway is of the 13th century, the two side ones are of the 15th. The whole is decorated with statues of various Saints —amongst others S. Germain, S. Vincent, and S. Geneviève holding her candle, which a hideous little demon is trying to extinguish. Round the tympanum, the subject of which is the Last Judgment, are the Wise and Foolish Virgins, the Apostles and the Martyrs. Abraham sits on one side holding a napkin on which are three little souls; while upon the other is a cauldron from the lower regions containing three lost souls (one mitred), and two horrible demons—one tormenting a soul with a whip, the other throwing a poor creature into the flames, having already torn his flesh into shreds. The gargoyles are peculiarly grotesque: a grinning savage is being ejected from the jaws of a hippopotamus; a man carries a hooded ape on his shoulders; and a showman is making a monkey dance. A corbel shows us a quantity of rats persecuted by a cat—the rats being the wicked who encumber the earth; the cat, the demon who awaits their souls.

The plan of the church is cruciform; the entire length is 240 ft., and the width at the transepts 120 ft. The interior is very plain, that is to say, what remains of the old church after the embellishments of the renovating architects of 1745. These gentlemen fluted the pillars of the choir, and converted the mouldings of the capitals into garlands and flowery festoons,

INTERIOR OF SAINT-GERMAIN L'AUXERROIS.

giving the whole a grandly Classic appearance. Happily they left the arches pointed, instead of filling them in with round-headed ones as at S. Séverin; and, likewise, we may be thankful that the nave was not "improved," and that the bosses and the ornament of the Lady Chapel were allowed to remain in their primitive beauty. Among the subjects of the bosses may be cited a S. Christopher crossing a torrent with the infant Christ on his shoulder; and a S. Germain in episcopal vestments, painted and gilt, may be seen upon an openwork ground in the Lady Chapel.

In 1744 the choir was enclosed by a magnificent screen, the combined work of Pierre Lescot and Jean Goujon;[*] but the *curé* and churchwardens, upon the suppression of the chapter, lost no time in destroying this work of art, in order to open up the east end of the church to the congregation—not the only case of its kind.

Had the modern improvers of the church only pulled this down they might have been forgiven, but they did not rest until they had appointed an architect named Bacarit to "purify" the church of its "*barbarie Gothique.*" Unfortunately for the reputation of the academicians of 1745, the project submitted to, and approved by them, appears to us, so far as it was carried out, to be a decided *barbarie Classique;* and even in the beginning of this century, when the Empire had introduced a sort of pseudo-Classic style, and made it fashionable, people of taste were no less severe upon the re-dressing of the old pillars and capitals in Greek garments: "Nearer to my residence, and of a kindred style of architecture, is the Church of S. Germain Auxerrois. The west front is yet sound and good. Nothing particular strikes you on the entrance, but there are some interesting specimens of rich old stained glass in the windows of the transept. The choir is completely and cruelly modernised. In the side chapels are apparently several good modern paintings; and over an altar of twisted columns, round which ivy leaves apparently composed of ivory are creeping, is a picture of three figures in the flames of purgatory. This side chapel is consecrated to the offering up of orisons 'for the souls in purgatory.' It is gloomy and repulsive. Death's heads

---

[*] Some of the bas-reliefs by Jean Goujon are now in the Renaissance Museum of the Louvre: a Deposition from the Cross, and the four Evangelists, the latter having been discovered in 1850, embedded in the wall of the staircase of No. 4, Rue S. Hyacinthe-S.-Honoré.

and thigh bones are painted in white colours upon the stained wall; and in the midst of all these fearful devices I saw three young ladies intensely occupied in their devotions at the railing facing the altar." *

The chapels of the *chevet* have niches in the wall surmounted by round-headed arches, and containing statues. There are in all thirteen chapels, but four of them have been converted into a sacristy and the north door, the exterior of which is a good specimen of Renaissance work.

The abbé Lebeuf attributed some of the glass of the choir to the commencement of the 14th century, but not a vestige of this remains; there is nothing earlier than the two following centuries. Here also the good gentlemen of the 18th century "improved" much; the church was dark and gloomy, and so, forsooth, the stained glass of the nave was taken out, and the colour, and golden *fleurs-de-lys* of the vaults and columns, were scraped off or whitewashed over. Thus was lost the history of S. Germain which formed the subject of the windows. But happily the rose-windows of the two transepts, four lights in the south aisle and two of the north aisle, still remain; but these being only of the 16th century, are consequently not in the best taste. Some have Gothic and some Renaissance surroundings, but the colour is, if rather bright, clear and rich. Unfortunately, time has obliterated many of the heads and hands; but enough remains to make out the subjects. In the north rose, the Eternal Father, in a Papal tiara, is surrounded by Angels, Cherubim, Martyrs, and Confessors; amongst whom may be recognised SS. Catherine, Vincent, Margaret, Agnes, Martha, Germain, and King Louis. Above and below are the four Fathers of the Latin Church. In the north transept the subjects are taken from The Passion, The Acts of our Lord, Scenes in the Life of the Patriarch Abraham, a gentleman donor accompanied by his sons, and a lady followed by her daughters, a S. Peter, and S. Anne instructing her daughter, and patronising another donor. In the southern rose, the Holy Spirit descends from Heaven in the form of a dove; The Blessed Virgin and The Apostles receiving light from above, with enthusiastic expressions upon their visages. In the southern transept: The Incredulity of S. Thomas; The Ascension; The Death of the Virgin; and The Assumption. Above, the Coronation of the Virgin and a well, recalling the attribute "Well of living water"

* Dibden.

given to her by the Fathers. There are a great many modern windows, but except those in imitation of the glass in the S. Chapelle, by MM. Lassus and Didron, they are of little artistic value. M. Lassus was the architect who superintended all the later restorations and decorations.

The chapel of the Blessed Virgin is a little church in itself, with stalls, organ, pulpit, screen and altar, all richly decorated. The reredos is the tree of Jesse which surrounds the Virgin with its branches. This is in stone, of the 14th century, and comes from a church in Champagne. Some restorations in 1838 brought to light a curious 16th century wall painting, representing a cemetery with the graves giving up their dead to the sound of the Angels' trumpets. Three statues were also found of the same date as the chapel, and serve as the retable of the altar: they represent the Blessed Virgin sitting, and S. Germain and S. Vincent (who are united in all the decorations of this church), standing on each side of her. The *banc-d'œuvre* was executed in 1648 by Mercier, from drawings by Lebrun. It is handsome in its way, and excellently carved, but utterly out of keeping with the rest of the church. It is composed of Ionic columns supporting a huge baldachino; and probably looked its best when it was filled with royal personages on high festivals and state occasions. Another exquisite example of wood carving may be seen in the chapel of Notre-Dame de Compassion, forming the retable. It belongs to the latest Gothic period, and is covered with a multitude of figures, representing the Genealogy and History of the Virgin, and the Life and Death of Christ. This came from a Belgian church. The organ, pulpit, and stalls are part of the old furniture, but are not remarkable in any way.

S. Germain was formerly a museum of tombs of the 16th and 17th centuries; but the only remaining ones are the recumbent marble figures by Laurent Magnier, of Etienne d'Aligre, and his sons, both chancellors of France, who died respectively in 1635 and 1677; two statues and several marble busts which belonged to the mausoleums of the house of Rostaing, formerly situated in S. Germain, and in a chapel of the monastery of the Feuillants; and an epitaph of a lady of Mortemart, Duchess of Lesdiguières, who died in 1740.* Under the church is a

---

* The fine recumbent statues of Louis de Poncher, *conseilleur et receveur-trésorier du roi François Ier*, and his wife Roberte Legende, now in the Renaissance Museum of the Louvre, were formerly in S. Germain.

crypt full of bones, symmetrically arranged as in the catacombs: it was excavated in 1746-7 as a burial place for the parishioners.

Amongst the tombs of a crowd of courtiers and statesmen were those of Malherbe, the poet; André Dacier, the *savant;* the painters Coypel, Houasse, Stella and Santerre; the sculptors Sarazin, Desjardins, and Coyzevox; the medallist Warin; the goldsmith Balin; the engraver Israël Sylvestre; the architects Louis Levau and François Dorbay; the geographer Sanson; and the Comte de Caylus, the distinguished antiquary; but they have all disappeared. The grandest tomb was that erected by Charles V. to his jester. Says Sauval, in his *History of Paris* (which was not published until after his death, in 1670): "Charles ne s'est pas contenté d'avoir des fous et des plaisants; il leur a encore dressé des mausolées, presque aussi superbes que celui du connétable Du Guesclin. Car j'apprends des registres de la chambre des Comptes, qu'il en fit enterrer un dans l'église de Saint-Germain l'Auxerrois. Sur une grande tombe de marbre noir était couchée de côté une figure peinte et grande comme nature, dont la tête et les mains étaient d'albâtre, les cuisses, les jambes, les pieds et le corps de marbre blanc, et qui servit de modèle au mausolée qu'il fit faire en 1375, à Thévenin, autre fou, dans l'église de Saint-Maurice (de Senlis), par Hennequin de la croix." But even in the time of Sauvel this curious work of art was no more.

A few fragments of former monuments have found a quiet resting-place in the Louvre, in the Renaissance Museum. Calvin lived near S. Germain; and at the dean's house, between the Louvre and the church, a celebrity of another kind died suddenly on Easter-Eve, 1599—"la belle Gabrielle d'Estrées." The Maréchal d'Ancre (Concini) was also buried at S. Germain after his assassination; but the body was torn from the grave the next day by an infuriated mob, who drew it through the street on hurdles, then hung it, and finally burnt it.

SAINT-GERMAIN-EN-LAYE.

The Château of S. Germain has existed since the time of Charles V., and has received additions during the reigns of François I., Henri II., Henri IV., and Louis XIII. It was given over to James II. of England, and in the church is his monument, gazed at, if bronze eyes can penetrate stone walls, by M. Thiers, who sits in an arm-chair outside.

THE CHAPEL OF THE CHÂTEAU OF SAINT-GERMAIN.

SAINT-GERMAIN DES PRÉS.

The Abbey of S. Germain-in-the-fields, of which nothing remains but the church and the abbot's palace, was, after Notre-Dame, the oldest foundation in Paris. It dates back to the earliest period of the French monarchy, and its history is interwoven with that of some of the best and noblest sons of France. The Saint to whom this church is dedicated was an early bishop of Paris, and must not be confounded with S. Germain of Auxerre, whose legend is described on page 178.

The foundation of the abbey was in this wise. Childebert I. having made a second expedition against the Visigoths in Spain, returned in 543 with much loot of various kinds: S. Vincent's tunic; a rich gold cross ornamented with precious stones, from Toledo; some vases which had belonged (so said tradition) to King Solomon; and a quantity of chalices, patens and golden covers for the Gospels. What could be more natural, in the 6th century, than to consult a holy man as to the future destination of such valuables? Accordingly, Childebert communed with S. Germain on the subject, and the bishop suggesting the foundation of a church as a fitting home for the treasures, the king laid the first stone amid the green fields and woods of what is now the densely populated Faubourg S. Germain. The enclosure extended from the Rue Jacob on the north, to the Rue Ste. Marguerite on the south, while upon the east and west the boundaries were the present Rue Lachaudé and the Rue Bonaparte. The buildings within the precincts were very numerous, almost forming a city in themselves, enclosed by walls and surrounded by a moat filled by the waters of the Seine. There were three gates: the Petit-Bourbon, Ste. Marguerite, and St. Benoit. The church was originally dedicated to the Holy Cross and S. Vincent, the consecration taking place upon the very day of Childebert's death in 558.* It was cruciform in plan; the roof, which was

* "Après avoir," says Grégoire of Tours, "été longtemps malade à Paris, le roi Childebert y mourut et fut enseveli dans la basilique de Saint-Vincent qu'il avait lui-même construite." The bones of Childebert and of his queen, Ultrogothe, were deposited (in 1656) in the centre of the choir. The religious placed them in a new marble tomb, and surmounted it with the antique one which had been repaired in the 11th century, when the church was restored by abbot Morard and his successors. Ultrogothe was a French S. Elizabeth: "Elle était la mère des orphelins, la consolatrice des pupilles, la bienfaitrice des pauvres et des serviteurs de Dieu, le secours des moines fidèles."

Another lady much vaunted by Grégoire de Tours was Ingoberge, the widow of Chérebert. She called in the aid of Grégoire in her last moments, and made many donations to churches; and what was better, "elle donna la liberté à beaucoup de personnes." She was a woman "d'une grande sagesse, vouée à la vie religieuse, assidue aux veilles, aux prières, aux aumônes."

covered with plaques of gilt copper, was supported by
enormous marble columns; the walls, decorated with paintings
upon gold grounds, were pierced with numberless windows;
and the pavement was laid in mosaic. At the end of the
church was the chapel of S. Symphorien, which in 576 became
the burial-place of good Bishop Germain, and was subsequently
the scene of many wondrous and miraculous cures, so many
indeed that the original patrons, S. Vincent, S. Symphorien,
and the Holy Cross, drifted into almost complete oblivion;
and S. Germain, getting the credit of the cures, became the
acknowledged and chief patron of the famous abbey. Before
the foundation of S. Denis by *le bon roy Dagobert*, S. Germain
served as the burial-place of the Mérovingian kings and their
consorts. Thus, during the 6th and 7th centuries, the following princes were interred there: the Kings Childebert I.,
Chérebert,* Chilpéric I., Clotaire II., and Childéric II.; the
queens Ultrogothe, Frédégonde, Bertrude, and Bilihilde; the
sons of Mérovée, Clovis, and Dagobert; the princesses Chro-
desinde and Chrotberge, daughters of the first Childebert.
Some of these tombs were opened in the time of Dom Bouillart (1655), who gives an account of the performance in his
Histoire de l'Abbaye. The bodies were swathed in shrouds
of silk and other precious stuffs; some of them reposed on
beds of odorous herbs, others were surrounded by phials of
aromatic scents. The coffins were of stone, without any exterior ornament, and contained, besides the bodies, fragments
of drapery, of crossbelts, and foot gear.† Some of these stone
coffins may be seen at the Hôtel Carnavalet, which, besides
having been the dwelling-place of Madame de Sevigné, is most

---

* In 1704, a tomb was found which Montfaucon, a Benedictine of the
congregation of S. Maur, considered to be that of Chérebert, but the
General of the order would not consent to its being opened. However,
in 1799, less reverent hands searched the spot, found the coffin, and
opened it, only to discover a skeleton vested in a tunic and mantle, its feet
shod in leathern shoes, and by its side the fragments of what may have been
a crozier, thus proving the remains to have been those of an abbot rather
than of a sovereign, but whether of the 6th or the 9th century it was impossible to decide.

† "Les tombeaux les plus considérables furent ceux du roy Childéric
II., de Bilihilde, son épouse, et du jeune Dagobert, leur fils, qui furent
tuez par Baudillon, dans le forêt de Liori. On trouva ces tombeaux dans le
chœur." In cleaning the coffin "Childre rex" was found engraved by the
side of the head.

interesting on account of its unique collection of curiosities. But we have been anticipating.

When the abbey was finished, S. Germain sent to its namesake, S. Symphorien at Autun, for some monks to serve it. At first they followed the rules of S. Anthony and S. Basil; but shortly after the foundation, they joined the order of the great legislator of the monks of the west, S. Benedict. In the 17th century a second reform took place, and they adopted the rule of S. Maur; and it was after this return to primitive discipline that the monks of S. Germain became famous throughout Europe by the works of Jean Mabillon, Bernard de Montfaucon, and other members of their order. The abbots were formerly all-powerful, exercising spiritual and temporal jurisdiction over the whole Faubourg S. Germain; but jealousies occurring there as elsewhere, between the ecclesiastical and the lay element, and squabbles arising between the bishops and the mitred abbots, it came about that the kings, uniting their forces with those of the bishops, were enabled to restrict the power of the abbots to the immediate precincts of their abbey. Among the famous persons who bore the dignity of abbot of S. Germain were Hugues Capet, Jean Casimir, King of Poland, several princes of the House of Bourbon, and many cardinals.

When the Normans swooped down upon France, Paris was their goal, and the monasteries and churches their desire. Over and over again they came; pillaging, burning and destroying all they could not carry off. Once in, or near Paris, S. Germain lay at their feet; its fame, its riches, its magnificence, made it a mark for attack; and upon one occasion, when King Eudes had driven out the barbarians, all that was left of church and monastery was a heap of ruins. But Morard, the twenty-ninth abbot, who ruled the community from 990 to 1014, undertook the entire restoration, or rather the rebuilding of the abbey; and it is to him that we owe the oldest portions of the nave of the actual church. Whether Morard left the work unfinished, or whether the monks resolved to improve upon his design, we know not; but about a hundred and fifty years later we find the choir being rebuilt upon a plan of great magnificence.

Situated as it was, amidst what was termed the *Pré-aux-Clercs*, the resort of students and other bellicose persons, it became necessary to guard against assaults and incursions, by surrounding the monastic buildings with fortified walls and a moat, strong gates and watch-towers, from whence to keep an eye upon dangerous neighbours. Later, when students at the University had become more civilized, when danger of civil war had faded away, and the Huguenots had been suppressed, streets took the place of the moat, and houses occupied the site of the fortifications. At the commencement of the last century the monks built several large houses from plans by Victor d'Ailly, for artisans and labourers; but for the privileges obtained by living within the abbey precincts they paid a heavy rental. These habitations formed the Rues Childebert, Ste. Marthe, Cardinale, Abbatiale, and de Furstemberg—all within the walls. Originally there were two cloisters situated to the north of the church, but with the exception of a portion of the larger one, which has been converted into dwelling-rooms, they have been completely destroyed. The round arches and Doric pilasters belong to the 17th century; the older part, which was built by Abbot Eudes, was cut through and improved away, for the completion of the Rue de l'Abbaye. The same streets, and the houses thereof, have also to answer for the destruction of the refectory, the chapter-house, the great sacristy, and the Lady Chapel, to which the little cloister gave access. The refectory was a large hall constructed during the life of Abbot Simon by the celebrated architect of the Sainte-Chapelle, Pierre de Montereau. It was filled with stained glass bearing the arms of France and of Castille, some fragments of which may be seen in the church. The stone statue of Childebert, that stood at the entrance gorgeous with painting and gilding, is now in the Renaissance Museum of the Louvre. Dom Jacques Bouillart, describing the refectory as built between 1239-44, speaks of this statue as "apparently modelled upon a more ancient one."* De Montereau was also the artist-builder of the chapel of the Virgin, commenced under abbot Hugues d'Issy, who died in 1247, and finished under Thomas de Mauléon, who resigned his dignities in 1255. This chapel had but one rival, the *chef-d'œuvre* of its architect; but

* "L'on a placé à la porte du réfectoire une statue de pierre qui représente Childebert, laquelle a été faite apparemment sur le modèle d'une autre plus ancienne. Elle est haute de cinq pieds et demi. Childebert a une couronne ornée de trèfles et une sceptre en la main dont l'estrémité d'en haut est cassée. Il a une robe qui descend jusqu'à la cheville du pied; sa ceinture est ornée, d'espace en espace, de petites roses façon d'orfévrerie; son manteau, qui ne le couvre que par derrière, est attaché au devant par un cordon qu'il tient de la main gauche; ses souliers, pointus par le bout, sont échancrés en ovale par le dessus, depuis la moitié du pied jusqu'à la ligature."

all authorities speak of the beauty and gracefulness of the Lady Chapel, and its similarity to the Sainte-Chapelle in style and plan. When the great architect died, in 1266, the then abbot Gérard de Moret, desiring to perpetuate the memory of him who had done so much to beautify the convent, caused a magnificent tomb to be erected in the chapel of his creation. Pierre was represented with a rule and compass in his hand, and the epitaph describes him as *Flos plenus morum* and *Doctor latomorum.** Gérard be Moret was the builder of the chapter house, an oblong edifice divided into two naves by a row of four central columns, paved with encaustic tiles and illuminated with stained glass. Passing behind the church down the Rue de l'Abbaye, is the abbot's palace, a handsome stone and red-brick building erected by the Cardinal de Bourbon, about 1586. At the summit of one of the pavilions is a figure of a woman bearing the arms of the founder upon an escutcheon. Fragments of the chapel of Our Lady, columns, capitals, gargoyles, balustrades, and other remains of ornament which were found in a garden hard by, have been placed in the grounds of the Hôtel Cluny; but the statue of the Virgin and Child, which was formerly upon a pier, was sent some years ago to S. Denis.

The gaol was rebuilt in the 17th century, and was flanked by four turrets. It was the scene of many horrors from time to time, the abbots possessing the power of punishing as well as of trying criminals; and during the Revolution it was filled with priests and nobles, who suffered for the crimes of their forefathers, as well as for their own, being the scene in 1792 of the hideous September massacres. It was afterwards used as a military prison, and in 1854 was pulled down. The library was justly celebrated for its manuscripts, printed books, and other objects of value; but was destroyed by fire at the commencement of the Revolution.

The only part of the church which contains any remains of Childebert's structure is the apse, into the triforium of which are built some early white marble capitals and some various coloured marble shafts; but inasmuch as they have been painted over, all interest in them is destroyed.

The earliest part of the present church dates from the beginning of the 11th century, the choir and apse from the second half of the 12th century. The best view of the apse

---

* The entire epitaph will be found upon page 7.

196 THE CHURCHES OF PARIS.

with its flying-buttresses is to be obtained from the garden of the abbot's palace; but since the clearing away of the houses which formerly were almost built on to the church, and the

SAINT-GERMAIN DES PRÉS.

planting of gardens round it, the view is very picturesque from any point. An insignificant 17th century porch leads to the west door, which is underneath the tower, and has, in its tympanum, a much mutilated bas-relief of *The Last Supper*.

SAINT-GERMAIN DES PRÉS.

The tower has been so much restored and renovated from time to time that little of the original remains. It has a high, but stumpy spire covered with slates. Dom Bouillart relates that on the 2nd November, 1589, Henri IV. mounted to the top of it (accompanied by only one ecclesiastic) to examine the situation of Paris; and, continued the monk, "He afterwards walked round the cloisters, and without speaking one word, departed." Of the other two towers which were formerly at the angles of the choir and transepts, nothing remains but the bases, which were considered necessary for the support of the church. It seems that they were pulled down about 1822, to save the expense of their restoration! a piece of vandalism which destroyed the originality of the building and the *raison d'être* for its nickname of "*l'Église aux Trois Clochers.*"

The building is 265 feet long, 65 feet broad, and 59 feet high. The nave is divided into five bays, the choir into four, and the apse into five; but these latter are much narrower than those of the nave. In the 17th century, the timber roof of Abbot Morard gave place to a stone vault, the transepts were rebuilt, and the nave much altered; but quite recently it has been restored to its primitive condition and decorated with frescoes by Hippolyte Flandrin. The church having been used during the Revolution as a saltpetre manufactory, the corrosive waters had so undermined the foundations of the pillars that they were obliged to be supported by enormous scaffoldings while the bases were repaired.

The choir and the apse are surrounded by square and polygonal chapels. The lower arches are round, the upper pointed; the intermingling being in no way inharmonious. Most of the present capitals are copies of the twelve remaining original ones which were transferred to the garden of the Hôtel Cluny; but they are of very inferior workmanship. The subjects treated are various: Angels, Saints, the Lamb of God, Daniel surrounded by the lions, priests celebrating the Holy Mysteries, Samson breaking the jaw of the lion. The old capitals are rough, but full of character, whereas the modern ones are utterly devoid thereof. A few of the old ones may be studied embedded in the walls of the aisles; the subjects being: The Visitation, The Birth of Christ, Warriors costumed as Roman soldiers, Syrens, male and female, surrounded by fish, interlaced serpents, hippopotami holding smaller beasts between their paws, and other quaint imagery peculiar to the Romanesque period. In the Hôtel Cluny may also be seen the upper part of an early ivory crozier belonging to the abbey, which was found in a coffin during some excavations in 1854—and some fragments of stone coffins. The choir, beautiful in its vigorous simplicity, remains as the 12th century left it. It was dedicated by Pope Alexander III., on the 21st of April, 1163; and on the same day Hubald, bishop of Ostia, assisted by three other bishops, consecrated the apsidal chapels. On entering the church at the west end, and looking towards the altar, it will be seen that the building deviates considerably from a straight line, which M. Guilhermy ascribes rather to difficulties of construction, which always occur when a new building is placed amongst older ones of which it is to be a part, than to the legend which attributes this arrangement (so common in Mediæval churches) to the position of our Lord upon the Cross. S. Étienne du Mont is even more out of a straight line—it turns more than any church I have seen. The columns resemble those of Notre-Dame in their massiveness. All the arches of the choir and chapels are round, but those of the apse and clerestory are pointed. The capitals of these choir pillars are all worthy of study, being in the best style of the period, and full of the quaint symbolism of the Middle Ages: human heads of a grotesque style, lions, harpies, birds pecking vigorously at the heads of men and women, griffins, and winged animals. The bases are all ornamented with foliage; but between the second and third chapels on the south side is an example of ornament which is probably unique, viz., two slippers, one embroidered and one plain, evidently those of a bishop or abbot.

A CAPITAL OF THE CHOIR.

The original High Altar, renovated in 1704, has been destroyed since 1792, up to which time it had existed in all its pristine beauty and splendour. The frontal was of gilt copper, with silver-gilt figures under canopies; and upon the retable rested the *châsse* of S. Germain, a magnificent specimen of smithcraft enriched with precious stones. It was made in the time of Abbot Guillaume III., about 1408 or 1409, and contained twenty-six marks two ounces of gold, 250 marks of silver, 260 precious stones, and 197 pearls. One would like to know what became of so many gems. Six of the cipolin columns of the baldachino, which were brought from the ruins of a Roman town upon the African coast in the reign of Louis XIV., are now doing duty in the gallery of paintings of the Louvre. The tomb of S. Germain, which was the scene of so many miracles and wonders, has been suppressed and covered up by the pavement. It was sunk below the level of the church, near the fourth column of the choir on the north side, and for centuries was a favourite spot for prayer and meditation. The chapel of S. Symphorien, at the end of the nave on the south side, is modern, having been consecrated by the great teacher, S. François de Sales, on the 27th April, 1619; the monument which marked the first burial-place of S. Germain being no longer in it. The chapels of S. Marguerite and of S. Casimir, in the transept, are ornamented with marble columns. That of the Blessed Virgin is modern, and in wretched taste; and the High Altar, the first stone of which was laid by Pius VII., is equally out of keeping with the rest of the church.

In an apsidal chapel are some fragments of 13th century glass, representing SS. Anna and Joachim, The Annunciation and the Marriage of the Virgin. In the south side of the nave is a large marble statue, called Notre-Dame la Blanche, given in 1340 by Jeanne d' Évreux to the Abbey of S. Denis. Placed at the Revolution in the Musée des Petits-Augustins, it was afterwards transferred to S. Germain. The marble statue of S. Marguerite is by one of the brothers of the convent, Jacques Bourlet; and that representing S. François Xavier is by Coustou the younger. The following tombs were partially restored in 1824: Jean Casimir, King of Poland, who, having renounced his throne, became abbot in 1669, and died in 1672 (the kneeling figure is by Marsy, the bas-relief by Jean Thibaut, of the Congregation of S. Maur); Olivier and Louis de Castellan, killed in the service of the king in 1644 and 1669 (the figures and medallions are by Girardon); William Douglas, eighteenth Earl of Angus, who died in 1611, and his grandson James Douglas, killed in 1645, near Douai, aged twenty-eight. The epitaphs, which the Academy set up in 1819 to the memory of Nicholas Boileau, of René Descartes,[*] of Jean Mabillion, and of Bernard de Montfaucon, which were formerly at the Musée des Petits-Augustins, were placed here on the dispersal of that museum. Boileau reposed formerly in the Sainte-Chapelle, and Descartes at S. Geneviève. What remained of the royal tombs was transferred to S. Denis. Of the riches of the Treasury nothing whatever was saved; it was all pillaged and dispersed.

The whole church has been painted in polychrome; red shafts and gilded capitals, a blue-and-gold starred vault. All round nave, transepts, and choir, just below the clerestory, are the exquisite frescoes by Flandrin, one of the few 19th century religious painters who has shown the possibility of uniting the sentiment of the early Florentine and Flemish schools with the, in some respects, superior knowledge of the modern. His work is so purely religious, and yet so essentially modern, that one wonders whence he drew his inspiration. There is nothing of the Archaic in his pictures; his figures are never attenuated, and yet the sentiment is as full of piety as in the work of Angelico: it is as if the Frenchman had drunk in the beauty of form of the Greeks, and amalgamated it with the faith of the Early Christians. And yet there is none of the false sentimentality of the modern school, the Saints who simper, and the milk-and-water misses bearing palm branches and crowns, and calling themselves martyrs. Flandrin's is essentially a masculine type of art; it is powerful as well as graceful, vigorous as well as refined. His Saints and Angels have all the sweet expression of those of Fra Angelico and Filippo

---

[*] DESCARTES DONT TU VOIS ICY LA SÉPULTURE,
A DESSILLÉ LES YEUX DES AVEUGLES MORTELS,
ET GARDANT LE RESPECT QUE L'ON DOIT AUX AUTELS,
LEUR A DU MONDE ENTIER DÉMONTRÉ LA STRUCTURE.
SON NOM PAR MILLE ESCRITS SE RENDIT GLORIEUX;
SON ESPRIT MESURONT ET LA TERRE ET LES CIEUX,
EN PÉNÉTRA L' ABISME, EN PERÇA LES NUAGES.
CEPENDANT COMME UN AUTRE IL CÈDE AUX LOIS DU SORT,
LUY QUI VIVROIT AUTANT QUE CES DIVINS OUVRAGES,
SI LE SAGE POUVOIT S' AFFRANCHIR DE LA MORT.

Lippi; while they are as perfectly modelled as a Greek Apollo, or the figures of Buonarroti and Raffaello. But Flandrin was not ashamed of calling himself a believer in the doctrines and mysteries of the Christian faith, and in the Biblical subjects which he was called upon to illustrate. The man who considered religious painting to be "the height of Art, and the most worthy employment of genius," and who wrote upon the door of his studio, "Thou, Lord, hast made me glad through Thy work, I will triumph in the works of Thy hands," could not have been, as a Christian, on a much lower level than Fra Angelico, who is said to have painted while assuming the attitude of prayer. Flandrin was the favourite pupil of Ingres, and won the Grand Prix de Rome of 1832. Humble-minded, gentle, courageous, he worked for love rather than for fame or money. His early struggles when he first arrived in Paris from his native place were terrible. He lived in a veritable garret with his brother, sacrificing anything in order to work at painting. Often in winter they went to bed at 5 o'clock in the afternoon to escape the cold of their attic. Their dinner was frequently some fried potatoes bought at stalls in the streets and squares; and it is probably to the privations endured for love of art that his bad health and early death may be attributed. But his enthusiasm carried him on; and he lived long enough to count his sacrifices as nothing compared to his successes. He stands out in this 19th century an example to all artists, and as the one man who can be compared to the blessed monk of Fiesole.

Like so many artists, he had to surmount many a home obstacle; and, being the fourth of a family of seven children, with two brothers devoting themselves to their father's calling, it is no wonder that the good mother wished Hippolyte to try some trade by which he could live. The father had been ambitious; but had been obliged to give up *genre* for miniature painting. The boys, however, plodded on, and sketched all that came in their way, which seems to have been mainly soldiers; and when a sculptor named Fayatier, happening to see their drawings, gave them a little encouragement, the mother's opposition melted, and they entered the studio of Magnin at Lyons. There and at the Beaux-Arts, they remained seven years, selling drawings and lithographs wherewith to gain a little nest-egg to enable them to go to Paris, the goal then, as now, of ambitious students. It was little enough, but the journey, being taken upon foot, the whole hoard was reserved for household expenses and lessons. Once in the capital, the brothers resolved to put themselves under M. Ingres, if he would allow them, and so encouraging was his welcome, that a friendship soon sprang up between master and pupils. Many traits in Ingres' character which came out in the history of the Flandrins' early artistic career prove him to have been sympathetic to the highest degree; and not a little pleasant is it to find that, when he heard of his pupils' forced asceticism, he exclaimed, "And I was taking their money!" Indeed, there are many anecdotes which prove as much the love of the master for the pupils as the devotion of the pupils for the master. He was inconsolable when Hippolyte failed to gain the *Prix de Rome.* "You have no notion how hard it is for a young man's hopes to be dashed to the ground!" he said to his wife; and he spoke of him as the "Lamb which had been slaughtered." He knew that it was unjust, and he felt the injustice as much as if it had been done to himself.

The account Hippolyte gives his brother Auguste of the whole affair is most touching.* "*Mon bon ami, mon cher* Auguste, I have experienced the last trial in competing for the *Grand Prix*, but it has been dreadful! The subject was a figure in painting, three feet high. I executed it, and yesterday was the day of the decision. I was satisfied with myself, and was hopeful, *mais tu verras*. M. Ingres, M. Guérin, M. Granet, and three other members of the Institute, on entering the exhibition hall, wished to place me first. *Mais non:* M. Gros and his party carried it otherwise; and instead of *first*, I have been voted *last*. M. Ingres, in despair, at length left the room, protesting with all his might against the proceedings of the meeting; and I have not been received. You may imagine what I felt when I heard I was excluded. . . . I dared not call upon M. Ingres; still I could not reproach myself; my figure was far the best; I can say so without pride. At last, in the evening, I determined to go. I found him at dinner, but he ate nothing. Several members of the Institute had come to comfort him, but he would not be consoled. He received me with, "Behold the lamb they have slaughtered!" . . . And all this with the accent of a heart so deeply moved that tears filled his eyes. He made me sit at his table,

---

* See *Les Lettres et Pensées d'Hippolyte Flandrin*, par H. Delaborde.

dine with him, and at last embraced me as a father would his son. I went away and was comforted. Oh! what do not I owe to this man who has already done so much for us, and who, on this occasion, has perhaps done more. . . . But sometimes regret seizes me, for this would have been the means of taking a great step. . . And then it was the only way to show my gratitude to M. Ingres; for to you, my brother, I can say that my good master had founded great hopes on my picture." The next year the same difficulties (want of money to pay for models, &c.) made him almost give up the idea of competing; but getting some portraits to do, and knowing that his master was keen upon the matter, he sent in his name. One of his sitters happened to be a *gen-d'arme*, whom he had promised to paint for 30 fs. When the portrait was finished, the man was so pleased that he said to the painter, "*I promised you 30 fs., but here are 35 fs.!*" Flandrin often said that he never was so pleased as when he received those additional 5 fs.

But a greater enemy to work than poverty appeared—cholera, the scourge of 1832. One of the competitors for the *Prix de Rome* died on his way to the school, and Hippolyte was attacked. He struggled against it, and, weak though he was, he went on working; but at length he had to give way, and for a whole month he was in bed. A few days before the time for sending in the pictures, he returned to work, and managed to finish his subject, which was at once pronounced as having the *Grand Prix*. At Rome, Flandrin was in his element; he studied the great masters, and drank in all their wisdom, working almost entirely upon religious subjects. Even Ary Scheffer, then at the height of his fame, felt the extreme beauty of his young rival's art. "No, I know nothing, nothing at all," he said to Hippolyte, on seeing the latter's picture of *Jesus with the Little Children.*

Flandrin's first commission for Church decoration was in his native city, S. Severinus of Lyon; his second, S. Germain; but his greatest work was the mural painting of S. Vincent de Paul, which he accomplished some years later.

On the 21st of March, 1864, Flandrin died at Rome of small-pox, whither he had gone for his health. He was buried at Père-la-Chaise; but the funeral service was held in the church he did so much to embellish; and, two years after, his friends placed a monument by M. Oudine to his memory, upon the wall of the north aisle. It is composed of white marble, four columns supporting a pediment, and resting upon a freize. Below the bust is an epitaph which is little in keeping with the man or the place:

À HIPPOLYTE FLANDRIN.

SES AMIS, SES ELÈVES, SES ADMIRATEURS, LYON, **22 MARS,** 1809,—ROME, 21 MARS, 1864.

Not one word of what he loved above all things, his home, his country, his art, and his God; and yet his friends, his pupils, and in fact everyone acquainted with him, must have known that such a man would have liked a few words upon his tomb which would have borne witness to the depth of his religious feelings. Here is an extract from a letter to his eldest brother which breathes through it his piety and his love of home: "You cannot imagine how I long to see you and embrace you, as well as the mother and father. Almost every night I fancy myself at Lyon, and yesterday I was really angry with Paul (his brother, helper, and fellow-student), because he awoke me just at the moment when I thought I was kissing you. I was crying for joy. . . . Remember that we agreed to pray for each other every evening. I never fail to do so, and I feel sure our poor mother never forgets: she loves us so much, and she is so far off. *Pauvre père, la bonne mère, vous n'êtes plus entournés par tous vos enfants.*"

The choir was the first part of S. Germain which was decorated, and it is the most successful, the nave pictures being somewhat flat, and faded in colour; but without the use of gold it was impossible to make the subjects effective with the bright polychrome surroundings, and Flandrin justly considered that the nave should be subordinate in splendour to the choir and sanctuary. On the right and left of the commencement of the choir are two large compositions: Christ entering into Jerusalem, and The Way of the Cross, both upon gold grounds. Above these are the twelve Apostles clothed in white, and the allegorical Virtues; and higher still are the founders of the church, Childebert and S. Germain, with the patron S. Vincent, Queen Ultrogothe, and abbot Morard. All these works are full of intense feeling, and the group of the Blessed Virgin and S. John have rarely been surpassed, from the pathetic point of view, by any religious painter. There is a certain modernness about them; the figures seem to emphasize the human element in our Lord's person, the sympathy, the love, and the sorrow; there is no weak sentimentality depicted—and yet the treatment adheres to the conventional traditions. The richness of the gold around, too, enhances the beauty of the compositions, and makes them almost as gorgeous as mosaics.

The frescoes of the nave occupy the space between the arches and the clerestory windows—in all, twenty compositions. The subjects are taken from the history of our Lord, and the corresponding Old Testament types. The two pictures forming one subject in each architectural division, show how perfectly the arts of painting and architecture may be made to harmonize, to be welded together as it were, although seven centuries separate the builder from the decorator. Except for a certain modernness of style, Flandrin might have lived and worked with the original architect, for his plan is that so often seen in the works of the Mediævalists, as for instance in the *Biblia Pauperum.*

In the first arcade on the left, on entering the church, we see The Annunciation and the Burning Bush, and under the window the text: "*Domine mitte quem missures es*" (Exodus iv. 13). The characteristic of the first of these pictures is the simplicity of the Virgin's expression, as she hears the Angels' message. Next comes The Nativity and its type, The Fall, with the legend, *Per hominem mors, per hominem resurrectio* (1 Corinthians xv. 21). The figures of Adam and Eve are excellent examples of the purity of form so commonly found in Flandrin's work. The Nativity is treated in the conventional manner, except that three Angels watch the child and its mother (who lie upon a rustic bed); while behind them, a Seraph bears a banner upon which is written: "*Gloria in, Excelsis Deo.*"

This is followed by The Adoration of the Magi and Balaam, the text being: *Habitantibus in regione umbrae . . . . lux orta est*" (Isaiah ix. 2). The Old Testament subject depicts the moment when Balaam, taken to the top of Pethor by Balak, blesses instead of curses the enemy. Before them is the altar; around them are the princes of Moab, angry and threatening; in the background are the tents of the children of Israel. The victims are ready for the sacrifice, but to the astonishment of the king and his followers, Balaam lifts up his voice and blesses those he was brought to curse. *How goodly are thy tents,* O

Jacob, and thy tabernacles, O Israel! This is one of the finest of the series.

In The Baptism we see the ascetic figure of S. John the Baptist pouring water upon Our Lord's head, while three Angels kneel upon the bank of the river, doing homage. Above is the descending dove and the verse: *Erit Sanguis Vobis in Signum* (Exodus xii. 13). In the Passage of the Red Sea, the majestic figure of Moses stands upon the shore, his hair and drapery blown by the wind. He raises his hand, and the waters close over the Egyptians, while the Israelites lift up their voices in triumphant songs, Miriam leading them to the sound of the timbrel: *Sing ye to the Lord, for he hath triumphed gloriously: the horse and his rider hath he thrown into the sea.*

The Institution of the Eucharist is treated from the purely Roman Catholic point of view. Our Blessed Lord is standing, holding up the wafer for adoration, while He places the other hand upon His side, symbolical of the gift of the sacred heart combined with His precious body. The Apostles form two groups, one on each side: *Novi Testamenti Mediator est* (Hebrews ix. 15). The Old Testament type is Melchizedek appearing to Abram: *And Melchizedec King of Salem brought forth bread and wine; and he was the priest of the most high God.*

The next pictures, close to the choir, are badly lighted, but both are very fine. The Treason of Judas, and Joseph sold by his Brethren: *Pro salute vestra misit me Deus* (Genesis xiv. 5).

And now we come to a subject into which Flandrin threw all his strength—The Crucifixion—which is not inferior in feeling to the great Angelico in the Convent of San Marco at Firenze. The divine expression of the dying Saviour, the heart-rending sorrow of the Mother, and the passionate grief of the Magdalen, are all exquisitely portrayed. So, too, The Sacrifice of Isaac, which is its type, is full of pathos and true religious sentiment. *Proprio filio non pepercit* (Romans viii. 32) is the text.

In the treatment of Jonah, the type of The Resurrection, the painter has avoided what must always be a difficulty—the great fish. Those who saw this *tableau* years ago at Ober-Ammergau must remember that even the good souls of that village could not divest the subject of the ludicrous element, and they did well, in 1890, to omit it. But Flandrin has got over the difficulty by making his prophet walking upon a beach, with waves breaking upon the shore around him. He has been ejected from the whale, and is giving thanks for his deliverance. *Signum Jonæ Prophetæ* (Matthew xii. 39).

That the Gentiles should be fellow-heirs and of the same body, and partakers of his promise in Christ by the Gospel, is the legend of the charge to Peter. *Gentes esse cohaeredes . . . promissionis in Christo* (Ephesians iii. 6). In the foreground kneels S. Peter, to whom Our Lord gives the keys of heaven and hell; but the rest of the Apostles stand around, and form part of the group: *Feed my sheep.* The type is The Dispersion of the Nations subsequent to the building of Babel; and Flandrin has most graphically described the wonder and amazement of the crowd, who, not being able to converse any longer, leave the town and scatter themselves over the face of the earth.

Above the frieze of subject-pictures are numerous personages in the panels which surround the windows, all from the Old Testament: Adam and Eve, Jacob Blessing his Children, Job, Samson, Aaron, Joshua, Miriam, Deborah, Judith, and ending with John the Baptist. Adam and Eve are, perhaps, the finest

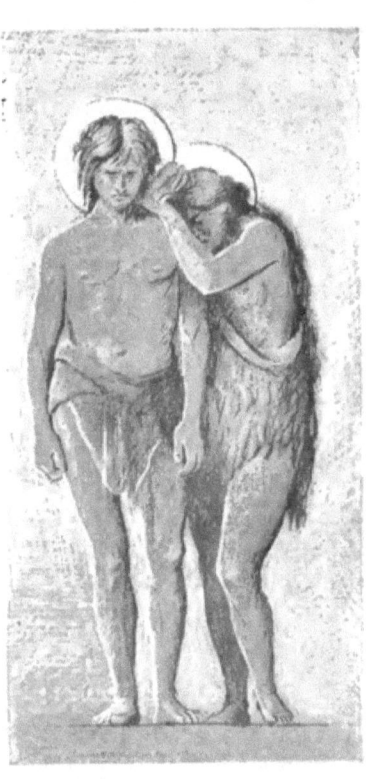

ADAM AND EVE.

of these figures. Adam stands erect, thoughtful, repentant, and ashamed; but his clasped right hand seems to indicate steadfastness of purpose to retrieve the past. Eve abandons herself to sorrow, and leans upon her husband's shoulder as if resolving in the future to depend upon him. The treatment is at once almost Classic in its simplicity, and realistic in its naturalism; the only discordant note being a something in the way in which Eve's hair falls upon her forehead, an echo, as it were, of the model, and the ugly fashion of dressing the hair peculiar to the thirties and forties, which so often shocks us in the Nymphs and Venuses by Etty, and gives them an unclothed appearance.

Formerly, judging from Dibden's account of the church, there was great display in the religious functions at S. Germain: "The immediate vicinity of S. Germain is sadly choked by stalls and shops—the West front has been cruelly covered by modern appendages. It is the church dearest to antiquaries, and with reason. I first visited it on a Sunday, when that part of the service was performed which required the fullest intonations of the organ. The effect altogether was very striking. The singular pillars of which the capitals are equally massive and grotesque, being sometimes composed of human beings, and sometimes of birds and beasts, especially towards the choir —the rising up and sitting down of the congregation, and the yet more frequent movements of the priests—the swinging of the censers—and the parade of the vergers, dressed in bag wigs, with broad red sashes of silk, and silk stockings—but above all, the most scientifically-touched, as well as the deepest and loudest toned organ I ever heard—perfectly bewildered and amazed me! Upon the dispersion of the congregation—which very shortly followed this religious excitation—I had ample leisure to survey every part of this curious old structure, which reminded me, although upon a much larger scale, of the peculiarities of S. Georges de Bocherville and Notre-Dame at Guibray. Certainly, very much of this church is of the twelfth century, and, as I am not writing to our friend N., I will make bold to say that some portions of it yet 'smacks strongly' of the eleventh."

I cannot say that I have ever noted much ceremonial, or any fine music, at S. Germain. Times have changed probably; certainly, its chief beauty now is the building itself— its grand architecture and beautiful decoration.

SAINT-GERVAIS-SAINT-PROTAIS.

There can be no doubt that the quaint inscription informing "les bonnes gens" that the church of *Messeigneurs Saint Gervais et Saint Prothais* was dedicated in 1420, refers to an earlier building than the present one. The Saints were twin-brothers, and are represented here as elsewhere, vested as deacons, although there is no evidence in their history of their having been in holy orders. The full inscription is as follows:—

> BONNES GENS PLAISE
> VOUS SAUOIR QUE CESTE
> PRESENTE ESGLISE DE
> MESSEIGNEURS SAINT GERVAIS ET
> SAINT PROTHAIS FUT DEDIÉE LE
> DIMÂNCHE DEUANT LA FESTE DE
> SAINT SIMON ET SAINT JUDE, L'AN
> MIL QUATRE CENS ET VINT PAR LA
> MAIN DU REUEREND PERE EN DIEU
> MAISTRE GOMBAUT, EVESQUE D'A-
> GRENCE, ET SERA A TOUSJOURS LA
> FESTE DE LA SAINTE DÉDICACE LE
> DIMÂNCHE DEUANT LA DICTE FESTE DE
> SAINT SIMON ET SAINT JUDE. SI
> VOUS PLAIS Y VENIR, GANGNIER LES
> GRANS PARDONS ET PRIEZ POUR LES
> BIENS-FAICTEURS DE CETTE ESGLISE ET
> AUSSI POUR LES TRESPASSEZ. PATER
> NOSTER AUE MARIA.

The twins were discovered as martyrs by S. Ambrose at Milano, when, in 387, he was desirous of founding a new church. The people called upon him to consecrate the building by placing some holy relics therein; and he, good bishop, was only too eager to gratify their wish. And so he had a dream, or a trance, or something between the two; for, while possessed of this desire to gratify the piety of his children, he, like a good shepherd, went to the church of S. Nabor and S. Felis to pray for his sheep; and as he knelt, he saw a vision of two beauteous young men clothed in white, standing with S. Peter and S. Paul. And it was revealed to S. Ambrose that these two young men were holy martyrs, whose bodies had been buried where he knelt. So he called his clergy-folk, and they all searched, and found two bodies of gigantic size separated from the heads, with much blood, and some writing recording their names. They were Gervasius and Protarius, who had suffered martyrdom under Nero. Having been sent bound to Milano, together with Nazarus and Celsus, they were brought before Count Artesius and accused of being Christians. Upon being commanded to sacrifice to Artesius' idols, they refused and were condemned, Gervasius to be beaten to death with lead-loaded scourges, Protarius to be beheaded. Thus they died, and a good man named Philip took up their bodies, and buried them in his own garden, where they rested until discovered by S. Ambrose. On the second day of the discovery, the bodies were borne with great solemnity to the Basilica; and many persons, touching the pall which covered the Saints, were cured of divers diseases, and of evil spirits. One man who had been blind for many years, Severus by name, and who had lived upon the alms of the wealthy, obtained permission to touch the bones of the holy martyrs, and was restored to sight; and then all the people rejoiced, for the man's infirmity being well known to everyone in the city, there could be no doubt that the cure had been effected through the intercession of the blessed saints. And this being so, S. Ambrose laid their bones under the altar, saying : " Let the victims be borne in triumph to the place where Christ is the sacrifice; He upon the altar, who suffered for all; they beneath the altar, who were redeemed by His suffering!" Then came the Arians, and scoffingly accused S. Ambrose of bribing Severus and others to aid and abet him in his miraculous performances; but the bishop defeated their wicked ways, and the church was dedicated to the twin brothers. S. Ambrose was buried in the same church, and subsequently its name was changed to that of Sant' Ambrogio Maggiore. In Italy the brothers were held in little rupute as time went on; but S. Germain, bishop of Paris, having in 560 carried some of their relics to France, they became exceedingly popular, and the patrons of several cathedrals and parish churches, besides being favourite subjects with some of the French school of painters, Le Sueur, Philippe de Champagne, and Nicholas Poussin.

In the History of S. Germain by Fortunat, a church dedicated to the twin brothers is mentioned, the door of which, when the good bishop desired to enter the building, flew open of its accord. S. Germain entered the church, and after much praying, restored his sight to a blind man, and worked other wondrous miracles through the intervention of the martyrs.

The present church is of Pointed and Classic architecture, the portal and *façade* being in the latter style.* Louis XIII. laid the first stone in 1616, Jacques de Brosse being the architect. A not very favourable, but tolerably just, opinion is passed upon it by our old friend Dibden :

"The next Gothic church to Notre-Dame in size and importance is that of *S. Gervais*, situated to the left, in the Rue de Monçeau. It has a very lofty nave, but the interior is exceedingly flat and divested of ornaments. The pillars have scarcely any capitals. The choir is totally destitute of effect Some of the stained glass is rich and old, but a great deal ha been stolen or demolished during the Revolution. There is a good large modern picture in one of the side chapels to the right, and a yet more modern one much inferior on the opposite side. In almost every side chapel, and in the confessionals, the priests were busily engaged in the catechetical examination of young people previous to the first Communion on the following Sabbath, which was the Fête Dieu. The Western front is wholly Grecian—perhaps about 200 years old. It is too lofty for its width—but has a grand effect, and is justly much celebrated. Yet the situation of this fine old Gothic church is among the most wretched of those in Paris. It is preserved from suffocation only by holding its head so high." The last remark is no longer applicable, as the church is now quite disencumbered from secular excrescences.

The interior is cold, dull, and dreary, almost the only part that relieves its monotony being the organ tribune, which is quaintly ornamented with Angels and Corinthian columns, a device of the 17th century. The statues of the Saints upon the altar are the work of Bourdin, a sculptor of the 17th century. The six candelabra and the cross of gilt bronze,

---

* The statues of the four Evangelists were the first important works of Simon Guillain, the sculptor of the fine bronze figures of Louis XIII., Anne d'Autriche, and Louis XIV. as a child, which adorned the Pont au Change, and which are now in the Renaissance Museum of the Louvre.

belonging formerly to the abbey church of S. Geneviève, are among the bronze *chefs-d'œuvre* of the 18th century. The stalls are finely carved, and bear various designs upon their bas-reliefs; but especially notable are the little histories upon the *misereres*: a writer at his desk; an architect measuring some blocks of stone, accompanied by his workmen; a baker putting his bread in the oven; a man stooping down with a fool's cap on his head; the vinedressers in a vat; a Genus sleeping upon a grave with his head resting upon a skull; two men squabbling; a shoemaker at his last, surrounded by a fine collection of foot-gear; two men roasting; a Syren, a crowned Salamander, a grotesque animal, a lion, and a pig gobbling in a gluttonous fashion; and finally a man in a boat traversing a river.

Some of the glass is fine, but much has been destroyed; and only the other day the Anarchists did their best to demolish the little which remains. In the choir the story of Lazarus, and the Pilgrimage to Mont Saint-Michel, were painted by Robert Pinaigrier, as well as the windows of the Lady Chapel; and another great *vitrier*, Jean Cousin, embellished S. Gervais with some beautiful golden-toned glass—The Martyrdom of S. Laurence, The Good Samaritan, and The Judgment of Solomon. On one fragment of the latter is the date 1531. The story is told most quaintly; Solomon sleeps surrounded by his books; and it is thus that he drinks in the wisdom which the Queen of Sheba, in the next panel, comes to enjoy.

Among the other subjects, we see S. Peter baptising Cornelius, surrounded by divers Scripture events. In the Lady Chapel a Tree of Jesse has survived, and also the Legend of S. Anne, attributed to Pinaigrier; but the latter is filled in with much that is modern—clever, but wanting in the vigorous drawing of the old glass painters, and the glorious transparency of the colours. One of the old panes shows us the Virgin weaving a curtain for the Temple, and being fed by an Angel. In this chapel there is a remarkable boss which descends from the vault. If is 6ft. in diameter, and falls 3ft.; and although iron has been used in its fabrication, it is, notwithstanding, a wonderful piece of masonry of the brothers Jacquet. It is a mass of carving—emblems of the Blessed Virgin; a fortified town (the Tower of David), and the Morning Star; attributes found in the offices of Our Lady.

A good many distinguished people were buried at S. Gervais:

Scarron, more celebrated as having been the first husband of the notorious Mme. de Maintenon than for his writings; that excellent, but insufficiently appreciated painter, Philippe de Champaigne; Ducange, the antiquarian and historian; the chancellors Le Tellier, Louis Boucherat and Charles Voysin; archbishop Le Tellier of Reims, son of the chancellor and founder of the library of S. Geneviève; and the poet Crébillon, author of *Rhadamistus*, *Electra*, *Catiline*, and other tragedies. The only monument which remains is that of Le Tellier, who reposes in white marble upon a black marble mattress, with allegorical figures watching over his slumbers. It was the work of Mazeline and Hurtrelle, members of the Academy, but not otherwise celebrated, as is occasionally the case.

In one of the chapels of the nave is a 13th century bas-relief of Our Lord receiving His mother's soul as she expires, surrounded by the Apostles; a fine old picture painted upon wood, of various scenes from the Passion, formerly attributed to Albrecht Dürer, but more probably by some master of the Flemish school. Many of the pictures by Lesueur, Bourdon, and Philippe de Champaigne, formerly in this church, are now in the Louvre.

LA TOUR SAINT-JACQUES.

This tower is all that remains of the church of S. Jacques de la Boucherie, which had to be demolished to make way for the Rue de Rivoli. It was commenced in 1508, and finished in 1522. The figure of S. James upon the little turret, and his friends the Evangelistic animals, by Rauch, were thrown down in 1793; but in 1836, when the municipality saved the tower by purchasing it, the statues were repaired and replaced. The church contained many tombs and slabs, some of which have found a home in the Hôtel Cluny. One of the most famous persons buried at S. Jacques was Nicholas Flamel, a member of the University, and librarian, who died in 1417, leaving large sums of money to the church. His effigy, and that of his wife, were to be seen kneeling at the Virgin's feet in the tympanum of the porch. He was venerated as their patron by the alchymists, for having, as was affirmed, discovered the philosopher's Stone; and several times his house in the Rue des Écrivains was rummaged in order to find some indication of his secret. His funeral tablet has the following epitaph engraven upon it, and is numbered 92 in the collection of the Hôtel Cluny :

LA TOUR SAINT-JACQUES, LOOKING TOWARDS THE HÔTEL DE VILLE

FEU NICOLAS FLAMEL JADIX ESCRI
VAIN A LAISSÉ PAR SON TESTAMENT A
LEUSORE DE CESTE ÉGLISE CERTAINES
RENTES ET MAISONS QU'IL AVOIT
ACQUESTÉES ET ACHETÉES A SON VI-

VANT POUR FAIRE CERTAIN SERVICE
DIVIN ET DISTRIBUCIONS D'ARGENT
CHASCUN AU PAR AUMOSNE TOU-
CHANS LES QUINZE VINS: LOSTEL DI
EU ET AULTRES ÉGLISES ET HOSPITEAUX
A PARIS.—SOIT PRIÉ POURS LES TRÉPASSÉS.

The Tour S. Jacques is an excellent example of what may be done with the remaining portions of demolished buildings. As it stands, surrounded by gardens, it is a most beautiful object, an oasis in the desert of streets, and trams, and omnibuses, a quiet spot where children may skirmish, and mothers can sit in the open air and knit their stockings. Why cannot we do likewise in London? If churches must be felled to the ground, why cannot we leave their towers as a centre to the burial-ground gardens, or remove and re-erect them in our parks? We might with advantage follow the example of Paris, both in the preservation of the old tower of S. Jacques, and in the arrangement of the garden of the Hôtel Cluny, where, also, fragments of churches are set up as ornaments.

It was from the top of the tower of S. Jacques that Pascal made certain experiments of the density of the air; and in memory of this, his statue, in white marble, was placed under the porch.

SAINT-JACQUES DU HAUT-PAS.

In no way remarkable, this church need only be mentioned as having been built between 1630-1684, in the Italian fashion. It is in the street of the same name.

SAINT-JEAN-SAINT-FRANÇOIS.

Founded in 1623, in the Rue Charlot, as a chapel for the Capuchins, S. Jean contains a statue of S. Francis of Assisi, by Germain Pilon, and a S. Denis, sculptured by Jacques Sarazin for the Abbey of Montmartre, by order of Anne d'Autriche.

SAINT-JULIEN LE PAUVRE.

In a little back street not far from S. Séverin is the old church of S. Julien, a fragment only of its former self, and all that remains of the ancient priory. Its locality is described in Guillot's *Dict. des Rues de Paris*, which gives a description in verse of the principal houses and streets in the city at the end of the 13th century, as follows :—

> Puis la rue de Saint-Julien
> Qui nous gart de mauvais lien,
> M'en revins à la Buscherie
> Et puis en la Poissonnerie.

And it appears that "il y avait jadis, près du Petit-Pont et la prison du Petit-Châtelet, une ruelle appelée ruelle du Carneaux,* qui conduisait au marché au poisson d'eau douce." This fish-market evidently occupied the site of the old annexe of the Hôtel-Dieu, and doubtless was in great requisition when the priory was inhabited by its fifty brethren.

Some years ago, when S. Julien was used as the chapel of the Hôtel-Dieu, it formed a picturesque object from the hospital garden, and no doubt was often a great comfort to some of the patients, who found within its walls a peaceful spot where they could be alone, and out of turmoil of sick wards and their accompaniments. But when the old hospital was pulled down, the church's very existence was threatened, and for some years it seemed as if Paris would have one more vandalism to lament. Happily its demolition was prevented, and it has been restored to God's service, for the use of members of the Greek branch of the Church.

INTERIOR OF SAINT-JULIEN.

Many were the Julians canonized by the Early Church, and it is difficult to say to which saint this edifice was dedicated, although the fact of the relics of S. Julien de Brioude, who was martyred in 304, having been placed upon the left-hand side of the High Altar, seems to point to him as the patron.

* The word is probably derived from *créneaux*, as the battlements of the Petit-Châtelet abutted upon one side of the street.

S. Julien was born at Vienne in Dauphiné about 270, and became a distinguished soldier in the Roman army; but having embraced Christianity, he was beheaded during the reign of Diocletian in 304, at Brioude in Auvergne, where he had taken refuge from his persecutors. There his remains were discovered by S. Germain d'Auxerre in 431, and forthwith the town became celebrated for the many cures performed at its miraculous well. "*Est enim ad hunc fontem virtus eximia*," said S. Grégoire of Tours; and Sidonius Apollinaris, who died in 489, also bears witness to the Saint's burial place in a letter to a friend who was travelling in Auvergne: "*Hic te suscipiet benigna Brivas Sancti quae fovet ossa Juliani.*" S. Grégoire, in his life of the Saint, gave a list of the churches dedicated to his memory; and although S. Julien le Pauvre is not enumerated, it would seem that it must have been one of them, as he speaks of lodging in a house attached to the little basilica, when he came to Paris, and called it S. Julien the Martyr: "*His diebus Parisius adveneram et ad Basilicam Beati Juliani martyris metam habebam.*"

Another S. Julien was a confessor, and first bishop of Mans. He was a Roman by birth, and upon being consecrated, was sent by Pope Clement to convert the Cenomans. He arrived at Suindinum (Le Mans) while the town was besieged and deprived of water. Entering it, he caused water to spring from the ground, and henceforth the well was called *Sanct-nomius*, or fountain of S. Julien. The bishop worked in his diocese over 40 years, and then retired to S. Marceau, where he died in 117, his decease being revealed in a vision to his first convert, a Gaul, surnamed *Le Défenseur*, who caused the Saint's body to be carried back to Le Mans, and buried with great pomp at Notre-Dame du Pré. In 840 it was translated to the cathedral, where many miracles were wrought. S. Julien is generally represented destroying a dragon, symbolizing paganism, or accompanied by a young girl carrying a pitcher of water, an allegory of the miraculous well. This connection of different Saints of the same name with wells is curious, and makes it difficult to decide the patronage of S. Julien le Pauvre; for there also are two wells, one the so-called "miraculous," just outside the eastern apse of the church, and another outside one of the windows of the 17th century *façade*. If, as many authorities think, the old 13th century west front occupied a space in advance of the present one, this well may have been originally inside the church, an arrangement frequently adopted by Mediæval architects, and still existing in some of our old churches. There is one of exquisite beauty in the south aisle of Regensburg Cathedral, and at Coutances there are two in the transepts. S. Germain des Prés also had its miraculous well, but it is now closed up. There is yet another one at the corner of Rues S. Jacques and

CHAPEL OF THE SOUTH AISLE.

S. Séverin, which formerly bore the name of Julien, but is now re-christened S. Séverin. It was re-constructed in the 17th century and bore the following inscription by the poet Santeuil:

DUM SCANDUNT JUGA MONTIS ANHELO PECTORE NYMPHÆ,
HIC UNA E SOCIIS VALLIS AMORE SEDET.

Which is prettily rendered by d'Amaury Duval : "Tandis que les nymphes, haletantes, montent vers le sommet de la montagne, l'une d'elles, éprise de la beauté du vallon, y fixe sa demeure."

The third saint who disputes the patronage of this particular church is S. Julian Hospitator, who watches over travellers, ferrymen, boatmen and travelling minstrels. He was a nobleman much given to the chase, and one day, while pursuing a deer, the frightened creature turned round, and cried out, "Thou followest me, thou who wilt one day kill thy father and mother."* Thereupon Julian rushed away to a far country, where he was made a knight, and much honoured by the king. But his parents, grieved at his loss, set off to try and find him, and coming to his castle, they made themselves known to his wife, who put them in their son's chamber, and left them for the night. In the morning she went to early mass to give thanks for this great mercy, and during her absence, Julian, finding the old people in his room, and not recognizing them in the dim light of dawn, turned upon them and slew them, as it seems, somewhat hastily. Then Julian resolved to depart and devote himself to some good work; but his wife would not let him go alone, so they journeyed until they came to a great river, where many people were drowned in trying to ford it, and there they set up a hermitage and a hospital, and a ferry boat for travellers free of charge. One day, when a leper presented himself, Julian not only ferried him over, but carried him in his arms to his own bed, and tended him with the aid of his good wife. And in the morning the leper arose, transformed, and saying, "Julian, the Lord hath sent me to thee; thy penitence is accepted, and thy rest and that of thy wife is near at hand," vanished out of their sight. And shortly after, both Julian and his wife fell asleep.† The Cathedral of Rouen possesses a window presented by the

---

* In the quaint old French of the *Légende Dorée* of Jacques de Voragine : "*Tu me suys, toi qui occiras ton père et ta mère.*"

† "Tout aussitôt, il apprend de sa femme, qui revenait de la messe, qui il a tué."

"Et quand il ouyt ce, il fut à bien peu demy mort et commença à plorer très amèrement et à dire :

"'Las! chétif, que feray-je, car j'ay occis mes très doulx père et mère, et ores est la parole du cerf accomplie.

"'Adieu, ma très aimée sœur, car je ne reposerai, dores en avant, devant que je sache que Notre-Seigneur aura recue ma pénitence.' Elle lui répondit : 'Loin de moi, ô mon très affectionné frère, la pensée de t'aban-

company of *bateliers-pêcheurs* in the 14th century, upon which this legend of the ferry is represented.

There can be little doubt that the church was originally dedicated to Julian the Martyr, as recorded by Grégoire de Tours, and that later the *culte* of the other two Julians was added; particularly as we find upon one of the houses of the Rue Galande, which abuts upon one side of the church, a curious 13th century bas-relief of this very legend of the ferry.

BAS-RELIEF OF THE FERRY.

donner: puisque j'ai partagé tes joies, je partagerai aussi tes souffrances et ta pénitence.'

" Et alors, sa femme et lui s'en allèrent ensemble delez (*vers*) un moult grand fleuve, où moult de gens périssaient, et firent un hospital en ce désert pour faire pénitence et pour porter oultre tous ceulx qui y voudraient passer, pour recevoir en hospital tous povres.

" Et moult de temps après ce, quant Julien se reposait tout lasse, environ minuyt, que la gelée était griesve, il ouyt une voix qui plorait piteusement, et appelait Julien pour passer, à voix piteuse.

" Et quant il se leva tout esmeu, il trouva icelluy qui mourait de froit, il le porta en sa maison, et alluma du feu, et se estudia à le chauffer, et comme il ne le pouvait eschauffer nullement, il se doubta qu'il ne défaillit par froit, et le porta en son lict, et le couvrit diligemment. Et, un peu après, celui qui lui était apparu comme malade et lépreux monta très resplendissant ès cieulx et dit à son oste: 'Julien, Notre-Seigneur m'a envoyé à toi et te mande qu'il a receu ta pénitence, et tous deulx reposerez en Notre-Seigneur dedans un peu de temps.' Tantost celluy s'évanouit (*disparut*). Et lors, un peu après, Julien et sa femme, pleins de bonnes œuvres et d'aulmônes, reposèrent en Notre-Seigneur."—*Légende Dorée*.

S. Julian and his wife are rowing the boat, apparently in opposite directions, and standing up is the passenger, no other than Our Lord Himself, as we see from the cruciform nimbus. Is it not probable that at some time, when repairs were going on, this bas-relief was removed from the church, and does not the situation of S. Julien le Pauvre, or *des* pauvres, close to a river and a fish-market, seem to be further proof that the Hospitator was one of the later patrons of the church? There are said to be nearly sixty[*] saints of this name, and as a proof of their popularity in France, we find no less than one hundred and sixty-two villages called after them. In Spain they were still more popular. Saint-Julien le Ménétrier, or des Ménétriers, was a hospital founded in 1330 by Jacques Grare and Huet le Lorrain, for fiddlers, jugglers, and acrobats. It was situated near the Rue S. Martin. One of the attributes of S. Julian Hospitator is a mask. He is thus seen on some of the windows at the cathedrals of Chartres and Rouen, the latter of the 14th century. His name also seems to have had virtue in it as an expletive, for in the *Chronique des Ducs de Normendie et des Rois d'Engletierre* the following exclamation occurs: "'*Par Saint Julian!*' *dist Hubiers Gautiers li bons archevêsque de Chantorbire* (Canterbury)."

S. Julien was also invoked by travellers:

> (Saint Ylaire) saint Juliens
> Qui héberge les Crestiens,

was a rhyme of the *Moustiers de Paris*, written in 1270; and a document of 1325 upon the *Churches and Monasteries of Paris* thus confirms the usefulness of S. Julien-le-Pauvre:

> Or m'en iray outre le pont
> Pour des autres moustiers trouver
> Que l'on ne puisse réprouver,
> Quar s'en mon dit faille de rien,
> Premiers trouverez saint Julien
> Le Povre, et bien ai regardé
> Que maint compagnon a gardé
> De mort, ce n'est pas mesprison
> Et d'estre en vilainne prison;
> Il les héberge et si les tence
> De héberger a la poissance.

---

[*] L'abbé Guérin: *Les Petits Bollandists*.

The early history of S. Julien is similar to that of all the other churches of Paris. Destroyed in 886 by the Normans,* it fell into lay hands, but was rebuilt in the 12th century, and became the property of Etienne de Vitry and Hugues de Monteler, who, in consequence of a vow made during sickness in the Holy Land, gave it over to the monks of Longport, near Monthéry, who rebuilt the church and erected a priory for fifty brothers.

The 13th and 14th centuries were periods of great intellectual activity. Students flocked to Paris from all parts of Europe, and the left bank of the Seine became a colony of colleges. According to Victor Hugo, there were no less than forty-two in 1465.† S. Julian was in the midst of these schools, and in the streets surrounding it were dwellings for the students of the various nationalities. The little Rue du Fouarre takes its name from *fourrage*, the straw upon which the students sat during the lectures; and so large was the attendance in 1535, that the authorities were obliged to erect two gates to prevent the circulation of carriages during the lessons. Brunetto Latini, **Dante** Alighieri, Petrarca, and Rabelais, were among the students of the Rue du Fouarre; the three last referring to it in their writings. Dante, especially, mentions his old master Sigier de Brabant in his *Divinia Commedia*:

> *Essa la luce eterna de Sigieri*
> *Che, leggendo nel vico degli* **Strami**,
> *Sillogizo' invidiosi veri.* (*Il* **Paradiso**, canto x.)

The poet also bears witness to the violent discussions which took place in the street, and adds that he found comfort in going to S. Julien to say his prayers. Ambroise-Firmin Didot speaks of Dante living in the Rue du Fouarre, *in vico stramineo*; and Mézières adds his testimony: "Il est allé chercher la science à Bologne et entendre à Paris, dans la Rue du Fouarre, de la bouche de Sigier, ces leçons hardies qui effrayaient ces contemporains."

The colleges and dwelling-houses of the students, together with the buildings of the priory, formed a small town. In an old plan of the church, and its dependencies in the precincts,

---

* So terrible were the Northmen, so outrageous the atrocities which they committed, that the canons of S. Geneviève chanted a line in their Litanies : "*A furore Normannorum, libera nos, Domine.*"

† In 1648, there were 50 colleges, 16 hospitals, and 190 churches and convents for the education of a population of 232,030 inhabitants.

during the 14th century, we find a number of most curious names attached to the houses: Maison d'Angleterre, de la Hure, de Picardie, de Normandie, de l'Ymaige Notre-Dame, du Paon, de l'Escu de France, de la Nef* d'Argent, du Sabot, du Soufflet vert, du Papegaut, des Carneaulx, des Deux Cygnes, des Lyons, de la Heuze, des Trois Boittes, des Quatre filz Hémon, de la Corne de Daim, du Lièvre cornu, de la Cuiller, des Trois Canettes, du Poing d'or, de la Main d'argent, du Turbot, les Étuves de la Queue du Reynard, l'Escouvette d'or, and la ruelle du Trou-Punais; la maison des Sept-Arts, à la nation d'Angleterre; les Escolles du Cheval Rouge à la nation de Picardie, et la maison de la Corne de Cerf; these are only a few of the names. Many of the houses were demolished quite recently to make way for the Rue Monge. Much as I love Paris and admire it, I sometimes wish a new street were not obliged to proceed upon its way in a perfectly straight line, thereby destroying all that comes in its path. A remnant of the houses attached to S. Julien may be seen in the Rue Galande, No. 42, *maison de la Heuze et de Saint-Julien*—the bas-relief of the old portal, mentioned above.

For several centuries the old church was the seat of the general assemblies of the University; and by a decree of Philippe le Bel, the Provost of Paris was obliged to go there every two years, to take an oath to observe the privileges of the students, who were under his jurisdiction. He bore the title of *Conservateur de l' Université* with much pride; but he must have had a troublous life, for the students were always quarrelling with the citizens; and in the reign of Charles VI., the then Provost, Hugues Aubriot, rebuilt the Petit-Châtelet (which was close to S. Julien), in order to defend the city against the nocturnal incursions of the scholars. To such a pass had matters come in 1601, that the Parliament issued the following decree: " La court a faict inhibitions et défences aux dicts escolliers porter espées et dagues sur le quay de la Tournelle ny commettre aucune insolence." There were several classes of students, *Boursiers* and *Pensionnaires* (*Convicteurs ou Portionnistes*) living with the masters; *Caméristes*, rich young men who lived without

* *Nefs* or *Navettes* were vessels in the shape of boats used by the church for incense—hence incense-boat. Later on, they took the form of complete ships, with ropes, yards, &c., often upon wheels, and placed in the centre of the table at banquets. They contained spices, wine, drinking-cups, and spoons, in order to guard the guests against that bugbear of the Middle Ages, poison.

control and were only provided with teaching and firing; *Externes libres*, or *Martinets*, troublesome students who gained their name because they rarely appeared before the Principal except for punishment with the rod or *martinet*; and the *Galoches*, who lived out of college (*externes*), and were named after the clogs (*patins* or *galoches*) with great nails which they wore to keep their feet dry in traversing the muddy or snowy streets. These were often older men whose presence at lectures flattered the professors. Up to the 16th century, S. Julien was also the scene of the election of the Rector of the Faculty of Arts, **Rector** *Magnificus de l'Alma Parens;* and upon these occasions, notably in 1524, the students seemed to have amused themselves, after their kind, by breaking doors and windows, wrenching knockers, and such like playful imbecilities. The next year Parliament decreed that the elections should take place elsewhere; the new localities chosen being, first the Mathurins, and then the College Louis-le Grand.

The University of Paris was established in 1200, but the word was not commonly used until the time of S. Louis. In the time of Philippe Auguste there were three schools in Paris, at Notre-Dame, and at the abbeys of S. Victor and S. Geneviève. Naturally to keep so many students in order was no easy task, and we can easily understand that upon every excuse, every small discontent of the citizens, the scholars were only too glad to help in the scrimmage. They were at first classified in nations, or Société de Maîtres; thus in 1169 we read of la nation de France, surnamed *Honoranda;* la nation de Picardie, *Fidellissima;* la nation Normande, *Veneranda;* and la nation d'Angleterre, *Constantissima.* In the "town and gown" rows between students and citizens, the members of the University were only amenable to the Provost of Paris, who gloried in the title of *Conservateur de l'Université;* and when this gentleman found the gownsmen in the wrong, the University suspended its lectures.

But S. Julien was not simply the centre of the University; it was also the head-quarters of many guilds and corporations, such as the Confraternity of Notre-Dame-des-Vertus, the Papermakers, the Ironfounders, and Roof-tilers.

Even before the Revolution, church property was not entirely exempt from taxation. The abbeys and other ecclesiastical communities possessed enormous privileges; but they were not enjoyed without certain obligations, as witness requisitions from the sovereigns to furnish supplies to carry on their little warlike pastimes. Sometimes the amount was sent in money, but more often in kind; a few silver saints, some golden shrines, and so on. S. Julien possessed a good revenue in the old days, but in the 16th century the priory had begun to decline in position and in wealth. The colleges moved up the "mountain" of S. Geneviève; teachers and scholars deserted the old quarters; the houses, which had been the greatest source of revenue, had begun to fall into decay; and the priors became indifferent to their business affairs, and were often absentees. At last things became so bad that, in 1643, a prior named E. Thiboust had to be deposed, and replaced, nominally by Pierre de la Valette, practically by Pierre Méliand, who accused his predecessor "d'avoir laissé dépérir l'église depuis l'an 1612 qu'il était entré en jouissance du prieuré. Et pendant cette jouissance, qui a duré 18 ans, le sieur Thiboust a laissé tomber une grande partie de l'église en ruine." Not only did prior Thiboust allow the buildings to fall into decay, but he must have kept back part of the revenues; for the next step was a petition to

THE SANCTUARY.

the King's *procureur-général* to beg him to oblige Thiboust to pay 16,500 *livres*, the repairs requisite having been estimated at that sum by the King's judges Villedo and Monnard. But notwithstanding this, Thiboust took upon himself to grant a lease to Nicolas Brossier and Edme Porrion for a certain stone quarry situated at Croix Faubin; and although the King confirmed Méliand in the priory, the audacious Thiboust pleaded youth at the time of his appointment, and subsequently shuffled out of payment of the whole sum.

The church was in a parlous state when prior Méliand began his repairs. The roof was in a miserable condition, with a temporary covering over the altar to keep out the rain and the door was almost in the last state of decay; so Messire Claude Menardeau was called in (he was a councillor of the King's, and a *commissaire*), and he decided "que des réparations seraient faites au plus tôt, d'autant que l'églize despérit journellement par la pluye et autres injures du temps, qui y tombent, comme en plaine campagne." Unfortunately the master mason, Bernard Roche, to whom the work was given, began by destroying the Gothic west front and portal, to make room for lodgings for the ecclesiastics. Then we read of plasterings, and a new front with pediment and Ionic columns, and all the Classicisms so much beloved in the 17th and 18th centuries.

In 1655 the priory and its possessions were made over to the Hôtel-Dieu; and thenceforth, until the demolition of the old building a few years ago, it was used as the hospital chapel. But previous to this, Cardinal Mazarin had turned over an annual payment of 2,500 *livres* to the Hôtel-Dieu from the revenue of his abbey of Saint-Étienne at Caen, and in his capacity of abbot in chief of the order of Cluny, he made a bargain which put an end to the independence of S. Julien. The prior was to resign, and all the revenues of the convent were to go to the establishment of a convalescent hospital; the Hôtel-Dieu undertaking, in return, to carry on Divine service in the church, and to fulfil the conditions of the different foundations belonging to it. At this time, 1660, the property of S. Julien consisted of thirty-eight houses and gardens in the neighbouring streets, besides certain lands in the Faubourg S. Jacques, at Montmartre, at Vitry, Villeneuve and Versailles, together with revenues in kind—corn and fodder, and donations made at burials; altogether amounting to about 2,400 *livres*.

It appears that the misfortunes of S. Julien were not over when it lost its independence, for Louis Roche required payment for his various "improvements," and so the poor church had to sell its plate. Nor could services be held there without the permission of the archbishop, as the *curé* of S. Séverin seems to have objected: "Défense lui (the chaplain of S. Julien) est faite de célébrer des messes hautes, de faire l'eau bénite, la bénédiction du pain, de reçevoir offrande, faire quête, chanter l'office et le salut, ni même exposer le Saint-Sacrament en ladite église, sans la permission de Son Eminence."

In 1705 an inventory of the furniture, vestments, and plate

was taken, and a very poor collection it seems to have been; indeed, at that time, even the hospital revenues were only about a sixth of the expenses. The inhabitants of Paris had largely increased, and famines and wars had brought many of them to the Hôtel-Dieu; so full was it that seven or eight patients were packed into one bed, which, even considering the width of an 18th-century sleeping place, must have been rather unpleasant crowding.

At the Revolution, the revenues passed over to the State, and God's House was converted into the "House of Humanity." The old church became a salt warehouse, the *asile*

EXTERIOR OF SAINT-JULIEN.

was pulled down, and it was only in 1826 that S. Julien was restored to its right use.

The first time I visited the church was before the Franco-German war, when I was taken over the hospital by one of the Augustinian sisters. Two or three patients were there pouring out their sorrows, or giving thanks for mercies received. Outside, in the garden, were a few more sitting about among the trees, making a charming picture, such as Fred Walker would have delighted in. All this is now changed, and the sisters are gone with the old hospital buildings and the quaint covered bridge—a second *Ponte Vecchio*. Whether the poor have gained anything by being nursed by lay-women instead of religious, we cannot say; but no one will deny that the sisters were devoted to their work—kindly, patient, sweet-tempered, of the same spirit as when, in the old time, they not only nursed, but "au plus fort de l'hiver," they broke the ice of the river, "qui passe au milieu de cet hôpital, et y entrer jusqu'à la moitié du corps pour laver les linges." It was in S. Julien that the White Sisters took the veil, and devoted themselves specially to the service of God and the care of His poor.

The Miraculous Well and some of the foundations are all that remain of the first Carlovingian church; the arcades of the nave and some of the columns date back to the commencement of the 12th century, but the rest of the building belongs to the end of that period. The tower, like the portal, was improved away by Master Bernard Roche, and the old bell has at present to content itself with a little pointed roof as a covering. Its inscription is dated, and is in French:

✠

J. H. S.

MARIE SUIS NOMMÉE PAR M. JEAN BOURLON, CONSEILLER DU ROY ET GREFFIER EN SA CHAMBRE DES COMPTES, ET PAR DAME MARIE PAJOT, FEMME DE M. ALEXANDRE REBOURS, CONSEILLER DU ROY EN SON CONSEIL D'ÉTAT ET PRIVÉ, ET PRÉSIDENT DE LA COUR DES AYDES DE PARIS ET V^E DE BARTHÉLEMY TOUSSAINCT MOUSSIER GOUVERNEUR DE L'ÉGLISE DE CÉANS DELAUNAY.

1640.

The plan of the church was originally a nave and aisles of six bays, each terminating in an apse, but in 1675 two bays were demolished with the entire west end, to make room for a forecourt. (It is said that, of all the churches of Paris, the two which stand most truly East and West are Notre-Dame and S. Julien.) Although parts of the interior have suffered from "improvements" and neglect, the two bays of the choir and the apsidal terminations have lost nothing of their original beauty. The single-shaft pillars, recalling upon a small scale those of Notre-Dame, the clustered columns which support the vault, and the little columns of the windows; the capitals, the bosses, and the mouldings are all in the best style of the end of the 12th century. The sculpture of the details is treated with the greatest care, and the ornamentation of the capitals (about one hundred and fifty in all) has all the variety of foliage and

SAINT-JULIEN LE PAUVRE.

imagery so dear to the Mediæval artists. The most curious example is on the south side of the choir. Springing from a mass of foliage are four figures of birds with female heads, bodies of feathers, outspread wings, and clawed feet. Some of the foliage is the acanthus, but still more represents the water plants which probably, in those early days, grew in the Seine; for it must be remembered that the sculptors of the Middle Ages were in the habit of taking their inspiration from the types of Nature which surrounded them. It is curious that one of the capitals in Notre-Dame, in the same position (the south side of the choir) is almost identical with the one just described.

On the right side of the altar is the *piscina*, which is said to communicate with the Miraculous Well; the water having been held in great veneration, people came to fetch it from far and near.

The church contains no monuments of any artistic value. A curious bas-relief with a very long inscription was erected to the memory of *Honorable et sage Maistre Henry Rousseau, jadis avocat en Parlement, seigneur de Chaillaut (Chaillot)* . . . *lequel trépassa l'an* 1445 *le IXe jour de novemlre. Dieu en ait l'âme. Amen.* The defunct left money to endow masses, and also for the Hôtel-Dieu. He is represented enveloped in a winding-sheet, addressing a prayer to our Lord, which is written upon a streamer. The words in italics are lost:

Peccavi super numer [*um arene maris et multiplicata sunt peccata mea* non sum
Dignus videre altidinem [*Celi pre multitudine iniquitatis mee $\overline{qm}$ irrita*] ram tuam.

Et malum coram te feci qm̄ ini [*quitate mea ego cognosco et*] delictum meum

Coram me est semper. Tibi soli pecca [*vi ideo deprecor*] majestatem tuam

Ut tu deleas iniquitatem meam miserere mei [*secundum magn̄a misericordia*] tuam.

The epitaph is in Gothic letters, and in an excellent state of preservation. Above the bordering we read :

Cy devant gist honorable homme et sage maistre Henry Rousseau, Jadis advocat en Parlement, seigneur de Chaillaut et de

Within the framing :

Compans en partie, lequel dès son vivant a fondé en cest hostel trois messes Par chascune sepmaine qui sont et doivent estre dites et célébrées à l'autel et Chapelle de Mons. S. Loys, jadis Roy de France, située et assise au milleu de cest

Ostel, aux jour de Mercredi, Vendredi et Dimenche. Cest assavoir au mercredi

De Requiem, au vendredi de la Croix et au dimenche de la Solennité du jour, ou

A la voulenté du célébrant, et en la fin de chascune messe qui ne serait ditte De Requiem, le célébrant est tenu de faire mémoire des Trespassez et pour ce

Faire a fondé le dit **Deffunct** et donné à cest hostel XII livres de Rentes que il ou ses hoirs

Doivent faire admortir, situées et assises sur une maison et estuves assises à Paris

Devant le Palais, à l'image Saint Michel, et, pour avoir la sépulture en cette chapelle

Below the border :

a donné la somme de cent francs que aussi en son vivant il a payiez
en six Livres Parisis de Rente assises sur plusieurs maisons à Paris declaires ès,

Lettres sur ce *faictes*, tout pour le salut de son âme et des âmes de ses père et mére, parents et amis, lequel trépassa l'an 1445 te IXe jour de novembre.

Dieu en ait l'âme. Amen.

The bas-relief was originally coloured, and at the corners of the border were armorial bearings. The slab was formerly in the church of S. Blaise and S. Louis, which was destroyed in 1765, and which belonged to S. Julien, only having been separated from it by a narrow passage. It is supposed to have been either a refectory or a private chapel. In 1476 the masons and carpenters of Paris made it the seat of their guild, and built the portal in the Rue Galande; in 1684 it was reconstructed.

Another monument, or rather statue, by Bosio, of Antoine de Montyon, was removed from the old Hôtel Dieu when it was pulled down, and placed over the last burial-place of the philanthropist. Originally interred at Vaugirard, M. de Montyon's body was afterwards placed under the peristyle of the hospital, where it remained until the demolition. M. de Montyon is principally known by his *prix de vertu* given annually by the Immortals of the Institut. But he left other legacies for prizes: to whomsoever should discover the means of rendering certain industries less unhealthy; to a poor French subject who should write a book the most conducive to morals; for the advancement of medical science or surgery; also for the poor who require aid on leaving the Paris hospitals. All the prizes are distributed by the Academy, and the whole sum left amounted to some seven millions of francs, a considerable fortune seventy years ago (1820) when M. de Montyon died. The principal prize, *pour l'action la plus vertueuse*, generally falls to the lot of some obscure person, who has passed years of self-sacrificing devotion to the old, the sick, or the poor; virtuous actions, in M. de Montyon's opinion, being those unrecorded works of love and charity which are done in simple homes, without excitement or glamour; works which become great because of their very monotony and which prove the patience and unselfishness of the true Christian.

À LA MEMOIRE
D'ANTOINE J. B. ROBERT AUGET DE MONTYON,
BARON DE MONTYON,
CONSEILLER D'ÉTAT,
DONT L'INÉPUISABLE BIENFAISANCE
ET L'INGÉNIEUSE CHARITÉ
ONT ASSURÉ
APRÈS SA MORT, COMME DURANT SA VIE,
DES ENCOURAGEMENTS AUX SCIENCES,
DES RÉCOMPENSES AUX ACTIONS VERTUEUSES,
DES SOULAGEMENTS À TOUTES LES MISÈRES HUMAINES.
NÉ LE 23 DÉC. 1733.—MORT LE 29 DÉC. 1820.
ICI REPOSE SA DEPOUILLE MORTELLE
TRANSPORTÉE DE LA COMMUNE DEMEURE DES MORTS
À L'ENTRÉE DE L'ASILE DES PAUVRES, SOUFFRANTS ET SECOURUS,
COMME À SA PLACE LÉGITIME,
PAR LA PIEUSE RECONNAISSANCE

DE L'AUTORITÉ MUNICIPALE ET DE L'ADMINISTRATION DES HOSPICES
AUXQUELLES SE SONT ASSOCIÉES
L'ACADÉMIE FRANÇAISE ET L'ACADÉMIE DES SCIENCES,
XXVI MAI M.D.CCC.XXXVIII.

M. de Montyon was a remarkable man, in that he refused the exalted office of Keeper of the Seals offered him by Louis XVI., for fear of his moral character deteriorating: "Dites à Sa Majesté que je suis confus de ses bontés. Si je fais un peu de bien dans la place que j'occupe, c'est que je ne suis pas en évidence. En acceptant celle que l'on me propose, je serais exposé à toutes les intrigues, à toutes les cabales de l'envie; je n'aurais peut-être ni le talent ni la force nécessaires pour y résister; dans le doute, je dois m'abstenir."

SAINT-LAURENT.

There is nothing in the present somewhat spick-and-span church to recall its former state in the 6th century. The patron of Nürnberg, of the Escorial, and of Genoa; the young martyr, who from the earliest beginnings of Christian art has been one of its most popular subjects; the saintly deacon, who, as painted by Fra Angelico, charms us by his expression of sweet sanctity, and who, when depicted by the disciples of horrors, makes us shudder and close our eyes—S. Laurence, the deacon, has always been a favourite, and many are the churches dedicated to him. He was a native of Osca or Huesca, in Aragon, and acted as deacon (although a priest) to Sixtus II., bishop of Rome, in the middle of the 3rd century. He had the care of all the precious vessels of the church, and of the money. Times were bad, and Sixtus was denounced as a Christian; then Laurence, following the example of S. Stephen, petitioned the good bishop to allow him to share the captivity. Before Sixtus died he ordered Laurence to distribute all the money and treasure amongst the poor, and predicted his disciple's martyrdom as worse than his own. Laurence went about the city and distributed the alms, which, when the tyrant heard thereof, caused him so much anger that he thrust the deacon into prison, where he converted his gaoler. But the Prefect ordered him to give up his treasure. Then Laurence gathered together the poor and the sick, and presented them to the Prefect; and he being enraged, concocted a new and terrible torture. He made a sort of gridiron bed, upon which the young deacon was laid, and fire being placed underneath, the victim was roasted to death. "Seest thou not, O thou foolish man, being roasted on one side, thou shouldst turn me over, that the other be well

SAINT-LAURENT.

cooked," are the words recorded to prove his steadfastness. Then he lifted his eyes to Heaven, and said, "I thank Thee, O my God and Saviour, that I have been found worthy to enter into Thy blessedness"; and so he passed away into bliss, and was buried in the Via Tiburtina.

Grégoire de Tours speaks of a monastery of S. Laurence in Paris; and S. Domnole, bishop of Le Mans, who died in 581, had been previously its abbot. This abbey has long since disappeared, and been lost to memory; and the parish, which since the 13th century has taken its place, became a dependency of the priory of S. Martin. The *façade* of the present building is no older than 1622; the nave and transept were erected in the 16th, the choir and apse in the 15th century. A niche containing a statue of S. John Baptist is commendable, and some of the details of corbels, gargoyles, cornices, and other exterior decoration are quaint and often grotesque: little beasties jumping about in foliage; small children in fool's caps tumbling about in grotesque attitudes; one little imp being whipped by the schoolmaster; Angels with animal continuations; a hunter shooting arrows at a salamander, and divers other monstrosities.

The interior is cold and uninteresting, the bosses being the best part of the decoration. They are of all manner of devices: S. Nicholas blessing his children; crowns, garlands, Angels' heads; foliage and draperies, and a mass of ornament and little personages—the Virgin and Child, S. John Baptist with his cross, S. Laurence and his gridiron, the scenes from the Passion, and many other conceits.

The apse has been disfigured, after the manner of S. Séverin and S. Germain l'Auxerrois, by Corinthian columns, pilasters, monograms, and trophies—the work of Lepautre. The *jubé* has gone, and divers other Gothic "excrescences," and the church remains a grand example of the last century barbarism. Well has Victor Hugo described those gentlemen, so-called artists, who fell down and worshipped Fashion, as set by its 18th century votaries: " Les modes ont fait plus de mal que les révolutions. Elles ont tranché dans le vif, elles ont attaqué la charpente osseuse de l'art; elles ont coupé, taillé, désorganisé l'édifice, dans la forme comme dans le symbole, dans sa logique comme dans sa beauté. Et puis, elles ont réfait; prétention que n'avaient eue, du moins, ni le temps, ni les révolutions. Elles ont effrontément ajusté, de par *le bon goût*, sur les blessures de l'architecture Gothique leurs misérables colifichets d'un jour, leurs rubans de marbre, leurs pompons de métal: véritable lèpre d'oves, de volutes, d'entournements, de draperies, de guirlandes, de franges, de flammes, de pierre, de nuages, de bronze, d'amours replets, de chérubins bouffis, qui commence à dévorer la face de l'art dans l'oratoire de Catherine de Médicis, et le fait expirer, deux siècles après, tourmenté et grimaçant, dans le boudoir de la Dubarry."

SAINT-LEU-SAINT-GILLES.

About the year 600, the town of Sens was besieged by Clotaire's general, Blidebodes, and grievous was the pain and suffering to which the inhabitants were subjected. But the bishop, Lupus,[*] Leu, or Loup was a holy man, and while the warriors fought he passed his time in prayer. Then he bethought him of a little stratagem. Ostensibly for the object of collecting the citizens for prayer, he set to, and vigorously pulled the church bell. The crowd rushed from all parts of the town, and following the example of their spiritual father, they threw themselves on their knees. Presently came the news that the siege was raised; at the sound of the bell, the enemy had fled precipitately. This, all but miracle, may be accounted for by the fact that bells were first introduced into France about this time (615); and if Clotaire's soldiers, coming from the north and west, had never heard any before, they may have felt much the same sort of terror as was said to have been instilled into the natives during the Ashantee war by the Scottish bagpipes.

Considering that the church has two patrons, it ought surely to be in some way remarkable; but the fact is, it is a very insignificant little building, and devoid of beauty of any kind. It formerly belonged to the Abbey of S. Magloire from which it was separated by only a small space of ground; the abbey having been situated in the Rue S. Denis, and the church in what is now the Boulevard Sebastopol. The latter must have been built in the 13th century, as the abbé Lebeuf found a notice in the archives of S. Magloire to the effect that some little bells had been placed in S. Leu. The church has been so repaired, so cut about (the east end was lopped off when the new boulevard was pierced); it has been so mutilated and travestied, that little remains of the old building. Some of the bosses are elegantly and curiously carved. We see S. Giles and his hind, and S. Loup in episcopal vestments; the 17th century marble bas-reliefs illustrating the Passion; quaint

---

[*] There was another Lupus, bishop of Troyes, who accompanied S. Germain of Auxerre to Britain, to confute the Pelagian heretics.

emaciated bodies and large heads are the characteristics of the crowd.

In one of the chapels, the first on the south, is a curious picture commemorating a terrible event, which led to a miracle. The inscription reads thus:

CETTE IMAGE A ESTÉ FAITE L'AN 1772
EN L'HONNEUR DU SIGNALE MIRACLE ARRIVÉ A PARIS A LA RUE AUX OURS PAROISSE DE ST. LEU ST. GILLES LE 3ME JUILLET L AN 1415 EN MEMOIRE DE QUOY.

LES BOURGEOIS DE LA DITE RUE TOUS LES ANS A PARCIL JOUR BRULENT L'EFIGIE

DU MALFAICTEUR QUI MALHEUREUSEMENT FRAPPA L'IMAGE DE LA SAINCT

VIRGE DE LA QUELLE SORTIT DU SANG ET FUT PUNI PAR ARREST DE LA COUR DE PARLEMENT COME IL EST REPRÉSENTÉ CY DESSOUS.

The picture represents the Virgin and Child sitting under an elegant baldachino, the curtains of which are borne by Angels, who are holding, at the same time, a crown over the head of the holy mother. The following description by Père Du Breul* gives the story of the miracle:

"Le troisième du mois de juillet 1418, veille de sainct Martin,† Bouillant, un soldat ou goujat sortant d'une taverne qui estoit dès lors en la rue aux Ours, désespéré d'avoir perdu tout son argent et ses habits à jouer, jurant et blasphémant, frappa furieusement d'un couteau une image de la Vierge Marie qui estoit au coin de ladite rue. Laquelle image rendit du sang en abondance; de quoy estant advertie la justice, il fut mené par devant l'image, fut frappé d'escourgées depuis six heures du matin jusques au soir, tant que les entrailles luy sortoient, et eut la langue percée d'un fer chaud. Au mesme lieu, tous les ans et à tel jour, on fait un feu pour souvenance de ce miracle. . . . Audit lieu se voit encores une image de Nostre Dame enfermée d'un treillis, auprès de laquelle, contre la parvy, le jour que ce faict ledit feu, l'on attache une tapisserie ou est représenté l'histoire susdite."

Horrors of this kind were common enough in the 14th and 15th centuries; indeed, when we think of Damiens' tortures, even the 18th century was no more humane or decent. In the account of the Black Death in 1348, when 500 persons were

---

* A Religious of the abbey of S. Germain des Prés.

† The summer festival of the Saint, being the day of his ordination, and also of his translation, 4th July.

buried daily, and Jews were tortured and burnt for poisoning the people (as the populace affirmed), an order of Philippe IV. was issued that all blasphemers should have their lips or tongues cut off, as a sanitary measure to dispel the plague. It is curious that such doings should be commemorated in a church dedicated to S. Giles, that gentle hermit who screened the wounded hind from its pursuers, and gave an eternal reproof to the votaries of the hunt. One can imagine what the hermit-Saint would have thought of thus torturing a man, being not only the protector of hunted animals and woodlands, but also of those specimens of human misery, the lepers. Yet for many years the hideous cruelty described above was celebrated as a sort of Guy Fawkes festival, with fireworks, and mannikins of gigantic size, which were marched about the neighbourhood to the terror of all the youthful inhabitants.

SAINT-LOUIS D'ANTIN.

Little need be said of the church which formerly belonged to the Capuchins who were transferred from the Faubourg S. Jacques to the new quarter of the Rue d'Antin in 1783. The church was built by Brongniard, but is of no importance whatever. It now forms a part of the Lycée for those connected therewith who do not find science and literature all that is requisite to their souls' weal.

SAINT LOUIS EN L'ILE.

This church stands upon the little island of the same name, and was commenced by Louis Levau in 1664 ; Gabriel Leduc continued the work, and Jacques Doucet finished it in 1726. Men are said to be happy if they are minus a history. Not so churches ; without it they are anything but interesting. And so we will pass on from the second S. Louis, just noting some of the modern woodwork as respectable.

SAINT-LOUIS DES INVALIDES.

Built by Libéral Bruant from 1671 to 1679, this church has a certain grandeur, and could the dome be seen from it by taking away the intervening partition of ugly painted glass, it would be very imposing. The latter, the burial-place of

Napoleon and of some of his generals, contains also monuments and statues of other military heroes. This part, the cupola (or Tombeau as it is generally termed), was built by Jules Hardouin Mansard, and dedicated by the Cardinal de Noailles in 1706. The exterior is very fine, and, with its gilding, forms a beautiful landmark for all parts of the city and suburbs. The interior, if somewhat pompous, and over addicted to

LE TOMBEAU DE NAPOLÉON.

yellow glass, is nevertheless very grand; and the general effect of the magnificent baldachino over the altar (just such an arrangement as was wanted in S. Paul's), and the subdued light, make a decidedly striking *coup d'œil*.

The statues of Charlemagne and of S. Louis are by Coyzevox and Nicolas Coustou; the cupola was painted by Charles de Lafosse and by Jouvenet. The statue of Turenne, which has at last found a resting-place, after having been shunted about since its departure from S. Denis, is the work of Tuby and Marsy. In the centre, under the beautiful dome, is Napoleon's tomb, sunk some feet below the surface.

In the chapel proper are rows of flags of all nations suspended from each side of the roof; but beyond these there is little that is picturesque except during the military mass on Sunday morning. Then, when the pensioners line the aisle, bearing their swords and halberds; when the drums beat at the Elevation, and the old men present arms, the effect is both grand and intensely pathetic. Formerly the military band played throughout the offices; now the duty is done by the organ.

LA SAINTE-MADELEINE.

If good materials and excellent workmanship can make a building interesting, assuredly the Madeleine ought to be so. Commenced in 1764 as a church, its fate was somewhat similar to that of S. Geneviève, for, in 1806, Napoleon, then busy in Posen, sent his orders that it should be finished as a Temple of Glory. The pediment was to bear the following inscription :—" L'empereur Napoléon aux soldats de la grande armée ;" and the 5th article of the decree was thus composed : " Tous les ans, aux anniversaires des batailles d'Austerlitz et d'Iéna, le monument sera illuminé, et il y sera donné un concert précédé d'un discours sur les vertus nécessaires au soldat, et d'un éloge de ceux qui périrent sur le champ de bataille dans ces journées mémorables. . . Dans les discours et odes, il est expressément défendu de faire mention de l'empereur."

Pierre Vignon carried on the work, and the building grew into a magnificent temple, planned upon the Maison Carrée of Nismes. The results of Waterloo turned it again church ways, but it was not finished until 1842. The bronze doors are perhaps the best work of Baron de Triqueti ; and the group of the Magdalen over the altar may be no more mundane and meretricious than is usual in Marochetti's performances. The picture in the vault over the altar is a jumble by Ziegler of sacred and secular personages, from the Magdalen and her Master down to Napoleon the arrogant. It is supposed to be an allegory of the history of Christianity, which Clovis introduced to France, and Napoleon patted on the back by means of the Concordat. The most important position in the picture is occupied by the last-named brigand—the poor Pope even being in a secondary place, somewhat inferior to the imperial eagle. The group in the baptistry is by Rude; the one opposite, in a chapel dedicated to marriage, by **Pradier**. It was in the Madeleine that some of the Communards were massacred in 1871. At the end of the struggle, about 300 of them were driven into the church; and there, before the altar where their victim, the abbé Duguerry had officiated, they were mown down in terrible retribution, with no more mercy shown them than they had accorded to the hostages.

In the interior fittings of the church, no expense has been spared, and what it lacks in beauty as regards sculpture and painting it possesses in its marble walls and its carved woodwork. The pulpit is an excellent piece of modern woodcarving; the details of the ornament are in the best style; and so are most of the worshippers; for it is one of the fashionable churches of Paris. There, especially at the lazy mass (as the old writer has it, "la messe des paresseux," which was said at "la plus haute heure du matin," at "unze heures,") you see "*des mondaines*" by the dozen; only the lazy eleven o'clock has become one in the afternoon. What in the world would the old chronicler have said to the swarms of fashionables who just save their souls by hurrying off after a comfortable *déjeuner* to those one o'clock masses? But there is a mixture at the Madeleine; old ladies of the *noblesse; nouveaux riches;* a few soldiers who like the music; half-a-dozen husbands who go as a duty to their wives; an old Bretonne gorgeous in chains and muslin, and velvet bodice; and two or three black women, charming in the yellow silk handkerchiefs which swathe their heads. It is a mixture, and what brings them? Probably the music, for at no church in Paris, and few elsewhere, do you hear such refined, soft, emotional strains as there. Sometimes the boys' voices are not of the best; but the artistic taste with which they sing is always there. S. Roch has a reputation for its choir, gained many years ago by its execution of the masses of Mozart and Haydn; but it no longer deserves it. S. Eustache also is celebrated for its music. But there is a special tone about that of the Madeleine one meets with nowhere else; it aims at raising one's soul from the earth upon which it is supposed to grovel; it certainly never interrupts prayer or disturbs thought. Even on Good Friday, when the old *Passione* by Haydn, or the new one by Dubois, is performed, refinement, not clatter, is the distinguishing characteristic. If only some of our London organists would take a leaf out of the Madeleine music-book ! Just think of the noise at a certain West-end church, which is the model of all that ritual should be. From its foundation, what we all loved was the refinement of its music ; it was the exponent of Gregorian chants and Plain song. Now the most elaborate compositions are performed for the edification and vanity of the choir. Church music ought certainly to be an aid to prayer, not a disturbing force ; but what else can it be, when organ and choir are all shrieking Haydn's Imperial Mass, or Beethoven in C, and each man or boy is trying to get the mastery? It is a bitter duel between organ and voices. All the great masters' masses are sung at the Madeleine ; but you can devote yourself to your own prayers all through them without being disturbed, if you so wish. Moreover, one hour suffices in Paris for what in London endures an hour and a half, or more. And is not the long, elaborate *credo* answerable for the objectionable Roman practice of sitting through the greater part of it? Of course church music should be of the most perfect kind ; but perfection is sure to be greater where less is attempted ; and the mere repetitions of words, and the placing of the accent upon the wrong note in the English translation, make these elaborate masses unsuitable in our churches.

PÈRE HYACINTH PREACHING AT THE MADELEINE.

The ceremonial at the Madeleine always gives strangers the impression of having been over-rehearsed. The black-clothed beadles walk about with measured steps, particularly the frog faced one ; the *Suisses* in their cocked hats leisurely saunter about with their halberds looking the essence of flunkeyism, and never issue from their stereotyped expression of importance and unmixed boredom, except upon occasions when

a foreigner fails to kneel at solemn moments. Why need the good Protestant remain sitting when the bell rings, feigning a kneeling posture by a sort of zigzag attitude? Up comes the *Suisse*, and shaking the back of his chair, tries to jerk him out of it. Why not stand, if rags of popery and scarlet women prevent you kneeling? Or why go at all, if you cannot do at Rome as Rome does? I confess to feeling a sensation of distress, and am much upset when that chair-tipping begins. And the worst of if is that, although the victim is innocent of what lies in store for him, we, who know the ways of the *Suisses*, anxiously anticipate the fatal moment. Sometimes, too, the British-born struggles to look pious, while he furtively reads his Baedeker, never dreaming that the benighted foreigner knows that Classic by its blood-red exterior. We are a great people, and are justly proud of our institutions; but we should be no less great if we had a little more respect for other folks, and other folks' manners and customs.

It is curious how the church beadle varies. At the Madeleine he is pure flunkey. His cocked hat is high and broad, like the old Bumble of our childhood; he is whiskered, but not bearded; he has an arrogant way with him as he precedes the priest who makes the collection; and as he carries the bag into which the alms are emptied from time to time, he looks the essence of important officialism. Likewise, when he demands, in a commanding voice, "Pour les pauvres, *s'il* vous *plait!*" few persons would say him nay. Not so the *Suisses* of S. Eustache; they have the military air; the cocked hat is low, and worn as by the Marshals of France. Such are they also at S. Roch, and at both churches they salute at the Elevation, *à la militaire*.

It has always seemed to me that the author of *Monsieur, Madame et Bébé*, pictured the Madeleine in his scenes of Madame at church; at all events I have often seen the like. She kneels on her velvet-covered *prie-Dieu*, and tells her beads; and then, between a *Pater Noster* and a new batch of *Ave Marias*, she turns round to a neighbour, "Ah! chère madame, comment allez vous? et monsieur votre mari? Et la chère petite Bébé?" "Merci, chère baronne, mon mari ne va pas trop mal; il a la migraine, voilà tout. Et Bébé, c'est un ange; elle est ravissante, le petit chou. Mais moi, je souffre, oh, comme je souffre! je suis tellement éreintée que . . . Je vous salue Marie, pleine de grâce." . . . "How

adorable is the Madeleine," said Dibden; but he meant its exterior at twilight, when the lights spring up on the neighbouring boulevards. And so it is in its way; but its way is to some of us not the most beautiful way.

Many are the functions which take place there; marriages and funerals by the score. At the latter, it affords ample room under its portico for that terrible French custom which forces all the family of the deceased to stand by the door and receive the condolences of their friends and acquaintances. How do they ever survive it? And why do they not rebel against the conventionality, and give it up? Because they are at once the most conventional of nations, added to the most revolutionary. The funeral terror is greater in France that here at home; it is one of the few things in which we a e ahead of our neighbours. We do not waste quite so much upon putting our friends underground, although we too are compelled to pay twice as much as we ought. But in some respects the French are far more decent. Men raise their hats at passing funerals, and I have never seen the undertakers sitting in the open car when returning from the cemetery; an indecent proceeding like the one immortalized in *Figaro*. "Mon Dieu! What strange people, ces Anglais! When they return from a funeral, the friends of the deceased ride upon the top of the hearse with their legs hanging over it!"

One of the beauties of the Madeleine is the flower-garden at its feet, and the tree-planted boulevards which surround it. How pleasant it is to be able to sit down in the air upon a warm evening; would that we could do likewise! Here, sunset is the last moment when we can breathe the air of most of the parks, without perpetually tramping round and round upon our weary legs. But in Paris we may sit and gaze upon the buildings by moonlight if we like; and certainly, that is the most flattering time for the Madeleine. Its portico, lighted up by the moon with the dark shadows thrown behind it, has a decidedly grand appearance.

SAINTE-MARGUERITE.

The church, dedicated to

> *Mild Margarete, that was God's maid;*
> *Maid Margarete, that was so meke and mild,*

in not of much importance. The popularity of S. Margaret was so great in the Middle Ages that it seems strange so little notice has been taken of her in Paris. Only think what a lovely dragon the sculptor of the monsters upon the towers of Notre-Dame would have contrived! We have only to look upon them to picture to ourselves the dreadful worm.

> Maiden Margrete tho (*then*)
> Loked her beside,
> And sees a loathly dragon
> Out of an kirn (*corner*) glide :
> His eyen were ful griesly,
> His mouth opened wide,
> And Margrete might no where flee,
> There she must abide.
>
> Maiden Margrete
> Stood still as any stone,
> And that loathly worm,
> To her-ward gan gone,
> Took her in his foul mouth,
> And swallowed her flesh and bone.
> Anon he brast—(*burst*)
> Damage hath she none !
> Maiden Margrete,
> Upon the dragon stood ;
> Blyth was her harte,
> And joyful was her mood.*

The church of S. Marguerite is in the Rue S. Bernard, Faubourg S. Antoine. The chapel of the Souls in Purgatory is a curious composition by Louis, dated 1765; and still more curious was the burying, in 1737, of the tomb of Antoine Fayet, one of the *curés*, because of the indecent nudity of the white marble Angels, a piece of astounding prudery in that peculiarly indecent period of French history. Some pictures illustrative of the life of S. Vincent de Paul are remarkable from the truthfulness of the portraiture; they were formerly in the Lazarists' Church. A marble *Descent from the Cross*, designed by Girardon, and sculptured by his pupils Le Lorrain and Nourrisson for the church of S. Landry, found its way to S. Marguerite in 1817, where it accompanies another *Descent* painted upon wood, and very excellent in its way.

SAINT-MARTIN DES CHAMPS.

Situated upon the east side of a square which lies between the Rue S. Martin and the Boulevard Sabastopol is the Con-

* Metrical legend in the Auchinleck MS. quoted by Mrs. Jameson.

servatoire des Arts et Métiers, formerly the rich priory of
S. Martin. As its name indicates, it used to be surrounded by
fields and gardens; now it is an oasis of antiquity, built up
upon every side but the square with huge modern houses. Its
old walls enclose a museum; its chapel contains hydraulic
machines, and its refectory is a public library. One of the
twenty or more turrets which surmounted the wall at intervals
still remains; but the chapel of S. Michel, which old Nicolas
Arrade founded in the 13th century as a tomb-house for himself and his descendants, the chapter-house, the tower, the Lady-Chapel, and several statues of royal personages, have all been
demolished—not by Revolutionists, but by the latter-day
monks, who also saw fit to rebuild their cloisters, and ornament them with handsome Doric columns. These acts of
barbarism were perpetrated some hundred and fifty years ago.
But in spite of adversity, S. Martin still gives us some idea of
a conventual foundation, and in Paris it is the only one which
has survived improvements by friend and foe. It still has its
gate leading into a large courtyard, with church, refectory, and
a portion of the cloisters.

Although the priory ranked after all the abbeys of Paris, it
was well-nigh as important, and as rich. The prior enjoyed a
revenue of 45,000 *livres*, and had the right of nomination to
sixty benefices, twenty-nine priories, and many curacies and
chapels.

The legend of S. Martin bestowing half his cloak upon a
beggar is well known, and a frequent subject for painters. But
he was given to other works of mercy, and one, healing the
leper, is said to have taken place upon the site of this particular
convent. S. Martin is the patron of soldiers. Born in the reign
of Constantine the Great, at what is now Stain, in Hungary,
Martin early became a Christian, but his parents being Pagans,
he was not baptized until comparatively late in life. His
father was a Roman soldier and tribune, and the son was
enrolled in a cavalry legion. Obliged to leave his native
country for Gaul, we find him in the year 332 quartered at
Amiens; and here it was that he performed the act which has
made him so famous in literature and art—the cutting of his
cloak in two to clothe a starving beggar. His namesake,
Martin Schoen, gives him such a voluminous mantle that one
feels the act of cutting it in half to have been that of a highly-practical mind—enough for you, and enough for me. But

other painters, on the contrary, depict the cloak as of such very small dimensions that one can only marvel that the Saint did not give it all to the beggar; for a portion of the garment could scarcely have benefited either party. This act brought him, however, praise from Heaven, and he hastened to receive baptism, being then twenty-three years of age. At forty he left the army, and was elected Bishop of Tours; and again we read of a similar story of clothing the naked, this time with his sacerdotal vestment during the celebration of mass.

S. Martin founded several churches and monasteries, and many more were dedicated to him after his death. Marmoutier, near Nantes, was a very celebrated convent; and in England there are a great many churches of which he is the patron. S. Augustine, when he came to Britain, found a chapel in the neighbourhood of Canterbury, which had been dedicated to S. Martin as early as the 5th century, and there he baptized his first converts. The church is certainly one of the earliest in England, and the font cannot be later than the 11th century; but whether it be the identical one at which King Ethelbert stood to be baptized in the 7th century is considered doubtful. Still, though much restored from time to time, the building retains numbers of Roman bricks incorporated into its walls; and that Queen Bertha worshipped in a church upon the same spot, or close by, is certain, tradition also pointing to a stone coffin in which she lies.

To return to S. Martin, the legend relates that when he was entering Paris, as Bishop of Tours, he met a wretched leper at the gate, and, filled with compassion and love, he embraced him, and thus healed him of his leprosy. This was the act which King Henri I. commemorated by founding the priory in 1060. His son Philippe I. dedicated the church in 1067, placing the new foundation under the patronage of the abbot of Cluny, of which monastery S. Martin des Champs was the third daughter. Its domains originally consisted of several acres of land, which, as time went on, became more and more valuable; and probably, in consequence of its great wealth, it was governed by a long succession of illustrious men; at first regular, and subsequently, titular abbots, of which class was his eminence the Cardinal Richelieu.

It is owing to the cession of the last of the turrets, built by prior Hugues IV. to the town in 1712, and to the erection of a fountain at its base, that we now possess this fragment of the old wall. The principal gate, dating 1575, and ornamented with statues of the two royal founders, was unfortunately demolished at the same time.

The church belongs to two distinct periods. The nave was built about the middle of the 13th century, and is without aisles or pillars. It is lighted by pointed windows, and covered by a pointed timber roof. The choir and apse belong to the middle of the 12th century, and are peculiar in their arrangement. The choir is raised from the nave, and round it on a lower level are double aisles, divided by clustered columns which support the vaulting. Thus, the choir is approached from the nave by steps in the usual manner; but to enter the apsidal chapels one has to descend three or four steps from the nave. There are a few fragments of tombs with effigies of the priors, and some mutilated stone coffins. All the rest of the contents of the church have disappeared; it is in fact, architecturally, an empty shell. The statue of the Blessed Virgin sculptured in wood, and held in great veneration by the faithful worshippers at S. Martin, was taken to S. Denis. The whole building has been gorgeously decorated in colour, and, if restored to its proper use, would be, after the Sainte-Chapelle, the most interesting church in Paris; but the desecration grates upon our religious sentiments, and the noise of the machinery in motion distracts one's nerves. The study of architecture is not rendered easier by the rattle of a dozen or more steam engines, compared to which the confusion of tongues must have been a very small clatter.

Tradition gives Pierre de Montereau as the architect of the refectory, which is a *chef-d'œuvre* of the 13th century. It is an oblong building with seven tall, elegant, single-shaft pillars down the centre, dividing it into two equal parts longitudinally. Upon the side walls are an equal number of columns reaching about half-way down, and supported by foliated corbels to match the capitals; the vault, springing from these and the pillars, divide the length into eight bays. The windows consist of two lights surmounted by a rose; but upon one side they have been blocked up. The reading pulpit, which is built into the wall, is a beautiful specimen of its kind. It is lighted from the back by three little windows, and approached by a staircase in the wall, with open arcading to give light upon the refectory side. The building has been decorated with colour, and a painting representing S. Martin dividing his cloak, mediævalized by M. Steinheil—the whole sufficiently harmonious.

The rest of the buildings are modern, or have been modernized; most of the destruction having been perpetrated by the monks, who, like all authoritative Paris of the last century, had Classicism on the brain. At S. Martin, as at S. Nicolas des Champs, S. Germain l'Auxerrois, and S. Séverin (not to mention other churches), Doric columns have taken the place of the old work—they must have been sculptured by the hundred. The chapel of the Virgin, the chapter-house, the old cloister, which, according to Piganiol de la Force, had not the like in Paris, and the statues of divers Kings and Saints, were all swept away to make room for modern improvements; but the refectory was left intact, and having been used as the library, the transformation of the convent into a museum has affected it less than the chapel. As we pass into it from the outer world of trams and omnibuses, with all the *va-et-vient* of a great city, we seem to be suddenly transported into the olden time—into a world which, if not a better, was certainly a more artistic and a quieter one.

THE REFECTORY.

SAINT-MÉDARD.

The French S. Swithin shares with his brethren on the opposite bank of the Seine, *les frères Gervais et Protais*, a predilection for drenching us on and after his *fête* day; so that, what with S. Médard's 8th of June, S. Gervais' and S. Protais' 19th June, and S. Swithin's 15th July, we who live upon our

respective sides of the ditch may reckon upon a good three
weeks of wet, over and above the forty days, if unhappily it
rains upon the earlier of those unlucky festivals.

> S'il pleut le jour de Saint-Medard,
> Il pleut quarante jours plus tard ;
> S'il pleut le jour de Saint Gervais et de Saint Protais,
> Il pleut quarante jours après.

But if S. Médard was vindictive in his ways, he compensated
us for his downpours by inventing that handy instrument
without which life would be unbearable. The French say
that an Englishman goes to bed in his hat, clutching his
umbrella, which is a polite way of reproving him for his
peculiar and insular practices; but how could he live without
his umbrella? and kind Médard, foreseeing the state of damp-
ness to which our northern atmosphere was leading us, turned
to account an accident which befel him. In was in this wise.
On a certain hot day in a certain hot summer, Médard and his
friends went a picnicing, when suddenly a storm disturbed
their innocent junketings. All were thoroughly soaked through
from head to foot, with the exception of the host, who suddenly
found himself protected from the rain by the outspread wings
of an eagle which hovered over his head. This was the birth
of the umbrella, which, as everyone knows, is of French, and
not of oriental origin. In Belgium the rainy Saint is one
Godeliève; in Germany the character is undertaken by the
Seven Sleepers, showing the wisdom of the Teuton in slum-
bering through his miseries. Amongst the flowers, the money-
wort is dedicated to S. Médard.

At the commencement of the last century, Jansenist pilgrimages and divers miracles took place at the little church, curing
those suffering from convulsions; young girls had fits which
gave them "comical twitchings of the nerves. Some would
bark all night, and others leaped about like frogs. Sister Rose
sipped the air with a spoon, as your babies do pap, and lived
on it forty days; another swallowed a New Testament, bound in
calf. Some had themselves hung, others crucified, and one,
called Sister Rachel, when nailed to a cross, said she was quite
happy. In their holy meetings, they beat, trampled, punc-
tured, crucified, and burnt one another without the least
sentiment of pain." All this was done under Louis XV., and
attested by thousands of witnesses, until at last the archbishop,

by means of a strong military guard, put an end to the folly. Thereupon some wag wrote upon a wall:

> De par le roi défense à Dieu
> De faire miracle en ce lieu.

Large packages of the earth were exported to work miracles in the provinces and in foreign countries. One of these marvellous cures is related, scoffingly, in a song of the Duchesse de Maine:

> Un décrotteur à la royale,
> Du talon gauche estropié,
> Obtint par grace speciale
> D'etre boiteux de l'autre pied.*

The church of S. Médard is in the Rue Mouffetard, and originally the ground belonged to the abbey of S. Geneviève. At first the monks only erected a small chapel, which they placed under the protection of the great Bishop of Noyon, who was the friend and chancellor of the early Mérovingian Kings. In the 12th century the chapel is designated as a church in the bulls of the popes, and up to the Revolution it was served by the regular canons of the abbey.

The church is of no importance, dating only from the 15th century. The pillars are without capitals; but, as in many of the other churches, the keystones and bosses are elaborately carved. Some of them represent the Annunciation, the Visitation, the Descent of the Holy Spirit, and other Scriptural subjects, besides monsters, griffins, and garlands of foliage. In one of the chapels a little glass of the 16th century remains; and a retable, upon which a Notre-Dame de Pitié is painted, is also worthy of note.

In 1784 an architect named Petit-Radel conceived the idea of transforming S. Médard into a modern temple of Jupiter, with not much success. Doric and Corinthian columns, palms and personages, adorn the sanctuary and the *chevet*. Better are the fragments of old glass which are interspersed with the new in some of the windows; a S. Fiacre, patron of cabs and coaches, a Holy Family, S. Michael, a Calvary, and many Angels; but they are the merest scraps of former grandeur. The chapel of the Virgin was built by the "artist" who mutilated and distorted the choir, and is in the same grandiose style. The academician, Olivier Patru, and Pierre Nicole, the theologian, were buried at S. Médard.

* *The American in Paris.*

SAINT-MERRI.

At the bottom of the **Rue S. Martin**, close to the Rue de Rivoli, is a spot which, during the ages of faith, was much reverenced for its miracle-working powers. In the 7th century, the whole district was a forest, and doubtless the King and courtiers hunted there; for are we not told that the Louvre, hard by, was in early days but a royal hunting-box. As is well known, Paris, the Lutetia of the Gauls, consisted only of the present Cité, the island upon which stands the cathedral. All around were forests, well stocked with game (animals more or less wild); and here and there, probably, small outlying settlements which we should now call villages and hamlets.

In the midst of the wood stood a little chapel dedicated to S. Peter, which was as much surrounded by trees and shrubs as the present church of S. Merri is by streets and houses. Adjoining this chapel was a cell, or hermitage, and it was there that S. Merri, and his disciple, S. Frodulphe, sojourned when on their way from Autun to the shrines of S. Denis and S. Germain. S. Merri was abbot of Autun, but he seems to have been glad of a change to the great city; for so it befel, that instead of returning to his abbey, he stayed in this little wooded retreat, undisturbed by aught but the singing of the birds and the sighing of the trees, for the space of three years. Then, on the 29th of August, about the year 700, he died, and was buried in the chapel. Many and wondrous were the miracles wrought at his tomb; and so famous did it become that S. Peter's patronage was forgotten, and the church was looked upon by the people as being under the exclusive protection of S. Merri.

About the end of the 9th century, a redoubtable warrior, **Eudes** de Fauconnier, desiring to celebrate his part in the expulsion of the **Normans from** the neighbourhood, erected a new church on the site of the little chapel, or in its immediate neighbourhood. This was dedicated to the two saints, S. Merri being placed before S. Peter. When this church, in its turn, was demolished in the time of François Ier, the remains of the founder were found in a stone coffin, the bones of his legs and feet being still shod in his gilt leathern boots. The coffin was re-buried in the choir, and an inscription placed upon a white marble slab: *Hic jacet vir bonae memoriae Odo Falconarius, huius ecclesiae, ora pro eo.* In the opinion of the abbé Lebeuf, this Odo was the famous warrior who with Godefroi defended the city against the Normans in 886. The surname *Falconarius* may come from Odo having been made the King's falconer, or from the kind of lance which he used, *falco*, because it was bent; just as Charles, the grandfather of Charlemagne, was known by the surname of Martel. The gilt leather boots denote a personage of the 9th century; similar *chaussures* may be seen in miniatures of the Carlovingian period. One of the monks of S. Germain des Prés, Abbon, has celebrated the heroic deeds of Odo, and testified to the ability of the surgical instrument makers of the 9th century:—

> UNA DIES ISTUM VOLUIT SIC LUDERE LUDUM,
> HIS DUCIBUS, GODOFREDO NEC NON ET ODONE;
> BELLIGERI FUERANT UDDONIS CONSULIS AMBO.
> IDEM ODO PRAETEREA OPPOSUIT SE SAEPUIS ILLIS
> ET VICIT JUGETER VICTOR. HEN! LIQUER UT ILLUM
> DEXTRA MANUS BELLO QUONDAM, CUJUS LOCA CINXIT
> FERREA, PENE VIGORE NIHIL INFIRMIOR IPSA.*

S. Merri was made into a parish church in the 12th century, and in the early years of the following century it became collegiate. It was called the third daughter of Notre-Dame, a title given to churches which were served by the clergy of the mother church, its chapter consisting of a *chefcier*, who filled the position of the *curé*, six canons, and six chaplains.

The present church was commenced in 1520 or a few years later, and finished in 1642; the architects adhering to the original plan, without any change of style, which is not often the case in churches that were so long in course of construction. The beautiful west front is a mass of rich ornamentation; its three portals, the pinnacles, corbels, niches, etc., being carved with various conceits—animals, human heads, flowers, vine-leaves, and so on, one little head having a cap such as is worn by the peasants of Auvergne. The statues, large and small, are modern, having been put in position in 1842, replacing those destroyed during the Revolution. Those round the *voussure* are copied from one of the portals of Notre-Dame, and consequently are two centuries too early for the church. Another blunder of the modern architect is the placing of a demon in the centre at the point of the arch, where the Mediæval artists invariably put the figure of Christ or of Our Lady. The lower part of the tower is contemporary with the

---

* De Bellis Parisiacae urbis (M. F. de Guilhermy, *Inscriptions*).

church, but the upper stories have been rebuilt in the 17th century, and consist of Renaissance arches and shafts. Upon the opposite side is a little turret of open woodwork, and from the roof some old gargoyles stretch themselves out. The church is cruciform ; unfortunately it is partly hidden by the Presbytery and other buildings. Indeed, like many Continental churches, it is so built about by surrounding houses that one only gets a view of it here and there. It is extraordinary that in such a city as Paris this is tolerated. At S. Germain l'Auxerrois there is (or was, not long ago) an extraordinary little wooden hut (presumably the dwelling of the sacristan) built in between the buttresses of the east end, and completely filling up two windows of the apse. The whole erection being in wood, it could easily be taken down ; for it is only supported on great wooden piles, and approached by a sort of ladder. Such a state of things only exists in Catholic countries, and the more Catholic—as, for example, Belgium— the more complete is this sort of desecration.

The havoc made in the interior of the church by the 18th century architects is deplorable. Windows have been destroyed, piers have been stuccoed over, and pointed arches turned into round ones. The pillars are late Perpendicular, or rather Flamboyant, shafts without capitals ; and round the nave, between the arches and the clerestory, runs a little frieze of foliage and quaint birds and beasts, a feature which is not common. All the bosses of the choir and apse are very richly decorated, and the vaulting is good, but both the choir and the *chevet* have been sadly " improved." About 1753 the brothers Slodtz were commissioned to convert the thirteen pointed arches of the choir into round ones, and to encase the pillars in panellings of stucco, which was marbled and gilt, the last bay being profusely decorated with golden sun-rays. One of these unfortunate brothers, Michel-Angelo by name, designed the pulpit, a mass of palm-tree decoration, surmounted by a female figure of Religion ; and to place this wondrous production, a whole bay of the nave had to be demolished. The year following three chapels were destroyed to make room for the new square, barn-like Chapel of the Communion ; which, besides being beautified by the Slodtz brothers' sculptures, was further embellished with a picture by Charles Coypel. The modest sum paid to these miserable, so-called artists, for hacking the church to pieces, was 50,000 *écus*.

SAINT-MERRI; NORTH-WEST DOOR.

The crypt is most interesting, and is said to have been a reproduction of the original one which contained the tomb of S. Merri. It was used for some time as a workshop by the cleaners of the church, and was the depository of brooms, brushes and lamps. It has a stumpy central column, from which spring the ribs of the vault, the capital being ornamented with vine-leaves. It is square, and divided into four parts. A few remains of recumbent tombs can be seen in the pavement; but of the monuments of Arnaud de Pomponne, ambassador of Louis XIV., and of Jean Chapelain, the author of *La Pucelle*, nothing remains. The crypt, with its solid central pillar, resembles that in the Louvre of the time of Philippe Auguste, which has lately been brought to light.

Much of the old glass has gone, the central portion of each window having been taken away, to throw more light upon the marbled stucco. What remains is in good 16th century style, the work, probably, of Héron, Jacques de Paroy, Chamu, and Jean Nogare, whom Levieil records to have been the artists employed. The subjects are from the history of SS. Peter, Joseph, John the Baptist, and Francis of Assisi; but it is most difficult to follow the designs, as not only are there the gaps of plain glass, but what was taken out has been used for repairing the other windows. Still a few subjects can be traced; the Raising of Lazarus; an Angel bringing food to the Virgin as she works in the temple; the Magdalen preaching to the people from a pulpit; the Beheading of S. John. In one of the chapels the history of Susannah figures—also Joseph and Jacob, and other Old Testament worthies. Three persons, identical in form and features, represent the Holy Trinity; they hold each other's hands in a circle, upon which is inscribed, *Ego sum alpha et omega, primus et novissimus*. On another window are the Sybils carrying the emblems of the Nativity and the Passion, the Cradle, a lantern, the Scourge, and the Cross.

The church possesses a very curious holy-water stoop of the time of Louis XII. It is about three feet high, more like a baptismal font than a stoop in size; it is octagonal, and stands upon a pedestal with a square base. The upper part is decorated with the arms of France and of Bretagne, and the instruments of the Passion. A small amount of carved woodwork of the Renaissance period remains—fragments of sculptured columns, pilasters, children, birds, and trophies. But a most remarkable picture of the 16th century arrests the visitor's attention as he saunters round the aisles, *S. Geneviève* sitting in a sort of Druidical circle surrounded by her flock of sheep—a rare combination of mystic Paganism and Christian legend.

A mosaic tablet of the *Virgin and Child* now in the Hôtel Cluny (No. 1795) was formerly in this church. It was given by Jean de Ganay, first president of the Parliament. Piganiol de la Force gave the continuation of the inscription as "*Opus magistri Davidis,* Florentini, Anno M.CCCC.LXXXXVI." Jean de Ganay went to Italy with Charles VIII., and took part in the campaign of 1494 and 1495, and for some time he was chancellor of the kingdom of Naples; but as he was not first president until 1505, the mosaic must have been sent to Paris subsequently to his sojourn in Italy. His epitaph runs thus:

> CY GIST LE CORPS DE NOBLE CHEVALIER
> JEAN DE GANNY DE FRANCE CHANCELIER
> ET ZELATEUR DE LA CHOSE PUBLIQUE.
> TARDIF A NUIRE ET PREST A CONSEILLER
> DU BIEN DAUTRUY CAR CESTOIT LE PILLIER,
> PHILOSOPHAL VRAY ARISTOTILIQUE,
> POURTANT HUMAINS UN CHACUN SE APPLIQUE
> PRIER JESUS PAR MESSES ET PAR DITS
> QUIL LUY PARDONNE ET DONNE PARADIS.
> OBIIT ANNO 1512.

M. de Sommerard attributes this mosaic to David Ghirlandajo.

SAINT-NICOLAS DES CHAMPS.

The patron saint of children, of schoolboys, of poor maidens and travellers, of merchants, and, above all, of pawnbrokers, was popular in Paris as elsewhere, and thus we find three churches dedicated to him. S. Nicolas was a performer of stupendous miracles. Thus it happened that during a time of famine, while he was visiting his flock, he discovered that a certain disciple of the Evil One murdered little children, and, cannibal-like, feasted on them. And so audacious was this fiend in human shape, that he impudently served up the dismembered limbs of a young babe for the good bishop; who, seeing this wickedness, went to the tub where the children's remains were being salted down, and making the sign of the cross over them, the babes all stood up. This is a favourite subject in art; and not the least beautiful of all the saints and martyrs in the processional frieze in S. Vincent de Paul is Flandrin's conception of S. Nicholas.* Why the Saint's three balls, which

PORCH OF SAINT-NICOLAS.

seem to have been purses given to three poor maidens, should

* See page 335

have become the sign of pawnbrokers, seems doubtful. Perhaps simply as being emblems of gold lent by merchants to impecunious customers. The story of the children is probably an allegory of the conversion of sinners, the tub being the baptismal font and the wicked host, the evil state in which all men are born. S. Nicholas is also the guardian of property, and in that form figures upon the windows of the cathedral of Chartres. The Saint's image was stolen by a Jew, and placed in guardianship over his treasures. Then came robbers, who carried off the property, which, the Jew discovering, led to the chastisement of the bishop's effigy. But S. Nicholas was equal to the occasion, and reproving the Jew, ordered the robbers to restore what they had stolen; and when the Hebrew saw the miracle, he became converted, he and his whole house. This, too, may be the reason for S. Nicholas' patronage of pawnbrokers, who are many of them, indeed most of them, Jews.

In the 12th century S. Nicolas des Champs was but a chapel built upon the domain of the priory of S. Martin. Two centuries later it was rebuilt; but in the 16th century, being too small for its parishioners, it was widened by turning the chapels of the nave into an aisle, and erecting fresh chapels outside it. Later on it was again enlarged, until it has become one of the longest of the Paris churches.

The *façade* in the Rue S. Martin is in the Flamboyant style, and not without some beauty, with its pinnacles and turrets, its niches and statuettes; but the most striking part of the church is the richly-sculptured doorway in the Rue Aumaire, a mass of niches, figures of Angels, and Flamboyant ornament of the most elaborate kind—birds, baskets of flowers, borne by pious little personages, and every kind of foliage, reminding us of the works of Germain Pilon.

The interior shows the change of style from shafts without capitals to the latest development in the way of Doric columns. The High Altar is ornamented with Corinthian columns, some stucco Angels by Jacques Sarazin, and a picture of *the Assumption* by Simon Vouet. The best picture in the church is M. Bonnat's early work of *S. Vincent de Paul*. An old panel of a *Calvary* is a very good specimen of one of the unknown artists of the 16th century.

A few celebrities were buried in S. Nicolas; the *savant* Guillaume Budé, who died in 1540; the philosopher Pierre

Gassendi; the historians Henri and Adrien de Valois; and Mdlle. de Scudéry; but their monuments have vanished. On the pavement are some stones bearing the names of Rochechouart, Crillon, Labriffe, Potier de Novion, Mesmes, and several others.

Here is one of the many curious epitaphs:

> LE CIEL L'ESTIMENT TROP POUR LA
> LAISSER PLUS LONTEMPS MORTELE,
> LAISSANT A SON ÉPOUX UNE FILLE
> POUR GAGE DE LEUR ÉTROITE ET
> INMORTELE AMITIÉ, DANS LAQU'ELLE
> IL SURVIT POUR PLEURER LE RESTE
> DE SES JOURS SA DURE SEPARATION
> D'AVEC CETTE CHERE ÉPOUSE, QUI' ÉTOIT
> RECOMANDABLE, PAR SA TRES GRANDE
> DOUCEUR, SA VIE PURE ET INOCENTE,
> ET SA PRUDENCE AU DESUS DE SON
> AAGE, QUI LUY ONT OUVERT LE
> CHEMIN DE L'IMORTALITÉ.
> REQUIESCAT IN PACE.

In the 16th century the acolytes of Notre-Dame celebrated their well-known *fêtes* at S. Nicolas, performing various antics *en route;* but as their disorderly conduct was great, and the "*facéties*" practised led to divers troubles and various abominations, the ceremony resolved itself latterly into a simple Benediction which the *enfants de chœur* chanted in honour of their patron.

SAINT-NICOLAS DU CHARDONNET.

This is an ugly church, with traditions going back to the 13th century, but with nothing thereof now to be seen, in the Rue S. Victor. The present building dates from 1656 to 1709. A picture by Lebrun, of *The Miracle of Moses*, adorns one of the chapels; and the tomb erected by him to his mother's memory, by Tuby and Callignon, is to be found in another. Lebrun's own tomb is by Coyzevox; Jérôme Bignon's, by Girardon. There are also pictures by Le Sueur, Coypel, Corot, Desgoffes, and Mignard.

Suzanne Butay, widow of Lebrun, was a generous body, and left a number of legacies to the poor of the parish, and divers other church institutions, which are recorded thus:

LADITE DAME SUZANNE BUTAY VEUVE DUDIT FEU S^R LEBRUN PAR SON TETA^MT.
OLOGRAPHE DE XIII SEPTEMBRE MDCXCVI RECONNU DEVANT VATRY, ET TORINON NOT^RES . . . . A LEGUÉ AUX PAUVRES HONTEUX, ET AUX PAUVRES MALADES DI CETTE PARROISSE LA SOME DE DEUX MIL LIVRES UNE FOIS PAYÉ, PLUS A LEGUÉ MIL LIVRES DE RENTE
A AYDIR A MARIER DE PAUVRES FILLES, ET A METTRE EN APPRENTISSAGE DE PAUVRES GARÇONS NÉS DANS LA PARROISSE. . . . .

NOTRE-DAME.

Sauval likens the island upon which the cathedral stands to a ship: "L'ile de la cité est faite comme un grand navire enfoncé dans la vase et échoué au fil de l'eau vers le milieu de la Seine;" and perhaps the Ship of Paris upon the Gallic sea may have owed its origin as the city arms to some idea of this sort.

The origin of Notre-Dame is enveloped in mystery. Whether its first bishop, S. Denis, or Dyonesius, was the Areopagite converted by S. Paul's preaching at Athens, and sent by S. Clement to preach the Gospel to the Parisians, or whether he was another personage of the same name who was sent into Gaul in the 3rd century and martyred during the persecutions under Decius, it is impossible to say, as there is no evidence of any value. Certain it is, however, that the first bishop of Paris bore the name of Denis, and that he suffered martyrdom with his two companions Rusticus and Eleutherius, on the summit of the hill now called Montmartre. Tra-

VIEW FROM THE SOUTH TOWER.

dition went so far as to point out the spot where they first gathered their followers together—the crypt of Notre-Dame des Champs; also the prison where Our Lord appeared to them and

NOTRE-DAME FROM THE PLACE DU PARVIS.

strengthened them with His Holy Body and Blood, at S. Denis de la Chartre ; the place, at S. Denis du Pas, where they suffered their first tortures ; and, lastly, Montmartre, where they were beheaded. But, with the exception of the latter, all these holy spots have disappeared. So, too, have the crosses which marked the route taken by the Saint, when he carried his head to the place chosen for his burial, at S. Denis. An ancient church covered the remains of the three Saints until the present splendid building was erected in the reign of Dagobert I.

Under the Roman dominion, Paris was comprised in the fourth Lyonnaise division, of which Sens was the metropolis. Hence the bishops of Paris acknowledged the archbishop of Sens as their primate, until 1622, when, at the request of Louis XIII., Pope Gregory XV. raised the see to an archbishopric. The succession has consisted of one hundred and nine bishops and fifteen archbishops, eight of whom have been raised to the dignity of Cardinal. Besides S. Denis, six have been venerated as Saints : Marcel, in the 5th century; Germain, in the 6th century; Céran, Landry, and Agilbert in the 7th, and Hugues in the 8th century. No less Saints, although uncanonized, are the three martyrs

ARCHBISHOP DARBOY.

of our own time—Sibour, who was stabbed by a discontented priest in the church of S. Étienne-du-Mont; Affre, who was shot upon a barricade in 1848, while negotiating with the insurgents, and whose last words pronounced him a true follower of his Master : " Puisse mon sang être le dernier versé ! " and Darboy, the liberal-minded and large-hearted, who was shot as a hostage by the fanatics of his own party. In former times the entry of the new bishop into his episcopal city was accompanied by much gorgeous ceremonial. All the municipal officers, mounted on horses, went to meet him at the Abbey of S. Victor. Thence they processioned, accompanied by the bishop, seated on a white palfrey, to the church of S. Geneviève, from which he was chaired by his vassals to the Rue Neuve-Notre-Dame, where he was met by the dean and canons of the cathedral, and after taking an oath upon the Gospels to uphold the privileges of the church, and to observe the engagements entered into by his predecessors, he was installed, and received the homage of the chapter. Mass was then said, and at the conclusion, the prelate was conducted to his palace, where he gave a sumptuous entertainment to all who had assisted at the ceremonies.

In 1674 Louis XIV. conferred the lands of S. Cloud, Creteil, d'Ozouer-la-Ferrière, and d'Armentières upon the archbishopric, a donation which was valued in the last century at a revenue of 140,000 *livres*. The old episcopal palace was situated between the cathedral and the river, and the whole must have been an imposing mass of buildings; but what remained of it twenty years ago was mostly 18th-century work, with the exception of a fragment of the chapel which was consecrated by bishop Maurice de Sully at the end of the 12th century.

The chapter of Notre-Dame was one of the most important in the Kingdom. Its revenue amounted to 180,000 *livres*, and its jurisdiction extended beyond its own clergy and officers, to the Hôtel-Dieu, and the churches which were called *les filles de Notre-Dame*. These were the collegiate bodies of S. Merry, the Holy Sepulchre, S. Benoit, and S. Étienne-des-Grès. Four other colleges, S. Marcel, S. Honoré, and S. Opportune, bore the title of *filles de l'Archevêque*.

Of the cloisters not the slightest vestige remains to determine their position or size. What was latterly termed the *cloître* was only a collection of narrow tortuous streets, with two or three houses and doorways which may have dated from the 15th century. One of these houses bore the reputation of having been the abode of Canon Fulbert, the uncle of Héloïse; but it could only have been built upon the site of the original one, which may possibly have existed in the 12th century, as some Roman foundations were discovered when it was demolished a few years ago. The *enceinte* of the cathedral enclosed two churches, S. Aignan and S. Jean-le-Rond, and a garden at the eastern end of the church, which the chapter called *Le terrain*, but to which the people, in their original lingo, gave the name of *Motte aux Papelards*.

The cathedral is now open on all sides, and the *coup-d'œil* is fine when seen from the Place du Parvis-*Notre-Dame, or from the garden at the east end; but to obtain these fine views many buildings of interest have been sacrificed,—the cloisters, the churches of S. Jean-le-Rond and S. Christophe, the episcopal palace, the oldest parts of the hospitals of the Hôtel-Dieu

THE EAST END, FROM THE GARDEN.

and Les Enfants-Trouvés, and the chapel constructed in the 14th century by Oudart de Mocreux.

It may not be uninteresting to give the number of religious institutions in the city of Paris before the end of the last

* From time immemorial, the space to the West of the church was called *Parvis paradisus*, the terrestrial paradise which led by the celestial Jerusalem.

century: 12 chapters; 59 parishes; 4 abbeys for men, and 6 for women; 11 priories; 124 monasteries and communities; 90 chapels (exclusive of those in Notre-Dame); and 5 hospitals; in all, 311 ecclesiastical establishments. When it is considered that all these corporate bodies possessed lands, were all exempt from direct taxation, and enjoyed other privileges, the storm that brought about their suppression is not to be wondered at, however much we may regret the results from an artistic point of view. Even at the commencement of the 18th century the suppression of a certain number of convents and the demolition of several churches was determined upon; but it was not until the Revolution burst that the main destruction took place. Had there been more men of the type of the *citoyen* Chaumette, who saved the sculptures on one of the doors of Notre-Dame by affirming that the astronomer Dupuis had discovered his planetary system therein, there would have been less loss to art to lament. As it is, the only remnant of all this ecclesiastical wealth besides Notre-Dame is a portion of the priory of S. Martin des Champs (occupied at present by the Conservatoire des Arts et Métiers), 12 parish churches, the Sainte-Chapelle, and the little church of S. Julien le Pauvre, which belonged to the old Hôtel-Dieu. These are the only buildings which have come down to us from the Middle-Age or Renaissance periods.

Some remains of altars dedicated to Jupiter, of the time of Tiberius, which were found under the choir of the cathedral, and are now in the Palais des Thermes, seem to suggest that the Christian church was built upon the site of the Roman temple, or that the latter was converted into a church by the early Christians, as at Rome, Ravenna, and other places.

The earliest authentic record of a Christian church in Paris is in the life of S. Marcel, where it is related that at the end of the 4th century one stood at the Eastern extremity of the island of the Cité. This is supposed to have been rebuilt by Childebert I. at the instance of S. Germain, for it is not probable that the building described by Fortunat, bishop of Poitiers, as rich in marble columns, glass windows, and magnificent ornaments, could have been the original edifice. Indeed, a discovery, made in 1847, seems to prove this. During some excavations which were made in the Place du Parvis it was found that some Roman houses had been demolished to make way for the foundations of Childebert's church; and, together with the Roman remains, were marble cubes which formed the pavement, three columns in Aquitaine marble, and a Corinthian capital in white marble. The Christians of the 5th century adhered in their church architecture to the style of building adopted by the Romans for their basilicas; in fact, in many cases the secular basilica was adapted to the purpose of Christian worship. Hence it is but probable that Childebert looked to Rome for the design of his church. These remains are in the museum and gardens of the Hôtel-Cluny.

From the 6th to the 12th centuries there is no record of Notre-Dame, but Grégoire de Tours and d'Aymoin, towards the end of the 6th century, speak of two churches close together, but distinct from one another—the one, S. Étienne, to the south of the present church; the other, S. Marie, towards the north-east. A rather doubtful tradition attributes certain works of construction in the church to bishop Erchenrad I. during the reign of Charlemagne. But it is known that in 829 the celebrated Council of Paris was held in the nave of S. Étienne; and in 857 the other church, S. Marie, was burned by the Normans, the bishop, Énée, only being able to save the former church. In the 12th century, archdeacon Étienne de Garlande, who died in 1142, made some important restorations to Notre-Dame, and Suger, the great abbot of S. Denis, gave it a stained glass window of great beauty—probably similar to those in his own church. So, too, the early Capétien monarchs frequently visited this *nova ecclesia* (as it was called to distinguish it from S. Étienne), and presented it with valuable ornaments.

We now come to the building of the present church. Maurice de Sully, the seventy-second bishop (1160-96), had scarcely mounted his episcopal throne when he determined to rebuild his cathedral by joining the two existing churches, and upon his epitaph in the abbey church of S. Victor he was accredited as the builder of Notre-Dame.

Bishop Maurice was the son of a poor woman named Humberge, who lived in a humble cottage on the banks of the Loire, under the shadow of the feudal castle of the Sullys; and, like many of the Churchmen of those times, he seems to have had only one parent; at all events his father was unknown, and consequently Maurice was obliged to go from *château* to *château*, and from convent to convent, to beg for bread and alms, for himself and his mother.

On April 21st, 1163, at the instance of Abbot Hugues de

Moneçaux, Pope Alexander III. consecrated the recently-constructed apse of S. Germain des Prés; and it is also affirmed that he laid the first stone of the new cathedral in the same year. In 1182, the High Altar was consecrated by Henri, the pope's legate, and three years later, Heraclius, patriarch of Jerusalem, who had come to Paris to preach the third crusade, officiated in the choir. Geoffrey, son of Henry II. of England,

ONE OF THE MONSTERS OF THE TOWERS.

and Count of Bretagne, who died in 1186, was buried before the altar of the new cathedral, and towards the end of the century the wife of Philippe-Auguste, Isabelle de Hainault, was laid near the same place. When Maurice de Sully died, the church could not have been completed, as he left 5,000 *livres* towards the leaden roofing of the choir. Indeed, the western façade was only commenced towards the end of the episcopate of Pierre de Nemours, 1208-19, although the work had been continued during the time of his predecessor, Eude de Sully, 1197-1208. According to l'abbé Lebeuf, the remains of the old church of S. Étienne were demolished towards the end of the year 1218 to make room for the southern part of the *façade*, and, amongst other finds, were some fragments of the Saint's tomb.

It is probable that the West front, as high as the gallery which connects the two towers, was terminated about the time of the death of Philippe-Auguste, 1223; and that the rich appearance of this *façade* decided the reconstruction of the portals of the transepts.

An inscription at the base of the southern porch attests that on the second day of the Ides of February, 1257, Master Jean de Chelles commenced this work in honour of the mother of Christ, S. Louis being then king of France, and Renaud de Corbeil, bishop of Paris; and, in spite of certain documents amongst the archives, there is no doubt that the little *Porte Rouge* and the first chapels on both sides of the choir belong to the same period and were the work of the same architect, for they are quite similar in style and are built of the same stone.

The history of Notre-Dame is in a great measure the history of France. It was there that the *Te Deum* was sung after successful battles, and where the standards which were taken from the enemy were suspended during the continuance of the wars. There, too, in the early part of the 13th century, S. Dominic preached from a book given him by the Blessed Virgin, who appeared to the Saint after an hour's silent meditation, radiant with beauty, and dazzling as the sunlight. Some fifty years ago, the cathedral, and, indeed, all Paris, was stirred by the *conférences* held there by one of S. Dominic's own children, Père Lacordaire, who, with his friends Lamennais and Montalembert, made an effort to free the Roman branch of the Catholic Church from the fungi which had grown on to it, an effort which was

PÈRE LACORDAIRE.

NOTRE-DAME AT SUNSET.

as fruitless as that undertaken by his predecessor Savonarola, 400 years before him.

On Easter Eve, the 12th April, 1229, the Count of Toulouse, Raymond VII., was absolved of the crime of heresy in Notre-Dame. As the old chronicler Guillaume de Puylaurens relates: "Et c'était pitié de voir un si grand homme, lequel par si long espace de temps avait pu résister à tant et de si fortes nations, conduit nu, en chemise, bras et pieds découverts, jusqu'à l'autel."

Here is a pleasant little example of some of the doings of the "good old times": Pierre Bonfons tells us that in 1381 the *prévôt* of Paris, one Hugues Aubriot, accused and found guilty of heresy and other crimes, was, through the instrumentality of the University, "presché et mitré publiquement au Parvis-Notre-Dame, et après ce, condamné à être en l'oubliette au pain et à l'eau."

On the 27th November, 1431,* the child, Henry VI. of England, was crowned King of France in the choir of the cathedral. But the pomp of this ceremony was soon effaced, for, on the Friday in Easter week, 1436, a *Te Deum* was sung to celebrate the retaking of Paris by the troops of Charles VII.

In the 13th century the Feast of the Assumption was celebrated with great pomp; the whole church was hung with valuable tapestries, and the pavement covered with sweet-smelling flowers and herbs; but two centuries later, grass from the fields of Gentilly seems to have sufficed to do honour to Our Lady on her *fête* day.

The same custom prevailed here as at the Sainte-Chapelle and other churches, of letting fly pigeons, and throwing flowers and torches of flaming flax from the windows in celebration of the descent of the Holy Spirit on the Day of Pentecost; and every year, on the 22nd March, the chapter went in procession to the church of the Grands-Augustins, where a mass was sung in memory of Henri IV.'s entry into Paris in 1594.

The original design of the church did not comprise the chapels which flank the nave and somewhat spoil the effect of the exterior. In this respect, the cathedral of Paris cannot be compared to those of Reims and Chartres, which have no chapels between the buttresses. They were added to Notre-

---

* This is the date given by Mézeray. Hénaut gives it as the 17th December.

Dame in 1270, Jean de Paris, archdeacon of Soissons, having bequeathed 100 *livres* for their construction. The chapels of the *chevet* were finished at the end of the 13th or beginning of the 14th century. An inscription at the entrance of one of them, S. Nicaise, placed upon the pedestal of a statue of

PIERRE DE FAYET.

Simon Matiffas de Buci, recorded that this chapel and the two next were founded by the bishop in 1296, and that the others were added subsequently. This precious relic was discovered at S. Denis among a number of others from different churches. One of these gives the name of Canon Pierre de Fayet* as the

* This slab is now in the Renaissance Museum of the Louvre. It is dated 1303, and bears the following inscription: " Maitre Pierre de Fayet,

donor of 200 *livres* towards the *histoires* which surround the choir, and some new glass; and another gives the names of the sculptors of these same *histoires*, the Masters Jean Ravy and Jean le Bouteiller, who carved them in 1351. It must be remembered that the great churches of the Middle Ages were more the work of the people than of the nobility, and thus we find that the armorial bearings upon old glass or upon the pedestals of statues are mostly those of the different trades-guilds, such as the bakers, the butchers, the woollen-drapers, the furriers, the shoemakers, and the like. These, either as individuals or as corporate bodies, enriched the old churches in money or in kind.

It must not be forgotten that the great churches of the Middle Ages were, in a sense, the schools of the period. The people, not being able to read, were instructed through the medium of sermons and stage plays; they saw the histories of Saints, the story of the Gospel, and legendary and historical matter carved in wood or stone upon all sides of them, and they learnt their moralities by picture tales and clerical discourses. Art was literally the handmaid of Religion, and the great teacher; and being enriched by divers gifts, the churches became receptacles for all kinds of treasures. Guillaume Durand, in his *Rational des Divins Offices*, speaks of rare things, such as stuffed crocodiles, ostrich eggs, and skeletons of whales, besides gold and silver vessels, *intagli*, and *cameii*, as attractions for the people, on the principle that he who comes to see may stay to pray. Churches were, in fact, museums, and places in which to transact business; the naves constantly being thus used.

Notre-Dame has two towers at the west end, and a *flèche* over the intersection of the nave, choir and transepts. This is modern; and why? Because, in 1787, an architect was found

---

chanoine de Paris, a donné deux cens livres parisis pour aider à faire ces histoires et pour les nouvelles verrières qui sont sur le chœur de céans." In the account of the church in 1763, the slab is thus described: "Avant la construction du nouveau chœur (par le roi Louis XIV.) on voyait autour de l'ancien chœur et en dedans les histoires de l'Evangile et des Actes des Apôtres en statues de pierre isolées avec des inscriptions au bas, et au-dessous l'histoire de la Génèse en bas-relief. A côté était un chanoine à genoux, dont la mort arriva en 1303, aussi ce bas-relief avait cette inscription derrière lui: 'Messire Pierre Fayet' . . . Mais depuis la construction du nouveau chœur, on a mis sa statue à la porte collatérale, vis-à-vis la porte rouge."

who considered it well to "amputate" the old one. Listen to Victor Hugo : " Un architect de bon gout l'a amputé, et a cru qu'il suffisait de masquer la plaie avec ce large emplâtre de plomb, qui ressemble au couvercle d'une marmite "—doubtless that strange species of turret so common in London, familiarly termed a pepper-box.

The western *façade*, though not so rich as that of Reims, is nevertheless exceedingly beautiful. It is divided into three parts in its width, and into four stories in its elevation.

Here is what our old friend Dibden says of it in his time : " Of Notre-Dame, the West front, with its marygold windows, is striking both from its antiquity and richness. It is almost black from age " (would it were so now !)—" but the alto-relievos, and especially those above the doors, stand out in almost perfect condition. These ornaments are rather fine of their kind. There is, throughout the whole of this West front, a beautiful keeping, and the towers are *here* somewhat more endurable, and therefore somewhat in harmony. Over the North transept door, on the outside, is a figure of the Virgin—once holding the infant Jesus in her arms. Of the latter only the feet remain. The drapery of this figure is in perfectly good taste, a fine specimen of that excellent art which prevailed towards the end of the XIIIth century. Above is an alto-relievo subject of the *Slaughter of the Innocents*. The soldiers are in quilted armour. I entered the cathedral from the Western door, during service-time. A sight of the different clergymen engaged in the office filled me with melancholy, and made me predict sad things of what was probably to come to pass! These clergymen were old, feeble, wretchedly attired in their respective vestments, and walked and sung in a tremulous and faltering manner. The architectural effect of the interior is not very imposing, although the solid circular pillars of the nave, the double aisles round the choir, and the old basso-relievo representations of the Life of Christ upon the exterior walls of the choir, cannot fail to afford the antiquary very singular satisfaction. The choir appeared to be not unlike that of S. Denis." Notre-Dame should be visited by lovers of plain song. To hear forty men and boys chant Gregorian tones, with *ad libitum* accompaniments upon a small organ, is a treat not to be forgotten. And note, the *small* organ, for the large one at the end of the nave is only used for voluntaries; thundering accompaniments to the voices being unknown in Paris.

All the six doors of Notre-Dame bear distinctive names—the Porte du Jugement, the Porte de la Vierge, and the Porte Ste. Anne, at the west end; the Porte du Cloître, the Porte

NOTRE-DAME DURING SERMON.

St. Marcel and the Porte Rouge, at the east end Each of these is divided into two openings by a central pier, supporting a figure and surmounted by a tympanum; over which

is a deep *voussure*, peopled with sculptures innumerable. Tradition formerly recorded a flight of thirteen steps rising to the west front; but the excavations made in 1847 proved this to have been a mistake. If steps existed anywhere, they were probably on the side of the episcopal palace near the southern tower and leading down to the river. At the same time there is no doubt that the church would gain in effect were it raised above the roadway as is the case at Amiens. At present it is even a little lower than the *place*, but allowing for the rising of the ground during seven centuries, it is quite possible that the cathedral originally had not the sunken appearance it has at present. In the niches upon the great buttress are four figures; S. Denis and S. Étienne at the extremities, and two women crowned in the centre. These represent a very common conceit of the Middle Ages, the Church and the Synagogue, the one triumphant, the other defeated.

Above the portals is the gallery of the Kings of Judah, the ancestors of the Virgin, and perhaps typical of the sovereigns of France. The gallery of the Virgin is still higher, and upon it in the centre stands the queen of Heaven with attendant Angels, Adam and Eve being above the side doors. Higher still we come to the tower galleries presided over by delightful monsters of various zoological tribes. Nothing gives a visitor to Notre-Dame a better notion of the richness of its sculptures than mounting to this gallery, whence he obtains a full view of the roof and the towers, with their numerous pinnacles, crockets, finials, gargoyles and statues.

Unfortunately the great central portal was hopelessly wrecked by Soufflot in 1771 in order to increase its width for processions; it is one of the many examples which prove the fact that the "stupidity of man" has done more harm to old buildings than time or even disastrous riots and revolutions. In 1773 and 1787, so-called restorations, by architects who ought to have known better, still further mutilated the church.

Listen to Victor Hugo once more : " Il est difficile de ne pas soupirer, de ne pas s'indigner devant les dégradations, les mutilations sans nombre, que simultanément le temps et les hommes ont fait subir au vénérable monument, sans respect pour Charlemagne, qui en avait posé la première pierre, pour Philippe-Auguste, qui en avait posé la dernière. Sur la face de cette vieille reine de nos cathédrales, à côté d'un vide on trouve toujours une cicatrice. *Tempus edax homo edacior*: le

temps est aveugle, l'homme est stupide." Sixty years have passed since this was written, but the great poet lived to see a restoration which he probably sighed over as much as over the

THE ROOF AND FLÈCHE.

mutilations of former times. Viollet-le-Duc did his work better than most restorers; but of the old church nothing remains but the shell—even the surface of the stone has been scraped and scrubbed, giving the building as new an appearance as that of the churches of S. Augustin and La Trinité. Hugo's words in 1832, directed against the architects of Louis XIV. and Louis XV., apply equally to those of our own time: "Si nous avions le loisir d'examiner une à une avec le lecteur les diverses traces de destruction imprimées à l'antique église, la part du temps serait la moindre, la pire celles des hommes, surtout des hommes de l'art." The great destruction occurred between 1699 and 1753. Louis XIV., the great destroyer of men and of their works, in order to carry out the "*Vœu de Louis XIII.*", made away with the old carved stalls, the

ANIMALS ON ONE OF THE TOWERS.

jubé, the cloisters, the high altar with its numerous *châsses* and reliquaries, its bronze columns and silver and gold statuettes, the tombs, and the stained glass. In 1771, the statues above the great west doors disappeared when Soufflot began his evil work of widening them. Another great loss to the church was the destruction of the statue of S. Christopher, a huge colossal figure as celebrated in the Middle Ages as the relics of the Sainte-Chapelle. It stood at the entrance of the nave, and was the work of Messire Antoine des Essarts in 1443, in gratitude to the saintly giant for having saved him from the Burgundians. Miracle-working Virgins, Philippe-Auguste posing as S. Simon Stylites, and two bishops of Paris, likewise upon columns, were amongst some of the former treasures. Whether three great figures in wax of Gregory XI., his niece, and nephew, which tumbled into decay in 1599, are equally to be regretted, is doubtful; but the description of an equestrian statue which stood in the nave, the man in armour, and the horse in emblazoned trappings, sounds fascinating. It was a Louis VI., or a Philippe le Bel—who knows? Perhaps the latter, erected as a thank offering to Our Lady for the victory at Mons, for Philippe founded solemn commemorations of that battle at Notre-Dame, at Chartres, and at S. Denis. But in spite of this evidence, Père Montfaucon pronounced in favour of Philippe de Valois, who rode into the church equipped and armed to give thanks for the victory of Cassel, and fulfil a vow made in front of the enemy. This same Philippe's effigy also rode a stone horse upon the *façade* of the Cathedral of Sens.

Du Breuil cites some quaint verses explaining the dimensions of the church, which were written upon a picture hanging near the statue of S. Christopher by the doorway:

> Si tu veux sçauoir comme est ample
> De Nostre-Dame le grand temple :
> Il a dans œuure, pour le seur,
> Dix et sept toises de haulteur,
> Sur la largeur de vingt et quatre ;
> Et soixante cinq sans rabattre,
> A de long. Au tours hault montées
> Trente quarte sont bien comptées,
> Le tout fondé sur pilotis,
> Ainsi vray que ie le te dis.*

When the revolutionary period began, little remained to be done in the way of destruction, but that little the votaries of Reason did pretty well as regards everything pertaining unto royalty; for to be just, we must remember that anything that could be construed into philosophy or art was spared. In August, 1793, it was decided that eight days should be allowed for the destruction of the "*gothiques simulacres*" of the kings upon the portals. Later on the Saints were ordered to share the same fate, but Citizen Chaumette, as we have seen, stepped in and saved the sculpture by assuring his colleagues that the astronomer Dupuis had discovered his planetary system on

---

* *Théâtre des Antiquités de Paris.*

one of the portals. Thereupon the Citoyen Dupuis was put upon the council for the preservation of public buildings, and in consequence much was saved from complete and hopeless destruction. We all know how a goddess of the class so dear to the kings of old, a vulgar Gabrielle or Pompadour in sabots and a Phrygian cap, was set upon the altar and worshipped in derision, a ceremony followed by others that "we leave under a veil which appropriately stretches itself along the pillars of the aisles— not to be lifted aside by the hand of history."* Robespierre and his friends must have been utterly wanting in a sense of humour, or they never would have instituted these curious ceremonies. In an old print† representing the great Feast of the Supreme Being upon the Champ de Mars, we see the President of the Convention in a fine blue coat, and bearing an enormous bouquet of flowers, discoursing to the multitude; and,

HÔTEL-DIEU AND NOTRE-DAME

after burning the statue of Atheism, sticking up Wisdom in its place. Young girls in the inevitable white of church processions, beadles, and singing men, with all the paraphernalia of the dethroned ecclesiastical pomp, are depicted; but only one man seems to have seen how ludicrous it all was: "*Tu commence à nous ennuyer avec ton Etre Suprême!*" said he to Robespierre, somewhat profanely.

* Carlyle.
† Exhibited at the Exhibition of Documents relating to the Revolution, held at the Tuileries in 1889

The prelates and sovereigns who succeeded to these stormy days endeavoured to restore Notre-Dame; but the ignorance which prevailed at the commencement of the present century with regard to Gothic architecture rather added to the destruction than mended it; and it was not until the Christian art and Liberal Catholic revivals led by Montalembert and his friends that a thorough and rational restoration of the church was commenced by the eminent architects, Viollet-le-Duc and Lassus.

The central portal is a mass of wonderful sculpture. The lower part of the stylobate bears lozenge-shapen compartments enclosing roses and lilies. Above this are the *Virtues and Vices*,* the former being figures of women bearing their emblems; the latter, little scenes describing each particular vice. It is interesting to see that the Virtues should be portrayed as women, Guillaume Durand giving the reason that they are men's nursing mothers; but Eve, having been supposed from all time to have been man's temptress, how comes it that the Mediæval sculptors exempted her and all other women from personifying the vice, for example, of curiosity? Courage our first mother undoubtedly had, and so this virtue on the front of Notre-Dame is represented by a woman with a shield bearing a lion. Equally certain is it that Adam was mean and cowardly, and so we find Cowardice painted as a man running away terror-stricken from a harmless hare. Amongst the vicious we see Judas in despair, an iniquitous Nero, an impious Mahomet, and a funny little Nimroud throwing a javelin at the sun, symbolic of that great warrior's attempt to build a high tower in order to attack Heaven itself.

Above the Virtues and Vices are the Twelve Apostles, placed over the Virtue which in their lives they especially displayed. Nothing in these sculptures was done without a purpose; thus S. Paul stands over Courage, and S. Peter above Faith; indeed the whole doorway was designed to carry out a particular idea,

* The twelve Virtues, according to Hermas, are Faith, Temperance, Patience, Magnanimity, Simplicity, Innocence, Peace, Charity, Discipline, Chastity, Truth, and Prudence. The counting of twelve Virtues lasted a long time, for we find in 1454 at a *fête* given at Lille by the Duc de Bourgogne, Philippe le Bon, that twelve Virtues dressed in crimson satin danced at the ball with the many knights who were present. They were the great ladies of the town; and perhaps the knights personated the Vices, as they were not improbably able to do with a considerable amount of truth.

and to illustrate the main doctrines of Christ, whose statue stands upon the central pier, giving the benediction to all who enter.

On each side of the doorway are *the Wise and Foolish Virgins*, and in the tympanum, which is divided into three zones, is *the Resurrection of the Dead*. Souls are being weighed; and under one scale a mean little demon may be seen pulling it down with a hook, in case the poor soul's sins should not be sufficient to weigh it down. It may be noted that the Mediæval theologians evidently considered the nails which pierced our Blessed Lord's body of more honour than the tree unto which he was bound; for here we see an Angel holding the cross with bare hands, while another envelopes the nails in a napkin. In the *Voussure* are rows of personages; the lower ones belonging to the Judgment, the upper ones to the Resurrection. Then come the Angels, Prophets, and Doctors of the church (taking precedence at Notre-Dame of the Martyrs, by reason of Paris being a great seat of learning). Following them are the Martyrs and Virgins.

ONE OF THE PINNACLES.

Didron* gives an account by an Armenian bishop of a visit to Paris in 1489-96, in which he describes these sculptures

* *Annales archéologiques.*

exactly as they now appear, and speaks of the beauty of their colouring and gilding.

The sculptures of the other two doors are of the same character as the Porte du Jugement, but the subjects are taken severally from the histories of the Blessed Virgin and of S. Anne. In the Porte de la Vierge, the *Mother and Child* hold the central place, and in the tympanum are the *Assumption* and the *Glorification of the Virgin*. In the stylobate are saints, a conspicuous one being *S. Denis carrying his head*, with Angels upon each side, to prevent anyone damaging his headless body. In the bas-reliefs, amongst other subjects is an almanac in stone representing the earth and the sea, the twelve signs of the Zodiac, and the occupations, mostly agricultural, of each of the months. Corresponding to these are the idlings of the season. The industrious man is warming himself by the side of his well-cured hams and sausages; the idle man is sitting enveloped in fur, enjoying a sleep by the fire. For April we see a personage with two heads, one asleep and one awake; and, showing that the climate was much the same in the 13th century as it is now, we see one side of him clad in the airy costume of our first parents, while the other is well wrapped up in warm raiment. May only wears pyjamas, while June prepares for a bath. The signs of the Zodiac follow the ecclesiastical year, which up to the reign of Charles IX. commenced at Easter. The custom of carving them on the exterior of churches is a very ancient practice, as it may be seen on the Catholicon at Athens, which is as old or older than the time of Justinian. Nearly all the great churches of France possess them. On S. Denis there are three: one is mosaic; another, a bas-relief on the exterior; and the third, an incised stone upon the pavement of one of the apsidal chapels.

The Porte S. Anne is the oldest of the three portals, and the sculptures being the most ancient of the church, it has been assumed that they were brought from an older edifice. The central figure is *S. Marcel*, ninth bishop of Paris, who died in 436. He is here seen standing upon a strange and venomous beast with a tail ending serpent-wise, issuing from a winding sheet—the vestment of an unfortunate rich and wicked woman whom the beast had consumed in punishment for her vices. Marcel, in spite of this just retribution, seems to have pitied the poor soul, and went forth to the forest to reprove the dragon; who, listening to the holy man's words, became repentant and showed his contrition by bending his head and flopping after the Saint for the space of three miles, wagging his tail like a dog. But S. Marcel could not forgive him. "Go forth," said the Saint, "and inhabit the deserts, or plunge thyself into the sea"; which he seems to have done, for no more was ever heard of the monster from that day forth.

The tympanum is ornamented with the *History of Joachim and Anna*, the *Marriage of the Virgin* and the *Budding of S. Joseph's staff*. Angels and a kneeling king complete the composition; the latter probably being Louis VII., the friend of Suger and the father of Philippe-Auguste, as he is presenting a charter of donations and privileges. On the other side is a bishop, bearded, mitred, and vested, but unlike the king, the prelate stands; he is probably the builder, Maurice de Sully. The older part of this doorway is similar in some respects to the *façade* of S. Denis. Abbot Suger, its builder, had only been dead about ten years when Maurice de Sully reconstructed the cathedral; and we see in the figures upon the Porte S. Anne the same Romanesque character as at S. Denis.

The beautiful ironwork of the doors of Notre-Dame are worthy their reputed origin; they are said to have been finished in a single night by his Satanic Majesty in consequence of the dilatoriness of Biscornette the blacksmith. The legend has probably grown from the design of a part of the ironwork, a little man with horns and the tail of a fish, who sits upon the branch of a tree. It appears that Biscornette was charged to forge the ironwork of the doors in a given time; but finding himself behind-hand in his work, he determined to call in the aid of the Devil. This personage arrived, put on the leathern apron, and set to work so vigorously that by dawn it was finished. Biscornette thanked his assistant, who politely, in recognition of the blacksmith's gratitude, presented him with his horns. Popular opinion always held that Biscornette could not forge the central door by which the Blessed Sacrament passed; and that a curse rested upon that of S. Anne, as it was never opened; but in these latter faithless days it has been found to do so as easily as the others. The sculptures of the tympanum of the Porte du Cloitre represent the *Legend of S. Theophilus*, the deacon, who lived in the 3rd century. This Saint was troubled in his mind, and abjured Christianity through the instrumentality of a Jew; thereupon he fell into the hands of the Father of Lies, and we see him on his knees between the hoofs of the demon. But he was reinstated in the good books of his bishop, in spite of the tempting whisperings of a little demon by his side. Then the Virgin enters upon the scene, and tears up the contract signed by S. Theophilus with his blood; and the demon enraged has the impertinence to seize the raiment of the Virgin, in order to profane her. But Theophilus is forgiven, and the bishop displays the contract, which is now hallowed by the episcopal seal, and upon which is written in Gothic letters: *Carta Theophili*.

At the foot of the Southern *façade* is the inscription which gives the name of the architect and the date of the church:

ANNO. DNI. M. CC. LVII. MENSE. FEBRVARIO. IDVS.
SECUNDO. HOC. FUIT INCEPTUM, CRISTI. GENITSIS, HONORE.
KALLENSI. LATHOMO. VIVENTE. JOHANNE. MAGISTRO;

John de Chelles was wise in his generation, for had he not thus taken care of his own reputation, we should have known nothing about him, there being no record of any other works by him. Chelles, the place of his birth, was celebrated for the abbey founded by S. Bathilde; and like Montereau, Bonneuil, and Lusarches, which gave birth to some of the most famous architects of the 13th century, it was situated in the diocese of Paris. The beautiful little Porte Rouge is of the end of the 13th century. In the tympanum a king and queen are represented kneeling at each side of our Lord and His Mother, very probably S. Louis, and his wife, Marguerite de Provence.

Formerly, in front of the grand portals there was a pillory, described by Père Du Breuil in the 16th century as raised upon a platform. The culprit knelt upon this with a paper, stating his offence, affixed to him; and then he stayed *longtemps mocqué et injurié du peuple*. Du Breuil lamented that this object of the spiritual justice and power was no longer to be seen at the abbey of S. Germain.

The interior of Notre-Dame is imposing, though somewhat heavy in character; and although the nave and choir were sixty years in construction, there is scarcely any difference in style, except in the details. There is a certain clumsiness about the great round shafts of the nave, but the carving upon the angles of the plinths and of the capitals helps to relieve this effect. Most of the capitals are ornamented with examples of

LA PORTE ROUGE.

the flora of Parisian fields. At the west end is a gallery now occupied by the great organ, but which formerly was the stage upon which miracle-plays were performed. The choir is by far the most beautiful part of the church; and being filled with stained glass, it has not that painfully cleaned-up appearance which is the result of over-restoration. Some parts of it, the bays which separate the side-aisles from the crossings, are of the 14th century; and the little Angels blowing trumpets which surmount the archivolt are beautiful specimens of sculpture of that period. The capitals of some of the choir columns being the oldest in the church (the early part of the 12th century) are very rich in the quaint style of decoration delighted in by Mediæval artists—masses of foliage, with heads of grotesque animals peeping out, and biting off the leaves and flowers. One capital (between the seventh and eighth southern chapels) is interesting as showing the transition between the use of personages and animals, and that of foliage only, which was customary in the later period. The subject is very unecclesiastical, as was so often the case in the 12th and 13th centuries —two Harpies, male and female, with human heads and bird bodies, issuing out of the foliage. Much of this is treated in the most realistic manner, and we find specimens of the oak, the ivy and the trefoil.

In many of the chapels are double *piscinæ*. From one, the water in which the priest washes his hands *before* mass, is ejected by a pipe; from the other, used *after* mass, the water descends into the ground. They are both ornamented with carved canopies.

The Lady chapel, or chapel of the Compassion, and the two on either side, are painted and gilded, a good deal of the old colouring having survived as a guide. There is some good carving, and in front of the tabernacle hang seven lamps of elegant design. These, added to the beauty of the old stained glass, make this end of the church by far the most beautiful part.*
The chapel also contains an inscription, bearing the name of the founder, bishop Simon Matiffas de Bucy, who died in 1304. In the chapel of S. George is the fine marble statue of the martyred archbishop Darboy, shot in 1871 by the Communists.

The alto-reliefs alluded to above, by Jean Ravy and Jean le Bouteiller, are supported upon an arcade of clustered columns

---

* For a detailed account of the cathedral see Viollet-le-Duc's *Dictionnaire raisonné d'Architecture*.

FOUNTAIN IN THE LITTLE CLOISTER.

and pointed arches fixed against the back of the stalls. Formerly they were continued across the *jubé* and all around the choir; but unfortunately, when the sanctuary gates were constructed, these sculptures were sacrificed. The subjects are: 1, the Visitation; 2, the Appearance of the Star of Bethlehem to the Shepherds; 3, the Nativity; 4, the Adoration of the Magi; 5, the Massacre of the Innocents; 6, the Flight into Egypt; 7, the Presentation in the Temple; 8, Christ disputing with the Doctors; 9, the Baptism of Christ; 10, the Marriage in Cana; 11, the Entry into Jerusalem; 12, the Last Supper; 13, Christ washing S. Peter's Feet; 14, the

TWO OF THE ALTO-RELIEVOS WHICH SURROUND THE CHOIR.

Mount of Olives. The mysteries of the Passion and Resurrection were on the *jubé*, the destruction of which we owe to the Cardinal de Noailles. On the South side the subjects are of later date (14th century): 1, Christ appearing to the Magdalen; 2, to the Three Maries; 3, the Apostles running to the Sepulchre; 4, the Journey to Emmaüs; 5, Christ appearing to the Disciples; 6, to S. Thomas; 7, to S. Peter on the Sea of Tiberias; 8, another Appearance to the Disciples; 9, the Charge to preach the Gospel in all Lands. Jean Ravy was represented kneeling with joined hands in the last of these alto-reliefs. The whole was finished by Jean le

Bouteiller in 1351; and it is recorded that a part was a votive offering in honour of God, of the Virgin Mary, and of Monseigneur S. Étienne, given by Guillaume de Melun, Archbishop of Sens—one of two bishops of the name who occupied the see in 1317-29 and 1344-96 respectively. The sculptures are all coloured and gilt, and a very good cast of them may be seen at the Crystal Palace.

The choir remained intact until 1638, when Louis XIII., putting his kingdom especially under the protection of the Blessed Virgin, registered that unfortunate vow that he would consecrate the sanctuary of Notre-Dame to the fulfilment of it. "*Afin que la postérité ne puisse manquer à suivre nos volontés à ce sujet, pour monument et marque incontestable de la consécration présente que nous faisons, nous ferons construire de nouveau le grand autel de l'église cathédrale de Paris, avec une image de la Vierge qui tienne entre ses bras celle de son précieux fils, descendu de la croix, et où nous serons représentés aux pieds du fils et de la mère, comme leur offrant notre couronne et notre sceptre.*" Louis XIII. died in 1643, before he was able to carry out his marvellous design; but unfortunately, his son, Louis XIV., was only too ready to embellish buildings in the miserable taste of his time, and so the altar is disfigured by a *Descent from the Cross* by Nicolas and Guillaume Coustou, and a pair of kneeling kings (the 13th and 14th Louis) by Coysevox. In themselves these sculptures are fine examples of the art of the period, but they and the eight bronze Angels by Cayot, Vanclève, Poirier, Hurtrelle, Nagnier and Anselme Flamen, are all equally out of place in a 13th century church. The bas-reliefs of the altar were by Vassé, and Du Goulon was the sculptor of the beautiful woodwork representing scenes from the life of the Virgin. The altar was destroyed in 1793, in order to erect a symbolic "*montagne*" upon "*les pompeux débris de l'antique imposture.*" The present one was reconstructed in 1803, the *Entombment*, in gilt copper, from designs by Vanclève, being conveyed from the chapelle des Louvois, in the old church of the Capuchins in the Place Vendôme. The cross and candelabra belonged to the cathedral of Arras before the Revolution; and the beautiful bronze lectern, as exquisite in design as in workmanship, is signed and dated, "Duplessis 1775." The statue of the Virgin, on a pillar at the entrance of the choir, had the reputation of working miracles. It was thrown down at the Revolution, but was found later at S. Denis and replaced

PART OF THE STALLS.

in Notre-Dame. Such is the history of the statue, but whether it is the identical figure, it is impossible to say. In any case it is mainly of the same date as the church, which cannot be said of the reliquaries in the treasury, that are also supposed to have survived the Revolution.

The choir is raised three steps above the transepts. The two arches which separate the side aisles from the crossings show evidences of a later style. As we have seen, many sculptures were saved by the deputy Chaumette, and by Alexandre Lenoir, as works of art worthy of preservation; but unfortunately, reliquaries were of more value as metal, and most of them passed through the melting-pot into coinage for the bankrupt National treasury. The reliquaries shown at the cathedral are mostly modern imitations of those which were formerly in the Ste. Chapelle. One, however, is said to be the veritable *Croix Palatine*. This is a double-armed gold cross of Byzantine workmanship, formerly belonging to S. Germain-des-Prés, to which church it was left in 1684 by Anne of Cleves, princess of Mantua and of Montferrat, widow of Edouard von Baiern. The prince received it from Jean Casimir, King of Poland, when he took refuge in France; it having been given to a King of Poland in the 12th century by Manuel Comnenus, Emperor of Constantinople. The princess and her daughter, the Duchess of Brunswick, attested to having seen the cross upon one occasion encircled by flames and coming out of the fire unhurt. In 1793 the constitutional *curé* took the cross and preserved it until his death in 1827, when he remitted it to the archbishop of Paris. The inscription is in Greek and covers the length and the two arms: *Jesus Christus cruci affixus qui exaltavit hominum naturum, scribit Comnenus Manuel coronatus.* The following are some of the enormous number of valuables which formerly filled the treasury. In the inventory of 1763 there were no less than four busts and two statues in gold, silver-gilt, and jewelled; six silver reliquaries, two of gold, and five of silver-gilt; a gold cross attributed to S. Eloi, six silver-gilt crosses, and a whole closet full of silver candlesticks; besides a number of chalices, patens, ciborium, pax, censers, cruets, and other vessels for the altar; but very few were anterior to the 16th century. Of these the following remain: the Holy Crown from the S. Chapelle (imitation); the Holy Nail from S. Denis, given to Charlemagne by Constantine V., placed in the treasury of Aix-la-Chapelle, whence it was carried by Charles le Chauve to France; the golden cross of the Emperor Manuel Comnenus, 12th century, which was bequeathed by the Princess Anne de Gonzague to the monks of S. Germain des Prés in 1683;[*] two silver-gilt chalices of the 13th century; the relic of the True Cross sent in 1109 to Galon, bishop of Paris, by Anseau, precentor of the church of the Holy Sepulchre at Jerusalem;[†]

---

[*] This passed through miraculous adventures at the Revolution and was restored to the cathedral by M. de Quélen.

[†] Its preservation is said to have been in this wise. Louis XVI. sent it to S. Denis to be in safe keeping, and in 1793 it was offered by the Convention to the municipality. Thence it passed into the hands of M. Bonvoisin in 1804, and in 1808 it was placed in its present crystal reliquary by Cardinal de Belloy.

the crozier of Bishop Eudes de Sully, of wood and copper; the crucifix belonging to S. Vincent de Paul, which he presented to Louis XIII. upon his death-bed; the "discipline" of S. Louis; portions of this king's raiment; and the *soutanes* of archbishops Affre, Sibour, and Darboy.

The high altar as originally arranged had brass bars at the sides from which hung draperies. Behind it was another altar, that of the Holy Trinity, or *les ardents*, raised so that it could be seen above the first one. Steps led up to this, and between them was a depository called the *conditoire*, where all the sacred vessels used at mass were kept. There was no tabernacle; as in most churches in the old times, the host was enclosed in a ciborium which hung in front of the altar. A figure in alabaster of the Virgin surmounted the *autel des ardents*. Above all were three rows of *châsses*, one above the other, as it were upon shelves, containing relics of S. Gendulphe, S. Séverin, S. Germain, bishop of Paris, S. Justin, S. Lucain, S. Ursula's young friends, and other martyrs. The reliquary of S. Marcel was behind the high altar, resplendent in gold and pearls and precious stones, an elaborate and beautiful work of art, by, said tradition, S. Éloi, the bishop of Noyon; but unfortunately, it was too valuable to escape the melting-pot, and its 436 marcs worth of gold found their way into coin of the Republic.

The church was rich in glass up to the year 1741, when a demon in human shape, one Levieil, the author of a treatise upon the art of glass-painting, set to work to re-adorn Notre-Dame. He describes the matter himself; what he found and what he transformed. In the choir and the apse the windows were ornamented with colossal figures 18 ft. high, representing bishops, vested and bearing pastoral staves, without the usual crook termination. A border of lozenge-shapen coloured glass framed the figures and filled up the divisions of the compartments. These windows Levieil dated no later than 1182, and he adds that there were many fragments of much older glass, probably emanating from the ancient basilicas, which preceded the present church, interspersed between the *grisaille* of the 12th century. In the tribune of the choir were windows given by a little personage whose effigy knelt at the bottom of one, Michel de Darency by name, chaplain of Saint-Ferréol, who died in 1358. The abbot Suger also gave some of the glass in the tribune, resembling that of his own church, S. Denis, which is so rich in resplendent sapphire blue. In some of the chapels were subjects such as *the Beheading of S. John Baptist*, a king

STEPS IN THE LITTLE CLOISTER.

and queen, possibly Philippe le Bel and Jeanne de Navarre, kneeling. All this, or most of it, was improved away, or re-arranged into floriated borders and armorial bearings upon white glass. A little remains of the 14th century: some small Angels holding the instruments of the Passion, a Pelican and its chicks, a Christ draped in red, and a little figure of the Virgin. This is all in the *chevet*. But the glory of the church is the glass of the rose-windows, which continue the subjects portrayed upon the sculpture of the doors over which they are placed. In the western rose the Virgin is in the central compartment, crowned and bearing a sceptre; on her left arm is the infant Christ giving the benediction. The twelve prophets surround her, and we see again the Signs of the Zodiac, and the work special to each month during the year. Virtues and Vices, Judges, Priests, Prophets, and Kings of Judah; Saints and Martyrs with the instruments of their martyrdom, or palms, decorate these exquisite windows, masterpieces of the art; equal to the windows of Metz and Strasburg, and contemporary with the stone walls which surround them.

Formerly the pavement was a mass of tombstones, erect or prostrate, bearing portraits of the defunct in brass or marble; but Louis XIV.'s architects thought well to improve many of them away, and substitute a marble pavement costing 300,000 francs. Many brass tombs had been melted up with the lectern some years previously. Among the celebrities who had formerly either effigies or epitaphs in the choir were the following. Princes and Princesses: Philippe, Archdeacon of Paris, son of Louis VI., 1161; Geoffroy, duc de Bretagne, son of Henry II. of England, 1186; Isabelle de Hainault, first wife of Philippe-Auguste, 1189; Louis, dauphin, son of Charles VI., 1415; Louise de Savoie, mother of François Ier, 1531 (only her heart was buried here); Louis XIII., 1643. Bishops of Paris: Eudes de Sully, 1208; Étienne II., called Tempier, 1279; Cardinal Aymeric de Magnac, 1384; Pierre d'Orgemont, 1409; Denis Dumoulin, patriarch of Antioch, 1447. Archbishops of Paris: Pierre de Marca, 1662; Hardouin de Péréfixe, 1671; François de Harlay, 1695; and an archbishop of Sens, who was also High Almoner of France, Renaud de Beaune, who died in 1616.

The few statues which are now in the church are modern: the marble monument by Pigalle, of the Comte d'Harcourt; of Cardinal de Belloy giving alms to a woman and child, by Deseine; and those of the three murdered archbishops, Sibour, Affre, and Darboy, who are buried in the crypt. The epitaph of Monseigneur Affre is as follows : *Le bon pasteur donne sa vie pour ses brebis. . . . Que mon sang soit le dernier versé.*

The bells of Notre-Dame were justly celebrated; but of the thirteen which were formerly in the towers, only one remains, the great *bourdon*, heard all over the city on great occasions; as, for instance, on Holy Saturday, when at High Mass, during

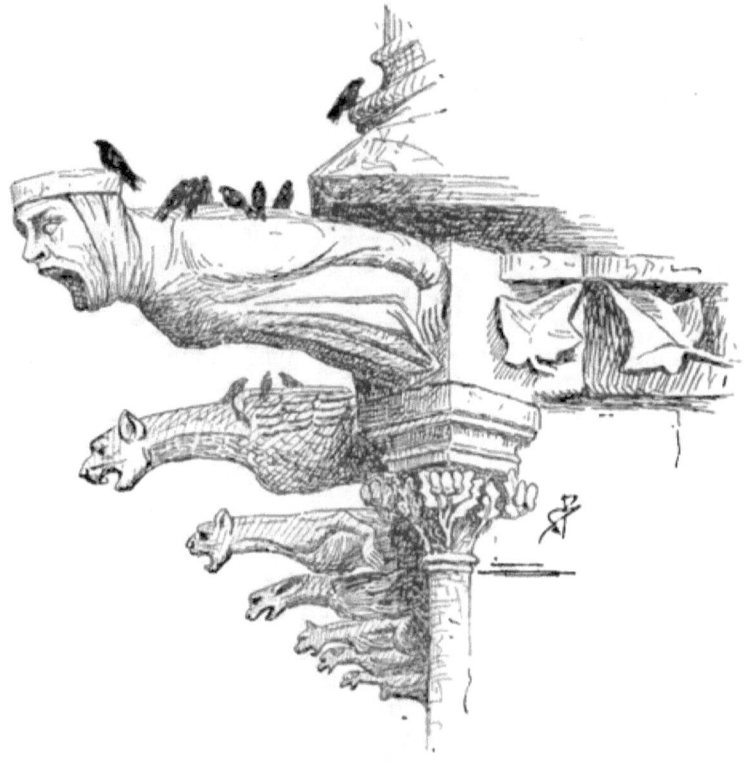

GARGOYLES.

the *Gloria*, it peals forth, giving the signal for all the other church bells to break their forty-eight hours' silence. It was given by Jean de Montaigu[*] in 1400, who named it Jacqueline, after his wife Jacqueline de La Grange; and in 1686 it was refounded and re-baptised—Emmanuel-Louise-Thérèse, in honour of Louis XIV. and Marie-Thérèse of Austria.

[*] Jean de Montaigu, beheaded in 1409, was a councillor, grand master of the palace, and brother of Gérard, 95th bishop of Paris.

The exterior decoration of Notre-Dame is very rich. Gargoyles, monsters of the most grotesque type, called also *tarasques* and *magots*, are there, encircling the towers, and disputing their importance with the Angel of the Judgment. The monsters stand, as they did centuries ago, gazing down upon Paris and its doings for good or for evil. Think of the events they have witnessed from the burning of fifty-four Templars in a slow fire by Philippe IV., to the horrors of the Commune. They must have seen the flaming villages and *châteaux* during the Jacquerie, and witnessed those useless *sorties* during the last war, when the Parisians vainly endeavoured to escape from the city and gain one of the outside army corps. They seem to look down in scorn upon humanity, whether in the form of the coronation of Henry VI. of England, so mean an affair that "un bourgeois qui marierait ses enfants ferait mieux les choses," or the misery of the famine of 1419-21. "Vous auriez entendu dans tout Paris des lamentations pitoyables, des petits enfants qui criaient, 'Je meurs de faim.' On voyait sur un fumier 20-30 enfants garçons, filles, qui rendaient l'âme de faim et de froid. One enterrait 100,000 personnes. Des bandes de loups courraient les campagnes et entraient même la nuit dans Paris pour enlever les cadavres." And all the ages through, the brutes have had the same expression of scorn, of spite, of diabolical ugliness, that one feels it to be a comfort that they are fixed safely to the gallery of the towers, out of the way of working mischief.

Amongst the great ceremonies which have taken place in the cathedral are: The marriage of Marie Stuart with François II., of France, in 1552; the marriage of Henri of Navarre and Marguerite de Valois upon a platform erected outside the great porch, to prevent Protestant contamination of the church. This was upon the eve of S. Bartholomew, the 18th August, just six days before the great work of massacre on the 24th. The coronation of Napoléon by Pope Pius VII., in 1804; the marriage of the Duc du Berry, and the baptism of the Duc du Bordeaux (Comte de Chambord) in 1816; the funeral of the Duc d'Orléans, son of Louis Philippe, in 1853; the marriage of Louis-Napoléon in 1853; the baptism of his son in 1857, and a certain number of episcopal consecrations.

There was a great procession organized in 1590, during the siege of Paris by Henri IV. Sermons were preached against

"Le Béarnais," the clergy took up arms, and the pope's legate promised the palm of martyrdom to all who fell in the holy cause. The day after the first assault, the procession took

DEMON WATCHING THE FIRES OF THE COMMUNE.

place. The principal heroes of the League, after shaving head and face, marched first, vested in "*camail and rochet,*" and bearing sword and "*partisan.*" Then came a number of monks in order of battle, shouldering their axes and arquebuses, "dans un accoutrement moitié religieux et moitié militaire qui avait quelque chose de burlesque et de terrible à la fois. L'Eglise militante chantant des hymnes entremêlées de salves de mousqueterie. Ils défilèrent devant le legat, qui les traita de vrais Machabées; pour que quelques-uns méritèrent à la défense des remparts." But it did not save them from starvation.

There was at one time a mass said for the idle at "la plus

NOTRE-DAME BY MOONLIGHT.

haute heure du matin. Ainsi qu'en d'aucunes paroisses de Paris, il y a la messe d'unze heures." This was suppressed in 1722 by the Cardinal de Noailles, archbishop of Paris. It was founded by the kindly regular canon, Jean Le Moyne, and its revenues were applied to the *bénéficiers machicots* and *clercs du matins*. The *machicots* were officers of the church of Notre-Dame inferior to the *bénéficiers*, and superior to the simple wage-singers. "The word *machicotage* se dit de certaines additions des notes, suivant une merche diatonique avec lesquelles on remplissait dans le plain chant les intervalles du tierces et autres." A number of corona hang from the vault, and in the crossing of the transepts is a huge one recalling that of Hildesheim. When lighted during the services of Holy Week, just giving a gentle diffused glimmer, the effect is very fine ; never, indeed, are these great churches so grand as at the evening services. The mass of men sitting in the nave (it is reserved for them), the deep roar of their voices as they sing the *Miserere*, the intense silence during the eloquent discourses of Père Monsabré or some other Dominican, the procession, dimly lighted, of old canons in every stage of decrepitude, the small boys, followed by a crowd of the most unharmonious specimens of humanity, carrying tapers, are elements forming a picture which is uniquely picturesque. In the old days before the war, the graceful, sweet-expressioned archbishop, bending to this side and that, while the faithful kissed his episcopal ring and received his blessing, added to the beauty of the scene. Had we known what was in store for him, it would have added also to the pathos.

NOTRE-DAME DE L'ASSOMPTION.

This building may be described as a dome and a portico, built from 1670 to 1676, by Charles Erard, director of the Academy of France at Rome, and decorated by Charles de la Fosse. The cupola is graceful, and if it were as well decorated as the Allerheiligen church of the palace at München, or the Apollinarus-Kirche at Remagen on the Rhine, it would be an imposing edifice ; as it is, it seems under a cloud, and is only used as a *succursale* or *dépendance* of the Madeleine. It belonged to the convent of Augustinian nuns, now turned into barracks, but still showing a few remains of the cloister. It is strange that no one in these days should desire to build a round church under a dome ablaze with mosaic decoration. It might have a sanctuary as at Aix la Chapelle for the Divine offices, with a pulpit in the dome, which would have the advantage of being placed so that all the congregation could see the preacher. I am thinking at this moment of the beautiful Russian church in Paris, which is gorgeous with colour and gilding. Such a building upon a large scale, built in the sumptuous style of the Brompton Oratory, of marbles and mosaic, and in the form of the church of the Assumption, would be a refreshing change from red brick and Doulton tiles, which seem to be inseparately mixed up with elaborate ritual, and are as infallibly correct as clothing for an Anglo-Catholic service as is chocolate colour for dressing up *pseudo-Grecian* temples surmounted by pepper-box turrets, which delighted the architects at the beginning of this styleless century.

NOTRE-DAME DE L'ABBAYE AUX BOIS.

If I say that the little church and cloister, which are all that remain of a monastery of Cistercian nuns, built in 1718, are situated in the Rue de Sèvres, hard by the Bon Marché, my readers will immediately picture their whereabouts. At the beginning of this century, the Abbaye became a genteel boarding-house for fashionable ladies who played at being weary of the world; but, although they retired into a monastic building, their *monde* followed them; and thus we find Madame Recamier receiving her admirers in her cloistered *salon*, and listening to their philosophical sophistries while she elegantly reclines upon a satin sofa with straight legs and curling arms.

NOTRE-DAME DES BLANCS-MANTEAUX.

When the white-mantled religious, the servants of Mary, came to Paris about the year 1258, they set up housekeeping in the street which is now named after them, the Rue des Blancs-Manteaux. Everyone who has been to Florence knows the chapel of the Annunziata, where during mass one day, the general of the Servites, Filippo Benozzi, saw a vision of the Virgin sitting in a chariot, and heard her voice calling upon him to draw near, and join himself to her servants, who, some fifteen years earlier, had banded themselves together. There were seven of them, all of noble family, and they gained their name from their especial devotion to the Virgin. As they wandered out to the church of the Annunciation to sing their *Angelus*, the women and children used to point at them and cry out, "*Guardate i Servi di Maria*"; and so, when they formed themselves into a community, they became known as the "Servi" or "Serviti." Benozzi was a medicine man of benevolent disposition, who, tired of witnessing suffering (perhaps of operations performed without anæsthetics), gave up his work, and retired, like another S. Benendict, to Monte Senario. His power in smoothing down the ruffled-up backs of the Tuscans in their many family squabbles was so great that he became a renowned moral healer; and in 1285, when he died, his order was flourishing all over Italy and France. It was soon after his beatification, about 1671, that Andrea del Sarto was called upon to decorate part of the cloisters of the Annunziata; and, as a result, we have the lovely Madonna del Sacco. At the end of the 13th century the hermits of Saint-Guillaume replaced the Servites at the monastery of the Blancs-Manteaux, and in 1618 the house was united to the Reformed Benedictines who erected a new church. The habit of the monks was then changed to black, but as the name of Blancs-Manteaux was still retained, the people called the fathers *les mal nommés*. The conventual buildings are now occupied by the Mont-de-Piété, another kind of service of the poor, in the shape of official and honest pawnbroking. If anyone wishes to study character, let him go into the great hall, and look at those rows and rows of physiognomies sitting upon the benches awaiting their turn to be served. Young, old, poor, and, apparently, rich, all go there for loans upon their goods; and you may pile upon the mountain anything you like, from a bundle of rags to a diamond butterfly.

NOTRE-DAME DES CHAMPS.

Legendary history records an assemblage of the first Christians of Lutetia in the fields where now runs the Rue S. Jacques, listening to the preaching of S. Denis, and strengthening themselves against the persecution which loomed in the distance. And legend further relates that a chapel was built upon this spot. But leaving the realms of tradition, we find an authentic account of a church in the 8th century which, in the next hundred years, was served by the Benedictine monks of Marmoutier. This remained the headquarters of a priory for about six hundred years. In 1604, Cardinal Bérulle introduced the Carmelite order as reformed by S. Theresa, and the nuns began to rebuild. The church they left intact with its 13th century porch, and its great statues of S. Denis, Moses, Aaron, David, and Solomon. This building disappeared, and a modern one arose in its stead, more to the West; but the crypt is supposed to be under the level of the street; and according to the abbé Lebœuf, a second subterraneous burial-ground of Gallo-Roman origin was discovered still lower down, with fragments of tombstones, slabs, pottery, and the like.

The present church contains a few *débris* of its former grandeur, a statue by Sarazin, of Cardinal de Bérulle, being the principal one.

The monastery was celebrated, during the 17th century, as the asylum of many distinguished ladies who sought a refuge from their troubles; amongst others, of the blessed Sœur Louise de la Miséricorde, who died there in 1710, in the odour of sanctity. In her mundane career this *Madeleine da la Cour* was Mdlle. de la Vallière, and she is said to have posed to Le Brun for his terrible picture of *La Madeleine pénitente renonce à toutes les vanités de la vie*, which was painted for M. de Camus as an adornment of this Carmelite church. It is now in the Louvre, which it in nowise adorns. Lebrun, as a decorative artist, painting allegories and battles, is bearable; but his religious pictures are only gross exaggerations of the Italian Eclectics. This Madeleine de la Vallière is in a tortuous state of agony at the thought of the vanities she enjoyed. With eyes turned up, with her flowing locks, and swathed in rich satin garments, which are blown by a gust of wind coming in at the open casement on the top of a cloud, she looks thunderstruck; it is astonishment at the discovery of her sinfulness, revealed by the heavens opening, and the Divine voice addressing her. Surely the moderns, the Bérauds, the Lhermites, the Dagnan-Bouverets, Uhde, Hitchcock, Pierce, and their followers, have far more religious feeling, although they clothe their personages as Parisian workpeople, and paint their Madeleines, like Henner, in the pastures (apparently) of the Bois de Boulogne—backgrounds, considering the subject, not altogether inappropriate.

NOTRE-DAME DE LORETTE.

An utterly uninteresting exterior encloses some good mural paintings by Orsel, Périn, and Roger. The church was completed in 1836 by Lebas, and were the weather always bright, the interior would not fail to impress the visitor; but it is too dark for a Northern clime, and it is therefore difficult fully to appreciate the frescoes. That over the altar is by Picot; the subjects from the life of the Virgin are by Dubois, Langlois, Vinchon, and Hesse; the choir is the work of Delorme; *the Presentation in the Temple*, and *Christ disputing with the Doctors*, are by Heim and Drolling. They are all inspired by a reverent feeling for the subjects, and are resplendent with gold

NOTRE-DAME DES VICTOIRES.

Louis XIII. laid the first stone of this church in 1629, and dedicated it to Our Lady of Victory, in memory of the famous battle of La Rochelle. It was part of the convent of barefooted Augustins, who were nicknamed the Little Fathers, by Henri IV., on account of the diminutive stature of some of the friars, and consequently the church was as often called Notre-Dame des Petits Pères as Notre-Dame des Victoires. Pierre Lemut was its original architect; and before it was completed, in 1740, by Cartaud, two other architects, Libéral Bruant and Gabriel Leduc, lent their aid. The cupola is decorated with an Assumption; pictures by Vanloo adorn the choir, and other chapels contain some by Perrault. Those by Vanloo represent the thanksgiving of the King and the Cardinal for the mighty victory aforesaid, the taking of La Rochelle. But the interest of, or the objections to, the church, according to the point of view from which we start, consists in the innumerable *ex-voto* tablets which cover the walls, and proclaim the answers to prayers by mothers, wives, husbands, sons, fathers, and daughters. They are emblems of the faith which saves. But would not the same earnest prayers, put up on other spots, produce the same results? Is it not a narrow notion that we are more likely to be heard in the Place des Victoires than in the Halles? Such is not the view of the *dévots* and *dévotes*, as the statue of the Virgin proclaims, for it is hung all over with costly jewels and ornaments; and whatever time of the day we may enter the church, we find it almost filled with troubled souls who come to gain an indulgence at its privileged altars, which are to those of a different sort of mind examples of what to avoid. For those persons having leanings to superstition, let me commend this church as an antidote; to others, it is neither æsthetically interesting nor, from a religious point of view, particularly edifying. To musicians it has one attraction, as being the burial-place of Jean-Baptiste Lulli, the charming fiddler, who died in 1687, and whose bronze statue by Cotton is in the transept.

L'ORATOIRE.

Built for the Oratorians, this elegant circular church is now given over to Protestant gloom of the least decorative order. It was constructed by François Mansard, and dedicated to Notre-Dame-des-Anges in 1634, upon the site, some authorities say, of the Hôtel of Gabrielle d'Estrèes; it may therefore be said to have passed from the good Gabrielle, through the better fathers, to the best Protestants; or, contrariwise, from the bad Demoiselle to the worse Catholics, and, worst of all, Calvinists. However, now all is calm, and passions have subsided; and a fine statue of Admiral Coligny is fixed to its wall, facing the scene of his murder on that fearful feast of bloodshed which S. Bartholemew must have been scandalized to find attached to his name.

SAINT-PAUL-SAINT-LOUIS.

In the Rue Saint-Antoine is the old church of the Jesuits, gorgeous in marbles, gilding and stucco, as is the wont of the architects employed by those wary fathers. It was built from the designs of François Derraud from 1627-41. The remains of the conventual buildings are now occupied by the Collège Charlemagne. The expenses of the building were defrayed by Louis XIII. and Richelieu, who celebrated his maiden mass there. It was the second cupola erected in Paris, the first being that belonging to the Carmelite church. It is Italian in style, the *façade* being very similar to that of S. Gervais, recalling the Gesu and S. Ignacius at Rome, and is adorned with statues of S. Louis, by Lequesne; of S. Catherine, by Auguste Préault; and of S. Anne, by Etex. Bourdaloue and archbishop Huet of Avranches are buried there, and in a crypt below lie the Jesuits who have died in the convent from its foundation until the suppression of the order. The numerous monuments were swept away at the Revolution: a rich sculptured coffer for the heart of Louis XIII., and another by Coustou le jeune, containing Louis XIV.'s heart. The tabernacle was of silver gilt, but it is no more. The only contents now of any interest are a picture representing the abbey of Longchamps, attributed to Philippe de Champaigne, and a fine work by Delacroix, *Christ in the Garden of Gethsemane*. Although his first known picture, it is an example of his splendid colouring and grand composition. Victor Hugo's first child was born in the parish, and baptized at S. Paul's, and to commemorate the event the poet presented two holy-water stoops, in the shape of shells, very beautiful in design.

SAINT-PHILIPPE DU ROULE.

"This church presents you with a single insulated row of fluted Ionic pillars, on each side of the nave ; very airy, yet consequential, and even imposing. It is much to my taste, and I wish such a plan were more generally adopted in the interiors of Grecian-constructed churches. The choir, the altar . . . the whole is extremely simple and elegant. Nor must the roof be omitted to be particularly mentioned. It is an arch constructed of wood, upon a plan originally invented by Philibert Delorme—so well known in the annals of art in the sixteenth century. The whole is painted in stone-colour, and may deceive the most experienced eye. This beautiful church was built after the designs of Chalgrin, about the year 1700, and is considered to be a purer resemblance of the antique than any other in Paris. Perhaps the principal front may be thought to be too close or servile a copy. It was erected upon the site of an ancient Gothic chapel, of which latter the author of the three quarto volumes of Parisian topography has given a vignette from the only known design of it, in aquatint, but very indifferent. This church, well worth your examination, is situated in a quarter rarely visited by our countrymen, in the Rue du Faubourg du Roule, not far from the barriers." *

I give this criticism of S. Philippe because it shows how taste has changed in architecture, as indeed in all else. From most persons' point of view the church is quite uninteresting ; indeed the only object in going there is, except to a certain number of fashionables, to hear some celebrated preacher. It was from the pulpit of S. Philippe that Père Didon poured forth those eloquent and learned discourses, stocked with liberal ideas, which brought him into disgrace and forced retirement, until quite recently.

It is curious, too, that the quarter should have so changed. It is now the centre of the English and American colonists, and withal well filled with persons who delight in the one o'clock mass. It is so convenient ; they can saunter in after *déjeuner*, say a few prayers, step into their carriages again, and go straight off to the races. Perhaps S. Augustin has bereft S. Philippe of some of its fashion ; but it has still plenty to spare ; it may be said to swarm with elegant *toilettes*, and not much else in the way of beauty. Let us walk on.

* Dibdlen.

SAINT-PIERRE DE CHAILLOT.

"Chaillot, très ancien village de la banlieue de Paris érigé en faubourg, sous le nom de la Conférence, par arrêté du conceil du mois de Juillet 1659. Le nom de ce faubourg lui fut donné à cause de la porte de la Conférence, située sur la rive droite de la Seine, vers l'extrémité de la terrasse du jardin des Tuileries."

The apse of this church is the only part that is old; the rest is Italian, and very poor of its kind, which makes the groined vault of the apse all the pleasanter to contemplate. Lately a new chapel has been added on in the Avenue Marceau, something between a Swiss *châlet* and a *café*, all ablaze with gilding and tawdry decoration.

The abbey of Sainte-Perrine de Chaillot was founded by Philippe le Bel about 1300, in the forest of Compiègne for the canonesses of the order of S. Augustin; and in 1646 it was transferred to La Villette. Later, the monastery was united to another community of the same order which was established at Chaillot in 1659. In 1760 the abbey ceased to exist, and the buildings gradually disappeared, with the exception of a few fragments belonging to some school buildings. Augustin's sisters may still be seen at Chaillot, working in the parish of S. Pierre, and observable by their quaint head-gear and their quainter clogs worn over spotless white stockings. By the way, why do Anglican sisters and nurses wear long gowns trailing about the wards of our hospitals? Are they not possibly receptacles for the germ and microbe population?

SAINT-PIERRE DE MONTMARTRE.

The first church of S. Peter is said to have been founded by Louis VI. and Alix de Savoie his wife, upon the site of a still older edifice; and its most remarkable event in those early days was the presence of S. Bernard at its consecration. Little remains earlier than the 15th century, except two *verd antique* columns and some of the pillars of the choir. Upon a slab may be read an inscription bearing upon the martyrdom of S. Denis and his companions, who suffered here upon the mountain; and in the open ground outside is a Calvary to which the pious world resorts. A splendid new church dedicated to the Sacré Coeur is being built hard by, to which a vast number of processions and pilgrimages now industriously and toilfully wend their way.

SAINT-ROCH.

Built by Jacques Lemercier, after the first-stone-laying by the *Grand Monarque*, this church became fashionable and much affected by the great ones of the City. Bossuet lived hard by in the Rue S. Anne, and was placed in the church he had often preached in, previously to being removed to his cathedral of Meaux. Another celebrity, Marie Anne de Bourbon, Princesse de Conti, daughter of Louis and his hand-maiden La Vallière, was buried in the chapel of the Virgin; and the sculptors François and Michel Anguier also found their rest here.

The portico was commenced in 1736 from the designs of Robert de Cotte. It is in no wise beautiful; but it is celebrated as having been the scene of the terrible 13 Vendémiaire An IV. (5 October, 1795). In the "*cul-de-sac Dauphin*" against the church walls the "young bronze Artillery Officer" set his guns. "The firing was with sharp and sharpest shot; to all men it was plain that there was no sport."* In a couple of hours it was all over; insurrection quelled; and the "Whiff of Grapeshot" proved so successful that it became the active power in subsequent doings of the dynasty of the "Man of bronze."

S. Roch is a vast edifice mainly conspicuous by its ugliness; but it contains much furniture that is worth noting. Over the altar is a fine crucifix by Michel Anguier, formerly in the Sorbonne. The group of the Nativity brought from Val de Grâce is by François Anguier. Saint-Jean-en-Grève has contributed the Baptism of Our Lord, by Lemoine; the Latin Fathers were sculptured for the Dome of the Invalides; the figure of S. Roch on the right of the choir is by one of the Coustou brothers; a dying Christ by Falconet. The bust of Lenôtre, by Coyzevox, was part of a monument; so was the statue of Cardinal Dubois by Gillaume Coustou. Mignard was buried here and has a memorial bust by Desjardins. Medallions also abound: the Maréchal d'Asfeld, the Duc de Lesdignières, the Comte d'Harcourt, and the Duc de Cérqui; also a monument to Maupertius, l'abbé de l'Epée; and an epitaph to

* Carlyle.

Pierre Corneille. Madame de Feuquières, in white marble, was treated after the manner of the kings and queens at S. Denis. Lemoine made her kneeling at her father, Mignard's feet; some one improved upon this, and turned her into a Madeleine at the foot of the cross.

Behind the choir is the chapel of the Virgin, with the Crucifixion lighted up after the manner of that terrible tomb at Windsor erected to the memory of the Princess Charlotte; but they vie with each other in popularity from the many sightseers who pass by. There is also an entombment which, on Good Friday, is visited by thousands of people; and in the chapel of the S. Sacrament, a reproduction of the Ark of the Covenant with the Mercy Seat and the Cherubim — about the most interesting part of the church; it is I believe, used as the tabernacle. "S. Roche is doubtless a very fine building, with a well proportioned front and a noble flight of steps;

A SISTER OF SAINT-ROCH.

but the interior is too plain and severe for my taste. The walls are decorated with unfluted pilasters, with capitals scarcely conformable to any one order of architecture. The choir, however, is lofty, and behind it, in Our Lady's chapel, if I remember accurately, there is a striking piece of sculpture of the Crucifixion, sunk into a rock, which receives the light from an invisible aperture, as at S. Sulpice. To the right, or rather behind this chapel, there is another—called the *Chapel of Calvary*—in which you observe a celebrated piece of sculpture, of rather colossal dimensions, of the entombment of Christ. The dead Saviour is borne to the sepulchre by Joseph of

Arimathea, St. John, and the three Maries. The name of the sculptor is *Deseine*. Certainly you cannot but be struck with the effect of such representations—which accounts for these two chapels being a great deal more attended in general than the choir or the nave of the church. It is, right, however, to add, that the pictures here are preferable to those of S. Sulpice, and the series of bas-reliefs, descriptive of the principal events in the life of Christ, is among the very best specimens of art, of that species, which Paris can boast of."*

The music at S. Roch gained much renown some years ago, and although it is not now in any way remarkable, its reputation is still great. People assure you that the best music in Paris is at S. Roch. True, we may hear the masses of Haydn and Mozart very fairly performed there; but neither voices nor organ equal the refinement of the Madeleine. In one respect, however, we may prefer S. Roch. The boys sit upon their little stools in the choir, and when they have to sing, group themselves with the singing men round a huge lectern, which stands out in the centre of the chancel. Thus they stand before the old noted service book, and in their picturesque costume of red cassocks, white albs, and blue or red sashes, they form a most picturesque *coup-d'œil*, very different from the other churches. At the Madeleine the choir sits behind the altar, and you hear the singing from invisible voices,—very charming if you did not see the boys in their *collégien* uniform pass round before the commencement of the service; but this gives a somewhat theatrical effect. At S. Roch the grouping of the men and boys and the double basses round the lectern gives the whole affair such a delightfully old-world appearance that it is most refreshing, and the effect of the huge service-book, with its plain-song notation up above the heads of the boys, takes one back hundreds of years. That S. Roch was much esteemed in the early years of the century our American's letter shows. His criticism of the sermon might apply very well to many a one in this year of grace, more especially here at home. The French preachers almost always speak well, and are eloquent, even if their matter be indifferent, dull, or twaddly. Englishmen unfortunately despise the manner, and think their hearers ought to be content with good matter only; and so it comes about that in a life-time only two or three great preachers stand out in one's memory—a Henry Parry Liddon and a Samuel

* Dibden.

Wilberforce. However, the "American," is of a diverse opinion. "Yesterday, being Sunday, I went to S. Roch's; I had the luck to hit upon the fashionable church; but the preacher was the *god of dulness*. The world, he says, is growing worse and worse; our roguish ancestors begot us bigger rogues, about to produce a worse set of rogues than ourselves. The Antichrist is already come. If he had said the antichrist of wit, anybody would have believed him, and yet this is the very pulpit from which the Bossuets and Bourdaloues used to preach. The church was filled almost entirely of women; one might think that none go to heaven in this country but the fair sex" (or perhaps the men require no help, he might have added). "The worshippers seem intent enough upon their devotions, but the wide avenues at the sides are filled with a crowd of idle, curious, and disorderly spectators. Give me a French church; one walks in here booted and spurred, looks at the pretty women and the pictures, whistles a tune if one chooses, and then walks out again. They have not spoilt the architectural beauty (!) of S. Roch's by pews and galleries. The walls are adorned splendidly with paintings; and here and there are groups of statuary, and the altar being finely gilt and illuminated, looks magnificently. When I build a church I shall decorate it somewhat in this manner. It is good to imitate nature as much as one can in all things; and she has set us the example in this. She has adorned her great temple, the world, with green fields, and fragrant flowers, and its superb dome the firmament with stars."[*] The trotting about at S. Roch is the same to this day, which makes it the least restful of churches.

SAINT-SÉVERIN.

The church of S. Séverin is particularly interesting as showing a gradual development from the 13th to the 16th century. Founded upon the site of an oratory by Henri I. in 1050, it was first rebuilt at the end of the 11th century.

There were two saints of this name; one, the founder of the Abbey of Châteaulandon, who miraculously cured Clovis I. of some sickness by placing his chasuble upon him; and the other, the patron of this church, a monk, or rather a hermit, who lived during the reign of Childebert I., in a cell near Paris, and was of course much given to prayer and supplications, and

[*] *American in Paris.*

other pious exercises. Considering the brutal manners and customs of the early sovereigns and their companions, it is a blessed sign that human nature, even in those dark ages, was not completely diabolical; and to find that some men and women cared for other matters than fire and sword and pillage. S. Séverin was one of these more peaceful souls; and

SAINT-SÉVERIN FROM THE TOWERS OF NOTRE-DAME

so well did he preach his pacific faith, that S. Cloud, or Clodoaldus, the grandson of Queen Clotilde, became one of his disciples, and received the religious habit of the Benedictine order from him. S. Cloud was the youngest of the sons of

Chlodomir, one of three brothers who suffered from the murderous inclinations of wicked uncles. What brigands they all were! Imagine a woman being asked in all seriousness whether she preferred death or the tonsure for her grandchildren. No wonder monasteries and convents flourished, for where else was there any culture, enlightenment, civilization, or even safety to life and limb? And yet Clotilde must have had some reason for her passionate answer, "Better they were dead than shaven monks!" for she must have foreseen that such an exclamation could only lead to assassination, and thus we find that S. Cloud alone of the brothers escaped death, and became a shaven Benedictine.

S. Séverin was probably buried near the oratory, and what would be more natural than that the disciple should consecrate the spot to the memory of his master? In 1050 Henri I. gave the patronage, which had been up to his reign in the hands of the kings, to the then Bishop of Paris, Imbert. At the end of the 11th century, it became an enormous parish, extending almost over the whole of the southern part of the city. It is now the centre of the Italian legion, models, organ-grinders, white-mice men, and plaster-image vendors; and it is a pretty sight on Sundays and *fête* days to see the church packed with emigrants from the sunny South decked out in all the splendour of their holiday attire. How a group of people can alter the whole aspect of a building, was once demonstrated to me in S. Paul's cathedral. Walking down that dismal and gloomy nave upon an afternoon to which the same adjectives might be appropriately applied, it seemed suddenly to become bright and light by the entrance of a group of three or four Italian women with their children, dressed in the familiar, and upon any other human beings, hideously crude violet, emerald-green, and raw-blue coloured garments; colours which are totally wanting in beauty and harmony of themselves, but allied to the snow-white chemises and trimmed with gold braid, and partially covered with silver ornaments, they seemed to drop into harmony with the church, and to completely change the general appearance of the melancholy background, as even a ray of sunshine fails to do completely. S. Paul's is so essentially Italian that its usual congregations, clad in blacks and browns, form an utterly inharmonious foreground to the architecture, and give one the idea that the building is *dépaysé*.

SAINT-SÉVERIN.

The present church of S. Séverin was re-built in the 13th century, in great part by money obtained by indulgences, which Clement VI. in 1347 accorded to the generously inclined among the faithful. In the next century this system was revived, and the churchwardens, with shrewd foresight, bought up more ground, with a view to the enlargement of the building. The first stone of the new part was laid in 1489, the chapel of S. Sebastian being built three years later. In 1490 the chapel of the Conception, which was situated near the east end, was demolished to make way for the lengthening of the north aisle. Five years later, Jean Simon, Bishop of Paris, consecrated the new portions of the church, including the high altar, and several of the chapels of the *chevet*. In 1498 the chapels on the south side were commenced by Micheaul le Gros; the sacristy and treasury being added in 1540, and the chapel of the Communion in 1673, to make an entrance to which the chapel of S. Sebastian had to be destroyed. Thus for four hundred years, more or less, the church was undergoing constant change and development. Then began the downward path, commencing with the destruction of the *jubé* and the "ornamentation" of the sanctuary to suit the taste of the devotees of Classic art. Originally, many of the Paris churches had *jubés* (rood-screens), but the only one now remaining is that of S. Etienne du Mont. A brass attached to one of the pillars gives the names of the donors of the screen, Antoine de Compaigne (illuminator) and his wife Oudette.

Were it not for the elegant little tower and spire, few persons would know of the existence of S. Séverin. It is out of the beaten track, beyond Notre-Dame and the "monuments" of the Faubourg S. Germain. It has to be hunted up; but it is well worth the trouble, and any one visiting the remains of the Roman amphitheatre of Lutetia, in the Rue Monge (now laid out as a public garden) can see S. Séverin at the same time.

The portal is profusely carved and bears an inscription upon the stylobate (the letters of which are of the 13th century), giving the various duties of the grave-diggers, amongst others the cleansing of the vaults of the roof as well as the lower part of the church on the feast of S. Martin, in order to be tidy for the dedication festival which fell two days later. As in many other churches, there are two lions on each side of the arch, probably the supports formerly of some heraldic shields. This, no doubt, is the origin of the formula, which terminates certain ecclesiastical judgments pronounced at the threshold of the temple, *Datum inter duos leones.* The tympanum bas-relief has been restored. It represents the charity of S. Martin, who is one of the patrons of the church, and whose mutilated mantle, or a portion of it, has been one of the cherished relics of S. Séverin since the 14th century. There is also a chapel dedicated to the venerable bishop of Tours, which was formerly completely covered with *ex voto* horse-shoes, the gifts of thankful travellers; for S. Martin having been on horseback when he divided his cloak, became the patron of the travelling community. The western *façade* is composed of portions of the portal of S. Pierre-aux-Bœufs in the Cité, which was demolished in 1837, and is, the little which has been left unrestored, of the 13th century. S. Pierre was situated in the Rue d'Arcole; the only fragment remaining being a *bas-relief* fixed against the wall of the house which occupies the site of the church, representing an *Ecce Homo*, surrounded with the emblems of the Passion. Above the porch of S. Séverin are an open work gallery, a rose window and a cornice upon which a party of little animals are playing among some foliage, all in *Flamboyant* style. The statue of the Virgin is quite modern. The whole of the chapels, as well as the greater part of the nave, are of the 15th and 16th centuries; but the first three bays of the nave are of a totally different style; the form of the arches and of the windows shows the craftsmanship of the 13th century artists. Birds and beasts, natural and grotesque, form gargoyles, shooting the rainwater from their open mouths. At the north-west end of the chapels, an elegantly carved canopied niche encloses the patron Saint, and near him is an inscription inviting the passers-by to pray for the souls of the departed

Bonnes gens qui p cy passes
Pries Dieu pour les trespasses.

The last word has been mutilated.

The interior consists of a nave and double aisles. The triforium is very similar to that of Westminster Abbey church; but at the commencement of the apse, the 13th century arches were filled in with round-headed ones, Cupid-like Cherubs being placed between the two to "ornament" the intervening space, and the pillars converted into marbled pilasters.

Some of the capitals and corbels of the south aisle are most droll—prophets, flying Angels, and divers kinds of animals, all

INTERIOR OF SAINT-SÉVERIN.

more or less grotesque, after the manner of the *miserere* seats at Wells cathedral. During the reign of Henri IV. Sibyls, and Prophets, Patriarchs and Apostles, were painted by one Jacques Bunel on a gold ground above the arches of the nave; but happily they have disappeared. It was Mlle. de Montpensier who caused the marbling of the choir to be undertaken in 1684, and who also bore the expense of the baldachino of the altar, employing the sculptor Tubi to carry out the designs of Lebrun.

In the side aisle, on the south, is a little door leading

SAINT-SÉVERIN.

through a garden, formerly the graveyard, to the *presbytère*. This, in summer, forms a charming little picture. In one of the side chapels (Notre-Dame de l'Espérance) is a 15th century wall-painting of *The Resurrection of the Dead;* and in the chapel of the *chevet* a *Preaching of John the Baptist*, also in fresco. In the apse are a series of fluted and spiral columns. The bosses are many of them ornamented with figures—the

Annunciation, S. Anne and S. Joachim at the golden gate, a Holy Face, and a chalice surmounted by the host.

A number of distinguished persons were buried at S. Séverin: Étienne Pasquier, an eloquent *Avocat-Général* under Henri III. who was mainly instrumental in causing the exclusion of the Jesuits from the University, and who died in 1615; the brothers Saint-Martre, celebrated men of letters living at the beginning of the 17th century; and Moreri, the author of the *Dictionnaire Historique*, who died in 1680.

There are only three ancient epitaphs remaining—that of Nicolas de Bomont, who died in 1540; Guillaume Fusée, president of the Parliament of Paris, and of his wife, Jeanne Desportes, who made several pious foundations in 1521; and Jean Baptiste Altin, *conseilleur au Châtelet*, who died in 1640. The first, Nicolas Bomont, his wife, and fifteen children, are represented as pigmy personages praying at the foot of the Crucified. The emblems upon the Altin slab have been borrowed from the Roman catacombs; and the epitaph is as follows:

> ALTINI PECCATORIS OSSA
> HIC JACENT,
> PIE JESU MISERERE EIUS
> TU VIATOR PRECARE PRO EO
> VIX ✠ AN ✠ PLU ✠ JUNIVS
> A ✠ C ✠ DIONYSIANO MDCXL ✠
> SENATOR FOIT IN CASTELL ✠ PAR ✠
> PŒNE QUADRAGEN ✠
> VALE VIATOR ET VALERE
> MANES IOBE

A modern tablet states that the first confraternity established in France under the patronage of the Immaculate Conception was founded at S. Séverin in 1311, but the chapels used by the association have disappeared.

The church contains no furniture of any value artistically, except perhaps, the organ and wrought-iron gallery, erected in 1747 to replace an earlier instrument of 1512; the original organ, given in 1358 by Maitre Regnaud de Douy, the master of the parish schools, is described as *une bones orgues et bien ordenées*.

A good deal of the stained glass is of the 15th and 16th centuries, and bears the figures and arms of the donors (some of whom appear by their long robes to have been magistrates), accompanied by their wives and families. The subjects are the usual ones taken from the New Testament, or from the lives of the Saints; but a few are somewhat out of the beaten track, as for instance: Two families of numerous members accompanied by, or superintended by S. Peter and S. Andrew; S. Michael clad as a warrior bearing a shield upon which are emblazoned the arms of France; S. Geneviève holding her demon-extinguished taper which an Angel relights; S. Anthony with his staff and bell, and holy fire under his feet, which is in dangerous proximity to his faithful porkling; and lastly, S. Thomas of Canterbury celebrating mass, while his murderers fall upon him with their swords. One of the chapels of S. Séverin was dedicated to the memory of the martyred archbishop.

Several modern artists have decorated the side-chapels—

Alexandre Hesse, Cornu and Flandrin; but the student of the latter painter must go to S. Vincent-de-Paul and S. Germain-des-Prés to fully appreciate this great master of religious art.

The symbols upon the slab mentioned above are very similar to those found in the cemetery of S. Marcel which occupied the site of the abbey of S. Geneviève. In the Breviary of Paris we read, in the office for the Translation of S. Marcel, that his body was put in a chapel, *ædicula*, named after S. Clement, and from which the Saint had driven out an enormous serpent. Coming from a neighbouring wood the monster had seized upon the remains of a rich woman who had been a great sinner, and was regaling himself therewith, when Marcel came to the rescue, and chasing him away three miles, forbade him ever to return. This miracle was popular upon the churches of Paris, and is still to be seen on the centre pier of the Porte S. Anne of Notre-Dame and in the *voussure* of the Porte Rouge.

On the slab at S. Séverin are the doves with olive branches and the sacred monogram. Below, the Lamb is standing upon the earth, from which flow the rivers of Paradise, Pison, Gihon, Hiddekel, and Euphrates, typical, according to S. Ambrose, of the Cardinal Virtues, Prudence, Strength, Courage, and Temperance. The epitaph is written between the doves and the Lamb.

LA SORBONNE.

Another institution which owes its initiative to S. Louis is the Sorbonne, actually founded in 1250 by Robert de Sorbon, a canon of Paris, for sixteen poor students in theology. The

TOMB OF CARDINAL RICHELIEU.

present church is a fine example of 17th century Classicism, such as the world of that day affected. Jacques Lemercier was the architect, and the great Cardinal the pay-master, and between them they certainly turned out a very respectable piece of work with a certain sense of grandeur, and a very fine dome, the first that figured in Paris. It was built between 1635 and 1659. Within, is the marble tomb of Richelieu, the work of Girardon (1694) from the design of Lebrun. The great man reclines gracefully upon a couch supported by a figure of Religion, and a weeping lady of Science at his feet. It has not the feeling of the Renaissance sculpture, and although Religion forms a principal part of the composition, it is purely and simply a secular design. It might be the memorial of a Pagan, and it would be just as appropriate in a town hall, a garden, or a theatre; but that perhaps gives it the more fitness as the monument of so singular a churchman and

THE OLD SORBONNE.

so farcical a Christian. The wary Cardinal turns up his face and piously gazes at Heaven as if that were his only thought; he appears overwhelmed with holiness and sanctity, a veritable Pecksniff arrayed in the gorgeous robes of a prince of the holy Roman Church. But artistically, the composition is fine, far finer than many of the works of the 17th century; and one feels that could the figure rise, it would move about with the same grace as that portrayed in the noble portrait of the great statesman by Philippe de Champaigne in the Louvre. As posthumous retribution for his crimes and vices, Richelieu's head was chopped off into three pieces in 1793, and remained fragmentary until 1861, when they were patched together. The church also contains a painting by Hesse of little value, *Robert de Sorbon présentant à S. Louis de jeunes élèves en théologie*, and some statues by Romy and Bure.

SAINT-SULPICE.

"Yonder majestic portico forms the west front of the church called S. Sulpice . . . . It is at once airy and grand. There are two tiers of pillars, of which this front is composed; the lower is Doric, the upper Ionic; and each row, as I am told, is nearly forty French feet in height, exclusively of their entablatures, each of ten feet. We have nothing like this, certainly, as the front of a parish church, in London. When I except S. Paul's, such exception is made in reference to the most majestic piece of architectural composition which, to my eye, the wit of man hath yet ever devised. The architect of the magnificent front of S. Sulpice was Servandoni; and a street hard by (in which Dom Brial, the father of French history, resides) takes its name from the architect. There are two towers—one at each end of this front, about two hundred and twenty feet in height from the pavement; harmonising well with the general style of architecture, but of which that to the South (to the best of my recollection) is left in an unaccountably if not shamefully unfinished state. These towers are said to be about one toise higher than those of Notre-Dame. The interior of this church is hardly less imposing than its exterior. The vaulted roofs are exceedingly lofty; but, for the length of the nave, and more especially the choir, the transepts are disproportionally short, nor are there sufficiently prominent ornaments to give relief to the massive appearance of the sides. These sides are decorated by fluted pilasters of the Corinthian order, which for so large and lofty a building have a tame effect. There is nothing like the huge, single, insulated column, or the clustered slim pilasters, that separate the nave from the side aisles of the Gothic churches of the early and middle ages.

"The principal altar between the nave and the choir is admired for its size and grandeur of effect, but it is certainly ill-placed; it is perhaps too ornamental, looking like a detached piece which does not harmonise with the surrounding objects. Indeed, most of the altars in French churches want simplicity

Y

and appropriate effect, and the whole of the interior of the choir is (to my fastidious eye only, you may add) destitute of that quiet solemn character which ought always to belong to places of worship. Rich, minute and elaborate as are many of the Gothic choirs of our own country, they are yet in harmony and equally free from a frivolous and unappropriate effect. Behind the choir is the chapel of Our Lady, which is certainly most splendid and imposing. Upon the ceiling is represented the assumption of the Virgin, and the walls are covered with a profusion of gilt ornament which, upon the whole, has a very striking effect. In a recess above the altar is a sculptured representation of the Virgin and Infant Christ in white marble, of a remarkably high polish; nor are the countenances of the mother and child divested of sweetness of expression. They are represented upon a large globe, or with the world at their feet; upon the top of which, slightly coiled, lies the "bruised" or dead serpent. The light in front of the spectator, from a concealed window (a contrivance to which the French seem partial), produces a sort of magical effect. I should add that this is the largest parochial church in Paris, and that its organ has been pronounced to be matchless.

"This magnificent church is the production of several periods and of several artists. Anne of Austria laid the foundation stone in 1636, under the superintendence of Levau. Levau died shortly afterwards, and was succeeded by Gittard and Oppenard. The finish was received by Servandoni, who, in the West front, or portico, left all his predecessors far behind him. The church was dedicated about the middle of the last century. The towers are the joint performances of Maclaurin and Chalgrin; but the latter has the credit of having rectified the blunders of the former. He began his labours in 1777; but both the South tower, and the *Place*, immediately before the West front, want their finishing decorations."

I have quoted this long dissertation by Dibden because I do not think a better description of the church could be given; but the writer is wrong in some of his details. The church was commenced in 1646, not '36, the first architect being Christophe Gamart. The finishing stroke was put by Jean Servandoni, the funds being provided by means of a lottery started by the energetic *curé* Languet de Gergy. I cannot endorse Dibden's praise of the chapel of the Virgin by De Wailly, the surrounding paintings by Vanloo, and the Slodtz

brothers' decorations. It is all very splendid with gold and
marbles, and the statue by Pajou is looked upon as a *chef-*

A PROCESSION IN SAINT-SULPICE.

d'œuvre. The cupola, with an Assumption painted by Lemoine,
is graceful; but the effect of light is theatrical to the last

degree, and the whole chapel is wanting in dignity and the religious feeling without which a building fails as a Christian church. Another statue of the Virgin, a Notre-Dame des Douleurs, by Bouchardon, a great tomb of the *curé* Languet de Gergy, by Michel-Ange Slodtz, and the pulpit given in 1788 by the Maréchal de Richelieu, are all very grandiose, but fail utterly to impress one; whereas the two shells serving as holy-water stoops, given to François I. by the Republic of Venice, are charming examples of pure Renaissance sculpture. The general effect of the church, by its enormous size alone, is exceedingly grand; but, being entirely of stone, it is cold and colourless. An Italian edifice wants Italian materials, which is the reason that the Brompton Oratory is so highly satisfactory, and perhaps the most magnificent example of Italian architecture on this side of the Alps. The details of glass, furniture, pulpit, &c., in S. Sulpice are utterly uninteresting, with the exception of the mural paintings by Delacroix in the chapel of the Holy Angels, which are splendid examples of the great artist's work. The subjects are: *Saint Michel triomphant de Lucifer; Héliodore terrassé et battu de verges;* and *La lutte de Jacob et l'Ange dans le désert.* In the west chapel, dedicated to the souls in Purgatory, are pictures by Heim; and in the other chapels, works by Abel de Pujol, Vichon, Lafon, A. Hesse, Drolling, and Guillemot. In the crypt, used as a chapel for catechising, are the statues of S. Paul and S. John Evangelist, by Pradier.

The organ is an enormous instrument by Cavaillé-Coll. It possesses 118 stops, 5 manuals, 20 composition pedals, and some 7,000 pipes. Exquisitely played by M. Widor, one is carried away from the unsympathetic surroundings, particularly when the Seminarists form in procession and pour out the solemn old Gregorian tones, the beauty of which no one can understand unless they have been heard by a mass of men's voices and accompanied by an organist who understands harmonizing with taste. The organ here, as at all the Paris churches, is at the west end of the nave, and is only used for voluntaries and solo performances, never to accompany voices, for which purpose a small instrument is always placed close to the choir, either at the side or behind the altar. This is a much better arrangement than our modern one of having a huge organ in the chancel thundering away and drowning the voices. Of course it necessitates two organists, but the gain in refinement is worth the outlay; and there is no reason why the choirmaster, who would accompany the singers, should necessarily be a first-rate player.

Although there are no remains of an earlier building, there was a parish church upon the same site as S. Sulpice as early as the 12th century; this was enlarged under Louis XII. and François Ier.

A brass slab incrusted in the pavement of the south transept

SAINT-SULPICE FROM THE LUXEMBOURG GARDEN.

indicates the meridian in a direct line towards the north—an obelisk. When the weather is fine, the midday sun shines through a little opening in the window of the south transept, and strikes the middle of the *plaque* in Summer, and the top of the obelisk in the Winter solstice. This meridian was established in 1743 by Henri Sully and Lemonnier, to fix the Spring equinox and Easter Day.

SAINT-THOMAS D'AQUIN.

This is another church for the smart people, but not the *nouveaux riches*, rather the old *noblesse* of the Faubourg S. Germain—tall, lean old gentlemen, with fine aquiline noses and *distingué* figures; and old ladies in sober black, much lace and old-fashioned grey curls. There was a story told in one of the newspapers of a lady wanting an anniversary mass said at S. Thomas, but, the price being 10 fr., she could not afford it. "Eh bien, madame, vous pouvez en avoir à S. Pierre du Gros-Caillou pour 7 frs. 50 c." I cannot vouch for the truth of the tale; but it is well-known that masses for the dead could not possibly be said in sufficient number in the city churches except by uniting many heterogeneous souls, which would not be pleasant to those who wish to spare no expense, and to run no chances of failure as regards the future of their dear relatives and friends; and so commemorative and anniversary masses are farmed out, like the poor babies, to country priests; which has the double advantage of aiding the departed souls and of augmenting the miserable stipends of the unfortunate provincial *curés*, who have to be "passing rich" literally upon forty pounds a year—and fees, which are no small items in certain places. The system of stretching out an income by fees is terrible. So much for weddings and burials at the High Altar; so much less at a side one; a little more at the altar of the Blessed Virgin than at that of S. Holobellou, and so on; by which means the *curés* of the rich churches, the Madeleine, S. Augustin, La Trinité, S. Thomas, S. Philippe and the like, multiply their incomes to an enormous extent. This is not the only country where equalization of the incomes of the clergy is desirable.

S. Thomas formerly belonged to the Jacobins; the conventual buildings are now used for the museum of artillery. The church was commenced in 1683, but only finished in 1740. The portal was designed by brother Claude, a religious of the monastery; the ceiling of the choir was painted in 1724 by Lemoine, and represents the Transfiguration.

L'ANCIEN ABBAYE DU VAL DE GRÂCE.

When Hannah of old obtained her desire, she dedicated

her son to God's service in the Temple; but Anne d'Autriche, under the same circumstances, went further, and built the church and founded the monastery of Val de Grâce, in the Rue S. Jacques. It it not often that the gratitude of sovereigns takes so magnificent a form. The Benedictine nuns of the monastery of Val Profond, which had been established near Bièvre le Châtel since the 13th century had been removed by the Queen to the Hôtel du Petit-Bourbon some years previously; but she did not commence the new buildings until she became regent. The little King laid the first stone of the church in 1645, François Mansard being the first architect; Jacques Lemercier continued the work, and Pierre Lemuet, Gabriel Leduc, and Duval finished it. The abbey is now a military hospital.

The decoration of the church points to the Birth of Christ as symbolising the birth of Louis XIV., in future years, known as the "Roi Soleil." In the great courtyard is a statue in bronze of Larrey, Napoléon's great army surgeon, by David d'Angers, the celebrated sculptor. The dome is exceedingly elegant, but the church below is, like the Invalides, too small as a basement. Both buildings give the impression of an elongated dome, and nothing else; hence they look far better from a point which hides the lower part of the buildings. The pavement is laid with rich marbles, and the baldachino, supported by six twisted columns, recalls that of S. Peter's. "If you wish to see the prettiest fresco painting in all Paris, you must go in here, and look up at the dome; the chapels, too, are full of virgins, and dirty little Angels." Why dirty, I know not; but the praise of the painting in the dome is not exaggerated. It is a mass of figures, a whole hierarchy of Saints adoring the Trinity, and Anne d'Autriche, introduced by S. Louis, presenting the model of her church. Like all Mignard's work, it is grandiose rather than grand, with exaggerated attitudes and hurricane-blown garments. In the chapel of the Communion are some works by Philippe de Champaigne.

Many were the royal hearts placed in neat little golden and silver-gilt boxes, which formerly adorned the church. It was privileged to entertain these appendages of Bourbon bodies, but the Revolution made light of them, and carried off the casings. Poor hearts, alive or dead, they were not worth much, except for their settings.

LA CHAPELLE DU CHÂTEAU DE VERSAILLES.

Consecrated in 1710, this chapel is, like the whole palace, an example of exquisite workmanship. Not a bolt or a hinge but is of the best bronze, exquisitely designed and gilt. We

CHAPEL OF THE CHÂTEAU DE VERSAILLES.

may not admire the style, but all Mansard's subordinates turned out the best work they could produce. Can anything be more worthy of praise in this respect than the staircases of the palace, resplendent with different coloured marbles, or the magnificent Salle des Glaces? The same may be said of the chapel. As a church it may fail; it certainly inspires no feeling of religion; but as a building it is magnificent.

The Kings sat in the gallery, and in consequence of the holiness of S. Louis, they were allowed a privilege only accorded to ecclesiastics—that of kissing the paten at mass; and when they received the Holy Sacrament, they were presented with as many wafers as there had been Kings in succession to Clovis—a custom which had come down from the time of Louis le Débonnaire, as a safe-guard against poison, Louis having been poisoned by a consecrated wafer.

LA CHAPELLE DU CHÂTEAU DE VINCENNES.

The beautiful chapel attached to the castle of Vincennes was begun in 1379, by Charles V., but was only finished by Henri II., who adorned the interior, and especially the glass, with the interlaced H. and D., which figure upon everything of the period, without the slightest shame. The apse contains glass by Jean Cousin, an exquisite Last Judgment.

At once a royal residence and a prison, the Château de Vincennes has a long history to recount. It was much beloved by S. Louis; he lived there, and delivered his judgments sitting under an oak in the forest. It was there also that he received those precious relics from the Emperor Baldwin, deposited for a time at the convent of the Minimes; and from Vincennes also the departure for those unhappy Crusades took place.

Louis X., Philippe V., Charles IV., and our own Henry V. died there; Charles IX. and Mazarin died there; and Henry IV. was imprisoned there. So was Mirabeau, who passed his time in composing *L'Essai sur les lettres de cachet et les prisons d'Etat.* Diderot was also a prisoner; and the Duc d'Enghien was shot within its precincts. Like the Bastille it had its *lettres de cachets*, and although less notorious, it was probably no less dark in its tales of legal and regal crimes. But for all that its woods were favourite hunting-grounds, a part having been enclosed by Philippe-Auguste to receive the stags and roebucks sent by Henry II. of England to his most Christian majesty.

Vincennes was also the birthplace of the Sèvres porcelain manufactory, started by one Charles Adam in 1745: but this is guide-book information, with no bearing upon the Paris churches. Let no one, however, visit the Chapel at Vincennes without sauntering into the wood, which is quite the equal, if not prettier than the Bois de Boulogne. You may pick violets

THE CHAPEL OF THE CHÂTEAU DE VINCENNES.

and enjoy a splendid view of the Seine and the Marne meandering among the valleys; but you will not enjoy *le monde*, which does not venture so far east of the Champs Elysées. If you require fashion, go not east of the Louvre.

SAINT-VINCENT DE PAUL.

Whether we consider this church from the architectural or the decorative point of view, it is quite worthy of its titular Saint, and is one of the grandest of modern churches to be seen anywhere. It is built on the plan of the early Roman basilicas. Begun by Lepère in 1824, it was finished from designs by Hittorf. The situation is fine, and the step and slopes leading up to it are at once grand and original. The subject in the tympanum is by Nanteuil, representing S. Vincent de Paul surrounded by Sisters of Charity and Angels.

S. Vincent de Paul was the founder of the picturesque grey Sisters we all know so well by their pretty flapping headgear, and of foundling hospitals in France. He was born in 1576 at Puy in Gascony, and being of a contemplative disposition, full of piety and sweetness, was fitted, his father thought, for the religious life; and so he was sent to a convent of the Cordeliers near by, and assumed the Franciscan frock at the age of twenty. For ten years he studied, and then an incident occurred which settled his destiny. Going to Marseilles to transact some business, and returning by sea, the bark was attacked by African pirates, and S. Vincent, with the others on board, was bound and sent into slavery at Tunis. Vincent spent two years in captivity, passing from one owner to another, when, one day, being asked by his master's wife to sing to her, he burst into tears, chanting, "By the waters of Babylon we sat down and wept," and "*Salve Regina.*" But the songs or the preaching converted the woman, and then her husband; which being so, they all escaped and landed at Aiguesmortes. Vincent went to Rome, and then to Paris, where he pleaded the cause of the wretched galley-slaves of Marseilles. We all remember the grand picture by Bonnat, of S. Vincent taking the place of a slave and having the fetters put upon him. I forget its exact name; it was exhibited, in London some years ago, and is now in one of the churches. The Saint began his good work by visiting the prisons or *dépôts*, whence the criminals were forwarded to the galleys. There he saw "des malheureux renfermés dans de profondes et obscures cavernes, mangés de vermines, atténués de langueur et de pauvreté, et entièrement negligés pour le corps et pour l'âme." S. Vincent then took up the cause of the street girls, and finally he instituted the Order of Sisters of Charity, nuns

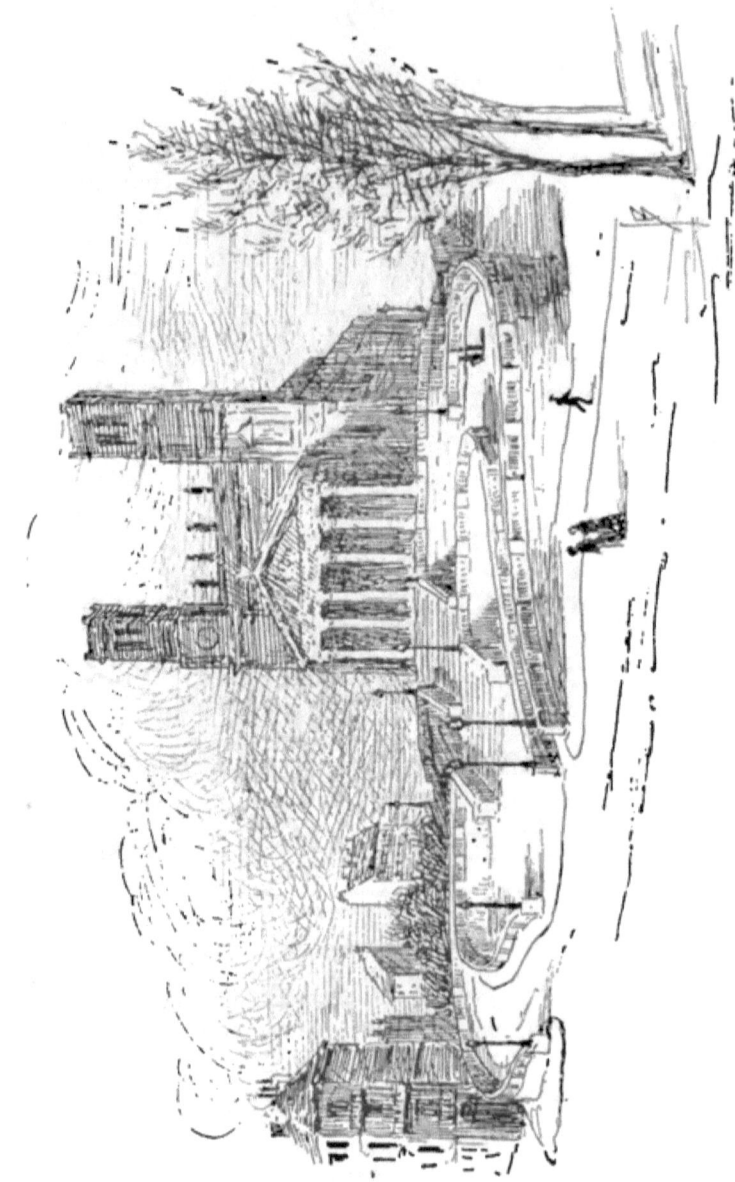

SAINT-VINCENT DE PAUL; FROM AN OLD ENGRAVING.

"qui n'ont point de monastères que les maisons des malades, pour cellules qu'une chambre de louage, pour chapelle que l'église de leur paroisse, pour cloître que les rues de la ville et les salles des hôspitaux, pour clôture que l'obéissance, pour grille que la crainte de Dieu, et pour voile qu'une Sainte et exacte modestie, et cependant elles se préservent de la contagion du vice, elles font germer partout sur leurs pas la vertu." Such was S. Vincent's idea when founding the Sisterhood, and such the Sisters are to this day, eminently practical, whether in their work or their quaint costume, which is short enough to clear the muddy street pavements, a model to most nurses in or out of hospital. They move with the world, but are not of it.

S. Vincent is generally represented carrying one babe and holding another by the hand, typical of his founding la Maison des Enfants Trouvés, which was the outcome of his first plan of gathering up children in the streets and placing them with his Sisters. Such an accumulation of little outcasts did he obtain that a special house had soon to be founded.

Nor was S. Vincent out of his element at Court, for he was friendly with Cardinal Richelieu, and attended Louis XIII. in his last moments. He died, in 1660, at S. Lazare, and was canonized in 1747; but, in the words of the people, he was "l'Intendant de la Providence et Père des Pauvres." When the fine new church, dedicated to S. Vincent de Paul, was built, Hippolyte Flandrin was at the height of his reputation. He had decorated S. Germain-des-Prés with exquisite pictures, telling the whole story of the Redemption from the Old and New Testament; the churches of S. Paul at Nismes and S. Martin of Lyons were no less great successes. But the frescoes of S. Vincent were to be the painter's crowning work. The church has a feature in common with S. Apollinare Nuovo, Ravenna, namely, a long flat wall space on each side of the nave and the west end, supported by pillars, and, in the case of the Paris church, forming a gallery. This it was that Flandrin was commissioned to cover with frescoes; and just as he had gone to the Roman catacombs for his inspiration for the Romanesque church at Lyons, so he looked to Ravenna for his designs for the Paris basilica. There is great similarity of idea in the two processions, and if S. Apollinare carries off the palm for its gorgeous mosaic, it must give way to S. Vincent in beauty of form and spirituality of design. Few, if any, churches can show pictures so full of beauty as this procession to Paradise (the "Christian Panathenæa" it has been called), a magnificent army of sufferers who have gained the crown. There they walk with stately steps, a hundred and fifty men and women, carrying their emblems and their palms; and yet there is no repetition; each one has his own individuality, his own idiosyncrasy.

M. Ingres was the first artist invited to undertake the work, then Delaroche; but happily, both of them declined, and Picot accepted the commission. The 1848 Revolution broke out and interrupted the work; then the new administration, struck with the beauty of the frescoes of S. Germain, wished to give over the decoration of S. Vincent to Flandrin. Naturally this

S. GREGORY AND S. LEO, BY FLANDRIN.

great artist did not relish ousting a brother brush, and so a compromise was arranged; Picot chose the choir, and the frieze of the nave was left for Flandrin.

The procession of men is on one side, that of women upon the other, both being marshalled into Paradise by Angels bearing crowns for the elect. These stand on each side of the sanctuary, symbolic of Heaven : " *Beati misericordis, Beati qui persecutionem patientur propter justitiam.*

Beginning with the Apostles, we see SS. Peter and Paul as the pillars of the Church and the two great preachers of Christianity. S. Matthew and S. John follow, accompanied by the rest of the twelve. Then come the Holy Martyrs, beginning with S. Stephen looking up at the "Son of Man seated on the right hand of God." S. Pothinus and S. Eustace lead the group of soldier martyrs, ended by S. Christopher bearing the Infant Christ upon his shoulders. Then follow the doctors of the Church: S. John Chrysostom, "the golden mouthed"; S. Jerome; S. Augustin, of Hippo; and S. Leo, said to be a portrait of M. Ingres. Of these I give slight sketches, as they seem to be peculiarly fine in expression.

The Bishops and Confessors follow, a notable figure for refinement and dignity being S. Nicholas with his three little chubby boys; S. Joseph bears the carpenter's rule instead of the palm, and a lily, emblem of chastity. Charlemagne, sainted, and S. Clodoald, his kingly robes being covered by the monk's habit, are followed by S. Roch, S. Francis of Assisi, S. Dominic, and a crowd of others it is impossible to mention.

S. NICOLAS, BY FLANDRIN.

Turning round we see first the Virgin-Martyrs, S. Cecilia bearing her harp, S. Ursula and her friends, S. Agnes, S. Geneviève, and S. Zita bearing her pitcher, one of the most beautiful of Flandrin's women. Interspersed, after the manner of the Ravenna mosaic, are palm trees dividing the groups. After the Virgins the Holy Women march along: S. Felicitas with her six little children is a charming group; S. Anne, old and feeble, walks with S. Elizabeth leaning on the boy S. John Baptist; S. Monica is alone, her son being amongst the doctors; S. Helena rests upon the cross, and is followed by the gentle Elizabeth of Hungary carrying bread, and S. Clotilde resting upon the shoulder of the young S. Clodoald.

The penitents follow: S. Mary Magdalen leading the group, S. Mary of Egypt, S. Thaïs burning her rich garments, and S. Pelagia trampling upon her worldly goods. The Holy Households follow: S. Eustache, S. Julian, and other heads of families who were converted by their wives, and whose children they dedicated to God.

Below the organ is the "Mission of the Church." S. Peter and S. Paul are teaching the nations. In the centre is an altar with the sacred monogram and a nimbed cross; S. Peter is on the left, holding the keys and preaching to the Western nations. A father and mother kneel at his feet and present their children that they, too, may be converted.

On the right is S. Paul, clasping his sword and announcing the glad tidings to the Eastern nations: Jews, Persians, Greeks, Arabians, and an African bearing his war arrows.

For beauty of form, purity of sentiment and spirituality, untainted by the least spark of sentimentality, which is the bane of most modern religious painting, this work of Flandrin's may be classed as the finest of our time. It is treated in the conventional manner; there is no intense realism such as we find in the work of Laurens, Lhermitte or Hitchcock, but neither is it inane, effeminate, or affected, as are the pictures of Ary Scheffer, Hesse, and a crowd of disciples of Overbeck and Cornelius. The latter called the frieze an example of a true Renaissance, and M. Ingres, who had helped his favourite pupil in analysing the details, looked upon it as a revival of true religious art, a vivification of the Old Masters. "Do you suppose it is to make copyists of you that I send you to copy the great masters? I wish you to get the juice of the plant and to plunder the bee." This Flandrin did. He studied the art of Memlinc and Van Eyck, of Fra Angelico and of Raffaello, but the feeling was his own. He went on his way calmly, thoughtfully working out his ideas in faith and prayer, scorning the world and indifferent to its inhabitants, and thus his painting is as instinct in religious sentiment as that of Angelico, while his mastery of drapery and his management of its folds are not surpassed by the Greeks themselves; indeed, he united Greek beauty of form with Mediæval purity of sentiment.

Flandrin's only weak point was his colour, but in the frieze it is sufficiently harmonious, owing to the flat gold backgrounds. In drawing he was perfect, never hesitating, never altering; beginning as he meant to finish, without any experiments, or changes in the designs he had sketched out.

Nor must Picot's part in the decoration of S. Vincent de Paul be overlooked. His *Christ sur un trône*, with the patron Saint at His feet adoring, is quite in keeping with the frieze, by the younger painter.

The wood-work of the church is finely carved, and, indeed, all the details of the building are magnificent, making it a glorious example of the perfect unity of the allied arts—architecture, painting, and sculpture; an example that is almost unique in modern times.

INDEX.

A.
Academy of Painters, 136.
Agnes, S., Legend of, 120.
Alleluiatic Victory, 180.
Anne d'Autriche, 147, 322, 327.
Anselme, 80.
Antoine, S., 1.
Apollinaris, S., 217.

B.
Barrère, 53.
Benoist, Curé of S. Eustache, 144.
Benozzi, F., 300.
Biscornette, Legend of, 283.
Blanc, J., 175.
Blanche of Castille, 2, 79.
Blancs-Manteaux, N.D. de, 300.
Boïleau, N., 12, 200.
Bonnat, 258.
Bontems, P., 47.
Bouillart, Dom, 197.
Bouteiller, J. le, 272, 286.

C.
Cabanel, A., 171.
Cameo, "Apotheosis of Augustus," 19.
Carlyle, T., 150, 279, 307.
Carmelites, Church of the, 1.
Champaigne, P. de, 213, 304, 327.
Chapelle, S., 2.
    ,,   ,, Ceremonies at, 11, 16, 17
Chapelle, S., Treasury of, 21.
Chapel, Valois, 38.
Charles VIII., Tomb of, 58.
    ,, le Chauve, 40, 58, 90.

Chavannes, P. de, 171.
Chelles, Jean de, 268, 284.
Clotilde, S., 158, 161.
Clovis, 158, 163.
Colbert, 125, 126, 139.
Columns, Memorial, 66, 67.
Coustou, 238, 307.
Coysevox, 189, 238, 259, 307.

D.
Dagobert, Tomb of, 49, 70, 71.
Darboy, Archbishop, 156, 262, 286.
David d'Angers, 169, 327.
Delacroix, 304.
Delaunay, J. E., 175.
Delorme, P., 49, 65.
Denis, S., 30.
  ,,   ,, Abbots of, 40.
  ,,   ,, Crypt of, 72.
  ,,   ,, Legend of, 34.
  ,,   ,, Tombs at, 44, 49, 50, 61, 74, 75.
Denis, S., Treasury at, 32, 89, 94, 95, 96, 97, 98.
Descartes, R., 200.
Dibden, T. F., 123, 165, 186, 208, 211, 273, 305, 309, 321.
Du Breuil, 125, 278.
Duguerry, L'abbé, 157.

E.
Early kings of France, Burial of, 44, 74, 192.
Elizabeth, S., 100.
Eloy, S., Legend of, 37.
Epitaphs, 7, 68, 69, 80, 83, 108, 132, 152, 164, 200, 214, 228, 229.

230, **231**, **236**, **252**, **256**, **259**, **260**, 317.
Étienne, S., **100**.
Eudes de **Fauconnier**, **251**.
Eustache, S., **116**.
„ „ Legend of, **118**, **119**.
„ „ Organ of, **154**.

F.

Félibien, 49, 73, 85.
Flamaël, B., **1**.
Flamel, N., **214**.
Flandrin, H., 197, **201**, 318, 334
Fléchier, 147.
—. François, Ier, Tomb **of**, 46, 49, 59, 65, 85.
François, S., **215**.
„ „ Xavier, **158**.
Fredégonde, Queen, 49, 72.

G

Galland, V., **176**.
Gaussel, J. 184.
Gems in Bibliothèque, 20.
Geneviève, S., Abbey of, 102, 103, 158.
Geneviève, S., Church of, 158.
„ „ Legend of, 159.
„ „ Tomb of, 112, 114.
Gérard, 170.
Germain, S., of Auxerre, 159, **178**, 179, 180, 181.
Germain, S., l'Auxerrois, **177**.
„ „ en Laye, 189.
„ „ des Prés, **190**.
„ „ Tomb of, **199**
Gervais, S., **209**.
„ „ Legend of, **209**.
Gilles, S., **235**.
Girardon, **320**.
Glass, Stained, 23, 109, 111, **112**, 130, 187, **194**, **199**, 212, 292, **317**.
Goujon, J., **186**.
Grégoire of Tours, **161**, **191**, **234**, 266.
Gros, Baron, **170**.

H.

Hébert, A.-E., **176**.

Helgaud, 75.
Henri II., Tomb of, 49, 64, 65, 66.
„ IV., **49**, 73, 197.
Hugo, V., **234**, 273, 275, **277**.
Hugues **Capet**, **75**.
Hulduin, **Abbot**, **35**.

I.

Ingres, 336.

J.

Jacques du Haut-Pas, S., **215**.
Jacques, Tour S., 213.
Jansenists, 249.
Jean, S., 215.
Joinville, 49.
Julian Hospitator, S., 219, 220, **221**.
Julien de Brioude, S., 216.
Julien the Confessor, S., 217.
Julien le Pauvre, S., 215.
Juste, J., **49**, **61**, **63**.

L.

L'Abbaye au Bois, N.D. de, 300.
Lacordaire, Père, 268.
Lamartine, 150.
Laon, Inventory of the Treasury of, 39.
L'Assomption, N D. de, **299**.
Laurens, J. P., **174**.
Laurent, S., 232.
„ „ Legend of, **232**.
Lebrun, **259**, **302**, **320**.
Légende dorée, **219**.
Lenepveu, **175**.
Leu, S., **235**.
Lévy, H., **171**.
Louvre, 47, 95.
Louis d'Antin, S., 237.
„ des Invalides, S., 237.
„ en l'Ile, S., 237.
„ VI., le Gros, 76.
„ VII., **77**.
„ IX., S., 2, 4.
„ „ „ Burial of, 9, 80.
„ XI., 81.
„ XII., Tomb of, 49, 61, 62.
„ XIII., 85, 86, 303, 304.
„ „ Vœu de, 277, 289.

INDEX.

Louis XIV., great generals of, 50, 51.
Louis XV., 165.
Lulli, 303.
Lupus, S., 235.
Lutrin, Le, 12.

M.

Madeleine, S., **239**.
Maid and the Magpie, The, 141.
Maillot, T., 173.
Maintenon, Madame de, **147**.
Marcel, S., Legend of, **282**.
Marguerite, S., 243.
  ,, de Valois, **83**.
Marie de' Medici, **83, 85**.
Martin des Champs, S., **244**.
  ,, S., Legend of, **245**.
"Mass of St. Giles," 90.
Massillon, **148**.
Médard, S., 248.
  ,, ,, Legend of, 249.
Merri, S., **251**.
  ,, ,, Legend of, 251.
Mignard, **125, 259, 307, 327**.
Millet, Dom, **31, 61, 69, 72**.
Mirabeau, **149, 329**.
Molière, **125**.
Montereau, P. de, **194, 195, 247**.
Montyon, A. de, **231**.
Music, **153, 240, 309, 324**.

N.

Nangis, Guillaume de, 71.
Nefs or Navettes, 223.
Nicolas des Champs, S., 256.
  ,, S., Legend of, 258.
Nicolas du Chardonnet, S., 259.
Notre Dame, Cathedral of, 260.
  ,, ,, Ceremonies at, **270, 296**.
Notre Dame de l'Assomption, **299**.
  ,, ,, de Lorette, **302**.
  ,, ,, des Champs, **301**.
  ,, ,, des Victoires, **303**.
  ,, ,, Tombs of, **294**.
  ,, ,, Treasury of, **291**.

O.

Oratoire, L', **303**.

Oriflamme, L', **41**.
Orléans, Tomb of the House of, **82, 83, 84**.

P.

Panthéon, **158**.
Paris, University of, **224**.
Pascal, B., **108, 109, 215**.
Paul, S., **304**.
Philippe, brother of S. Louis, **79**.
Philippe, S., **305**.
Pierre de Chaillot, S., **306**.
Pierre de Montmartre, S., **306**.
Pilon, G., **47, 65**.
Pils, **137**.
Pius VII., Pope, **151**.
Poirier, Dom, Notes by, **54, 55, 56**.
Pressoir Mystique, **110**.

R.

Rameau, **151**.
Ravy, J., **272, 286**.
Relics, **4, 5, 6, 17, 18, 19, 139, 142**.
Renaissance Museum of Louvre, **47, 132, 186, 188, 189, 211, 271**.
Richelieu, Cardinal, **319**.
Rigord, 77.
Robert, King, 75.
Robespierre, 279.
Roch, S., **307**.
Rochelle, La, **303**.

S.

Sauval, **109, 189, 260**.
Scarron, **213**.
September massacres, **1, 195**.
Servandoni, **321**.
Servites, **300**.
Séverin, S., **310**.
  ,, Legend of, **311**.
Sibour, Archbishop, **112, 262**.
Simon, L'Abbé, **129, 156**.
Sorbonne, La, **319**.
Soufflot, **165, 275**.
Suger, Abbot, **37, 69, 76, 77, 78**.
  ,, Vase of, **95**.
Sully, Bishop Maurice de, **266**.
Sulpice, S., **321**.

T.

Thomas d'Aquin, S., 326.
True Cross, Relic of, 4, 5, 6, 17.
Turenne, 51, 68, 147, 238.

V.

Val de Grâce, 45, 326.
Vallière, Mlle. de la, 302.
Valois, Marguerite de, 83.
Vase of Suger in Louvre, 95.

Versailles, 328.
Vincennes, 329.
Vincent de Paul, S., 321.
Voragine, J. de, 219.

W.

Winepress, Allegory of the, 110, 111.

Y.

Yeowell, J., 180.

www.ingramcontent.com/pod-product-compliance
Lightning Source LLC
Chambersburg PA
CBHW032351230426
43672CB00007B/665